*Your Country, My Country*

# Your Country, My Country

## A *Unified History of the United States and Canada*

ROBERT BOTHWELL

OXFORD
UNIVERSITY PRESS

# OXFORD

UNIVERSITY PRESS

Oxford University Press is a department of the
University of Oxford. It furthers the University's objective
of excellence in research, scholarship, and education
by publishing worldwide.

Oxford   New York

Auckland   Cape Town   Dar es Salaam   Hong Kong   Karachi
Kuala Lumpur   Madrid   Melbourne   Mexico City   Nairobi
New Delhi   Shanghai   Taipei   Toronto

With offices in

Argentina   Austria   Brazil   Chile   Czech   Republic France   Greece
Guatemala   Hungary   Italy   Japan   Poland   Portugal   Singapore
South Korea   Switzerland   Thailand   Turkey   Ukraine   Vietnam

Oxford is a registered trade mark of Oxford University Press
in the UK and certain other countries.

Published in the United States of America by
Oxford University Press
198 Madison Avenue, New York, NY 10016

© Robert Bothwell 2015

Library of Congress Cataloging-in-Publication Data

is available

ISBN 978-0-19-544880-1

1 3 5 7 9 8 6 4 2
Printed in the United States of America
on acid-free paper

*To my students, who have had
to listen to so much of this.*

# Contents

# Acknowledgments

MANY THANKS ARE due to my indefatigable research assistants, John Dirks, Tina Park, Susie Colbourn, and Jenn Bonder, who from time to time had to streak away and find apparently crucial material. Special thanks and gratitude are owed to Ira Gluskin, whose generosity created the May Gluskin chair at the University of Toronto, on whose resources I drew in the composition of this book. Not only did it pay my expenses, but it allowed me to ignore entirely the time-wasting procedures that accompany petitions for research grants. This spared me weeks if not months of irritation and wasted time. To my editors, Jennie Rubio of Oxford University Press in Toronto and Susan Ferber of Oxford University Press New York, I am grateful for their patience, enthusiasm, and strict supervision. Any stylistic solecisms that survive are my responsibility alone. Finally to my wife, Gail, I am grateful for patience, endurance, and support during this process.

*Your Country, My Country*

# Introduction

IF THERE WERE ever a prize for the most apparently futile academic study, Canadian–American relations would be an earnest contender. Over time, whole forests, presumably Canadian, have been cut down and pulped to produce shelves of books and reams of articles on Canada and its "great neighbor."[1] In times of crisis in Canada the occasional television pundit flashes onto the screen so that American television audiences can manage to be both startled and bored at the same time. An exception in 2013–4 was the reaction to Toronto's telegenic mayor, Rob Ford, who became America's best-known Canadian, far out-snorting the Canadian prime minister, the thin-lipped Stephen Harper.[2] Certainly Ford gave Canada exposure and raised justifiable questions about the people who elected him. These are not flattering questions but at the same time, as kindly Americans have pointed out, the same questions have frequently been asked about similarly buffoonish American politicians. This book attempts to answer some of these questions, and it takes as its starting point that sympathetic insight—if you've got them, we've got them too.

Commentary on Canadian–American relations usually follows the curve of population. The ratio in population between Canada and the United States flops around ten to one, with the ten signifying the United States and the one, Canada. California alone has a bigger population than Canada. GDP is roughly twelve to one, varying with the exchange rate between the Canadian and American dollars, but of course always in favor of the United States. The national origin of the thousands of works or studies on Canadian–American relations is also between ten and twelve to one—but this time the ten represents Canada, and the one, the United States.

Volume is not the same thing as impact. Great Britain, France, Japan, and Israel (among many other countries) are better known in the United States than is Canada. Canada is a state of vagueness on the other side of a "frontier," a place where (bad) weather comes from, and the home of the Toronto Blue Jays in baseball or the Vancouver Canucks and a few other hockey teams. Since 1999 it has occasionally been regarded as a potential source of terrorists slipping into the United States—an unsought and unappreciated distinction.[3] Taken together, weather and sports account for the overwhelming majority of references to Canada in the American media and in the American consciousness. Sports and weather data are embedded in a kind of cultural and economic soup, business excursions flavored with oil and sprinkled with moose and beaver, with a dash of Mountie-red for color.

In an age of mass communication and mass travel, fewer Americans visit Canada than they did in 1970, though in certain states or regions—Florida for example—the chances of meeting Canadians are fairly high. This is because although fewer Americans visit Canada, many Canadians visit the United States, despite the increased incidents of "border theater"—the frontier rituals designed to make Americans and Canadians feel more secure in the face of a threatening world. Canada in the twenty-first century is also harder for Americans to get to than in the nineteenth or twentieth, and vice versa if you are traveling south.

Meeting Canadians is one thing; the chance of finding them memorable or even distinctive (unless they are French Canadian) is considerably less. It used to be that Americans might easily meet resident Canadians—those who had crossed the border to live and (they hoped) prosper. As recently as 1970 Canadians were the third largest group of immigrants in the United States, as signified by border-crossers like John Kenneth Galbraith, Norman Jewison, Peter Jennings, Judith Shklar, Charles Krauthammer, Charles Bronfman, and, a bit more recently, John Candy and Justin Bieber;[4] but in 2010 Canadian immigrants were far down the list of foreign-born in the United States. That, perhaps, was because the bulk of immigrants, if they existed, would have to be middle class. An American immigrant to Canada explained the situation to an American journalist: "If you want to see your name in lights, go to the United States. If you want a stable middle-class existence, go to [or stay in] Canada."[5]

Canada always projected an image to Americans that was wholesome, if more than a little dull. The phrase "worthy Canadian initiative" won a contest for the most tedious headline in an American newspaper. "Dudley Do-Right"—a cartoon representation of a Canadian Mountie—cavorted with moose and contended with villains, whom he usually bested, and usually accidentally, for Dudley was not too bright. There was a sense of superiority in American attitudes, just as in the reciprocal Canadian vision of America or Americans there was a thick vein of self-righteousness. But in the oblivion that usually covers Canada these are traits that only occasionally achieve recognition or even consciousness. A Canadian has to go a long way to violate these cultural norms before he, or occasionally she, is noticed—as in the Rob Ford case, noted above.

The point is not that Canada's public image was different from that of the United States; it is that there *was* a public image, that it was consistent over time, and that the worst that could be said of it was that it was neutral or, on balance, positive. If Rob Ford resembles some (hopefully few) Americans, so does Dudley Do-Right. Some "Canadian values," if there was such a thing, resembled some American values. More concretely, individual Canadians or groups of Canadians had the same thoughts on many issues as individual Americans or groups of Americans. They were citizens of different countries and members of distinct political systems— yet the formal structures of Canadian government and the political parties that ran the government were recognizable though not identical across the international border. And over many generations, since the eighteenth century in fact, similarities of political context and political culture were mirrored in economic thought, social organization, religious practice, and attitudes toward the world at large.

And so, since this is a book written by a historian, we arrive at history. Explanations of Canadian–American relations, comparisons of Canadian– American values, and discussions of Canadian–American differences fall into the category of "deep history"—they go back to the origins of northern North America and beyond, to the ideas and motivations of the European settlers of the Americas, including those of France in Canada's case, but also, and mainly, those of Great Britain, where the origins of Canadian and American shared attitudes may be found.

"Rule Britannia," a song that dates from the era of North America's colonial origins, hymned Great Britain's unique virtues—its exceptional nature. The British colonists in America absorbed the sentiment and fed it into a sense of superiority—over nature, over the natives, over the French. There is, of course, no point in being unique if it means that you are actually uniquely or exceptionally inferior.

How then does uniqueness or exceptionalism fit with the great disruption in Anglo-American history, the American Revolution and the consequent separation of North America into a northern, British, half, and an American republic? The Revolution was directed at, or against, the British Empire. After the Revolution, some Americans, Loyalists and "Late Loyalists," remained British North Americans. Citizens of the republic and visitors to the North American continent over the next couple of generations compared the two groups, and generally concluded that they were not all that different, although they usually added that the British (North) Americans were a tad slower than their republican cousins. Americans, a twentieth-century Canadian historian once remarked, got up earlier and worked harder.[6] And yet, he might have added, they were essentially the same species.

In 1782, as the British Empire was dividing and the American republic was taking shape, a French diplomat observed at a dinner in Paris that the newly independent colonies would become a great empire, presumably to rival if not surpass Great Britain. The Scot who was secretary of the British delegation negotiating peace replied that independence for America might indeed have that effect, but there remained one important link. "Yes, sir, and they will *all* speak English; every one of 'em."[7] Seen from that viewpoint, the remaining colonies that would make up the future Canada were an inconvenient codicil, an appendix that served no useful function but that could not be got rid of unless the future Canadians themselves decided to follow their American brethren. Until then, however, a formal British connection as well as an informal British cultural link would shape the Canadian colonies.

Like many ambitious truisms, the notion of a connection based on the English language foundered when it came to Quebec. Without doubt the existence of a substantial French-speaking population gave the future Canada a distinct political culture, based on both confrontation and conciliation between "Canadians" and the "Canadiens." Yet not all dissonances were language based.

There was also race. When the British pulled out of the thirteen colonies they left behind the smoldering question of race. Black chattel slavery was embedded in all the colonies, British, French, and Spanish, and thus on the territory of present-day Canada as well as the United States. The United States inherited most of the race and slavery question on the North American mainland through the southern states. Slavery was abolished in Great Britain itself in the 1770s, and in British North America in the first decades of the nineteenth century, as in the northern states in the same period. Finally, in the 1830s, slavery was abolished in the whole of the British Empire.[8] As we shall see, this development provided both a link and a contrast between the future Canada and the United States.

To emphasize the continuities in North American history does not mean ignoring the constitutional break that occurred in the 1770s. The political culture of the American republic, after all, found its source in the repudiation—as effectively "un-British"—of the British government and its works. It also reflected the failure to find within the British Constitution a form of government that could bridge the Atlantic gap. Something new was required, and something new was found. In constructing a new constitutional structure the American revolutionaries solved, to a large extent, the problem of governing vast and distant spaces, through federalism—the creation of linked orders of separate governments. That federalism in turn would have a profound effect on the shaping of British North America into a recognizably similar federal structure in the 1860s.

For the time being, between 1783 and 1812, British Americans and American Americans wished each other ill success, and in 1812 were swept up in a war that from the American point of view was intended to clean up unfinished business. The matter was resolved, however, in a stalemated peace, but more importantly by the expansion of the United States across the continent to the Pacific and southward into Mexico. British North America remained intact, preserved by its British connection, but also by American preoccupation with other concerns and the growing realization that the fragile and limited British colonies were in no way a threat to the expanded United States.

British North America and the United States of America were both settler societies. The mix of settlers varied, and British America included, as we have noted, what had been French America. (So did the United States, but, crucially, the proportion of French speakers there was much smaller, and the French element was consequently swamped.) All told, however, the individuals and families who came to live in northern North America expected that by doing so they were bettering their lot, socially, politically, but also, invariably, materially. They were, in David Potter's phrase, "peoples of plenty." They dreamed "the American dream," or "the Canadian dream," or its French-Canadian analogy, but they all, after the first gruesome generations of settlement, believed that they lived better than their ancestors had and better than their cousins who had remained in Europe. Admittedly there was a hierarchy in dreams, and over time hundreds of thousands of Canadians, both English- and French-speaking, took up the American option. "The noblest prospect a Scotchman ever sees," wrote the eighteenth-century savant Dr. Johnson, "is the high road to London." And so it was, with destination altered, for generations of Canadians. Canadians were not exceptional in joining the American mainstream; those who immigrated to the United States were only living their dreams more fully.

It was easy as well as profitable to move, because (English-) Canadians and Americans found each other mutually recognizable—both creatures of prosperity, with the optimism that goes with prosperity, with the same language, and members of the same broad political tradition—that is the theme of this book. The French Canadians reached the same conclusion by dint of geography, though without benefit of language. Similarities inclined people on both sides of the border to decompress their anxieties about the other side. It was what might now be called "soft power." Hard British power supplemented and enforced political separation, which remained real and even expanded in the thirty years that followed the American Revolution. That "fact"—British power—is more than a historical curiosity. It helps explain why the North American fragment of the British Empire got treated differently from the United States' other neighbors—Spain and France and their successor states, Mexico and the islands in the Caribbean.

Cultural, geographical, and historical proximity, and the involvement of Great Britain, were the dominant features of Canadian–American relations well into the twentieth century. While Americans had their own unique institutions and their own distinct patriotic narrative, the resemblance between Canadians and Americans was an accepted fact of life—a comment on the "exceptional" nature (or not) of the United States. Canada was comfortable with a United States that did not go forth in search of foreign monsters to destroy (unless they spoke Spanish).

Canadian autonomy mingled with membership in the British Empire was something many Americans found difficult to comprehend, as did many Canadians, but Canada's ambiguous position did not figure significantly in Americans' view of their large neighbor in the 1920s, fed as it was by a common lifestyle: opportunity, mobility, and prosperity were the signatures of North American life in the 1920s, even if many Canadian exercised their mobility to find opportunity and prosperity in the United States.[9] It was also fed by the common disasters of the Great Depression and the prairie dust bowl in the 1930s. Because the Depression was worldwide, it did not cause many North Americans to re-think their sense that their continent was peculiarly blessed, and hence did not diminish their sense of exceptionalism. The Depression merged into the Second World War, and that war into the Cold War, all calling forth a sense of common purpose and shared objectives. Canada and the United States fought Nazism and then opposed communism with no serious contradiction to their shared values. But on the way, the United States, already Canada's much larger twin, became a superpower, which changed considerably Canada's relations with the United States.

Having shared insecurity in the 1920s and 1930s, Canada and the United States shared security during and after the war—interpreting security to mean security from harm or want, for individuals and families. The United States was known to be more forward in social security than Canada—more liberal, as the word would be interpreted in the twenty-first century. American liberalism and Canada's relatively less liberal policies suggest the two countries were in some important respects out of phase; but then in the 1960s their relative politics would be reversed, with Canada becoming more liberal, with American social policy either paralyzed or in retreat.

This phenomenon—a difference in social policies and social attitudes that has found reflection in politics—has received various interpretations, some apocalyptic, in which the present is projected on the past and the past mined for explanations of a predetermined problem. Examining the fluctuations of American and Canadian life in the twentieth century doesn't afford much comfort. It is likely that Canada and the United States have diverged, with the United States becoming more conservative and Canada more liberal between, say, 1960 and 2000, but it would be a rash historian who projected this difference, which may be occasional or opportunistic, into a deep division that will lead into the indefinite future.

There was a more certain change. The United States, which had not had "allies" since the eighteenth century, suddenly found itself the center of an alliance system that stretched into every corner of the globe, sustained by American economic and military aid, American bases, American atomic weaponry, and American fleets. Canada became one ally among many, a fate against which the trans-Atlantic British struggled, in pursuit of a "special relationship" with the United States. In the eyes of many Americans, the job of the allies was to be decorative and loyal in return for American protection. Fortunately successive American governments managed relations with the allies fairly skillfully, extracting help where they could and feeding back appreciation. American policy might sometimes have been imperious or insistent, but on the whole it responded to real problems with solutions that were rational and understandable, or at least appealed to the allies' own concerns.

That was just as well, for it kept a sense of confidence as well as purpose in Canadian–American relations in particular. In the age of atomic terror there was no time for lengthy contemplation and deliberation, which meant assigning the allies' fate, including Canada's, to American politicians and generals whom Canadians had not voted for or otherwise appointed. The Americans did not try very hard to involve Canada in adventures like the Vietnam War; and as we now know, many American leaders at the time had substantial misgivings about that war—misgivings shared by a substantial proportion of the American population. Canada could sit out the Vietnam War in part because many Americans and many Canadians had the same doubtful impression of it. As the Cold War stretched on and abruptly came to an end, and the need for instant response to incoming attacks dwindled, the relationship between the United States and its allies did not fundamentally change, even if the enemy— communism—had disappeared in a puff of historical smoke in 1991.

The United States then became the sole superpower. The allies did little enough to question this perceived American role, even as it became obvious during the 1990s that by themselves the allies, even the Europeans, were ineffective or at best supporting actors in the crises of the decade. That was as true economically as politically, though on the economic side the Canadians could at least claim strong ties to the United States, measured in trade and investment, and ratified a free trade agreement with the United States in 1989, and the North American Free Trade Agreement of 1993.

The twenty-first century has brought strains to Canadian–American relations. Canadians responded sympathetically and promptly to the al Qaeda attack on New York City in 2001, affording aid during the crisis, and sending troops in pursuit of the terrorists in Afghanistan. But when President George W. Bush pushed his luck and strained his budget by intervening in Iraq in 2003, Canada did not follow. Canada had a Liberal government, which evidently the Bush administration, or parts of it, did not appreciate; but soon enough Canada had a Conservative government that in many respects shared the same assumptions and policies as American conservatives.

Ironically, no sooner had Canada turned to the right than the United States turned, if not exactly left, then away from the right, in electing Barack Obama as president in 2008. George W. Bush, when he looked at Canada, saw a country that had turned away from its common past with the United States, from comradeship in wars and shared assumptions of an anglospheric role in the world. Barack Obama, looking north, saw a country whose government after 2006 had turned its back on a century of shared progressivism, as expressed through science and scientific administration.

What seems clear when we look at the past three hundred years of northern North American history is the close resemblance of Canadian and American society, on virtually every level. Resemblance is not identity, and closeness is not harmony. It is true that if parts of Canadian society and parts of American society are segregated and placed in tandem, the resemblance is sometimes striking—even to the point where opinion in one country can be said to virtually represent opinion in the other. What can be found in the United States can be found, soon enough, in Canada. But it is seldom found in the same proportions, and it frequently occurs at different times.

# *I*

# *Exceptional America*

## SOVEREIGNTIES IN NORTHERN NORTH AMERICA

INTERNATIONAL RELATIONS IN North America long pre-date the invention of countries labeled *Canada* or *the United States*. The many native nations of the Americas traded, exchanged populations, and warred among themselves for millennia before European ships appeared on the Atlantic horizon. Those ships disgorged their cargoes of settlers, arms, weapons, and disease, with dreadful results for the native peoples. In the resulting chaos of depopulation, European colonies took root—first Spain to the south, in the Caribbean and Central America; England in the center, in Virginia and Massachusetts; and France to the north, in Acadia and New France, the eventual components of what would be Canada.

To survive, the European colonists accommodated themselves to the societies they found, for even aboriginal nations disrupted by disease and depopulation greatly outnumbered the Europeans. The colonies were vulnerable not just because the settlers' numbers were tiny, but also because they sat at the end of a very long supply line, measured not just in distance, but in time. Voyages to and from Europe took two or three months, so that drawing on the home countries' resources was difficult and sometimes impossible. Sometimes military power and superior organization, not to mention daring leadership, altered the case. The Spanish conquests of Mexico in the 1520s and of Peru in the 1530s were military triumphs— although neither would have succeeded without substantial and crucial assistance from native allies.

What took the Spanish two or three generations took the English and French much longer. In part this reflected a changing Europe. The early Spanish conquistadores belonged to a Europe that was religiously united in the Roman Catholic faith. But thirty or forty years on—the time it took for the English and French to begin dreaming of imitating the Spanish— that was no longer the case. The Protestant Reformation divided Europe and divided the countries of Europe. France, Germany, England, and Scotland—among others—went to war with themselves. Two kings of France were assassinated, in England bishops were burned at the stake, and the Scottish queen lost her head—essentially as a testimonial to her religion. Spain, at some cost, maintained religious uniformity and, because of the riches that poured in from Mexico and Peru, could afford armies and navies—and losing one, could always buy another.

The Spanish example was impressive for the kings and occasional queens of other European powers. Visions of medieval splendor to the contrary, the monarchs of Europe possessed extremely limited resources and small treasuries. Their administrations and their armies were tiny. Their revenue depended on the willingness of their subjects to allow themselves to be taxed. Riots, rebellions, and sometimes revolutions checkered Western European history in the sixteenth and seventeenth centuries.

There are obvious parallels between the histories of Spain and other Western European countries and those of England and France. And over time, developments in Spain and the Spanish colonies would affect events in England, France, and their empires. But contacts and contrasts between England and France were more direct, and more important. England and France had been in intimate contact throughout the Middle Ages. For three hundred years and more, the language of the royal court as well as the courts of justice was a variety of French. Their royal families and their nobilities intermarried. They regularly invaded one another or assisted rebellions. In the sixteenth century, religious antagonism—Protestant versus Catholic—was added to the extensive list of subjects that could be fought over. For much of the time from 1560 to 1600, and again during the 1620s, 1640s, and 1650s, France and its monarch were distracted by civil wars, which sometimes were combined with wars against Spain and Austria.

Not surprisingly, royal governments in England and France seldom had the resources to establish and maintain colonies. Naturally they hoped to benefit from them, and for that reason licensed or chartered companies to go abroad and claim land, raid, trade, and settle. Indeed, the most lasting aspect of the early explorers and adventurers was the formal claim to land, on which all trans-Atlantic sovereignties were subsequently based. In the early seventeenth century, New France, Massachusetts, and Virginia were established by chartered companies, associations of merchants and gentlemen. They may have been, and often were, inspired by religious fervor, but they also depended on the hope of profit from what were assumed to be their unlimited economic prospects. Only when that hope proved illusory did governments in Europe begin to give thought to the longer-term proper governance of their trans-Atlantic territories.

There was some reason for governments to be concerned. The history of the early colonies was anything but peaceful. The European settlers made shifting alliances with their native neighbors—alliances for trade, sometimes, but mainly alliances for protection, and for war. The natives were hardly passive in all this, and as time passed many of the native nations became increasingly alarmed by the steady, if slow, increase in the numbers of the settlers, and by the consequent encroachment of settlement on native lands. The Iroquois Confederacy, the Five Nations, proved particularly skilful at guerrilla warfare against the French, blockading New France on the landward side, seriously discouraging immigration from France, and eventually forcing the settlers who dared to come and stay to look to old France for a solution to their troubles.[1]

The first generation of colonists saw themselves as direct participants in the society, even the politics, of their native lands. Samuel de Champlain, the founder of New France, was a figure in the literary and religious culture of his homeland. His writings, and the writings of the various missionaries drawn to the colony to convert the natives, had a resonance at home. The early settlers of New England were participants in the religious struggles of old England, "Puritans" opposed to the corruption, as they saw it, of the Anglican state church. Much has been made of the remark by an early governor of Massachusetts that his colony was "a city upon a hill"—but the point was that the hill should be high enough to be plainly visible to his religious sympathizers back home.[2] Some of the more prominent early settlers of New England easily and swiftly left the colony to participate in the English Civil War of the 1640s. Luckily for them, their side won, for the time being. The king, Charles I, Charles Stuart, was put on trial and beheaded in 1649.[3] A Puritan Commonwealth, headed by Oliver Cromwell, replaced the monarchy.

For the colony the price of religious satisfaction was unexpectedly high. With godly republicans in charge in old England, who could be bothered to gaze upon the "city on a hill" in New England? The political model, for example, was now in the old world, not the new. The same fate awaited the godly Catholic colony of New France, as old France turned to other pursuits. But, paradoxically, as the governments of England and France— and it is roughly now that we can begin to call them each a government as opposed to an extended royal household—reluctantly began to take a larger and stronger interest in the ordering of the colonies, the colonies became less interesting and less significant in the life of old Europe. But European developments were to have profound political, intellectual, social, and economic effects on the North American colonies, and it is appropriate to turn to events in Europe. The colonists were too few, too poor, too unprotected to do without a connection to the home country. The inhabitants of New England called themselves English and thought of themselves as part of English political society; similarly, the settlers of New France and Acadia were French and subject to the French monarch. England and France thus became protector, inspiration, and model for their colonists. New England and New France moved from the center of attention and fashion to the periphery, from innovative colonies to provincial status in the reforming and authoritarian monarchies in England and France.

## *The European Template*

The English republic did not endure, the English Civil War was not resumed, and the French civil wars, which had lasted on and off for almost a century, came to an end. But the memory of the republic, or Commonwealth, as it was called, lingered inside and outside the British Isles. There were two parts to the recollection. First, for ten years England enjoyed highly effective and purposeful government, and through the 1650s was consistently successful in its wars abroad. Second, despite its popular origins, Oliver Cromwell's government at home was tyrannical and arbitrary, and after Cromwell's death in 1658 its authority swiftly drained away, leading to the return of the monarchy in the person of Charles II, eldest son of the executed king, in 1660. Cromwell got posthumous justice: Charles II had his corpse exhumed, hung in chains, and beheaded. It took several centuries for Cromwell personally to be readopted into the English political tradition, but arguably his spirit and his ideas lived on, thanks to the light-headed governments of the later Stuart kings, Charles II and James II.

What had happened once might happen again, and indeed for the next fifty years England added to its reputation among the powers of Europe for turbulence and disorder. Louis XIV of France, cousin and contemporary of the Stuart kings of England, cited England as a horrible example of what might happen in the absence of a powerful monarch and an absolutist state. Louis was, after 1660, unchallenged domestically, and he used the resources of his large, rich, and populous kingdom to build an army of a size and efficiency not seen in Europe since the fall of the Roman Empire a thousand years earlier. Louis demanded obedience and uniformity from his subjects, and that included religion, for Louis was a bigoted Catholic. Protestants ("Huguenots") could convert to Catholicism, or they could, officially or unofficially, emigrate. Louis thus produced the first modern refugees.

Charles II maneuvered skillfully past sometimes hostile parliamentary majorities, in a political climate where taxation and religion were the dominant issues. For a time he even did without a parliament, since there was no absolute requirement for it to meet at any stated interval. The bad example of his cousin Louis was hardly reassuring to English (or Scottish or Irish) Protestants in the three countries where Charles was king—or, for that matter, in the colonies, which were even more uniformly Protestant than their home country. (The colonies were reminded of their subordinate status when Charles pursued some of the men who had signed his father's death warrant even across the Atlantic; but the colonists successfully concealed them so that they died in their beds of natural causes rather than at the end of a hangman's rope.)

England and Scotland were strongly Protestant countries, where the number of Catholics had been reduced to a tiny minority, of possibly 5 percent. The Protestants of whatever variety—and there were several—were determined to keep it that way. Despite this, the royal family, the Stuarts, inclined to Catholicism. The king, Charles II, was the official head of the Protestant Church of England, and by that token he was the Protestant champion. But his brother James converted to Catholicism and later married a Catholic. The prospect of a Catholic king disturbed many in England, and in the Protestant colonies too. Catholics were believed to be addicted to bigotry and persecution, and a Catholic occupying the highest office in the land was thought to be a definite risk. Louis XIV's persecution of the Huguenots fulfilled every Protestant fantasy. Nevertheless, on his deathbed Charles became a Catholic.

When he succeeded to the throne in 1685, James lived up to the worst expectations of his most pessimistic subjects. As king, he believed himself above the law, but just to make sure, he purged the administration, including the judges. Obedient courts produced the verdicts James desired and ratified his odd ideas about absolute executive authority. James "dispensed" with laws with which he disagreed—those discriminating against Catholics for example—and suspended their execution.

Conservative Anglicans (the term *Tory* was just coming into use to describe them) were placed in an impossible dilemma. Anxious to revere and obey the monarch under almost all circumstances, they found him threatening their religious institutions, and thus, as they saw it, the English state. Protestantism was embodied in the law, but James considered himself above the law. Those who were not Tories—less inclined to worship the office of the king, more inclined to suspect the king's motives and behavior, and especially skeptical of James II—came gradually to adopt the name *Whigs*. As Whigs and Tories pondered, James assembled a professional army and stationed it outside of London; many of its officers were Catholics, and many of the soldiers were recruited from his other kingdom, Catholic Ireland. A Jesuit lurked at James's side and was said to be more powerful than the king's ministers.

The tipping point was reached in the summer of 1688. Many Tories had been prepared to put up with James for his lifetime, because his heirs, his two daughters, were both Protestant. But when James's queen produced a son who would become king, displacing his sisters in the line of succession, it seemed clear that England would have Catholic monarchs in perpetuity. A group of disillusioned notables wrote James's Protestant nephew, William of Orange, the stadtholder[4] of Holland (a term for which there is no easy equivalent) and begged him to relieve them of their royal burden. William was also married to James's daughter Mary and thus was doubly attractive. William came to England with a Dutch army. James's own army disintegrated. The queen fled dressed as a washerwoman, and James himself eventually followed, almost certainly with William's anxious, if secret, connivance. James II spent the balance of his life stirring up his fellow king, Louis XIV of France, to set him back upon the throne, and indeed James' branch of the Stuarts were able to foment two large rebellions as well as many smaller incidents over the next sixty years. Such was the impression that James II had left on his kingdoms that these uprisings never came close to success.

The "Glorious Revolution" of 1688, much more than the English Civil War, set the mold for the dominant English political tradition in the eighteenth century. A tyrannical Catholic king had been displaced. Justice was not only certain; it was quick. William landed in England in early November 1688 and was in London by the middle of December. William had no effective opposition, and his battles were no more than skirmishes. By the first week of February, he and his wife Mary were king and queen, acclaimed by a "convention" Parliament—one in which the Whigs held the majority in the lower house, although with a substantial Tory minority.[5] The Whigs had no problems with the Glorious Revolution and hoped to consolidate it by limiting arbitrary royal power and enhancing that of Parliament, without, however, getting rid of the monarchy. Many Tories had only recently preached unconditional obedience to royal authority, and for them to admit that James had violated their trust was a substantial and painful concession. The House of Commons resolved that James had "endeavoured to subvert the Constitution of the Kingdom, by breaking the Original Contract between King and People; and, by the advice of [the Catholic order of] Jesuits and other wicked Persons, having violated the fundamental Laws; and having withdrawn himself out of this Kingdom; has abdicated the Government; and that the Throne is thereby vacant."[6]

In the Whigs' recollection, swiftly embodied as "tradition," 1688 was a true revolution, Glorious in both its process and its legacy. William's triumphal march to London, and James's ignominious flight, featured in this version. A patriotic nobility led the revolt in this legend, sustained by a patriotic and Protestant public. As to its being a true revolution, historians are inclined to agree, but unlike the triumphant Whigs, they now point out that James's overthrow could not have been accomplished without substantial coercion of his supporters. In many parts of England and Scotland, hysteria swept the population. Mobs ruled the streets, Catholics were roughed up and intimidated, their property was plundered, and Catholic chapels were sacked if not burned to the ground. Not all opposition was quelled, though even after James was deported voices were heard in public calling for him to be invited back, on the grounds that true subjects should be "obedient in all things to Kings." Such opinions were by then no longer taken seriously, even by most Tories—but that they could be uttered at all without reprisal is worth noting.[7]

The Whigs made sure to delineate the Constitution as they understood it, first in a Declaration of Rights, presented to William and Mary in February 1689 and tacitly accepted by the new monarchs, who became William III and Mary II. The Declaration enumerated James II's constitutional transgressions—his packing of the judiciary, his "dispensing" with laws, his arming of Catholics and disarming of Protestants among other things—and then listed a series of remedies, including free and frequent parliaments, freedom of the subject to petition the sovereign without fear of retaliation, free elections to Parliament, and a prohibition on "cruel and unusual punishments." Later in 1689 Parliament embodied the Declaration in a statute, and it remains to this day part of the British Constitution. A separate Act of Settlement regulated the succession to the English throne, barring Catholics from the office. Taking the oath as king, William (and all his successors) promised to maintain the reformed Protestant church in England—meaning, for most purposes, the Anglican church.

William III and Mary II did not merely become King and Queen of England, but King and Queen of Scotland too. (Ireland, though technically a separate kingdom, took its kings and queens automatically from England.) In Scotland the majority Presbyterians had been actively persecuted by both Charles II and James II, on behalf of the Anglican Church. (There was in fact a substantial Anglican minority.) The Scots drove a hard bargain, but in the end the dominant Presbyterians had little choice but to take the Protestant monarch and repudiate his Catholic father-in-law. Naturally Presbyterianism, not Anglicanism, became the state religion. There was a flurry of civil war in Scotland, swiftly put down, but the real conflict occurred in Ireland, where James was still in possession, and he soon arrived with a French army to enforce his claim. Protestant Ulster (the island's northeast quadrant) resisted James, and the arrival of William III and his Dutch army in 1690 did the rest.

James did leave a symbolic legacy. He had been, or had hoped to be, a tyrant. He believed he was not bound by law and custom, and he did his best to subvert the English (and Scottish) Constitution. Perhaps James did not conspire to accomplish his will in the technical sense, but he acted in concert with soldiers, politicians, and judges who were willing to do his bidding, whatever it might be. He was, of course, also a *Catholic* tyrant, and thus confirmed for his subjects for the next two or three generations that Catholicism and tyranny were intimately linked. The 1688 Revolution was accordingly justified as Protestant resistance to Catholic tyranny, and that principle became one of the foundations of English or British political thought in the century that followed. Because it was such a powerful principle, politicians were tempted to invoke it, and, being politicians, they frequently indulged the temptation. As a result, the concepts of tyranny and conspiracy were familiar enough—close enough—in the eighteenth century, as was the notion of justified popular resistance. Of course, if tyranny lodged somewhere else—France, for example, or Spain—then the inheritance of the Glorious Revolution strengthened the hand of the English nation and its government. But what if tyranny returned and took up residence again in London?

## *Revolution in the Colonies*

By 1688 England's colonies had spread along the Atlantic seaboard from the Carolinas (named after Charles II) to New England via New York (named after the Duke of York, who became James II, the king who fled in 1688), Pennsylvania, and New Jersey. The colonies operated according to royal charters granted to their colonizers or proprietors, sometimes permitting a fair amount of autonomy to the inhabitants to elect assemblies and even to select governors—all operating in the name of the distant king in London.

Unluckily for the colonists, the distant king, James II, saw a purpose for the colonies: to feed his appetite for revenue independent of any parliamentary grants.[8] The colonists by 1690 numbered in the hundreds of thousands—210,000 by current estimates, or four times the number in 1650. James was already the proprietor of New York and New Jersey, and his servants had been active in the administration of those colonies. (Some of James' appointees were, in fact, quite able.) James expanded their jurisdiction to New England, whose colonies he amalgamated into a single "dominion." He arbitrarily altered the colonial governments, discarding the colonial charters, instead appointing his own servants to be governors, while dissolving the colonial assemblies. Most notably, James' governors could levy taxation, confiscate land, and select judges and juries to try cases. Behind the governors sat the army, to remind the colonists of the fate in store for them should they resist. The governors denied that the colonists maintained the rights of Englishmen. These had been abandoned, they said, when the colonists had left English shores. If they disobeyed, they could expect fines, imprisonment, and confiscation of property or, in some cases, all three.

Under the circumstances, news of James II's displacement was joyfully received in Boston and New York. There were rebellions in New England, New York, and Maryland. The former king's governors fled or were arrested. The New England dominion was spontaneously disassembled, and the colonies resumed their colonial charters. The reasoning was the same as in England and Scotland, that "Almighty God" had saved the people of "the Three Kingdoms from the horrible brinks of Popery and Slavery."[9]

Or had tried to. William III's government used the occasion to rein in some of the colonial privileges, particularly the near-republican autonomy of Massachusetts. Only parts of Massachusetts's privileges were restored in a new charter, granted in 1691. Governors would henceforth be appointed by the king or his deputies in London, as in all other colonies except, remarkably, Connecticut and Rhode Island, which down to 1776 and after elected their own governors, councils, and assemblies. In the other colonies, now called provinces, governors representing the king or queen coexisted with elected assemblies, sometimes happily, sometimes not.

New York kept its name, and an effusively loyal nomenclature guaranteed that these notable events would never be forgotten—Ulster and Orange counties proliferated, while even the queen's sister, Princess Anne, and her husband, Prince George, appeared in county names. Virginia's College of William and Mary was located in Williamsburg, the colonial capital—named, of course, after William III.

In all this flourishing culture of loyal designation, there was one considerable change of name. In 1707, during the reign of Queen Anne, the previously autonomous realms of England and Scotland merged, into the new, united, kingdom of Great Britain. Anne became the first *British* monarch, and her subjects on both sides of the Atlantic quickly called themselves "British"—an invented nationality, to which they became strongly attached. The song "Rule Britannia," composed in 1740, expressed—may indeed have helped create—the identity of this new people.[10]

Annapolis, Maryland, is not the only town (nor the only colonial capital) to bear that name. In 1710 *British* forces captured the tiny capital of the French colony of Acadia and renamed it after their queen. Better still, they were colonial British forces, from Massachusetts, traveling on board a British fleet. Acadia was renamed too, becoming Nova Scotia, the first fruit in North America of the wars between Protestant Britain and Catholic France. A treaty in 1713 ended the war and kept Nova Scotia, and Annapolis, for Great Britain.

Britain's Protestant identity had been reinforced by an influx of French Protestant refugees, the Huguenots, fleeing royal and Catholic persecution in France in the 1680s. Estimates vary as to their number: a conservative figure would be 200,000. The Huguenots dispersed throughout Protestant Europe, including Great Britain, and almost immediately many moved on to the colonies in America.[11]

France and Britain—France especially—took a much more active role in the development of their colonies after 1660. Louis XIV turned New France into a province of France, with a governor and other officials appointed by himself, and with the various aspects of government subordinated to the king's ministers in Paris. To sustain them, the king sent money. To fight off the Iroquois, the king sent a small army. Then and later, the king's soldiers and governors successfully defended the new

province against native marauders, and their success was crowned by a
Great Peace signed at Montreal in 1701. New France's survival against
native attack was never again in doubt.

New France's survival against other enemies was much more in question. Dutch weapons, bought by the Iroquois, were used in attacks on
French settlements. France's frequent European wars had North American
consequences. In 1629 an English fleet forced Champlain to surrender
Quebec. It was not returned until 1632, after peace was made between
France and England. War between Louis XIV and William III brought another English fleet, based in Boston with two thousand Massachusetts soldiers, up the St. Lawrence River to Quebec in 1690; but by then King
Louis's forces were sufficient to see the English off.

Not all contact was warlike, but there was, and could be, little trade
across a frontier that consisted of hundreds of miles of trackless wilderness. Swamps, mosquitoes, and disease played their part in keeping
French and British colonists apart, at least on the North American mainland. In Acadia and in Newfoundland things were different. The fishery
brought fishing fleets, competition, rivalry, and occasionally violence.
Because the fishery was worth something, and had a direct connection to
Europe via annual fishing fleets, the coasts and islands and fishing boats
of the Gulf of St. Lawrence sometimes played more of a role in international affairs than the settlers and traders of the interior.

There were also the inhabitants of the frontier, who made the swamps and
forests their own—what one historian has called "the Middle Ground" between French and British America.[12] European settlement followed the
coasts and river valleys. Roads were few and poor, and travel slow and restricted. In Newfoundland, it was debatable whether there was any permanent settlement; certainly there was no regular government. Thirty miles
from the coast or the navigable rivers, and the colonies ceased to be, except
as sources for or recipients of trade, or in cartographers' fantasies. In 1700,
the native inhabitants, the native *nations* of North America, still outnumbered
the European settlers. Those in contact with the Europeans on the eastern
seaboard belonged to two great linguistic groups, Algonkin and Iroquoian.
Of the Iroquoians, the most powerful were the *Haudenosaunee*: the "People
of the Longhouse," the Five Nations, or the Iroquois to the English. The Five
Nations spent most of the seventeenth century in conflict with the French and
their Algonkin allies, or so it must have seemed to the beleaguered French.

By the eighteenth century, after a "Great Treaty" between themselves
and France in 1701, the Iroquois played one nation, the English or British,

off against another, the French. The British and French both had their supporters inside the Five Nations, and a fair number of the Iroquois had actually migrated to New France to dwell close to the French and to share their Catholic religion. Some historians have argued, not without force, that the French approach to the natives was more civilized than that of the English or British. The French did not wage a war of extermination against the natives of the St. Lawrence valley as the English did against the original inhabitants of New England or Virginia—but on the other hand, the original Iroquoian inhabitants of the valley had disappeared by the time the French got there. There were far fewer European immigrants to New France than to New England or Virginia, and less pressure to displace the natives along the frontier. Moreover, the French maintained a lucrative trade in furs with the natives of the interior, which presumed co-operation rather than belligerence as a basic policy. And, of course, there were not enough French settlers or soldiers to make a policy of war and conquest or extermination feasible.

War with the natives, then usually called "Indians," was no light matter. The natives could slip through the forests beyond the frontier of settlement and pick off isolated farms or villages or even forts. Burned houses, kidnapped wives and children, and scalped bodies left behind in the ashes made the Indian a fearsome, almost supernatural, being—and for many of the devout Protestants along the colonial frontier, the incarnation of Satan.[13] Indian warfare therefore had, over time, a psychological impact that may well have been greater than the actual physical fact of war and battle—a kind of multiplier that made the natives much more powerful and terrifying than their actual numbers would justify. That in turn enhanced the Indians' value as warriors and allies.

The French, already thinly spread, extended themselves further into the interior, founding Fort Detroit in 1701 and a couple of posts along the Gulf of Mexico soon after. In 1718 they established New Orleans and organized the colony of Louisiana, which stretched north along the Mississippi to meet New France around the Great Lakes. This was a conscious imperial policy, designed to hem in the British colonies along the Atlantic seaboard, and it certainly looked impressive on a map. It was, however, less impressive on the ground. The distances between France's posts in the interior were great, and the French garrisons at Detroit (Fort Pontchartrain), Kaskaskia (Fort de Chartres), and Natchez (Fort Rosalie), the way stations along the water route to New Orleans, were tiny. It was essential for the French to maintain good relations with the neighboring

Indian nations, which greatly outnumbered them. To prove the point, when a foolish French commander at Natchez gravely offended the local natives, he, his troops, and his fort, not to mention French settlers around the fort, were wiped out in 1729.[14] The French had their revenge—most of the Natchez nation were killed, and those who surrendered were sold into slavery in the French colonies in the West Indies. The episode suggests that amicable relations between the French and the natives were as much a function of numbers and power as any special affinity or inclination to seek peaceful relations. And of course, numbers and power could just as easily work in reverse. At Detroit, a powerful alliance of native nations demanded and got French aid in a bloody war against the Fox nation. But when, in a second war, the French tried to finish the job and exterminate the Fox, their allies deserted, and there was nothing the French could do to induce or compel them to fight.[15]

The French would have had difficulty in quickly reinforcing their interior forts. The estimated total European-derived population of New France in the early 1700s was about fifteen thousand and that of Acadia about eleven hundred. By comparison, the population of the English colonies had passed 250,000, would double in a generation, and double again in the next generation, to almost 1.2 million in 1750. True, New France also doubled and redoubled in that same time period, but the resulting number was sixty thousand—more than a million less than the British colonies.

The New French were not only fewer, but poorer. It is impossible to put a precise number on it, but one economic historian has calculated that in 1700 the average per capita gross domestic product—put in contemporary currency and using the values of 1990—of New France and Acadia was $430 and that of the British colonies $527.[16] The gist is that the French colonists were not as well off as their British counterparts, by about 20 percent. The disparity was to be a constant in Canadian–American comparisons (indeed a recent estimate puts the difference in income between Canadians and Americans at—20 percent).[17] There are many explanations, ranging from the reluctance of the French to leave their fertile and sunny homes in Europe (though French Protestants did, at the point of the king's bayonets), to the relative lack of fertile land in New France (true, but not all the arable land had been taken up by 1750), to the abominable cold in winter and prevalence of mosquitoes in summer (true, but the colder climate was discouraging to diseases as well as to the potential victims of disease; as for the insects, the British colonies also had them).

The French colonists were disadvantaged relative to the British colonists, but not when they were compared with the French of France. The standard of living did improve in the North American colonies, whether British or French, by the early eighteenth century. Travelers remarked that the colonists were well fed and well clothed, and they were increasingly better housed. By the early eighteenth century, in the British colonies, rich merchants and plantation owners were building large and comfortable mansions in the growing towns, or country houses outside of town. There were great estates, and great houses, along the Hudson River in New York, in Pennsylvania, and in the southern colonies—where they were naturally staffed by slaves.[18] This marks a contrast with New France, where houses might be commodious, but nevertheless lacked the space and style, and the luxurious furnishings, of their British counterparts.[19] Formal social standing had nothing to do with it. The French did make an attempt to install a semi-feudal nobility and succeeded in creating a "gentry" class— the seigneurs, who lived in manor houses on their seigneuries. But, as one observer put it in 1737, the seigneurs were likely to be "as poor as artists and as vain as peacocks." Nonetheless, life by the middle of the eighteenth century was secure and, compared with peasant life in Europe, solid and prosperous.[20]

Culturally, the colonies replicated the styles of their European homelands. Domestic architecture followed the models of the English or French regions from which the settlers had come. In New France, the model was Normandy and the Atlantic coastal provinces of France. New England resembled East Anglia in England, while the southern provinces took their cultural forms from the English–Scottish border, with an admixture of Ulster in Ireland.[21]

What the French had, the British coveted. What the French had was land, or at least claims to land, and as the British colonies grew, so did their appetite for real estate. The problem was the land was inhabited. To both the British and the French, the most powerful and most familiar inhabitants were the Iroquois, now the Six Nations. The Iroquois, like the French, practiced the politics of territorial grandeur, in claiming land far beyond their ability to populate it, or even defend it. In the late seventeenth and early eighteenth centuries the Iroquois steadily expanded their influence over their native neighbors, stretching at times into what are now Illinois, Indiana, and Kentucky. This certainly made them more formidable on paper, and prestige and legendary strength were, as always, diplomatic assets. The native nations of the Ohio Valley for the time being added greatly to Iroquois strength, multiplying it by three or four times. That was just as well, because observers put the actual strength of Iroquois arms at no more than two thousand warriors in the 1720s and as few as eleven hundred in the 1750s.

## The State of Britain and the British State

The British were already nibbling at the margins of France's North American empire, an aggressive policy that at the time seemed almost to be counter-intuitive. France, after all, was the larger country in territory and population, in arable land, and in wealth. But the English had managed to compensate for their demographic weakness. In countering Louis XIV's ambitions, the English (and then the British) reorganized their public finances, making it much easier for the British government to raise and spend money, while Louis XIV and his successors creaked along with a system that ultimately derived from the Middle Ages. If the French government chose to spend money, it placed a strain on the financial system. Even if that was a matter of indifference to the kings of France and their aristocratic ministers, it should not have been, for it did ultimately affect the stability of the state, as the unlucky Louis XVI discovered many years later. In England, Charles I had paid with his head in 1649 because of his inability to raise money by legal means; the same fate would befall his distant cousin of France in 1793.

As a result, in the wars of the long eighteenth century between France and Britain, France's obvious strategic advantages of size were negated by its much smaller rival, which was, at the same time, undergoing an economic and a political revolution. Turbulent Britain was becoming stable Britain as the settlement of 1689 took hold on British politics. When the Stuart dynasty expired with the death of Queen Anne in 1714, she was peacefully succeeded by her Protestant cousins (also the descendants of James I and Henry VII and the medieval kings of England), the House of Hanover in Germany. George I arrived from Germany in 1714 understanding little English, but at least grasping that as king of Great Britain he was a much more consequential figure than he had been as Elector of Hanover, his previous eminence.

George relied on his ministers, and as the ministers emerged into the political spotlight, the monarch receded. This was the great political development of the eighteenth century. If William III's government, like James II's, was the king's government in a very real sense, with the king as chief executive officer, that was no longer true of the governments of George I or his son George II. William and his sister-in-law, Queen Anne, had presided over meetings of the ministers, in what came to be called the cabinet. Beginning with George I's reign, the king was still a most important political figure, but the real action now took place outside the royal palaces and in the precincts of the British Parliament. There was now a chief minister, who, in the absence of the king, presided over the cabinet. The actual title of *prime minister* was not officially recognized until the mid-nineteenth century (the term *First Lord of the Treasury* was used before that), but in fact there were effective prime ministers from the 1720s onward. In 1735 the position received a home within walking distance of Parliament, 10 Downing Street, occupied from that day forward by the head of government and prime minister of Great Britain.

This may seem a pointless excursion in political nomenclature, but it is important because of the very novelty of these developments in the eighteenth century. When the revolutionaries of 1688 spoke of the office of king, they were referring to the head of government, a person with real and even decisive power, even after the Revolution clipped his political wings. But George I, George II, and George III were not kings like William III: they confided their governments into what they believed were good hands and hoped for the best. Above all, these kings dreaded having to manage politics directly in the kingdom, for experience showed what could happen if king and Parliament were out of sync. Parliament was elected every seven years, in a process that was certainly imperfect and unrepresentative of the majority of British adults. To meet the deficiency, political theorists invented the notion of "virtual representation"—so that whether one could vote or not, every Briton was "represented." Under virtual representation, British subjects wherever they were had a voice in the British Parliament, which represented them all, thanks to political theory. The theory had not yet been put to the test.

It followed that the primary requirement of the king's first minister was to command a majority in the House of Commons. This was not always easy, for the norms of party politics were not yet set. It was not at all accepted that there should be such a thing as party politics. Should not government be as one, engaging all well-intentioned and patriotic subjects? Partisan politics were often condemned as "factional," and there was much truth in the label, since politics centered on—or even derived from—the interests of the great landed aristocracy and their assorted followers. Broadly speaking, these were Whigs, supporters of the constitutional settlement of 1688 and generally favoring limitations on the royal power, but there were also some Tories, who took a much more favorable view of royal authority. Political leadership was not just a simple matter of inheritance: it took skill and management, and money. It was true that the voters could sometimes be bought, but not always, and shifts in the composition of the House of Commons could mean shifts in the office-holders at the top. And it goes without saying that not every prominent British politician was skillful or prudent in managing the king's business, as the many shifting governments of the 1740s and early 1750s showed.

Shifts in British politics and events on the continent of Europe drew Great Britain into the War of the Austrian Succession (1744–8),[22] known in the British colonies as King George's War. Though most of the action was in Europe, the war was fought on a global scale between the British and the French. Frontier raids in North America resumed after a pause of thirty years, mostly afflicting New York, New England, and Nova Scotia. On the other hand, an Anglo-American army landed on Cape Breton Island (owned by France) to besiege the fortress of Louisbourg. Fantastically costly to build, Louisbourg guarded the sea lanes from France to Quebec City: its loss was a humiliation for the French, as well as a strategic peril to New France, and a triumph for the British forces, particularly those from Massachusetts. Not surprisingly, some in Massachusetts saw a higher power at work in the fall of Louisbourg: "[Let] our Joy rise higher," one minister intoned, "that hereby a great Support of Antichristian Power is taken away, and the Visible Kingdom of Christ enlarged."[23]

Unluckily for Massachusetts, the Kingdom of Christ shrank back to its original dimensions in 1748 when Great Britain made peace and traded Louisbourg back to France for Madras in India and the status quo in Europe. In Massachusetts the return of Louisbourg to France was seen as rank betrayal, although the British government did try to soften the blow by sending a large amount of money to the province to pay its costs during the war.

For the French and especially French officials in New France, the peace of 1748 was a reprieve, of which they needed to take advantage immediately. War could easily break out again, they reasoned, though they did not pause to consider whether the outbreak would not be hastened by their own efforts. On Cape Breton Island the French reoccupied Louisbourg, but they did not stop there. The French administration encouraged the French-speaking Acadians from mainland Nova Scotia to leave their homes and come to Louisbourg, and a great many did. Raids on British settlements by the French and their Indian allies made it clear that a real peace had not been secured. In the words of a French missionary, Abbé Jean-Louis LeLoutre, "I think that we cannot do better than to incite the Indians to continue warring on the English." He had his wish, but one consequence was the embitterment of relations between local British officials and the Acadian inhabitants of Nova Scotia, who refused either to take an oath of allegiance to King George or to bear arms on behalf of the British Crown. Up until that point the situation had been tolerated. Now it seemed to be a clear danger to British interests. The authorities in Quebec City did their bit as well. British wealth and power in the American colonies threatened not just New France, but old France, by altering the balance of power across the Atlantic in Britain's favor.[24] Taking advantage of the weakening of Iroquois power around the Great Lakes, the governor of New France in 1753 sent an expedition into the Ohio country, as it was called, the land drained by the Ohio River. It was quite a force, the largest ever raised in New France up to that time—three hundred regular troops, seventeen hundred Canadian militia,[25] and two hundred Indians. They built a road from Lake Erie to the nearest tributary of the Ohio and established forts in what is now Western Pennsylvania to guard it. It was a considerable achievement, but it cost four hundred lives due to sickness—a very substantial loss for a small colony whose total population was around fifty-five thousand. While these military adventures went forward, in London, the king's chief minister, the Duke of Newcastle, complained of "the wild French governors in America."[26]

The French forts attracted the attention of the governor of Virginia, who sent an officer, George Washington, to warn the French off. Washington got a courteous reception and a dusty answer: the land belonged to the king of France, and that was that. This was grave news back in Virginia, where land speculators had already carved up the land and had large expectations of the fortunes to be made from real estate deals. In 1754 Washington returned to the Ohio country with a small force and fought briefly and unsuccessfully against the French, who captured and then released him, once again to bear dismal news back to the Virginian capital at Williamsburg. The next year, 1755, it was the turn of the British army under General Edward Braddock, with Washington as his aide de camp. Near modern Pittsburgh Braddock and his army were massacred, leaving Washington once again to take the news back to tidewater Virginia. Washington's excursions and Braddock's defeat took place before war was officially declared between Great Britain and France. When it was, in 1756, it set the clock running on what would be called the Seven Years War.

Braddock was the first of a series of unlucky British generals sent to fight the French in America. There were a few victories, the most important of which was the capture of a French fort on the frontier between Acadia and Nova Scotia in 1755. Once again New England sent troops, which, together with British regulars, captured the fort in June 1755. Two months later, those troops were used again, this time to solve the "Acadian problem," as the British saw it. The Acadians were offered one more chance to take the oath to King George. Refusing, they were bundled on board ships and deported to colonies further south. New England settlers, eight thousand of them, arrived to take their place between 1759 and 1766, with the expectation that Nova Scotia could become another New England colony. Meanwhile, at the other end of the province, on Cape Breton, another Anglo-American army besieged and took Louisbourg in 1758. This time Louisbourg was blown up and its inhabitants dispersed. Nova Scotia would now be a permanent addition to the thirteen original provinces of British North America, New England's northernmost outpost.

The capture of Louisbourg was the first sign of a turn in British fortunes. The government had changed, with the appointment of a new ministry under William Pitt, despite King George II's longstanding dislike for the Whig politician. (All the significant politicians were Whigs, so it was not party prejudice.) Pitt led the government in the House of Commons and inspired it to find the formula for victory over France in the Seven Years War. Shoveling money and soldiers into the American colonies, Pitt successfully raised fifty thousand troops from the American provinces, which served alongside the regular British army in the invasion and conquest of New France. It was admittedly a political and financial strain on the British taxpayer, but in the face of urgent need, that consideration could be put aside for the moment. The French were crippled by British naval power at one end of New France and by progressively worsening relations with their erstwhile native allies. The culminating event was the siege and capture of Quebec in 1759, in which the commanding British general, James Wolfe, snatched victory after months of frustration and in the face of a growing fear of failure, and died heroically in the battle of the Plains of Abraham outside the city. Less noticed, but equally if not more important, was the Royal Navy's success in severing communications between France and its North American colony. Soon after the fall of Quebec, the navy destroyed the French fleet at Quiberon Bay on the west coast of France; the French navy did not recover for the balance of the war. There would be no rescue for the isolated French garrisons in America, and they duly surrendered to the British in 1760.

The French army sailed away to France, taking most of the colonial officials and a fair proportion of New France's elite. Left behind were around sixty thousand "Canadiens"—Canadians—the name the inhabitants of New France had given to themselves from the term *Canada* used by Jacques Cartier for the valley of the St. Lawrence. Isolated and insulated in the valley of the St. Lawrence, almost entirely Catholic thanks to French policy, they now fell under the rule of an English-speaking, Protestant kingdom, many of whose subjects saw France and the French as slaves to tyranny, and in any case "antichristian." It promised an interesting future, because the terms of the capitulation of Montreal guaranteed the inhabitants the freedom to practice their Catholic religion and to keep their existing French code of law.[27] At the very least, British government in Canada would be founded on a contradiction between ideology and expediency, between keeping New France functioning by working with and through Catholics, and the deeply held beliefs of millions of anti-Catholic British Protestants.

The fall of Quebec was the triumph of the British Empire—adding to the joy and self-esteem of its already proud inhabitants.[28] Joy was universal, from the British Isles through the British colonies. The *Pennsylvania Gazette* announced that the fall of Quebec "has entirely broke the French power in America," and effectively, it was right, though the last French military remnant did not surrender until the fall of Montreal in September 1760.[29] Bells rang, solemn services of thanksgiving were held, and the triumph of Protestantism and the British race was duly celebrated. A monument to Wolfe was carved in Westminster Abbey, and a painting of the "Death of Wolfe" showed the hero-martyr in a largely fanciful but affecting setting. In death, Wolfe became an enduring icon of the British Empire, a fate that probably would not have displeased him.

## North America in 1763

The Treaty of Paris of 1763 reflected the triumph of British arms but also, indirectly, of British finance that had paid for the arms. To secure peace, France ceded all its mainland possessions in North America east of the Mississippi River to Great Britain. The balance of Louisiana was ceded to France's ally Spain, to compensate the Spanish for the loss of Florida to the British. France kept two small islands off Newfoundland, St. Pierre and Miquelon, and retained some fishing rights in the area. The French did regain some territory conquered by the British, especially the sugar islands in the West Indies, which in terms of trade were worth much more than the ice and snow and fur of New France. As for New France, France had no further role, though in the treaty, as in the surrender of Montreal, the practice of the Catholic religion was permitted, as far as the laws of Great Britain allowed.

The British victory retrospectively seemed inevitable. The English, then the British, had developed a superior financial system, which sat on top of an expanding economy, and could pay for a large and dominant fleet, which permitted a massive flow of immigrants across the Atlantic. The disparity between the populations of the British and the French colonies, large in 1689, was overwhelming by 1760. Yet the stalemate in the war of the 1740s, King George's War, and the early French victories in the war of the 1750s, the Seven Years War, indicated something different to contemporaries. The desperation with which British politicians confronted the possibility of defeat in 1756 and 1757 suggests that another outcome was conceivable.

But the other outcome did not happen. Everyone recognized that the situation of the British colonies was greatly improved. Great Britain now owned the entire Atlantic coast of North America and half the Mississippi valley too. The colonies held roughly two and a half million people including hundreds of thousands of African slaves—a sad but real indication of prosperity. The American empire was divided into seventeen provinces (later eighteen), of which fourteen, from Nova Scotia to Georgia, had governors mostly appointed by the government in London and elected assemblies.[30] The exceptions were East and West Florida, acquired from Spain, and the newly renamed province of Quebec, which had no elected assemblies. The treaty of peace did not give the Catholics of Quebec the right to vote, which was denied also to Catholics in the British Isles, or the right to hold office. Quebec and Florida apart, the administration of the colonies depended on the consent of the governed and the co-operation of the king's subjects. In the last resort, by pushing and hauling and bribing and influencing and occasionally threatening, the consent had been given.

It was quite a distance from the edge of British settlement along the Appalachian mountains to the Mississippi. The trans-mountain territory was almost entirely inhabited by native peoples divided by language, culture, history, and geography. Land speculators in the British colonies were determined to change that, and it took no imagination at all to predict conflict, especially as thousands of settlers arrived in New York, Philadelphia, and Charleston. But after 1763, there was no international frontier and no French governor in Quebec to appeal to.

And yet, paradoxically, the government in London now substituted itself for the French as the arbiter between the American provincials and the natives. In a sense, having got rid of one enemy, the British government unintentionally created a replacement. London had over time developed policies with the aim of conciliating and allying with the native nations, particularly the Iroquois—"our best friends," according to Sir William Johnson, the British "Indian superintendent," "or our most dangerous enemies."[31] Successive British governments attempted to separate Indians—and especially "Indian" land—from British settlement, first by a royal proclamation (1763) and then by treaty (1768), but these were at best temporary impediments to the flood of settlers. The government had few tools available to it—if the colonists chose to ignore instructions from London, there was little recourse. At best, and at worst, there was the British army, which ministers in London were doing their best to reduce, in the interest of economy. The army, in turn, was a very blunt instrument. Until 1763 it was employed not to discipline the Americans, but to protect them and advance their interests. After 1763 it was a very different matter.

## 2

## *Patriots and Loyalists*

BETWEEN 1763 AND 1783 the British Empire suffered a political collapse, followed by a bitter, eight-year civil war, which would later be called the American Revolution. When the war ended, British North America contracted. Its southern frontier was no longer in the Gulf of Mexico, facing Spain's colonies, but along the Great Lakes, facing the new United States of America. Its population shrank too, from 2.5 million to 300,000, most of whom did not speak English. The largest city in this shrunken empire was no longer Philadelphia, but Quebec City. A surrendering British army marched into captivity with its band playing a current tune, "The World Turned Upside Down." At least the losing British general, Lord Cornwallis, had not lost his sense of irony.

Money, or the lack of it, lay at the root of the American Revolution. The British government needed money, or thought it did, to pay off the debts it had accumulated during the Seven Years War. The war had been largely fought in North America, and its greatest beneficiaries, so they argued, were the American colonies. Surely the colonies could contribute to paying off money that had been spent on their behalf? So reasoned British politicians and, in 1763, many Americans too. There was a flaw in the argument: the war had been fought for British purposes as well as British-American ones, and the windfalls of the peace treaty, including Canada, benefited Great Britain as well as British America. The concentration on British America as a revenue target was risky, as well as unsound.

It was unsound because of constitutional incoherence. Incoherence need not doom a constitution; almost all political–constitutional systems harbor some contradictory elements, which, with luck, never connect. Fundamental to the British Constitution was the principle that a subject might not be taxed without giving consent. Fundamental, too, was the principle that the institutions of the Constitution, the monarch, and the Parliament represented the whole kingdom, from which it followed that their decisions—decisions by the king-in-Parliament—bound the whole kingdom. But the British House of Commons—representing only the kingdoms of England and Scotland—was based on an allocation of seats that last made sense in the sixteenth century, as far as England was concerned. Many seats had no resident voters, and many more were "owned" by rich proprietors who had no desire to lose their privileges or their influence. And so was invented the concept of "virtual representation"— whether or not a subject had the vote, or could exercise it, he was "represented" anyway and was bound by the result. It was a theory that justified the exclusion of the female 50 percent of the population[1] and of subjects who did not earn enough to meet the property qualifications that attached to the privilege of voting. There were other arguments too, less polite than virtual representation and founded on conceptions of the immutable superiority of the male and of the property-holder, and so on.

The British Empire was a shared experience—common history, common laws, common delusions, and common problems. The common history stretched back through the Reformation, the English Civil War, and the struggles against the Stuart kings, especially the tyrannical James II, with his design to subvert the Constitution and strip his subjects of their ancient liberties. English common law bound at least the English part of Great Britain to the colonies. Some lawyers moved to the colonies, but as the eighteenth century wore on and American prosperity increased, American students traveled back to London to study the common law at the Inns of Court. As for problems, the greatest problem had been the French, and the French, through a common effort, were now disposed of.

It would later be said that the British Empire had grown in a fit of absence of mind, but the same might have been said of the British Constitution. The colonies were created and first settled at a time when colonial dependence was an abject fact, and when the colonies for their survival relied on boats and supplies and, ultimately, money from home. Colonial governance replicated what Britons of the seventeenth century were used to—an executive or governor who ruled on behalf of a distant monarch or for proprietors, like the Penn family in Pennsylvania. In Connecticut and Rhode Island the monarch was exceedingly distant, for governors were elected locally; elsewhere they were selected by the authorities in London. The executive could not levy taxes without the consent of an elected assembly, and from tiny Georgia and Nova Scotia up to populous Virginia and Massachusetts, every British province had its house of assembly. Every colony—or province as they were all called by the eighteenth century— also had a council to advise the governor. And every province had its own miniature political system whose main task was to authorize revenue and supervise how it was spent. Put rather more crudely, politics in the American provinces, as in Great Britain itself, focused on jobs and money—lucrative salaried appointments under the Crown or the disposal of Crown assets to the privileged and the deserving. Judges, tax collectors, sheriffs, and governors and lieutenant-governors all collected salaries, or fees, and as a result enjoyed both security and an elevated position in a society that set store on hierarchy.

The rule of absence of mind also applied to those appointments made from London. Governorships gratified the connections of the king's or queen's ministers, political hangers-on whom it was useful to reward. Some governors lived in London and seldom if ever visited their provinces. Others moved from provinces of lesser importance to larger ones, and thus, desiring promotion, were more concerned to please London than they were to satisfy local needs and interests. By later standards, many were corrupt, and some were corrupt even as the eighteenth century saw such things.

It was an unhappy accident that an "English gentleman of third-rate abilities," Francis Bernard, was appointed governor of Massachusetts in 1760.[2] Bernard's predecessor told him that Massachusetts was a gentle, uncontroversial appointment—nothing to fear or to worry about. Nor was it absolutely out of the ordinary for Bernard to appoint his lieutenant-governor, Thomas Hutchinson, to be at the same time the province's chief justice. There were three problems with this appointment. First, Hutchinson was not a lawyer—not an insuperable difficulty, but all those who were already lawyers were offended at the implied comment on their professional abilities. Second, he kept the three government jobs he already had, and the salaries that were attached, thus depriving two others of money and place. Third, he was a well-known political figure, with more rivals and opponents than he had supporters. He was, it is true, very intelligent—he had graduated from Harvard College at the age of fifteen—but his intelligence did not warn him that he was exposing himself to political danger. There was accordingly a fourth problem: Hutchinson could not see danger coming and lacked the political skills to avert it. If he had to defend an unpopular or controversial policy, he brought little political strength to the party.

Political ability and political strength were needed. First, a local notable challenged the way the customs law was administered—a significant question at a time when customs duties, easy to levy and collect, were the most important segment of the government's revenue. Customs stimulated smuggling, and for a province with abundant ships and imports, evading duties was almost a national sport. That raised the question of who authorized the customs duties, and where the revenues went, the answer being, as everyone knew, that they went to London. And so for the first time the legitimacy of imperial regulation was called into question. By itself the issue might eventually have been smothered and the interested parties bought off, but then another and more serious question arose.

In 1764 the government of the day, pursuing its objective of having the American colonists pay for the war or for the visible consequences of the war, the British garrisons in America, passed through Parliament a Sugar Act that greatly increased the complexity of customs collections in America; this was followed by a Stamp Act in 1765. The American provincials were at least used to customs duties, however much they resented them, but the Stamp Act (called the Duties in American Colonies Act) was a direct tax— requiring a payment for every piece of legal paper produced in the colonies. On payment of the tax, a stamp would be given, hence the title.

The government was not entirely reckless in drafting and passing the Stamp Act. Ministers consulted some of the agents of the provinces in London, especially Benjamin Franklin, the Pennsylvania agent. Not only did Franklin see no difficulty, and certainly no great issue of principle, but he also immediately sought the job of Stamp Act agent in Pennsylvania for a friend of his. So it was that not only the British government was taken by surprise, but many if not most Americans too, by the strenuous objections of provincial politicians. The most extreme protests came from Massachusetts and Virginia.

In Virginia, the House of Burgesses (or assembly) passed five resolutions, the most radical of which appropriated the exclusive power of taxation to the Virginia assembly; that resolution was, however, withdrawn by the assembly the next day. What remained was an assertion of "British freedom" that "internal policy and taxation" required local consent. There were also two resolutions that were apparently not debated; certainly they were not passed. One stated, "That any person who shall by speaking or writing maintain that any person or persons other than the general assembly of this colony have any right or power to impose or lay any taxation whatsoever on the people here shall be deemed an enemy to this his majesty's colony." Those who drafted this resolution were not averse to suppressing contrary opinions, but the time to do that had not yet come. Not in Virginia anyway.

At the heart of political events in Massachusetts was a minor politician and lawyer named Samuel Adams. Adams was undoubtedly a skillful politician and a clever manipulator—and it was Adams's genius to form a secret cabal, called the Loyal Nine,[3] which came to dominate Boston's town government, and which formed a mutually beneficial connection with what would now be called a local gang, centered on the docks. Adams was a man of radical views who had imbibed pure Whig doctrine and by that token was prone to a conspiratorial interpretation of events. Conspiracy theorists were not rare at the time, and sometimes, of course, the conspiracies they spotted were close enough to reality, as in 1688. Adams, like the Virginians, argued that because the colonists were unrepresented in Parliament, they could not be taxed by that body. The assumption by Parliament of the power to tax the colonies suggested to Adams that there were malignant forces at work, in the government in London and through their minions in the colonies, with a design to reduce the colonies to "slavery." At any rate, Adams had formulated a conspiratorial narrative, and his story, or perhaps fable, was easy to understand. Adams's ideology and his political ability transformed a bunch of local rowdies into a purposeful mob, which he and his friends used to intimidate their opponents. As the historian and later judge Hiller Zobel put it, "The force which Samuel Adams and the Loyal Nine summoned into the argument destroyed the possibility of accommodation."[4]

Conspiracy theories are not the sole property of one side. Friends of the government in Massachusetts were pleased to characterize Samuel Adams as a plotter and schemer to the manner born. Even opponents paid tribute to his capacity to attract, hold, and convince an audience. As a hostile witness put it, "He understood human Nature, in low life, so well, that he could turn the minds of the great Vulgar as well as the small into any Course that he might choose."[5]

The mob could be construed as an expression of popular will. It needed a name, and a British politician, Isaac Barré, supplied one, "The Sons of Liberty." The Sons now marched around Boston, intimidating anyone who might be inclined to co-operate with the Stamp Act and assist in its enforcement. One prominent target was the unpopular lieutenant-governor and chief justice, Thomas Hutchinson. On August 28, 1765, Hutchinson's large and elegant house was sacked by the mob. A witness, no particular friend of Hutchinson, recounted that the mob "broke his Windows, threw all his Furniture out of his House, stamp'd upon the chairs, Mahogany Tables, very handsome large gilt-framed Pictures, the Pieces of which lay in Piles on the Street, open'd his Beds and let all the Feathers out, took ten thousand Pounds in Cash, took all his Cloathes, Linnen, Plate and every Thing he had, cut the Balcony off the top of his House, pulled down all the Fruit-Trees in his garden, and did him in all £25,000 Damage."[6] There was no one who could help. The notion of a police force was strange and repellent in eighteenth-century Anglo-Saxon political culture, and apart from a few constables, Boston had none. The magistrates and judges, some of whom hated Hutchinson, were inert. The governor was power-less. Even if he had wanted to call upon the military, there were no regular soldiers in the province.

The Boston riot was a turning point, though its lingering importance was not immediately perceived. Opposition to the Stamp Act acquired an edge, not to say a force. The Sons of Liberty proliferated, and with them their pecu-liar code of conduct.[7] Agents of the Crown could not be protected against mob violence, and those appointed under the Stamp Act prudently resigned. There were of course petitions and representations, resolutions by the var-ious provincial legislatures, and meetings, including a Stamp Act Congress that sought to unite the colonies in opposition. These traditional, "constitu-tional" forms had their effect, and gave a kind of respectability to the opposi-tion to the Act. But behind the remonstrances there was force, applied or implied. As a recent historian gently put it, after 1765 "an individual's stand on imperial legislation held tangible effects for their personal well-being."[8]

Not all the colonies were equally affected. In Nova Scotia, largely set-tled by New Englanders, there were protests and demonstrations. But in Halifax, the provincial capital, there were soldiers, and in the harbor, the Royal Navy. Protest in Halifax could only go so far. Quebec and the Floridas were ruled directly by governors and councils, with no elected assembly and no effective political society that could disturb official tranquility, at least on this issue.

Astounded and perhaps frightened by the reaction, the British govern-ment fractured. There was quickly a new government, and early in 1766 the new government withdrew the Stamp Act, which it could see was un-enforceable. In withdrawing the Stamp Act, the government put a resolu-tion to Parliament, denying that what it was doing meant any limitation on the ability and the right of Parliament to legislate on any subject, including taxation, for the whole British Empire. The resulting Declaratory Act passed almost unanimously.

The repeal of the Stamp Act brought a lull in the theatrical confronta-tions between radical leaders in the colonies and the politicians (and king)

in Great Britain. The conflict nevertheless fueled radical politics. Its leaders were known, and known to be effective, and it had a mob on its side.
On the other side, Governor Bernard and other provincial officials had
noticed that they had nothing to protect them, and that under some circumstances, not hard to imagine, they might need protection.[9]

The next year, those circumstances returned. There were new taxes,
applied not "internally," on the ground, but at the ports, as duties. Further
protests took place, following the template set in 1765. With that experience behind them, this time the British government was prepared to do
something. The rhetorical temperature rose, again there was disorder and
with it the prospect that even the customs laws were or soon would be a
dead letter. Meanwhile the radicals organized a "nonimportation" campaign, what would today be called a boycott of imports from Great Britain.
Such boycotts need general support to be effective, and once again intimidation was the instrument. Once again there were committees and enforced oaths to obey the boycott. Once again there was a spectacle of
disobedience and disorder. What if America proved to be ungovernable?
The general commanding in America, Thomas Gage, urged the government to "Quash this [rebellious] Spirit at a Blow, without too much regard
to the Expence, and it will prove Oeconomy in the End."[10] and at Governor
Bernard's request, they sent troops to Boston, the center of disorder.

The arrival of the army in November 1768 looked impressive, and it
was meant to be impressive. Unfortunately, the radicals were not impressed.
The army might have arrived, but it had arrived in a time of peace. It had
no jurisdiction and no function unless called upon by the local authorities,
and the local authorities were paralyzed. The army was limited to giving
"every legal Assistance" to the magistrates—but what if the magistrates
failed to call? And so the army sat, miserably, through a Boston winter, and
then another. Relations between the radicals and those who opposed them
deteriorated. How could they not? Since the radicals demanded a united
front of colonial opposition to the government, a united front could only
be achieved through the intimidation or violent suppression of those who
disagreed. That was especially the case if the opposition case was well put,
as it was by John Mein, the editor of a "Tory" or pro-government newspaper in Boston. (If the Whigs were the virtuous "patriot" party, then it
followed that the Tories were the tools of the ministry in London.) Mein
wrote well, and sharply, as his description of John Hancock, a rich Boston
merchant and prominent radical (or "Patriot") suggests: Hancock was
"A good natured young man with long ears—a silly conceited grin on his

countenance—a fool's cap on his head—a bandage tied over his eyes—richly dressed and surrounded with a crowd of people, some of whom are stroaking his ears, others tickling his nose with straws, while the rest are employed riffling his pockets."[11]

Such irreverence toward a revolutionary hero or proto-hero could not be countenanced. Mein knew he was in danger, but appeals to the authorities brought no help. He sought refuge in a military guardhouse where, admittedly, the mob could not reach him. Governor Hutchinson told Mein he could walk safely abroad, which, if he had had no concern for his health and life, he might have done. Finally he slipped out of Boston on a Royal Navy ship. The mob, with the full co-operation of the Boston magistrates, was now effectively in control of the streets of the town and, as a historian later put it, "The rule of law was near an end in Boston."[12] The harassed British soldiers could do little except suffer verbal and sometimes physical abuse, and store up resentment.

A Boston shopkeeper, Theophilus Lillie, published an essay commenting on the public's intolerance toward anyone who differed in opinion from what had become the dominant political doctrine. "If one set of private subjects," he wrote, "may at any time take upon themselves to punish another set of private subjects just when they please, it's such a sort of government as I never heard of before; and according to my poor notion of government, this is one of the principal things which government is designed to prevent; and I own I had rather be a slave under one master (for I know who he is [and?] I may perhaps be able to please him) than a slave to a hundred or more whom I don't know where to find, nor what they will expect of me." The local enforcers soon called upon Lillie and made it plain that they found his views unwelcome even though, as their actions showed, they were entirely accurate. At first, he was able to relocate elsewhere in Massachusetts, but in 1776 he left the province altogether, dying in exile in Halifax, Nova Scotia.[13]

Matters came to a head in a riot on the streets of Boston on March 5, 1770. Blows were exchanged between rowdies and soldiers, and the soldiers were taunted with cries to "fire." The crowd believed that the soldiers would not dare to use their weapons and that therefore they could abuse them to their heart's content. A soldier did fire, and then several others, and five of the mob were killed. The captain commanding the soldiers and eight of his men were arrested, charged with murder, jailed, and held for trial, which was held in the fall of 1770. Defended by a rising young lawyer, John Adams, six were acquitted and two convicted of manslaughter.[14] The soldiers remaining in the city were removed to an island in Boston harbor, and the immediate military occupation of Boston came to an end. The incident itself was labeled "the Boston Massacre" and received a solemn annual commemoration until after the Revolution.

The occupation of Boston showed the limits of military power and inadvertently exposed the limits of the British government's authority in the colonies. In some respects, it showed the limits on the power of any eighteenth-century government. The military could be effective, but only in warlike conditions, such as the Jacobite rebellions in Scotland in 1715 and 1745, or during the Gordon Riots in London in 1780. In the latter, anti-Catholic rioters sacked several foreign (and Catholic) embassies and burned the house of the Chief Justice, Lord Mansfield, among others. The regular army was called out and ordered to fire on any group of more than four people. By the time order was restored roughly 285 people had been killed and 200 wounded. It is at least arguable that faced with an identifiable enemy and given clear and legal commands to open fire, the army could restore order. But Boston never approached the violence of the Gordon Riots, and the authorities could not bring themselves to issue orders that could pre-empt rather than merely respond to violence.

In effect, the army had been sent to Boston as "peacekeepers," whose mere presence was intended to impress and overawe, rather than as peace enforcers. But this mere presence inflamed the Whigs and led them to make a connection that can only be called paranoid between the unhappy and inert Boston garrison and the supposed plots of the king and his ministers to enslave the colonists. The paranoia, in turn, drew on a century of Whig political tradition, stretching back to the Stuart kings and the Glorious Revolution. An imaginative politician might have been able to predict this outcome, but imagination was in short supply among the king's ministers and in surplus in the colonies. Partly for this reason, there was a gradual drift to the conclusion that only force, and large-scale force at that, would bring a conclusion.

Taxes once again supplied the catalyst. There was plenty of warning of this. At each stage of the American crisis, the king's ministers drew back, but never all the way. After each concession, the ministers insisted that they could, nevertheless, still impose taxes, and, unfortunately, they did. The Stamp Tax was revoked, but replaced by new duties in 1767. Those were cancelled, all but one, in 1770, with the latest prime minister, Lord North, arguing that it should signify Parliament's power to tax the colonies. The one remaining duty was a tax on tea, a favorite colonial commodity.

In 1773 the tax was revised, conceding a monopoly to the East India Company, in order to help that company's financial woes. That was of no concern in America. As before, there were remonstrances, boycotts, and committees to enforce the boycotts. The committees operated freely, without any serious interference from provincial authorities—in any province, for the anti–tea tax agitation drew in all the colonies. In Boston, the radical opposition frustrated the tax by throwing the imported tea into Boston harbor, the so-called Boston Tea Party. The Tea Party occurred in December 1773, and news of it reached London a month later.

The response came in the form of four acts of Parliament, collectively known as the Coercive Acts on the British side and as the Intolerable Acts in America. The port of Boston was to be closed until the destroyed tea was paid for and order restored. The powers of the Massachusetts governor were enhanced, allowing him to appoint virtually every official in the province. Local government meetings were drastically curtailed, a reflection of the fact that local authorities had refused to enforce the law, turning a blind eye and a deaf ear to the mobs of Boston and other communities. Government officials or agents accused of any crime could be tried in England, or in another colony if the governor thought a fair trial in Massachusetts was impossible. The accommodation of troops was made easier, probably a wise provision because more troops were on the way.

As this package of legislation moved through Parliament, it coincided with a fifth Act, organizing the new province of Quebec, known as the Quebec Act, which expanded the boundaries of the province around the Great Lakes, while permitting the employment of Catholics in the courts and administration, and on the governor's council. It did not make provision for an elected assembly, leaving all authority to the appointed governor. As far as the cabinet was concerned, this Act had given them the most difficulty, because it allowed Catholics, for the first time since 1688, to participate in government and gave the church the right to raise its own revenues by tithing the Catholic faithful. Seen in terms of British political orthodoxy since 1688, this was provocative stuff, seemingly linking the state and church—the wrong church.

There may have been another connection to the Coercive Acts, because by extending Quebec as far as the Ohio River, it cut off land speculators from their real estate and would-be settlers from their land. In doing so it struck at the heart of colonial politics and perhaps even at the roots of colonial society.[15] Massachusetts got a new governor too, General Thomas Gage, the commander-in-chief of the army in North America. General

Gage had been urging just such a firm policy, and it was only appropriate that he should be given the mandate to implement it.

The passage of the Intolerable Acts was in retrospect the end of any prospect for serious negotiation over the constitutional future of the colonies. There were, then and later, ideas put forward by moderate Americans that sought to bridge the gap between "virtual representation" (i.e., no representation) in the British Parliament and actual representation, in which the Americans would have a defined role and part in decision-making for the whole British Empire. Various Loyalists—people who would later discover that they were fundamentally opposed to the rebels—suggested constitutional changes that would raise the standing of the colonies and at the same time restrict or abolish the ability of the British Parliament to tax or even legislate for the colonies. A Continental Congress was convened in Philadelphia in September 1774 to coordinate resistance to the government's policies, which most delegates believed aimed to undermine the constitution and enslave the Americans. After a relatively brief meeting, the Congress dispersed, leaving behind a boycott of British goods and the means to enforce it, through an intercolonial system of committees. Finally, there would be a second Congress, to meet in May 1775 to consider further measures.[16]

The Intolerable Acts were the signal not for effective government, but for the collapse of all government. Defying Gage, the Massachusetts provincial assembly reconstituted itself as the provincial "congress." Gage soon found his authority limited to Boston and its immediate environs, effectively the amount of territory he could secure with his troops. In Concord, a county town thirty miles west of Boston, "the townspeople were now starting to punish some men and reward others on the basis of their conformity to popular views."[17] Militia officers thought to be loyal to the governor lost their posts. On the island of Nantucket, a Loyalist teenager, Kezia Coffin, summed up her reaction to Whig tyranny: the Whigs were "rebel low lived fellows," adding "O! how I loath and detest such creatures! It is Liberty which they pretend they are fighting for yet don't allow others liberty to think as they please."[18] New positions were created on "committees of correspondence" that kept radical Whigs in touch with each other around the province and elsewhere too. Other committees looked to "safety" and "supplies." Similar committees had been created in England during the Civil War of the 1640s. With another civil war in prospect, they were reconstituted. Arms and ammunition were smuggled through Boston and past General Gage's sentries.

General Gage was becoming alarmed. He had three thousand troops, which in the summer of 1774 he had thought enough for the task at hand, and which he had believed was overawing the provincials. The provincials had refused to be overawed. By October, thoroughly frightened, he was asking for more—many more. As he wrote to the relevant minister, Lord Barrington, "If you think ten thousand men sufficient, send twenty; if one million [pounds] is thought enough, give two. You save blood and treasure in the end."[19] Gage had crossed the line from peacekeeping to peacemaking, while the provincials had moved from resistance to insurrection. It would only be a matter of time. Radicals (or Whigs) formed "Associations" and demanded signatures and oaths; those who refused to swear or to sign were then identified as enemies to America. Naturally, Americans sympathetic to the Crown, "Tories" or Loyalists, as they were beginning to be called, began to pack their belongings and move to Boston, where at least they would be safe under the protection of Gage's troops.[20] General Gage begged governors in adjacent provinces to send him what they could. The governor of Quebec, General Sir Guy Carleton, sent two regiments, leaving only eight hundred troops available to defend his province.

The civil war finally broke out in April 1775. Gage attempted to raid a provincial arms dump in Concord. The locals heard about it and sounded the alarm. The local militia, "minutemen," mobilized, shots were exchanged, and Gage's troops barely made it back to Boston, with thousands of armed men on their heels. The rebels, as they now were, settled in for a siege, while the British government sent generals and troops. General Gage departed before the end of the year, and his successor as commanding general, Sir William Howe, pulled his army out of Boston onto shipboard, and sailed for Halifax in March 1776. With them sailed upward of eleven hundred Loyalists, men, women, and children.

## *The Civil War*

All the mainland American colonies joined the Revolution, except for the remote Floridas, Quebec, and Nova Scotia. In most American histories, they may as well have dropped off the face of the earth.[21] They had not joined the rebellion, did not become part of the United States, and thus must have been too different, to put it politely, to become American. Different, too, were the native nations beyond the frontier of settlement, of whom the most exposed were the Six Nations, in Western New York.

Finally, there were the Loyalists, followers of the king, who slipped away from the consensus of American republicanism—the first un-Americans.

Certainly the Loyalists had a different narrative from the American mainstream. Instead of British atrocities and oppression, there was the tyranny of the majority and the suppression of freedom of speech and debate; instead of liberty, there was persecution; and instead of freedom, for many Loyalists, there was slavery.[22] In their view, the revolutionaries had not won the right to represent America by anything resembling fair debate. In the rebellious provinces, the same process of boycott, association, intimidation, resistance, and eventual insurrection took place. In all of them, Loyalists were subjected to varying degrees of persecution, which, in many cases, prompted them to flee.[23]

The rebellious colonies, thirteen of them, sent delegates to a new Continental Congress, meeting in Philadelphia. The Congress, in June 1775, appointed George Washington of Virginia to command its army outside Boston, and it was the Congress that, a year later, dared to issue a Declaration of Independence on July 4, 1776. "We must, indeed, all hang together, or most assuredly we shall all hang separately," Benjamin Franklin told his fellow signatories, underlining what they all knew, that the success of the war with Great Britain was most uncertain.[24]

It was even more uncertain, Franklin might have added, because large numbers of his fellow Americans devoutly hoped that the Revolution would fail. These were scattered throughout the colonies. Many were Anglicans, who especially in the north were attached to government or had achieved high social standing; but many were ordinary people from all walks of life, of all religious persuasions, and all geographical areas. Though it does not fit the usual repertoire of deep or significant motivations, an attachment to stability in society and government assuredly played a role, both positively, in linking individuals to familiar institutions, and negatively, in causing them to resent those who were disrupting the rhythms of life. It is difficult to claim that the "patriots" were inherently individualistic, for while they stood for "rights" they were collective rights—the rights of all Britons, or, later, the rights of all Americans. Moreover, the means they used to enforce their views showed little respect for the opinions of those who might differ from Whig orthodoxy.[25]

Put in political terms, some Loyalists took their stand for ideological reasons, believing that a limited monarchy was best, and that republics, like the new United States of America, were doomed to chaos and failure. Others opted for the king and Parliament because they believed that

British power would be decisive in the future, as it had been in the past. All religious denominations were divided, including even the small American Jewish population.[26] While religion certainly played a part in cultivating and defining group loyalties, all Loyalists shared a secular cause. Loyalists were offended by the pressure put on them by their neighbors and by the coercive tactics of the radical Whigs.

In all probability, the largest number of Loyalists was to be found in the middle provinces, New York, New Jersey, and Pennsylvania. Loyalists were fewest proportionately in New England, and there they are most likely to be remembered as the inhabitants of "Tory Row," the great mansions in Cambridge, outside of Boston. But many came from humbler occupations and out of the way regions. On the island of Nantucket, off Cape Cod, the teenaged Kezia Coffin prayed that Franklin's prediction would come to pass: "She greeted the Declaration of Independence with the exclamation 'Horrible! I wish [the members of the Continental Congress] and all their well wishers had been strung 50 feet in the air.' "[27] The British knew that many Americans felt as Coffin did, and they based their hopes of subduing America on that fact.

The British government now determined to follow General Gage's advice from 1774 and mobilized an army to subdue the colonies, hoping that by defeating the Whig army they would restore freedom of political action to the Tories or Loyalists and allow the restoration of legal government.[28] A British armada carrying the army appeared off New York in July 1776. Landing on Long Island, the British general, Sir William Howe, defeated Washington in the battle of Long Island, captured New York City, defeated Washington again north of the city, and then, in November, invaded New Jersey, heading toward the rebel capital of Philadelphia. The objective was as much political as military, and certainly it was more than simple conquest. The presence of the army, in great force, should finally put an end to the terrorizing of the Loyalists who, some believed, made up a third or more of the colonial population. "I never had the idea of subduing the Americans," a British general explained. "I meant to assist the good Americans to subdue the bad."[29] The rebel army, deeply demoralized, began to show signs of disintegration, while in New Jersey Loyalists took the occasion to revenge themselves on their persecutors. Hundreds of Loyalists in a single county, Monmouth, volunteered for British or British-sponsored military units.[30] Disorder spread through the province, as the professional British soldiers indiscriminately plundered both friend and foe. The revolutionaries, it was observed, plundered only Loyalists.[31] The revolutionary government in Philadelphia packed its bags. Howe issued a proclamation offering amnesty to all who would take the oath of allegiance to the king and renounce the rebellion. It was, historian David McCullough wrote, "an immediate success." A young Whig militiaman years later recalled the mood in New England at the news of Washington's retreat, brought by a major in the revolutionary army: "I spent the evening with him, in company with many devoted Whigs. We looked upon the contest as near its close, and considered ourselves a vanquished people. The young men present determined to emigrate, and seek some spot where liberty dwelt, and where the arm of British tyranny could not reach us."[32]

The arm of British tyranny chose that moment to go into winter quarters. Its general, Howe, returned with many of his troops to comfortable New York City, leaving the rest of his army in garrisons scattered around northern New Jersey. Washington, having regrouped such troops as he could find, attacked, and rolled up the British forces. Howe and his main army would fight another day, but they had lost a key psychological moment in the war and, with it, their best prospect of victory. The British had not lost everything: there was still an army in New York, a naval base in Halifax, and another army in the province of Quebec. There were Great Britain's native allies. And on the ocean connecting Britain with America, there was the Royal Navy, essential to any kind of war. The navy would be indispensable, if not decisive, as it had been in the Seven Years War. Together, the navy and the Indians kept the revolutionaries at bay in the north.

## Revolution and Counter-Revolution in Nova Scotia and Quebec

The Revolutionary War was a near-run thing in both Quebec and Nova Scotia. In both cases geography favored the British. Nova Scotia was isolated by land, and its various pockets of population were conveniently reachable only by water. Despite the activity of rebel privateers and the abundance of shipping in the New England ports, the Royal Navy still commanded the waters between Massachusetts and Nova Scotia. The provincial capital, Halifax, had both a naval base and an army garrison, and there were small numbers of troops scattered around the rest of the province, which in the 1770s also included what is now New Brunswick.

Yet Nova Scotia was only a few days' sail from Massachusetts. Its institutions mirrored the New England origins of most of the population, and as the political crisis worsened in New England in 1774–5, its inhabitants showed the same reluctance to support government measures aimed at bringing Boston and the other colonies to heel.[33] While the governor was secure enough in Halifax, the hinterland by late 1775 was refusing to obey his attempt to use the militia to defend the province. The presence of the navy and the army undoubtedly made a difference in Halifax, but bringing the rest of the province behind the government was another question. It was the most distant parts of Nova Scotia that flared up—the St. John River valley and the isthmus of Chignecto. However, the would-be rebels were unable to get help from George Washington outside Boston, or from the Continental Congress in Philadelphia, whose energies and resources were already fully committed to, among other things, the invasion of Quebec. Before the end of 1776, the brief rebel uprising in Nova Scotia was suppressed. At the same time, the sympathies of the inhabitants began to shift, as they found themselves subject to raids and privateering activity out of New England. Mutual affection was replaced by mutual grievance, and Nova Scotia's connection to New England frayed. It was no longer a natural adjunct to the other New England provinces.

Quebec had recently and successfully been invaded, in 1759–60, by a fleet sailing up the St. Lawrence, from the Atlantic; by troops in bateaux coming down the St. Lawrence, from the Great Lakes; and by an army marching along the corridor formed by the Hudson River, Lakes George and Champlain, and the Richelieu River. The first expedient was unavailable to the revolutionaries, and the second would have required the co-operation of the Six Nations, who were aligned for the most part with the British. That left the Hudson–Richelieu corridor and, improbably, the seldom-traveled route through the wilderness of Maine over the Appalachians to Quebec City.

As everyone knew, Quebec was not only a very recent province, but overwhelmingly French and Catholic. It had no tradition of representative government and was ruled autocratically, as it always had been, by a governor in Quebec City. That governor, Sir Guy Carleton, had pressed the British government to draft and pass the Quebec Act of 1774 that gave legal recognition to the French language and the Catholic Church. Eventually, under the pressure of worsening events in the colonies, the king's ministers—and the king—gave way. Precedent or no, Catholics now could hold office without disabilities in Quebec. French common law would prevail in civil matters and English law for criminal cases. There would be no assembly, and thus no elections.

The reaction in the other colonies, and among English-language merchants (the so-called "old subjects" as opposed to the Canadien "new subjects") in Quebec, was not favorable. The merchants, most of them, had hoped for a Protestant ascendancy in Quebec as in England or Ireland, with their Protestant selves as the electorate. Since there would be no assembly, it was clear that the Quebec Act promoted arbitrary power as well as a tyrannical religion. "Does not your blood run cold, to think an English Parliament could pass an Act for the establishment of Popery and arbitrary power?" the young Alexander Hamilton wrote to a friend.[34] The Quebec Act seemed to be a blueprint for the future of the other colonies. In signing the Act, George III had violated his coronation oath—yet another reason why the king should no longer be obeyed and why the government must be resisted.

The anti-Catholic reaction in the colonies certainly played a part in mobilizing opinion—it played to one of the deepest sentiments in British society. At the same time, the Whigs would have preferred to get Quebec on the side of the other colonies, and so sent propitiatory letters, one in the fall of 1774, the next in the spring of 1775, to "Quebec"—though to whom in Quebec was a question, there being no assembly that could appoint delegates to Congress, as in the other provinces. The letters did not dwell on the tyrannical nature of the Catholic Church, but on the denial of equality under the law and just political representation to the inhabitants of the province. The letters were not ineffective: Carleton reported to London that "a report was spread that at Montreal that letters of importance had been received from the General Congress," and meetings had been held "breathing that same spirit, so plentifully gone forth through the neighbouring Provinces."[35]

Governor Carleton believed that he had secured, just in time, the gratitude of the French inhabitants of Quebec. He would need it, because the revolutionaries were nibbling at the frontiers of his province. By November 1775 the rebels were closing on Quebec City. Carleton had no more than eight hundred regular soldiers, and when the militia were called to arms almost nobody came. Appeals by the Catholic bishop and exhortations by the gentry, the seigneurs, had no positive effect; in fact, the appeals from above may well have stiffened the resistance of the ordinary farmers, the habitants. Carleton could not even get enough militia to defend Montreal.

That is not to say that individuals, especially in the towns, did not assist the beleaguered governor, but at the same time some Canadiens joined the rebel forces.[36] Most, however, hung back. Their reluctance may have been hesitation in many cases: it was hard to know who would win, and the invading rebels had threatened to burn their farms. In other cases, it was insubordination, and in still others it was dislike of the "English" and contempt for the instrument of the English, the Church. "You are an Englishman," the parishioners of Saint-Thomas-de-Montmagny shouted at their curé, "and you want to force us to submit and to become English too."[37]

Quebec was besieged. Fortunately for Carleton, the city had walls, and there were enough soldiers and volunteers to man the ramparts. The rebels did not have artillery powerful enough to make an impression, and so, on the night of December 30–31, 1775, they attempted to storm the fortifications. The American general, Richard Montgomery, a former British officer, was killed, along with thirty of his men; 450 were made prisoners. John Coffin, a Massachusetts Loyalist, was one of the volunteer defenders, and was singled out for praise for his role in defeating the rebels.[38] Coffin, it must be admitted, was certainly motivated. For the time being, Carleton could not get out of the city, but the rebels could not get in. In the occupied part of the province, centered in Montreal, the rebels proceeded as they had elsewhere, harassing and imprisoning Loyalists. As elsewhere, the rebels paid for supplies in paper money, which, the inhabitants rightly suspected, was worthless. This too began to drain some of the credibility from the rebel cause. There was time for a political mission sent by the Continental Congress, consisting of three delegates and a Catholic priest, and headed by Benjamin Franklin. Franklin spent not quite two weeks in fruitless negotiations with local personalities, including some of the clergy. Hearing that British reinforcements had landed at Quebec and that the rebel army was retreating, Franklin prudently departed for more congenial, and much safer, locations in time to assist with the American Declaration of Independence in Philadelphia.

The rebel army retreated to Montreal and then back up the Richelieu. Carleton moved slowly in pursuit, allowing most of the rebels to escape. Carleton's delays and sluggish leadership were severely criticized, both at the time and since. If Howe had spoiled a huge opportunity in New Jersey, Carleton missed the chance to dispose of the northern revolutionary army before winter. When the next year's campaign began in the spring, it would still have to capture positions and make up distances that Carleton with much less effort could have secured. Carleton could then turn to the question of Quebec's doubtful loyalty during the invasion.

Three commissions of inquiry were set up to visit every parish, chronicle what had happened during the invasion, and identify those who had sympathized with the rebels or, worse, collaborated with them. The good news, duly reported to the governor, was that in every parish there had been loyal subjects; the bad news was that Loyalists had had to remain passive and await a favorable turn of events. In this there was little difference between Quebec and the other colonies. Carleton did little by way of retaliation: he had established a policy of leniency toward rebel prisoners, most of whom were allowed simply to go home, and he adopted the same policy for Canadiens who had failed in their duty, as he saw it, under rebel occupation. They received official forgiveness, but inwardly Carleton was disillusioned. He reported to the colonial secretary, Lord George Germain, in September 1776 that as for the Canadiens, "I think there is nothing to fear of them, while we are in a state of prosperity, and nothing to hope for when in distress. I speak of the people at large; there are some among them who are guided by sentiments of honour, but the multitude is influenced by hopes of gain, or fear of punishment."[39] The governor also blamed what he called "the American Spirit of Licentiousness and Independence"; more rightly than wrongly he saw a clear resemblance between the behavior of the people of Quebec and that of the people of the colonies to the south.[40]

Resistance to official orders in 1775–6 had an anti-clerical tinge in Quebec. Carleton and the British government had gratified the Catholic Church by the Quebec Act, and had reaped the fervent support of the Church hierarchy. Many Canadiens had ignored or denounced the efforts of local priests to get them to support the government and had even used violence. For these, Bishop Jean-Olivier Briand reserved special treatment. Rebel sympathizers were denied communion and not readmitted to church until they showed proper public repentance. In one notable example, on New Year's Eve, 1776, twelve imprisoned rebel sympathizers were led to the cathedral door with ropes around their necks, there to apologize in public and to crave God's, and the king's, pardon. They were then sent to their home parishes to repeat the performance. Throughout, Briand and Carleton maintained close contact, conferring on the proper punishment to be given to those clergy who had sympathized with the invaders.[41] The failure of the Revolution in Quebec had much to do with Briand's and Carleton's firm response to overt disloyalty and disrespect.

Carleton's time in Quebec was by then limited. He soon resigned, giving way to the Swiss-born (and Huguenot) general, Frederick Haldimand, who presided over the later stages of the war in the north and west.[42] The Revolution was not quite finished as far as Quebec was concerned. When France joined the war on the American side, there was some nervousness about what might happen if the French army reappeared in the valley of the St. Lawrence. But the French army fought elsewhere, and another invasion, American or French, never came. Throughout the war Quebec was a base for British troops and a conduit for troops and supplies to British and Loyalist units fighting in Western New York and the Ohio country. And it was in and through Quebec that British Indian policy was reorganized.

## The War in the North and the Fate of the Native Nations

In the mid-eighteenth century, British native policy suffered from multiple contradictions. Essentially, the British focused on two things—warriors and real estate. Great Britain needed allies in the struggle with the French and cultivated a close connection with the Six Nations of northern New York. At the same time, naturally enough, the British wanted a peaceable frontier, especially in New York and Pennsylvania, where European settlement pushed up against native territories.

The Six Nations, that is, the Iroquois Confederacy, were both the neighbors of and the middlemen for the British colonies. The Iroquois could claim to speak for many other nations, and it was in the British interest to take them at their word. At the same time, British Indian agents could claim to speak for the British Empire, when they had no control either over provincial governments or over settlers encroaching on Indian lands. When the British government in London issued a proclamation drawing a line of settlement and jurisdiction between the settled provinces and the Indian lands to the west, it was virtually a dead letter from the moment it was issued. Yet because the Indians remained a significant military factor, and because there were major economic interests involved in trade with the native nations, it was preferable to get along peaceably—and that was especially the case for a government in London that was anxious to reduce military expenditures and practice budgetary economy, at least until 1774.

Relations with the Iroquois were the particular responsibility of Sir William Johnson, "Sole Agent and Superintendant [sic] of the said Indians." Johnson was a major frontier entrepreneur, with large estates in New York's Mohawk Valley; but he was also a merchant and a military contractor and, in the Seven Years War, a militia general. He maintained relations and kept the peace partly through a larger-than-life personality, but more importantly through his common-law wife, Molly Brant.[43] Molly

Brant is less known than her brother Joseph, but in the matrilineal Iroquois society she was the more influential—and because of her family connection, very influential indeed. Molly Brant presided at Sir William's mansion in the wilderness, Johnson Hall, and it was largely thanks to her that Sir William could bend the Iroquois to his desires.[44]

Johnson could not prevent settlers from crossing the mountains of Virginia and moving into the Ohio Valley, where they were resisted by native nations that were, in theory, subjects of the Iroquois. It was a full-time occupation to keep whites and Indians apart, especially when the whites illegally annexed Indian land and tried to extend British law to Indians who regarded themselves, with reason, as allies and not subjects of the Crown. In July 1774 Johnson held one last great occasion designed to keep the peace: he summoned the Iroquois to a conference at Johnson Hall, in the course of which he suffered a fatal stroke. General Gage, who by that time knew that he needed Johnson's help badly, wrote that "The king has lost a faithful, intelligent servant, of consummate knowledge in Indian affairs, who could be very ill spared at this juncture, and his friends an upright, worthy and respectable man, who merited their esteem."[45]

Johnson had heirs, but not replacements. His indolent son, Sir John Johnson, wanted nothing better than to live the life of a rich country gentleman, which, thanks to Sir William's business acumen, he could. Sir William's nephew, Guy, succeeded to the position of Indian superintendent and would eventually prove that he was not the man for the job. When the Revolution broke out in the Mohawk Valley the next year, the Johnsons fled to Montreal and England, to the disgust of Sir Guy Carleton. Carleton was a strong believer in hierarchy as well as duty. When the Johnsons returned to the tasks at hand, raising troops and seeking help from the Iroquois, they found they were subordinate to Carleton and his successor Haldimand as governors of Quebec. Sir John raised a Loyalist regiment and participated in the war along the frontier, eventually becoming a brigadier general. Nevertheless, he remained a figure of the second rank, while Guy was eventually removed from office and summoned to London to justify major discrepancies in his accounts.

Carleton was unwilling to use the resources he had to hand—not only the many Loyalist refugees who streamed north to his province after being persecuted and dispossessed by their rebel neighbors, but also the Iroquois who, thanks to Molly Brant and her brother Joseph, were—most of them—strongly inclined to take the British side in the war.[46] Through 1775 and 1776 Carleton did his best to discourage raids along the frontier, a policy designed to conciliate subjects who, he hoped, were not yet irretrievably committed to the rebel cause. The effect of this undoubtedly humane policy was to allow the Whigs of the Mohawk Valley to secure local dominance unchallenged, and to use their power to persecute their Loyalist neighbors. British strategy, however, dictated an invasion of the rebellious colonies from the north, which obviously had its best chance if it invoked the fearsome Indians to terrorize frontier settlers. And so Joseph Brant and most of the Iroquois joined a small British army that would attack along the Mohawk River, while the main force under General Burgoyne proceeded south along Lake Champlain toward the Hudson River. The Mohawk and four other Iroquois nations fought on the side of the British in the battle of Oriskany in August 1777; but on the other side were the Oneida nation, as well as rebel troops. The British won the battle, but casualties were heavy; and on the Hudson Burgoyne's army was defeated, surrounded, and forced to capitulate.

The British subsequently adopted a strategy of frontier raids, which proved remarkably effective in sowing terror along the frontier. So too were rebel counter-attacks, which from 1777 to 1779 drove the hostile Iroquois from their homes to seek refuge with the British at Fort Niagara. In doing so, the rebels were effectively recruiting for the British, because the dispossessed Iroquois, seeing their homes burned and their families abused and in some cases killed, were very inclined to take revenge. The Loyalists were similarly motivated, and the resulting raids kept the frontier in a constant uproar from 1777 to 1781.

The outcome of the war was decided not in frontier battles, but by the expansion of the war in 1778 and 1779 to include France and Spain, on the side of the rebels, by the impact of the French navy at crucial moments in the conflict, and by the surrender, in 1777 and 1781, of two British armies. The defeat of the British, however, was not merely military, but political, and the main factor in the political defeat of the British Empire was the failure to restore royal government in the colonies.

## *The Conclusion of the War*

Inept politics in Great Britain had produced the war, but the British prosecution of the war was not inept. The British government, once it grasped the problem it had helped to create, raised money and troops and kept a very large army in North America, three thousand miles away, for eight and a half years. Their objective was, clearly, to keep the colonies within the Empire and to restore civilian government. There was no single reason why this could not be done. General James Robertson in 1776 had said that he had come to help the good Americans overcome the bad. He presumed that there were plenty of good Americans, and he was probably right. Current estimates place Loyalist sympathizers at 20 percent of the population, and in some places, like New Jersey, northern New York, or Georgia, they were probably equal in numbers to the Whigs. Current estimates also suggest that the Loyalists mustered twenty thousand soldiers for the British forces—a very formidable total.[47] Some battles were fought entirely between Tory Americans and Whig Americans.

For the Whigs the stakes were high. Rebels in British history had not generally fared well, as a long history of beheadings and hangings showed, especially in Ireland. The rebels had used violence, intimidation, and confiscation of property to neutralize their Loyalist neighbors, and it was natural to expect that if the tables were turned such measures would be applied to them. Many Loyalists naturally hoped that would be the case, and sometimes, when they had the chance, they made it so. When Benjamin Franklin referred to hanging while he was signing the Declaration of Independence, he was not entirely joking.

The Loyalists, many of them, had predicted that British power, when exerted, would be awesome, and it was conceivable that many or most of the population, duly awestruck, would give in and take the oath of allegiance to King George. This had begun to happen in New York and New Jersey in 1776, and it happened wherever the British appeared or reappeared in force, from Montreal in 1776 to Philadelphia in 1777 to Savannah in 1778 to Charleston in 1780.

In the southern provinces the arrival of British ships or British armies had special significance. All the colonies tolerated slavery, but in the south most of the economy depended on it. Many slaveholders were rebels, like George Washington or Thomas Jefferson, and an obvious stratagem of war was to deprive them of their purported property. The last British governor of Virginia, Lord Dunmore, as early as 1775 promised freedom to escaping slaves who could reach British ships or outposts. Whenever British forces appeared in a slaveholding region, they found willing volunteers. At least two dozen of Jefferson's slaves joined the British forces as they marched through Virginia in 1781. "All told," historian Maya Jasanoff concludes, "approximately twenty thousand black slaves joined the British during the revolution—roughly the same number as the whites who joined loyalist regiments."[48]

The Loyalists' hopes and exertions were in vain. It was the rebels, assisted by the French, who won the war and the British government that gave up. Lord North, the prime minister, lost a vote of confidence in the House of Commons early in 1782 and resigned, much to the disgust of George III, who was forced to appoint a ministry committed to seeking peace through recognizing American independence. The new government, headed by the Earl of Shelburne, sent out a new commander-in-chief to America, Sir Guy Carleton, the former governor of Quebec, with instructions to wind up the British-held enclaves at St. Augustine in Florida, Savannah, Charleston, and New York.

The evacuation involved upward of 100,000 people: troops, dependents, and Loyalist refugees. Not all the Loyalists decided to go, but those who stayed realized there was no effective guarantee of their safety. And so they left from the southern posts in the course of 1782, sailing away on British ships to the West Indies or Bermuda, or to New York, whose abandonment was still some distance in the future, or even to Nova Scotia, far to the north. Many of the most prominent chose to go straight to the British Isles.

Shelburne's government wanted not merely peace, but conciliation, and in negotiating peace with the Americans British plenipotentiaries repeatedly gave way. Negotiations began in 1782 in Paris between the British and the Americans, as well as the French and Spanish. The result was a set of treaties between Great Britain and its various enemies.[49] The British did refuse to give up the remaining provinces to the north, Nova Scotia and Quebec, but on virtually every other issue they were remarkably accommodating. New England kept its fishing rights off Newfoundland and in the Gulf of St. Lawrence, including the valuable inshore fishery.[50] The new United States secured a boundary along the Ste. Croix River, the Saint John, and the Appalachians, then along the forty-fifth parallel to the St. Lawrence, and thence along the St. Lawrence to the Great Lakes as far as the west side of Lake Superior, and on to the Lake of the Woods. All the British posts in the West were abandoned. The Loyalists were a major point of contention, since the British delegates had been instructed to represent their interests, but there again the Americans did little more than nod at the principle of allowing compensation or a right of return, without any commitment to enforcing Loyalist rights.

In Quebec City, Governor Haldimand, when he read the peace terms, was appalled at what he considered a shameful surrender. As he wrote to a friend, "My soul is completely bowed down with grief at seeing that we (with no absolute necessity) have humbled ourselves so much as to accept such humiliating boundaries. I am heartily ashamed and wish I was in the interior of Tartary."[51] As governor of Quebec, Haldimand had to explain the terms not only to Loyalist refugees sitting in camps outside Montreal, but to Britain's Indian allies, especially the Iroquois, who lost their ancestral lands to the United States. The Americans did not, in fact, treat all the Iroquois as badly as they did the Loyalists, offering to pay Molly Brant for her confiscated lands, a proposition she "rejected with the utmost contempt."[52] At least two thousand Iroquois and their allies moved to what was left of British territory, principally along the Grand River under Joseph Brant, and on the Bay of Quinte under John Deserontyon.

The Treaty of Paris between Great Britain and the United States did one other thing, quite unusual for its day. It allowed inhabitants of the pre-war colonies to choose their allegiance. Those who considered themselves republicans and who identified with the anti-British struggle became American citizens. Those who favored the king, or who identified with the British government, or with Great Britain more generally, remained subjects of George III.[53] *Subject* defined an older form of identification or allegiance, to some eyes almost feudal and certainly traditional, while *citizen* carries a whiff of modernity. The Loyalists, however, chose to remain in the British Empire. They were subjects *by choice*, both their original choice in the 1770s when they faced violence, ostracism, and confiscation of their homes as a result, and in 1783, when they chose to leave their homeland.

The Loyalists finally left New York in the summer and fall of 1783. Carleton and George Washington, his opposite number on the American side, were told to make such arrangements as they could contrive. Washington had hoped that the British would return his escaped slaves, but Carleton gave him no satisfaction. Even before he met George Washington, he had arranged the departure of all registered black Loyalists, including Harry Washington, formerly part of George's property at Mount Vernon.[54] That George Washington could have a member of what we may call his extended household fighting on the other side of the Revolution was not unique. Not merely territory was divided, but families, while social patterns and economic ties were disrupted.

## Disrupting Old Societies, Creating New Ones

The war and the prelude to war replaced some old patterns and rituals with new ones. The creation of an annual commemoration of the Boston

Massacre actually shows the transition, when officers of the British garrison in Boston attended the event and hissed to show their disapproval of the pious solemnity of revolutionary ritual. A sacred ceremony for some was quite the reverse for others. "Those sanctified hypocrites," Jonathan Sewall called the victorious Americans, "rebellious, ungenerous, ungrateful sons of bitches." In the 1750s and 1760s in pre-Revolutionary Massachusetts, Sewall and John Adams had been close friends. When Adams was selected as a Massachusetts delegate to the First Continental Congress, Sewall begged him not to go: the power of Great Britain, he told Adams, was "irresistible" and would sweep rebellion, and Adams, away.[55] Instead, it was Sewall who fled, and thousands like him, and it was John Adams who, as one of the American delegation negotiating peace, had opposed even mentioning the Loyalists in the treaty. After the war, in London, Adams sought out Sewall, and the two held a brief reunion. But Sewall and his wife would not dine with the Adamses; for them the war had created a gulf that could never be bridged.

The war had created associations as well as symbols and ceremonies. Old occasions celebrating British royalty, or the habit of naming towns after British politicians, ceased in America. Very often the existing names were not changed, but no new ones were added. Instead, Washington, Adams, and Jefferson flourished in American nomenclature. The Fourth of July encapsulated what had occurred, and friendships and experiences in the revolutionary army created new bonds and new memories. In Boston Evacuation Day, March 17, the day the British left, has been celebrated as Patriot Day since 1901; but in the twentieth century it may have had more to do with Boston's Irish population and the hope that eventually the British would leave Ireland, too. In New York City Evacuation Day was November 25, but after eighty years it was merged with Thanksgiving Day, which falls close to the same date. July 4 is the main celebration, and often includes a faithful reading of the Declaration of Independence, bombarding contemporary ears with events and philosophy straight out of eighteenth-century Whiggery, a living monument to the conspiratorial theories embedded in British political culture in 1688.

The Loyalists are not mentioned in the Declaration of Independence, and in historical discussions of the Revolution they play a distinctly secondary role. Most often, they are treated as the option doomed to fail, or the road not taken. Sometimes historians give them a closer scrutiny, so as to determine what was wrong, or what was missing, in the makeup of these Americans that caused them to make the wrong choice. Were the

Loyalists an anachronism, devoted to concepts like "king" and "royal authority" that made them less liberty-loving, or less opposed to taxation, or less careful of the privileges of the colonies? The answers to these questions are doubtful. Many Loyalists firmly supported the jurisdiction of Parliament, and thus the constitutional settlement of 1688—as did their Whig opponents. Thomas Hutchinson, though a firm supporter of parliamentary supremacy, also opposed the Stamp Act as unwise and injudicious. Other Loyalists right up to July 4, 1776, and after tried to work out some compromise that would keep the British connection and preserve the ties of sentiment and history that linked Great Britain to its colonies. What the Loyalists did have in common among themselves were coercion and confiscation at the hands of Whig committees and resistance to what they considered illegitimate authority and arbitrary taxation at the hands of congresses and committees they had no hand in choosing. The Revolution broke the social and political compact between the Loyalists and their erstwhile neighbors. What it did not do was shatter the resemblance between the Loyalists and their former neighbors. Related before the Revolution, they remained similar thereafter.

# 3

## *The Unfinished Revolution: 1783–1815*

IN OCTOBER 1789 President George Washington paid a ceremonial visit to Salem, Massachusetts. Washington was doing a grand tour of the New England states, to show the citizens of his new country their new president. For his entry into Salem, Washington "quitted his carriage and mounted a beautiful white horse," riding through Salem as canons fired and people cheered. In the crowd watching Washington was Dr. William Paine, a Massachusetts Loyalist who had recently returned to the United States. It had been a good parade and a worthy occasion, Paine wrote. Washington had been the center of attention, and he had lived up to his role. "There is something in his looks, that is very noble and interesting, his situation, he fills with Dignity and in his Manner, he is very like Lord Dorchester: which in my opinion is paying him a handsome compliment."[1]

Washington might not have thought the comparison appropriate, or complimentary. He and Dorchester had met, in May 1783, as commanding generals of their respective armies. In those days Lord Dorchester was merely Sir Guy Carleton, the former governor of Quebec, and later the general sent to wind up the British occupation of New York, and to evacuate all the Loyalists who chose to leave. Carleton had made a particular point of sending off former slaves who had escaped from their American owners before Washington and his fellow slaveholders could reclaim them, as the peace treaty allowed.

The two men never met again, but in 1789 Carleton, now Lord Dorchester, was once again Washington's British counterpart, commanding British forces and acting as governor-in-chief for the remaining British provinces to the north. As in the 1770s, he was also governor of Quebec, and as before, the province still stretched from the Gulf of St. Lawrence to the Great Lakes. It was a truncated province. The Americans had occupied most of the territory south of the Lakes and were awaiting the delivery—stipulated in the treaty of peace of 1783—of the British-occupied western forts from Oswego to Michilimackinac, and American settlers were flooding into lands that in an earlier time still belonged to Great Britain's allies, the Iroquois. The people of Quebec had also changed. There were more of them, thanks to a high birth rate, but there were also more English speakers, settled along the shore of Lake Ontario—Loyalists, who had arrived from "the States" either before or after the peace treaty of 1783, and who were trying to scratch a precarious living out of the forests.

We can never be sure precisely how many Loyalists there were.[2] The usual figure for those who stayed in North America is about forty-four thousand who moved to the northern provinces of Quebec, Nova Scotia, and St. John's Island (now Prince Edward Island). Of these the great majority were located in Nova Scotia, about thirty-five thousand; the province was promptly divided into three, Cape Breton Island; mainland Nova Scotia, with the existing capital at Halifax; and New Brunswick, centered on the Saint John River valley, with a new capital at Fredericton. About eight thousand moved directly to Quebec. And finally about eleven hundred re-emigrated from Nova Scotia to Africa, where they founded Sierra Leone, a free black colony within the British Empire. These figures are, however, fluid, as Loyalists during the 1780s moved from one province to another; to and from Britain; in the case of the black Loyalists, to Africa; and sometimes back to their old homes in the new United States.

The Loyalists were of course refugees who had suffered for their loyalty to king and country. There was still a British Empire, still a British government, and still a British Treasury. From the siege of Boston through the end of the war, the British authorities provided relief, money, and transport to the Loyalists. They hoped that at war's end they could reclaim their property or recoup their losses in their old homes, but the American negotiators in Paris had firmly refused, agreeing only that Congress might recommend consideration for the Loyalists to the several states. The British, anxious to end the war, did not insist. Abandoned by the Shelburne administration in the rush to conclude a peace treaty, they had the mixed satisfaction of watching Shelburne's government fall on the issue in a vote in Parliament. The terms of the treaty were not affected, to be sure, but Parliament's sympathy was evident.

More practical was the establishment of a commission to look into Loyalist losses and to make recommendations for compensation. The five commissioners were overwhelmed by the volume and size of the losses, which documents presented to the commission estimated at £10,033,091.

The totals must have surprised the government: ten million pounds was about 40 percent of its average budget in the mid-1780s, according to one estimate.[3] Remarkably, however, at a time when the British government had its mind fixed on reducing expenditure and paying off the national debt, it found more than £3,033,091 to pay Loyalist claimants, a measure of the moral urgency of rewarding fellow subjects who had lost everything in the British cause.[4] In fact, the commission's task was unprecedented, but having set the precedent, it would have many descendants, beginning with relief for refugees from the French Revolution in 1789, and for Loyalists suffering losses in the Irish rebellion of 1798.

That was not all the compensation the Loyalists got. There were also pensions, nearly six hundred of them, and there was land. Land was abundant in Nova Scotia and Quebec, and if the Loyalists wished to take it up, they or their descendants might eventually be able to replace what they had lost. Non-military Loyalists got 100 acres for each family head, and 50 acres for each family member. If the grantee was unlucky enough to be a bachelor and not otherwise qualified, the grant was a mere 50 acres, which, after clearing the land, should have been enough for a living. For military veterans, land grants started at 100 acres for privates and ranged up to 1,000 acres for "field officers"—majors, lieutenant-colonels, and colonels. In Quebec only one Loyalist general, Sir John Johnson, got a grant, a substantial one; and in New Brunswick there was General Benedict Arnold, who had switched sides in 1780 after a military career that had greatly damaged the British cause and that of the Loyalists. Arnold spent an uncomfortable couple of years in New Brunswick among people who had every reason to resent his earlier life before he decamped for Great Britain.

British largesse took a particularly practical turn when it came to placing the Loyalists on the land, while supporting them until the land could produce. Once the government in London had decided on peace, it began to make preparations in the remaining northern provinces. Thus the governors of Nova Scotia and Quebec had long notice of the arrival of the Loyalists. Governor Parr of Nova Scotia started buying and stockpiling supplies of lumber and food at the end of 1782. Surveyors were hired to delineate farms and building lots for the refugees. Soldiers were transmuted into construction crews, doing their best to make the land habitable. In the Great Lakes region, earlier informal impressions of the land were turned into surveyed townships and, once negotiations with the local Mississauga nation were completed, into land grants. For Governor Haldimand of Quebec, these lakeside townships had the great advantage that they were distant from the settled Canadiens of the lower St. Lawrence. As the historian Christopher Moore observed, "Quickly, almost casually, Haldimand made the momentous decision that would create an English-speaking Ontario beside the French-speaking Quebec."[5]

The Loyalists had started to organize themselves before they left New York, and they disembarked in recognizable companies. Very soon there were difficulties. What seemed good in principle, government aid, was often lacking in practice. What was promised, what was expected, and what was performed were often sadly divergent. The refugees protested, only to discover that the official response was dusty. The refugees were insubordinate, in the opinion of Benjamin Marston, a Massachusetts Loyalist and surveyor for the government of Nova Scotia. What he saw at Shelburne in 1783 reminded him of what he had left behind in 1775: "This curs'd Republican Town Meeting Spirit." His impression was underlined by a later historian, Maya Jasanoff: "American loyalists could shockingly resemble American patriots."[6]

In Western Quebec, along the St. Lawrence and Lake Ontario, whole military units moved to their destinations before they were disbanded. Other Loyalists were more fortunate in their new homes. The Saint John River valley—contrary to the forebodings of Halifax officials—was fertile and welcoming. Shelburne, near the southern tip of mainland Nova Scotia, was not, and after a valiant effort its settlers began to desert. Despite good intentions, the flow of supplies from the government to the settlers was sometimes interrupted and even sporadic. Soon there were grumblings, to the effect that the Loyalists were not being treated as they deserved, and demanding a separate colony. In 1784 the province of New Brunswick was duly created, and a governor dispatched from London—Colonel Thomas Carleton, the brother of Sir Guy.

Carleton fitted in well with the prominent Loyalists of the Saint John valley, many of whom he appointed to his council to help him organize the province to make it the "envy of the American States,"[7] and accordingly organized so as to avoid "the American Spirit of innovation." Carleton relied on prerogative and executive power, and on the prestige and influence of his Loyalist friends, to manage the provincial legislature, and for a brief time everything transpired as he intended.[8] The legislature did not meet for over a year, and when it did, it proved to be the governor's faithful ally. But the "American Spirit of innovation" was missed, after all, because the economic progress of the colony was slow, if not deficient, and even the province's Loyalist majority was aware of the fact. "This Province would by this time have had thrice the Number of Inhabitants it now has, had not its Government been inimical to its Settlement," wrote one critic, himself a former military man, though not a Loyalist.[9] The resulting clash set the tone for New Brunswick's politics—a tone that was not, after all, very different from the politics of the pre-war American colonies or, indeed, very different from that of the other postwar British-American provinces.

Colonial officials and the British government struggled to concoct institutions and constitutions that would withstand the "American Spirit of innovation," or, worse, "the curs'd Republican Town Meeting Spirit." In the course of the war, in an effort to remove the issue of taxation from the political agenda, Lord North's government passed through Parliament a declaratory act, properly The Taxation of Colonies Act of 1778, renouncing the power to tax the colonies for revenue. That Act remained on the books (until 1973, when there were almost no colonies left to tax), and it is true that it removed the grievance of "no taxation without representation." It did not, however, solve the question of how the colonies were to be governed. In Massachusetts, for example, the governor had found himself adrift, without even the help of his councilors, for the provincial council was, of course, elected by the assembly. That too was a lesson that was absorbed by British politicians and officials.

Future colonies would have to be much more firmly structured. When finally organized, the northern colonies were divided into six: Nova Scotia, Cape Breton Island, St. John's Island (renamed Prince Edward Island in 1798), New Brunswick, Lower Canada, and Upper Canada. Newfoundland remained a special case, with a distinctive (and arbitrary) government and a very distinct society. Lower Canada and Upper Canada were created and organized by the Constitutional Act, passed through the British Parliament in May 1791. The government that drafted and passed the Act was headed by William Pitt the Younger, who called himself an "independent Whig." Pitt was entitled to his preferences, but his government was politically conservative, closely identified with the king, George III, and as time passed merited the name "Tory." Certainly the Act it produced bore a conservative stamp. While it conceded elected assemblies, it created not one but two appointed councils—one, an "executive council," equivalent to the British cabinet, the other, a "legislative council," equivalent to the British House of Lords. Its members would qualify for noble titles. The assemblies would meet once a year and vote taxes, but the government, through land grants, land sales, and licenses, would have revenue of its own. The Act also made provision for an established church, Anglican as in England

and pre-revolutionary provinces such as Virginia and South Carolina.[10] The most tangible form of establishment was money, and Pitt made provision for the Anglicans to draw revenue from land grants—one-seventh of the province of Upper Canada was constituted as "clergy reserves."[11] It was a clever ploy, because it avoided placing a direct tax on the inhabitants, showing that the British government had learned something from the Revolution.

There was one more dodge. Upper Canada in 1791 lacked many of the fundamentals of an organized political society. There was no possibility that its tiny population, mainly engaged in subsistence farming, could afford even the rudimentary government of a British province. And so official salaries were determined to be not a provincial expense but a charge on the British taxpayers, who paid £7,000 a year for the privilege of keeping a lieutenant-governor, a chief justice, and other officials in the frontier province. That was not all. The cost of the garrison of Upper Canada would also be charged to Great Britain, not the colony.[12] Supporting soldiers would never again be a direct issue between colony and mother country—but in turn this guaranteed that eventually the cost of the colonies would become a *British* political issue as much as a colonial one.

There was one more economic policy to be applied, and to the new settlers it was a familiar one. The British had always regulated colonial trade through Navigation Acts, directing the colonies' exports to Great Britain or to other parts of the Empire, and ensuring they got British products in return. The system encouraged British shipping and British commerce, and tied colonial interests closely to the mother country. In the pre-1775 world, New England fishing boats plied the Grand Banks off Newfoundland or the fisheries in the Gulf of St. Lawrence and exported salted fish, agricultural supplies, and timber to the British sugar (and slave) islands in the West Indies, receiving sugar and molasses in return. New England mariners ventured to Africa and joined in the slave trade, which enriched the merchants of Rhode Island in particular. British and colonial British shipping filled another purpose—it was a kind of floating naval reserve, whose sailors could, in time of war, be "pressed" onto naval vessels. This national security consideration was frequently decisive in persuading British politicians to reserve trade and commerce for ships and sailors that in time of need would be available for defense.

The Treaty of Paris preserved the Newfoundland fishery for New England, but it did not save the West Indian market. That market, the British government hoped, could be filled from Nova Scotia and New

Brunswick, but even if that argument required some imagination to believe, there was always national security. National security called for a new Navigation Act to preserve the nursery of British seamen, the merchant marine, by handing British ships the privilege of ferrying goods to and from the colonies; it was accordingly passed in 1786. The immediate effect was to bring on a commercial depression in the newly independent states, shrinking their revenue and raising their taxes. It was another reason that British North American ratepayers paid far less tax, proportionately, than their neighbors. The contrast was especially marked between Upper Canada and New York state: New Yorkers were paying five times the rate for their government as their British cousins across Lake Ontario.[13]

## Was "British North America" Fundamentally Different from "America"?

The historical evidence that supported the Canada Act—all of it very recent—was not lacking, but the conclusions to be drawn from it varied, not least between the politicians in London, their governors in America, and the inhabitants of the remaining British colonies. The early history of the northern provinces suggests that the principle of "loyalty," an identification with the traditions and institutions of Great Britain, and especially its king, did not guarantee that British North Americans were on other questions very different from their erstwhile compatriots to the south.

This has sometimes escaped the notice of commentators anxious to generalize about the nature of the Loyalists, Loyalism, and, eventually, the character of Canada as compared to that of the United States. In the twentieth century a whole school of thought emerged on the question,[14] following in the footsteps of an American student of Canada, Seymour Martin Lipset.[15] Lipset, his followers, and his opponents debated the question for fifty years, and while like many intellectual questions the issue can never be fully resolved, it is worth considering whether evidence matches the theory. Lipset was unusual, though not entirely unique, in his generation in making Canada an important part of his work, and he returned to the subject from time to time over his career. One of his students quipped that "'Lipset's ideas were so compelling' that he could even 'make Canada interesting to Americans.'"[16]

Essentially, Lipset argued that Canada and the United States diverged fundamentally at the time of the American Revolution. "Canada was a country defined by its rejection of the American Revolution," according to a Lipset disciple, through its "Tory tradition," in Lipset's own summary.[17] The United States, the argument continues, is a unique country and has been since its foundation, and the phrase "city on a hill," is invoked to explain its world-historical role. Lipset is not alone in his argument, though it is not easy for historians to agree with him completely. It is even possible to use the argument in an anti-American direction, by claiming that Canada is not only different, but, because of the difference, actually superior—presumably not quite the conclusion that Lipset anticipated.[18]

There is no doubt that if one follows the model laid down in the Constitutional Act, Canada, and perhaps British North America as a whole, was intended to be radically different from the United States. The popular elements of the Constitution, the assemblies, were limited, and hopefully controlled, by the conservative forces built into the Act—the councils, the established church, and the ever-present direction by Great Britain, except on taxation. As Pitt said in the parliamentary debate, its purpose was "to let the sovereign authority of Britain over the colonies be asserted in as strong terms as can be devised and made to extend to every point of legislation and the exercise of every power whatsoever except that of taking money out of their pockets without their consent."[19] But taxes were a large exception, and ultimately if government were to be supported and effective, voters, elections, and the assemblies that would vote revenue for government as a whole were an inescapable part of the process. Good feeling and loyalty might be enough to point government in the right direction, but if government faltered or veered in an unpopular direction, it would not take long for the impasse that had plagued the old colonies to revisit the new.

And so to call even the Constitutional Act entirely or effectively conservative is to ignore the conundrum at its core.[20] Lipset was optimistic to call the post-revolutionary settlement in Canada conservative or traditional, or to go further, as some of his allies have done, feudal. Nor does it suggest, as Lipset does, that the difference between the United States and the future Canada after 1776 is the logical result of European-style conservatism. Naturally as a social scientist he gave his use of history a contemporary meaning. "Conservatism in Europe and Canada," he wrote, "derived from the historic alliance of church and government, [and] is associated with the emergence of the welfare state."[21] Yet the main reference to church and state in the Constitutional Act, the creation of the clergy reserves of Upper Canada, is a self-evident dodge to support the church without involving the popular arm of the state, the assembly, with its potentially contradictory taxation powers.

Lipset was even more optimistic (or doctrinaire) when he attributes twentieth-century political choices to an instinctive and traditional Canadian preference for government action. He notes that in late-twentieth-century surveys Canadians were much more likely to prefer government-sponsored health insurance than Americans. And, no doubt, the surveys that Lipset cites confirm that there is a difference between Canadians and Americans on the issue. Is this a fault line that traverses the continent, or does it, perhaps have to do with the fact that when the surveys were done Canadians had had thirty years of government health insurance, and Americans had not? Put another way, Canadians had experience to guide them; Americans had chimeras.[22]

There remained, however, one inescapable difference between the new United States and the British provinces. Where the Constitutional Act did differ—somewhat—from American practice was in its treatment of Lower Canada. The barriers to French and Catholic participation in politics and government were swept away. This was not in itself a contradiction to what was going on in the United States, where religious tests had been abolished with the Revolution. There was, it is true, a "feudal" remnant in the preservation of the seigneurial system in Lower Canada, along with French common law instead of English, but "feudalism" sat lightly on the Canadiens living in seigneuries, and it did not exist at all in the towns and cities. Ironically, a number of seigneuries had passed into English-speaking hands through purchase or marriage, and some of the notional "feudal lords" bore names like Grant.[23] Local notables had influence over their neighbors to be sure—but so did the much richer landlords of the Hudson Valley and the great planters of the southern states. The pursuit of feudalism as a differentiating characteristic, like the relations between church and state, does not hold much promise. The real difference is what for Lipset was "the road not taken"—the acceptance of a majority French-speaking and Catholic enclave within British America.

## Land, Citizenship, and Culture

The Treaty of Paris allowed the inhabitants of British North America to choose their own citizenship. The Loyalists could reject American citizenship simply by moving out of the new United States; legally, the United States had no claim on them once they were gone, just as Great Britain renounced any jurisdiction over those who stayed. This provision, and the movement of refugees that gave it force, seemed to be clear enough.

Moreover, the various states had passed acts of attainder on exiled Loyalists, confiscating their property and forbidding them to return. Behind it were resentments from the war, which seemed to be especially acute along the New York frontier, but could be found in every state from north to south. In many cases Loyalists who attempted to return were reminded forcibly of the mob rule that had driven them out in the first place. There was the spectacular case of Benjamin Franklin and his Loyalist son, Sir William Franklin, the former governor of New Jersey. The elder Franklin had seen his son off to jail and then confinement in a salt mine in Connecticut, from which he was eventually exchanged for an equivalent rebel prisoner of the British. Attempts on Sir William's part to repair the rupture with his unforgiving father after the war were futile.

Yet it is clear that as time—and not much time—passed animosity diminished. Not all Loyalist property had been confiscated, and in many cases the owners returned to claim it and were supported by the courts. Most of them did not feel uncomfortable—barring changes at the top, in political structures, things were much as they had always been. The courts still functioned, the common law was what it was, and books, luxuries, and fashions still arrived from Great Britain. In some cases, returning refugees brought with them the compensation awarded by the British for their suffering as Loyalists, and, ironically, some brought their British pensions. In Massachusetts, former Loyalists settled comfortably into their old society and in some cases resumed membership in their old clubs that had survived the war. The children of Loyalists, themselves too young to remember the war, came back to their parents' homeland, sometimes urging the parents to come too. They tended to be on the conservative side of society, but they found there were plenty of former Whigs who shared their conservative views on society and even government.[24]

Cultural influences continued to flow across the Atlantic, not just in terms of fashions, but in science and literature. "Science and literature are of no party and no nation," in John Adams' opinion, and separation from Britain "made no breach in the republic of letters," in the view of Benjamin Rush.[25] Some prominent Loyalists found a congenial home in the Federalist party and even accepted George Washington as a plausible replacement for George III, or at least Lord Dorchester. If they worried about democracy, which in their memories equated to the mob rule they had experienced in 1775, it was a concern they shared with their conservative Federalist friends. By 1793, they could add to fears about democracy a phobia about the traditional enemy, France, and its fearsome new form of government, Jacobinism, as devised by "the monster Robespierre."[26] These too they shared with other Federalists.

Forgiveness for the past had its limits. The Loyalists did not, could not, exalt their devotion to the king or to Great Britain. The terms *Loyalist* or *Tory* were for many Americans synonymous with treason and remained so for several generations. When in the 1840s a conservative historian from Maine, Lorenzo Sabine, resuscitated the memory of the Loyalists and published a collection of Loyalist biographies, he was showered with abuse even in New England. "We are at a loss to conjecture the motive for writing a book like this," one newspaper wrote. "The Loyalists—traitors they might be called—seem to be the peculiar objects of [Sabine's] respect." A Maine journalist sneered at the Loyalist emigration to the "*loyal* provinces of Blue-nose-dom," an unaffectionate reference to the Bluenoses of the Canadian Maritimes.[27]

In Virginia, Washington and his fellow gentry resumed their purchases of British goods—china, wallpaper, silverware, fabrics, and furniture—to adorn their houses, and exports flowed again to Great Britain to pay for the imports. The imports included more than personal luxuries—for example, a British firm got the contract to supply iron water pipes for New York.[28] British books and magazines, often in pirated "American" editions, informed Americans of what was happening in London—the impeachment of Warren Hastings, the expansion of British power in India, the founding of New South Wales, and Britain's dangerous rivalry with Spain in the Pacific. The cultural influence was overwhelming. Life in London went on almost as if the war had never happened, and when Londoners were finished with an item—a play, a book—it was exported to the United States. On the American side of the Atlantic, animosity from the war was soon swallowed up in concern for other matters—designing a constitution, establishing a country, and preserving it against disunion.

The same could be said for those who remained north of the border. Contact with the United States did not cease. Families exchanged letters and even visits, not just among the prominent, rich, and well connected, but on a much humbler level. They were encouraged, remarkably enough, by official policy.

The eight thousand Loyalists and two thousand Mohawks of Upper Canada were a tiny and shaky foundation for British power. American settlement was moving steadily toward the border, and the forts the British still held on the American side of the line would probably not remain British forever—unless of course there was another war. If more were the immediate goal, the government would not ask too many questions at the border. Immigrants arriving from the United States had all, or almost all except for infants, been born British subjects, and if they wished to remain British, or to revert to being British, that was enough. The rabidly anti-republican Colonel John Graves Simcoe, lieutenant-governor of Upper Canada in the 1790s, heartily approved of American, or, as he saw them, ex-British, immigrants—some of the "thousands of the inhabitants of the United States whose affections are centered in the British Government & the British Name."[29] Already adapted to North America, these "Late Loyalists" would easily fit in beside their former neighbors, the Loyalists— if the Loyalists would let them. How this immigration actually worked is not often seen, but there are sporadic accounts that illustrate both the attractions of Upper Canada for humbler Loyalists and the links those Loyalists sustained to their former homes in the United States.

Consider the case of the Bowerman family of Dutchess County, New York. The Bowermans had landed at Plymouth, Massachusetts, in the 1620s, moved on to a series of towns on or near Cape Cod, propelled by their Quaker beliefs, or rather by the persecution that the Puritans of Massachusetts reserved for the Quakers—for in Massachusetts there was no toleration of deviant sectarians. In the middle of the eighteenth century they moved to Dutchess County in southern New York where they leased a farm or farms on the "Beekman Patent." Quakers were no longer persecuted as a matter of course in the eighteenth century, and they did mostly retain their pacifist beliefs and a characteristic unwillingness to swear to oaths.[30] When the revolutionary authorities in Poughkeepsie insisted that they swear loyalty to the new regime, many of the Quakers were disinclined to do so. Ichabod Bowerman, the family patriarch, was listed as refusing to take the oath, and consequently his house was repeatedly searched by enthusiastic Whigs looking for British agents and notorious Tories. His son Thomas, aged twenty-one, was jailed in May 1781 for the offense of "comforting, aiding and abetting robbers," meaning Loyalist raiders operating from the British lines around New York City.[31]

If prison was intended to intimidate Thomas, it failed to do the trick. Thomas next took the un-Quakerlike step of joining the King's Royal Regiment of New York, according to the historian of the Beekman Patent, and as a result by 1789 had received a land grant in what is now Prince Edward County on the Bay of Quinte.[32] By 1789 it was safe for him to return unmolested to his former home with word of available land—available to own, not rent. This was good news for the tenants of the Beekman estate. His mother and fourteen of his sisters and brothers forthwith emigrated from New York to Canada, leaving three siblings to carry on the family name.[33] They and their many, many children became landowning farmers and, presumably, they also appreciated George III's largesse in improving their standard of living and social status. The Upper Canadian Bowermans frequently returned to Dutchess County, to buy supplies, to renew—or form—family connections, and to tend to the affairs of the Society of Friends, their Quaker Church, which also linked Upper Canada with the Friends of New York state. Thomas Bowerman brought two successive wives from Dutchess County back to Upper Canada, striking evidence that connections across the border survived and flourished for at least a generation after the Revolution. Bowerman had the satisfaction of a prosperous choice—according to the census of 1808 he had six hundred acres, a herd of cattle, four horses, and other livestock, not to mention a lucrative business in barrel staves.[34]

The Bowermans' immigration to Canada—if that was what it was, because until 1783 origin and destination were all part of the same country—does have a political component, but except for Thomas, politics was probably not the decisive factor. The most senior member of the family, Ichabod, had refused the revolutionary oath, but does not seem to have suffered any serious harm as a result. Most of the family, as far as the records show, remained passive, probably but not certainly sympathizing with the Crown. And when the war ended, they remained peacefully on their leased farm and remained members both of their Quaker Church and of the Dutchess community. When offered an opportunity to better themselves, the Bowermans had no hesitation in leaving for Canada, but if Canadian land had not been on offer, they might very well have joined the stream of migrants leaving the overpopulated farms of the eastern states, for the American "West," that is, to Western New York or Ohio or Kentucky.

Canadian land was directly competitive with American land. As the historian Alan Taylor commented, "One of the great ironies of the American Revolution was that it led to virtually free land in British Canada while rendering land more expensive in the United States." The American states were desperate for money, and one of their few valuable assets was land. Land therefore was sold to speculators, who in turn would sell it to migrants, for their own profit. The year the Bowermans left for Canada, 1790–1, the New York state government sold more than five million acres to speculators for the impressive sum of $1 million.[35] The speculators then resold the land at a profit. Upper or Lower Canada, with the resources of the British government behind them, and with settling the land an imperial as much as a local priority, did not need to do that. The United States was obviously a good place for individual speculators riding the market; Canada was a better place for individual families, who also paid attention to market forces and decided accordingly. When John Graves Simcoe wrote of settlers "whose affections are centered in the British Government & the British Name" he was half right—the British government had paid for those affections and in return the settlers adopted the British name.

The impact of new American settlers, "Late Loyalists," was considerable. The population of Upper Canada rose from six thousand in 1785 to fourteen thousand in 1791, to sixty thousand in 1811.[36] Their economic interest in living in Upper Canada is clear—they had a choice to make, and they made it. What of their political views? Crossing any frontier to live in another country is to some degree a political act. Some Late Loyalists were probably acting out their political views, once they had the opportunity. For others, maybe most, the new republic had only a slight claim on their loyalties and affections. The United States was very new, its government was uncertain, and even some of its supporters were unsure whether it would last. The same might be said of the two Canadas—for some Americans crossed the frontier into the southern counties of Lower Canada, as well as into the Upper province. Many Late Loyalists could have wished to take first things first, to settle, to farm, and then to see what time and opportunity brought. In the meantime, to revert to the official point of view, they strengthened British America by their economic contribution, and that strengthened the colony's chance to become viable.

## The Great War, 1793–1815

Between 1783 and 1793 Great Britain recovered from the American Revolution. This might not have seemed a sure bet. In 1782 Britain was diplomatically isolated, at war with two European powers (France and Spain), close to war with several others, and defeated in its contest with the American rebels. British politics were in chaos, as politicians struggled with each other and with the king to form a government that could last more than six months. After two years of political instability, George III entrusted the government to a most improbable candidate, William Pitt the Younger, twenty-four years old when he became prime minister; he remained in office, without interruption, until 1801. Pitt was a supreme political manager, with an extraordinary sway over his cabinet colleagues and over Parliament, and, plainly, over the king; and when the king went mad, in 1788–9, Pitt managed for a time without him. Public expenditures were reduced and the armed forces limited to about a third of the national budget, and it followed that Pitt's policies were popular with taxpayers. This was sound, if limited, government, and it enabled Pitt to attract and keep the support of the politically influential, as well as that part of the population that could afford to cast ballots.

But the politics were not the main event. The government, more than it knew, floated on a steadily growing economy. The statistics for the period are imperfect, but later estimates suggest that the economy was growing by about 50 percent in every decade.[37] As contemporary observers saw, even the landscape was changing, as canals snaked across England and Ireland and Scotland, bearing coal to factories, for blast furnaces or for steam engines. It would take time for these changes to register in the British upper class, but they showed up very soon in the ability to raise revenues, when needed. That the government had been able to afford the American war for more than seven years was a testament to its ability to raise money, and that ability, in turn, derived from what the economy could produce. The American war had been more affordable than the Seven Years War, and the war that was to come in 1793, despite its length, would be more affordable than either.[38]

At the same time, national prestige was restored. The Empire expanded in India and Australia, which would mean, eventually, that what was understood by empire shifted too. The government drew conclusions from the Revolution, and legislated accordingly, and the small size and financial dependence of the remaining settlement colonies did the rest. The growth of the national economy meant that government spending took a smaller and smaller proportion of the gross domestic product. There were sporadic clouds—a crisis with Spain, resolved without war, occasional grumblings with the United States, but nothing that would affect the steady, happy, diminution of the national debt. It was a notable contrast with France, whose chaotic finances had been pushed over the precipice by France's heavy expenses in supporting the Americans during the Revolutionary War. Out of the war, France had gained an alliance with the United States, still in effect in 1789 when France's financial crisis turned into a political crisis. Over the next three years France slid into a revolution. In August 1792 the thousand-year-old French monarchy was abolished, and a republic proclaimed. The king and his family were arrested and imprisoned. To top it all off, the alliance with the United States lapsed, a consequence of American disapproval of the course of the French Revolution, which French aid to America had helped to cause. All this could be seen as France's own affair and, as far as the British government was concerned, that was what it should remain.

This remained true until January 1793. On January 21, in Paris, the king, Louis XVI, was guillotined. The revolutionary Danton exclaimed, "The kings of Europe would dare challenge us? We throw them the head of a king!" (He would later lose his own, to his revolutionary colleagues, the Jacobins.) War had already begun, in 1792, between France and its monarchical neighbors—all but one, Great Britain. The execution of the king made keeping the peace impossible for Pitt, and so Pitt, reluctantly, and George III, with rather more enthusiasm and of course with fellow feeling for the deceased monarch, began to prepare for war. The French Republic moved first, and on February 1 declared war on Great Britain (and the Netherlands, for good measure).

What followed was a conflict that lasted twenty-two years, with a brief intermission. From 1793 to 1802 the war was between Great Britain and assorted other European monarchies and the French Republic. That republic was on its last legs when, in 1802, the "First Consul" (head of state and government) of France, Napoleon Bonaparte, concluded the Treaty of Amiens with the British government, then headed by Henry Addington.[39] Though peace was widely welcomed in both countries, it was doomed almost from the outset. Bonaparte hardly conducted himself with restraint; among other things, he sent an army to reconquer Haiti, which had revolted against France, and forced Spain to hand back Louisiana, which had been under Spanish administration since 1783. These and other events convinced the British government—and with it most of the British political class—that they could make no lasting deal with Bonaparte. In May 1803 war resumed, still against the French Republic but after December 1804 against the emperor Napoleon, Bonaparte's new constitutional incarnation. This time there was no hope of compromise—Napoleon was assumed throughout to be an intransigent foe, whose word could not be trusted.[40] Whatever his other accomplishments, in foreign policy Napoleon looked for immediate gratification: his instruments were blackmail and, if that failed, war. "Napoleon's psychology and political outlook, however explained, should be regarded or classified as criminal," as the historian Paul Schroeder put it.[41] Revolutionary France under Robespierre might have been a tyranny, an example of what could happen under mob rule, but Bonaparte easily fit the definition of a tyrant, and because of his extraordinary military prowess, a dangerous tyrant. So strong was the British conviction on this point that they fought much of the war without allies and were always ready to subsidize or otherwise encourage resistance to the French, culminating in the ultimately successful Peninsular war in Spain, from 1808 to 1814.

The republican character of the first phase of the war was important, as it had been during the Revolutionary War, and a common republican ideology might have been thought to link the United States and revolutionary France. But American memories of the Revolutionary War were of France as it had been, sending a contingent of noble officers along with an army to aid the United States. As the French Revolution progressed, it degenerated into what was called the Reign of Terror, during which the extreme revolutionaries, the Jacobins under their leader Robespierre, arrested what they considered to be suspicious or treasonable personalities; after farcical trials, many of these were sent to the guillotine. Marshal Rochambeau, who had commanded French troops in America in 1780–1, was arrested and barely escaped the guillotine. His comrade in arms, the Marquis de Lafayette, who had been an American general during the war, had to flee the country in 1792, as the Terror was beginning. Lafayette had shown in the 1770s that ideology transcended borders in the struggle for the rights of the colonists against British tyranny. He would again be an example, this time to illustrate the inhumanity and depravity of his Jacobin enemies in revolutionary France.

As the guillotine chopped away in Paris, removing enemies of the republic, and the British and French navies tried their first maneuvers in the English Channel and the Mediterranean, Canadians and Americans took note. Louis XVI, so recently the embodiment of French tyranny, was reinterpreted in Upper Canada as a "mild and beneficent sovereign," like George III. The colonies' safety depended on keeping Great Britain secure, especially if, as might have seemed logical, the American and the French republics made common cause.[42]

To conservative Britons, and also to conservative Americans, the ideology of the French Revolution was more fearsome than a French invading army, because its ideas could easily be imported, spread, and adopted: liberty poles, liberty caps, unhappy peasants yearning to become happy in a revolutionary way, and then the guillotine. Panic spread, in England, and then New England, Lower Canada, and anywhere else that the revolutionary vision could travel. The reverse of panic was enthusiasm, and the revolutionaries had plenty of that, so that the two sides tended to reinforce one another. There were plenty of precedents for panic as a factor in war, and plenty of wars where ideology was the motivating force—most obviously, the recent Revolutionary War, the English Civil War, and the religious wars against Spain in the sixteenth century.

In Lower Canada the Catholic Church abandoned any lingering sense of identity with the government of old France. Clerical refugees from the Terror—fifty-one emigrated from France to Canada—spread the word. George III, already the legal king of Canada, became the unwitting bulwark of traditional Catholicism and hence an instrument of providence. Bishop Jean-François Hubert of Quebec was not being ironic when in November 1792 he wished a colleague in Paris "as happy a lot as ours in this country, where we enjoy, at least on the government's part, liberty for our holy religion, without worry and without dissension."[43] The government could count the church as a firm ally. British victories were duly celebrated, in response to requests for "enthusiasm" from the church.[44] The church, however, did not speak for all the people.

There *were* Canadian Jacobins and Jacobin plots, and consequently arrests, trials, and an execution for treason. There was never much chance that Jacobinism could overthrow the government; help from France was virtually impossible, and though there was some American meddling from Vermont politicians, it too was speedily frustrated. Historians have argued that the war and fear of Jacobinism marked a turning point in Lower Canadian politics, driving English speakers into increasingly fervent support of the government and its policies. The evidence for this contention is rather mixed, but it places too low a value on the Catholic Church's unswerving support of the British cause in the Great War. Indeed, the Lower Canadian assembly—majority French—voted £20,000 for the prosecution of the war, a rather tangible indication of its sentiments.

The Great War was also profitable for the Canadian colonies. The emperor Napoleon made a determined effort to reverse the British blockade, by coercing the countries of Europe not to trade with the British. The Royal Navy needed timber for ships, and especially tall straight logs of the white pine, perfectly suited for ships' masts. Timber cutting was at first centered in the Saint John valley, in New Brunswick, but soon after 1800 it moved to the St. Lawrence basin. With European supply limited or even cut off, the navy depended more than ever on Canadian timber—nine thousand loads in 1802, twenty-seven thousand loads in 1807, and ninety thousand loads in 1809.[45] War was especially responsible for the health of the economy in Lower Canada, and when the profits from supplying the British garrisons are included (the army spent around £250,000 per year in the Canadas), it is clear that the British military effort was a significant factor in buoying the various provincial economies.[46]

Through the twenty-two years of war, the Royal Navy kept the French fleet bottled up in its home ports, and the short-lived escapes of French naval squadrons resulted, most of the time, in disaster for the French and in celebrations in the loyal cities of the British Empire, including Quebec, Montreal, and Halifax. Jacob Mountain, the Anglican bishop of Quebec, proclaimed in 1799 what to Loyalists must have been obvious, that "we form an integral part of the Empire and with it we must stand or fall."[47] The merchants of Montreal erected a column to Admiral Horatio Nelson, who destroyed the French fleet at Trafalgar in 1805, opposite what is now Montreal's city hall. In Upper Canada, Nelson's victories were "Glorious, Glorious news," and the British stood for "the cause which was that of all humanity" in the war against Napoleon.[48]

Many Americans agreed. The Federalist party, the party of George Washington and John Adams, the first two presidents, was objectively pro-British and identified Britain with resistance to mob rule and tyranny. This obviously was a position that would have resonated with most Loyalists. On the other side of politics there were differences. In Canada it was impolitic if not dangerous to speak out in favor of the French Republic and, later, the French empire, but in the United States it was possible to say "The cause of France is the cause of man" and to argue that the United States must honor its alliance with France.[49] This President Washington chose not to do, and on that point he had overwhelming support.

Washington was shrewd as well as principled; with Great Britain at war with a formidable enemy across the Channel, it was a good time to approach the British about the nagging issue of the frontier forts, which the British had retained when the Americans had refused to honor Loyalist claims for losses. There were other issues. In the first year of the Great War the British had confiscated 250 American ships and their cargoes, and their owners wanted compensation. American slaveholders still wanted to be compensated for the slaves who had won freedom by joining the British army during the Revolutionary War. And the British wanted American debts to British merchants paid. In 1794 the United States and Great Britain negotiated a treaty to address these issues—or most of them. The issue of the slaves was clearly a non-starter and was dropped by the chief American negotiator, John Jay. The American shipowners were compensated,

and the British merchants were promised payment by the federal government if their debts could not otherwise be recovered. British subjects and
American citizens, and the native nations, could freely pass the border into
one another's territory. There would also be limited access for American
vessels into the British West Indies. Boundary questions outstanding from
the 1783 treaty were to be arbitrated. And most importantly, the British
agreed to give up the western forts. In 1796 the British duly evacuated the
frontier forts. Somewhere along the line the treaty was dubbed Jay's Treaty,
after John Jay.

The treaty was highly controversial in the United States but, with
Washington's prestige behind it, it was ratified. Subsequently American
historians have been divided as to whether the treaty was a good deal or
not. Certainly the Americans did not get all they wanted, but the Loyalists
once again got nothing. The British did not give way on any measure that
might weaken their blockade of France, and the Americans failed to get
recognition of what they called "neutral rights." Probably most importantly, the treaty averted war or the probability of war, especially over the
issue of the western forts.

Instead, the United States nearly went to war with France and actually
did go to war against the pirate states of North Africa, the so-called Barbary
pirates. By then the Federalists were out of office, and the opposition, the
Republicans, were in power under President Thomas Jefferson. It was a
period of inter-party feuding, an extreme politics that found expression
through a kind of anti-politics. As Alan Taylor perceptively writes, "Paradoxically, [the] dread of parties drove each group to practise an especially
bitter partisanship."[50] Jefferson was an odd combination of practical politician and dogmatist. Hating the British he nevertheless perceived the greatest threat to the United States to be the French repossession of Louisiana
under Napoleon, combined with the dispatch of a large French army to
reconquer Haiti. If Haiti were disposed of, it was possible the army would
sail on to New Orleans. It was one thing to have the enfeebled garrison of
a second-rate power, Spain, in New Orleans, but France was the leading
military power in the world, and its national leader was a general who very
seldom lost battles. And New Orleans would be once again French territory.

Accident intervened. The army was decimated by yellow fever and defeated by the Haitians. Napoleon's brother-in-law, the army commander,
died of disease, and his coffin reached Paris in January 1803. In May, the
long-anticipated war broke out again with Great Britain. With the European
war in mind, Napoleon cut his trans-Atlantic losses. On the last day of

April, 1803, American emissaries in Paris, rather to their surprise, bought the Mississippi watershed to the west of the river, all the way to the Rocky Mountains. The sum was large, but the value of the purchase was incalculable. In a stroke, France was removed from North America and the United States became the largest power on the continent—and larger still when the purchase was finally peopled. Although the event did not involve Canada or the British Empire directly, it would have a decisive effect on the development of Canada. It ensured that the United States was and would become a much larger power, with a reservoir of rich agricultural land in the West, which settlers could access easily enough, using the east–west river systems that flowed into the Mississippi. The Canadians, when they started to think about it, had the rocks of the Canadian Shield between them and the lands of the Hudson's Bay Company in what is now Western Canada; and even the large fragment of agricultural land of Western Canada from (eventual) Manitoba to Alberta was a fraction of the size of the American equivalent.

Admittedly, the Louisiana Purchase was for the time being merely a promissory note of greatness. Jefferson as president had many more problems, some systemic, some opportunistic, and some imaginary. The imaginary problems were not insignificant. As a later historian put it, "Jefferson seems to have generated his identity as an American from his hatred of England."[51] Jefferson was not alone in this—for the first generation of Americans there had to be some explanation for the existence of two nations where there had been but one, and the readiest formula was that Great Britain was irretrievably wicked, "our natural enemies" where the United States was concerned. France, he argued, was the "true mother country" and if France prevailed in the war with Britain, he hoped to be in London on the day of victory to dine with the victorious French general so as to "hail the dawn of liberty and republicanism in that island."[52]

For Great Britain, averting such an outcome was an obvious war aim; more generally, the British position in the French Revolutionary Wars and the wars that followed was essentially defensive. Once Napoleon became the French dictator and then emperor, there was also what Paul Schroeder has called his "hatred of the only rival which had successfully defied him."[53] Defeat for Great Britain would not have been pleasant, judging from what Napoleon did to the defeated Austrians and Prussians, and tried to do to the Spanish.

For Jefferson and those who thought like him, the Revolutionary War had not ended and would never end until the British were completely expelled from North America; perhaps it would not end until Great Britain had been conquered or had had its own revolution, or both. As president, his relations with the British started coolly and ended up in a deep frost. If he needed confirmation of his prejudices about Great Britain, it was easy to find it. The key was in a facility called re-export. The British early on in the war interdicted trade between French colonies and France, and when Spain allied itself with France, between the Spanish colonies and Spain. Spanish and French ships were swept from the seas. But if American ships picked up cargo in Spanish or French territory, brought it to the United States, landed it and paid a nominal duty on the goods, it could be re-loaded as an American export and conveyed on to its destination.[54] Effectively the United States replaced the French and Spanish merchant fleets, and the number of American ships doubled. The expansion of American shipping required—demanded—more labor, and there was only one source for that: Great Britain. As Andrew Lambert pointed out in a study of the naval war of 1812, "A project to surrender all British sailors in American ships in return for the British ending the impressment (forced enlistment) of actual Americans was quietly dropped because half of all skilled seamen in American merchant ships were British."[55] The chances of finding British seamen on American vessels were accordingly excellent.

The Royal Navy was stretched at all times to secure an adequate number of seamen. Wages and working conditions were better on merchant ships, and better still on American merchant ships. Those ships were English-speaking, and so as easy to work in as British ships. Some British seamen enrolled directly, while others took the chance of deserting from the Royal Navy. These facts were well known, and naval vessels regularly stopped and inspected merchant ships, including American ones, for renegade sailors. Captains desperate for experienced hands would not look too closely at citizenship, and it was in any case a world in which forged papers were readily available and widely used. Investigation showed there was considerable justice in the British complaints. Though the British claimed there were twenty thousand Britons on American ships, a certain exaggeration, they must have numbered in the thousands.[56] Often enough, genuine Americans ended up labeled "British" and toiling for King George on one of his men-of-war. Impressment thus joined the blockade as an American grievance.

Then there was the question of ships and cargoes, which could also be seized under certain conditions. The British were aware that re-export was just another means of preserving French and Spanish overseas trade. In a ruling in 1805, an Admiralty court determined that "the true purpose" of trans-shipment was to create a "fraudulently circuitous voyage" and to allow an ostensibly neutral ship to serve the enemy's purpose. The British position was that neutral ships conveying enemy cargo were serving the enemy and could not be exempt from reprisal. The British navy was block-ading French ports, and the prevention of enemy cargoes traveling on the high seas was an extension of the blockade. It remained theoretically pos-sible for American ships carrying American-originated cargo to deliver it to France, provided they were inspected in a British port first and were given a British certificate. The French position was the reverse: if the vessel had called at a British port, it could be seized.

The United States could do little about it. The Royal Navy outnum-bered and outgunned the United States' small navy. This was something the British easily could afford, as the Industrial Revolution steadily ex-panded the British tax base. British defense spending had shot up after 1793, from £8.1 million that year to £28.7 million in 1798, to £45.2 mil-lion in 1809, the year James Madison took office.[57] In 1810, the British had 152 ships of the line, the battleships of the day; the United States had none. In frigates, medium-sized warships, the Royal Navy had an advan-tage of 183 to nine.[58]

The cost was worth it from the British point of view. A French invasion of the British Isles would win the war for Napoleon, and at various points between 1793 and 1815 the danger of a French descent on England or Ireland was very great. If the Royal Navy were destroyed or even distracted, the French could win the war. Year after year hundreds of British ships sat along the coasts of Western Europe keeping the French in and the Americans out. Only the most daring American ships by 1809 or 1810 tried to reach French ports; the profits were great, but the risk of capture and seizure was greater. If stopped, American ships could expect to be inspected. This happened to an American naval ship, the *Chesapeake*, in 1807. The British suspected there were deserters aboard, and there prob-ably were. The *Chesapeake* declined to co-operate, and so there was a fight, which the British won, and they then proceeded to take off the men they had wanted. In retaliation for British procedures, Jefferson defaulted to a tried and true strategy of his youth—the boycott. He knew that the United States was unprepared for war—at this point he would not follow his rhetoric to its logical conclusion, and so a measure short of war was indicated. Jefferson embargoed American trade. If the British would not leave American ships alone, then there would be no American ships. Trade would wither, trade was important, the British would give way. But the British did not. They found other markets in Latin America, cut adrift from Spanish trade restrictions by the Napoleonic invasion of Spain.[59] Trade indeed withered, American ports were shut up, and merchants faced ruin, but Jefferson's embargo proceeded nonetheless.

The embargo had no effect on British policy, though it undoubtedly caused some economic harm, and accordingly Jefferson left office in 1809 with Anglo-American relations in a state of constant irritation. No doubt he considered this to be their natural state, at least until a republic was installed in England and a committee of safety ruled in London. Jefferson's successor, James Madison (president 1809–1817), was younger but, like Jefferson, part of the revolutionary generation. Jefferson's and Madison's party, the Republicans, was able to defeat the opposition Federalists thanks to the immigrant (Irish) vote in Philadelphia and New York, thus winning enough states and allowing Madison to win the election, despite the economic ruin that Jefferson had inflicted on the seaports.[60]

Madison must have looked enviously at the situation in Europe, where Napoleonic France dominated the continent from the Atlantic to the frontiers of Russia. Even the outbreak of war in Spain, provoked by Napoleon, who had kidnapped the Spanish royal family to install his brother Joseph as king, seemed no more than a minor distraction, despite the arrival in the Iberian peninsula of a small British army under Sir Arthur Wellesley (soon to be ennobled as Lord Wellington). This produced the Peninsular War, between Britain, Spain, and Portugal on one side, and France and its Spanish collaborators on the other. In fact, the arrival of the British in Spain was a good sign for the US administration, because it tied them down on the continent, with no resources to spare for America. It might not have been unreasonable to believe that Napoleon would cope with this problem as he had so many others. French power seemed unassailable on land, even if the British could hold out at sea, a situation that could well last indefinitely.

Not all American grievances or fears were maritime. While American traders might look eastward, toward the Atlantic, American settlers looked west, toward the lands of the native Americans. Until 1796, the native nations could come, as they always had, to the British posts along the lakes and receive gifts, sometimes including arms, and encouragement from British officials. The British Indian Department and its agents were careful to keep themselves in favor with the natives of the American

Northwest. If there were war with the United States, the king would need his native allies, as he had in the past. While few, the natives were still a most effective guerrilla force in the heavily wooded Great Lakes region. More effective still was their ability to strike terror into the settlers and soldiers on the American side.

Without British help, there were more settlers and soldiers than the native nations of the Ohio Valley could handle. Slowly but very steadily they were pushed back across what soon became the state of Ohio (1803) into Indiana and Michigan. In an engagement at Tippecanoe, in Indiana, a native alliance was decisively defeated by American troops in 1811 while its war leader, the Shawnee Tecumseh, was away. Surviving, Tecumseh had little choice but to cast his lot with the British, if the British wanted him. In the meantime, fear of the Indians merged with fear of the British among Republican party supporters. There were many who believed, and many more who wanted to believe with Jefferson, that the British government, and perhaps the whole British political establishment, would not rest until it had subdued the United States and gotten revenge for the defeat of 1783. Republican zealots, also wanted revenge for what they took to be thirty years of malevolent British policy. The British had to be punished, and the instrument was at hand—the exposed and under-defended provinces of British Canada.

The British colonies were useful as a means of putting pressure on London, but Jefferson hoped for much more. Writing in 1807, as relations with the British touched their lowest point, he predicted that in the event of war "we will take Canada which wants to join the Union," and when that was done the United States could add Spanish Florida, which in his view would force the British to stop their interference with American shipping. This was muddled thinking, to be sure, but through the confusion shines the desire to make the United States sovereign over the whole of North America. Jefferson never changed his view, and it encouraged him when war finally broke out. "The acquisition of Canada this year," Jefferson wrote in 1812, "as far as the neighborhood of Quebec, will be a mere matter of marching, and will give us experience for the attack of Halifax the next, and the final expulsion of England from the American continent."[61]

By 1811 Madison's patience was exhausted while the fears of his fellow citizens were growing.[62] Sharp partisan divisions meant there could be no compromise on the issue of relations with Great Britain: the Republicans and the Federalists could find no common ground. Many, and probably most, Federalists believed that Great Britain was not the enemy of their country; many also believed that in a contest between imperial France and imperial Great Britain, Britain was definitely preferable. The British side was the side of liberty, struggling against tyranny. Naïve, vacillating, fearful, and deluded as to the true state of affairs in Europe, Madison and his Republican party in Congress placed themselves in a position where their grievances against the British had to be satisfied, with war as the only alternative. National honor demanded no less. That the British were not seeking war with the United States is obvious today, as it should have been at the time. The British were slow to respond. The British government revoked some of its most obnoxious restrictions on American trade and shipping, and was prepared, too late, to make an effort to compromise.

The news of British concessions, made in London on June 16, 1812, arrived too late. Before news of the British action could reach Washington, Madison recommended, and on June 18 Congress passed, a declaration of war on Great Britain. Admittedly, Congress was divided, and war passed in what was roughly a sixty–forty split in the Senate and the House of Representatives. The declaration of war was denounced in New England and by Federalists generally. Six days later, Napoleon and his Grand Army, 600,000 strong, marched into Russia, an adventure that would undermine his power and eventually lead to his overthrow. When that happened, the British could turn their whole attention to the United States, if they chose. Paul Schroeder has pointed out the irony of Madison's choice to go to war, "that an infant democratic republic should have entered this titanic world struggle on the side of one of modern history's worst tyrants. Was it perhaps that one emotion linked Jefferson and Madison, great theorists of democracy, with Napoleon, a great military despot: a visceral hatred of Great Britain?"[63]

Madison certainly saw a linkage. He confessed that in 1812 he had believed that Napoleon would defeat Russia and that when that happened the British would make the necessary concessions to the United States, ending their restrictions on trade and impressment of sailors.[64] He did not add that he had expected, when it came time to make peace, that the United States would have seized most of Britain's American colonies and, presumably, would not have to give them back.

## The War of 1812

The War of 1812 may be briefly summarized. It had two parts, an interior war along the Great Lakes and St. Lawrence River, and a naval campaign in the Atlantic. The land war is more remembered than the war at sea, and the land war was the one with the longest-lasting and most significant consequences. The land war was important because it prevented the United States from securing its primary objective, the defeat of the British Empire and its expulsion from North America. By 1814 the armies around the Great Lakes were essentially stalemated. This fact by itself was not enough to make the Americans give up. That required two further developments—the defeat of Napoleon and peace in Europe, and victory for the British in the war at sea. The defeat of Napoleon removed President Madison's European partner, a major strategic blow. Nevertheless, it was the war at sea that won the war for the British and consequently for their Canadian colonial subjects.

The Americans invaded the two Canadian provinces at various points in 1812 and repeatedly thereafter. The major invasion was decisively defeated by an energetic and capable British general, Sir Isaac Brock, at Detroit, with the invaluable and probably indispensable assistance of Tecumseh and his native warriors. An American incursion at Queenston Heights on the Niagara River in October 1812 was also decisively defeated, though at the cost of Brock's life. These two actions saved Upper Canada, not merely by keeping the Americans out, but by showing the Upper Canadians that the British forces were not doomed to defeat and surrender, and that, therefore, it was prudent, and even intelligent, to support the British. Psychologically, this was the war's turning point.

In invading Upper Canada, the Americans had put the population on notice not to resist them, or they would face unpleasant consequences. When American proclamations referred to the tyranny of British rule, even the American-born found the notion laughable. Tyranny, in the view of an American Baptist preacher working in Upper Canada, "was a mere notion—for if [the population] had been under any, they could at any time have crossed the line to the United States." Michael Smith, the missionary, continued that Americans serving in the Upper Canadian militia, however reluctantly, were "considerably exasperated against the invaders, for they think it is hard that they should feel the misery of war who have no agency in the councils of England."[65]

The lesson was confirmed the following year, 1813, when the Americans had more success in invading Upper Canada. They were dismayed, and then enraged, to find that the population did not rush to join them. Aligning themselves with some Upper Canadian renegades, the Americans began a campaign of plunder and arson on the Upper Canadians. The

British and Canadians retaliated, with the result that both sides of the Niagara River and most of the north shore of Lake Erie were laid waste. The best-remembered episode was the burning in April 1813 of the public buildings at York (Toronto) the tiny provincial capital, and the looting of its inhabitants' houses. Symbolically, York supplied a raison d'être for the British-Canadians to fight against the Americans, both at the time and long afterward. Also symbolically, the British-Canadians responded to the renegades by trying fifteen of them for treason and hanging eight at Burlington Heights in July 1814.

American military performance did improve over the course of the conflict, and regular battles in 1814 were both bloody and competently conducted on both sides. Nevertheless, even with more and better troops the Americans were unable to break through, and the British-Canadians remained in control of most of the province (and Fort Niagara in New York state) until the end of the war. Further east, incompetent American generals defeated themselves and failed to reach Montreal, even though the city was barely thirty miles from the American border. The capture of Montreal would have cut off the British troops in the interior and might have led to their defeat; but it was not to be.

The war at sea was quite different, and different too are both the reality at the time and the prism of memory through which the sea war was interpreted. It is best captured by an incident almost 150 years later, when the Canadian prime minister, John Diefenbaker, was visiting the president of the United States, John F. Kennedy, at the White House in Washington. On the wall of Kennedy's office was a painting depicting the capture and burning of a British ship, the *Guerrière*, by an American one, the *Constitution*, in August 1812. This was how the Americans remembered the naval war of 1812—how American frigates stood up to and defeated the great Royal Navy, David and Goliath at sea. If Americans remembered the *Constitution* and the *Guerrière*, Diefenbaker and Canadians remembered something different. And so Diefenbaker sent down to the president another painting, this one of the battle between the American ship *Chesapeake* and the British ship *Shannon*, off Boston in June 1813. The result of that battle was a stunning British victory, for the American ship was considered to be superior in strength to the British. Kennedy's reaction to the gift went unrecorded, but it is true that Diefenbaker became a less-than-favored guest in Kennedy's Washington.

Duels between men-of-war are a natural and favorite subject for naval painters. There are fewer pictures of ships on blockade duty, sitting off the

American coast, but the British blockade of the United States played a larger role in the outcome of the war than is generally granted. The blockade was slow to start, because for some months after the American declaration of war the British government treated the conflict as somehow an enormous mistake, given that the British had revoked the orders-in-council that were its ostensible cause. Using Bermuda and Halifax as its principal bases, the Royal Navy began to blockade American ports. The British started with the southern ports, to retaliate against those parts of the United States that had voted for the declaration of war.[66]

A British naval squadron under Admiral George Cockburn located itself in Chesapeake Bay and proceeded to raid and blockade the towns round the bay. The British even seized an island and turned it into a base. It not only supported their cruises and raids, but also served as a magnet for slaves escaping from the plantations around the bay; they were promised freedom, money, and land after the war. The slaves—upward of six hundred of them—were promptly enlisted as marines in the British service.[67] The blockade gradually extended northward, to New York, Rhode Island, and finally Boston. Naturally the blockade strangled shipping, as it was supposed to, but it also deprived the American government of a large part of its revenue, based on customs receipts. American public finance, already chaotic, now became truly catastrophic.

Finally, in April 1814, an alliance of European powers led and financed by the British defeated Napoleon, invaded France and took Paris, and forced the French emperor to abdicate. He was given a tiny principality on the island of Elba, in the Mediterranean. All attention now concentrated on Vienna, where allied and French diplomats met to work out the terms of a lasting peace—only to be interrupted by the news that Napoleon had escaped from Elba and that one more campaign would be necessary to subdue him. Napoleon's final defeat came in June 1815, at Waterloo. The fallen French dictator was shipped to the island of St. Helena in the South Atlantic to spend the rest of his days justifying himself to his entourage, and, through them, to a large and gullible public. He died, still a prisoner, in 1821.

## The Peace of 1814

In 1812, at the outset of the war, the British offered peace on the basis of the status quo ante bellum; in other words, everything was to remain as it had been. At the time, Madison refused, believing he could do better.

Defeat and stalemate in Canada disabused him of the notion that he could easily conquer and absorb the British colonies into the Union. The United States lost eastern Maine to a British force. The defeat of Napoleon deprived him of an ally, however peculiar. Finally, the British naval campaign deprived him of most of his revenue.

That was not quite all. With peace at hand in Europe, some of the victorious British army was detached and shipped to Quebec, giving the British clear superiority in numbers of professional troops in North America. A British raid on Washington in August 1814, ostensibly to retaliate for the burning of York the year before, deprived the president of house and home. The "Executive Mansion" was burned by the British, but only after their commander sat down to a dinner that Madison's wife had left on the table before decamping. Repainted after the war to conceal the burn marks, the mansion became the White House. On the other hand, the British were repulsed at Baltimore some weeks later and at Plattsburgh in northern New York state.

Madison's secretary of the treasury had already strongly recommended peace. American and British negotiators met at Ghent, then part of the neutral country of the Netherlands. At first, relying on their recent victories in Canada, Maine, and Chesapeake Bay, the British wanted to revise the frontier and establish an autonomous native state in the center of the continent. A combination of factors—the American victory at Plattsburgh, the uncertainty of events in Europe, and, not least, the "lessons learned" during the Revolution of the futility of a land campaign in North America—persuaded the British government to settle for the status quo ante, that is, what they had offered in the first place, in 1812. Meanwhile the American delegation got the news that their country had defaulted on its national debt in November and that American credit stood at zero.

On December 24, 1814, the Treaty of Ghent was duly signed. It left matters where they had been—the boundaries of 1783, American sovereignty south of the Great Lakes, American fishermen on the Grand Banks, and North American natives divided between the United States and British North America.

The United States had entered the War of 1812 for a number of stated reasons, having to do with "neutral rights," freedom of commerce, and impressment of sailors. There was resentment of what was held to be British interference in Indian policy in the Northwest, even though the American victory at Tippecanoe had erased most of Britain's ability to interfere on American territory. En route to settling the West and clearing the seas for US commerce, the American political class expected to pick up Canada, and expected, too, that they would not have to give it back. This, as far as Jefferson and Madison were concerned, would have completed the work of the Revolution. They had been obliged to compromise, as they saw it, in 1783 by allowing the British to retain a foothold in North America. Its existence aggravated and offended purist Republicans in the United States, who wanted a total victory instead of the partial achievement of 1783. In that ambition they failed. They did not get Canada, and as Alan Taylor has pointed out, they alienated almost all the support they might have expected from American settlers in the Canadas. Politically, the American position was worse after 1812 than before.

British memories of 1776 were still vivid. A very large British army had not sufficed to subdue the United States in the Revolution, in a very difficult war. There was no appetite to repeat the process in 1814. The British had, after all, been successful: they had stood off an invasion from the country that had defeated them in 1783. It might not be a great epochal victory, but it was certainly not defeat.

It was also possible to claim that the United States had not lost the war, because it had not lost any territory; put another way, the Americans were not worse off because of a war that they had started and persisted in, when in 1812 the British offered to settle. The Americans did not see the War of 1812 as separate from events in Europe, and they hoped to benefit from the victorious French invasion of Russia. Napoleon's defeat was an American defeat too. As late as 1815 Thomas Jefferson was hoping that a French victory at Waterloo would set the world to rights—by defeating the British.

There was a lesson in Jefferson's disappointment. The ill-advised War of 1812 had been politically costly and financially ruinous. The British had clearly demonstrated the superiority of the Royal Navy in waging economic war on the United States and bringing the US government not merely to the edge of bankruptcy, but over the brink. A repetition of the war was inconceivable and remained so for the next fifty years. A mute recognition of the meaning of the war was the construction of large forts along the northern border and up and down the American Atlantic seaboard.

Canada (properly, British North America) therefore remained part of the British Empire, and the Revolution was completed in a way that Jefferson had not imagined. Politically separate, Canada and the United States—and Britain too—contrived to live as neighbors. Thanks to the Louisiana Purchase, the United States would expand west, not north, and the War of 1812 receded into myth.

# 4

# *Postwar, 1815–1854*

ALONG THE CANADIAN–AMERICAN border from the Gulf of St. Lawrence to the Great Lakes, and along the Atlantic coasts of Canada and the United States, stands a long series of forts and artillery batteries. Collectively, they are a monument to the War of 1812. To a later generation, the forts are useful mainly for tourism and as a challenge to parsimonious Canadian and American governments to pay out money for history and "heritage." To the generation of 1815, however, they were the last word in protection and deterrence. Their function on the Canadian side of the border was first to overawe the Americans, and if that failed, to delay the advance of American armies until the British army could be dispatched to the Americas to rescue the British North American provinces. They represented a world in which Great Britain could afford to, and did, rule the waves in all the world's seven seas. On the western side of the Atlantic Ocean, British bases in Halifax, Bermuda, and the West Indies were a distant reminder to the United States of the reality of British sea power. That sea power had protected the British colonies in North America in the War of 1812; it would do so again if there were another war.

The war that really counted in the memory of British politicians (and consequently for British policy on Canada) was not the War of 1812, but the Great War against France from 1793 to 1815. Memories were very long. The prime minister in 1865, Viscount Palmerston, had actually served in the wartime government that had defeated Napoleon, and his successor as prime minister, Earl Russell, had entered the House of Commons in 1813 (as Lord John Russell). Britain had often stood alone against the whole of the European continent allied with or intimidated by Napoleon. Unable to get secure supplies from the continent, the British had to rely on what could be grown at home or imported from the distant overseas, from Latin America, the United States, and British North America. The North American colonies supplied fish, some agricultural products, and most of all, timber to build ships for the Royal Navy. The long war against

France must have seemed like a vindication of the Navigation Acts, demonstrating the wisdom of linking colonial supply to metropolitan demand. Colonial imports were subsidized or given preferential tariffs, along with products from Great Britain itself. The colonies were worth subsidizing and worth protecting, but the subsidy system also linked the colonies' interest to that of British farmers. British grain (known as "corn") was good grain, reliable grain, whether it came from Canada or from Hampshire. Security of supply had more than proved its value in the opinion of most British leaders—at least as long as the memory of defeating Napoleon endured.

Naturally many colonists had an interest in maintaining the colonial, preferential, system, and even those who objected to British rule or resented inclusion in the British Empire did not do so for economic reasons. Nor was British patriotism purely an economic commitment. There was immense pride in being part of an empire that had just won a world war and in the good cause of defeating the tyrant Bonaparte. There was no doubt that British power had won the war for its embattled colonial subjects. In York, in Upper Canada, the Anglican archdeacon John Strachan naturally rejoiced that Canada remained British—that the war had confirmed that it would and should.[1] Association with a world power—with *the* world power—was an important point for the colonials and also a factor to be considered as they looked across the border at the United States.

Most of the obvious irritants between Great Britain and the United States disappeared with the end of the War of 1812 and more importantly the end of the Great War. There was no more need for impressment, no more need to talk about "neutral rights" in a world where nobody was at war. The British had abandoned the natives of the American Northwest, and the notion of an independent or autonomous native state vanished in the face of relentless settlement, pushing on to the Mississippi and beyond. In British North America, too, native affairs retreated from the political agenda into an administrative and budgetary backwater. For the natives to be allies and to be treated as such there had to be something to be allied against. The Treaty of Ghent resolved that, though not to the credit of Great Britain.

The postwar British government thought of economy, reducing the army and navy, and paying down the national debt. In 1817 like-minded governments concluded an agreement providing for naval disarmament on the Great Lakes (the Rush–Bagot Agreement), and in 1818 Britain and the United States signed a convention regulating the border between the lands of the Hudson's Bay Company and the Louisiana Purchase. It now extended along the forty-ninth parallel to the Rockies. There was as yet no agreement on who was to own the land on the western side of the Rockies between Spanish California and Russian Alaska, and so it was agreed it would be jointly owned, a British–American condominium ("Oregon"). These were important and significant actions, stabilizing American possession of the southern Great Plains, but there were events more important still to the south.

In a period of about fifteen years, the Spanish Empire in the Americas virtually disappeared. By 1826, only the Caribbean islands of Puerto Rico, Santo Domingo, and Cuba were left, and all the rest had proclaimed and enforced their independence. This particularly included Mexico, which eventually adopted a republican government as "the United States of Mexico" in 1823. Spain disappeared as the United States' southern neighbor, and a great (or formerly great) European power was removed from the continent. At the same time, Portuguese Brazil became independent.

The revolutions in the Spanish and Portuguese colonies left Great Britain as the only major European empire with more than a foothold in the Americas. (France was represented by a few Caribbean islands and St. Pierre and Miquelon, off the coast of Newfoundland, and Russia by remote Alaska.) Many of the successor states, including Mexico, were immediately convulsed by fierce internal political struggles and even civil wars. There was the possibility that Spain—which had its own civil war in 1823—might try one more time to subdue its Empire, this time with help from friendly European countries. However one might characterize what had happened in Latin America, there had been revolutions, and they had produced republics, and any thoughtful European monarch was able to draw a parallel between revolutions *there* and revolutions *here*.

Victory over Napoleon and over France had not produced self-confidence in the European ruling class. Victory might just be a temporary respite, as the revolutionaries regrouped and gathered their forces to overthrow the existing monarchical and traditional order. The revolutionary idea had a name, *liberal*, which by 1820 was identified as a political tendency looking toward individual freedom, reform, and progress. Fearful governments in Germany, Austria, and Russia coordinated repressive measures; the French government veered steadily to the right; and even the British government dabbled in repression of "reform" which in that country increasingly meant parliamentary reform—making the House of Commons more representative and politics more inclusive by broadening the franchise or suffrage. These struggles defined not only *liberal* and *liberalism*, but *reactionary* and *reaction*, clinging to or attempting to restore hierarchy and privilege as the only basis for a stable society.

The British government increasingly diverged from its erstwhile allies against Napoleon. The Tory government might stand for repression at home, but the foundations of British politics and of the British Constitution were revolutionary, from the Glorious Revolution of 1688—as were those of the United States. Awareness of British history stimulated a more nuanced view of liberalism and a willingness to support regimes abroad that Tory ministers might have frowned upon at home. British public opinion, they reflected, would not stand to see their government colluding "with great despotic monarchs," in the words of the British foreign secretary, George Canning. As the quotation suggests, the absolute monarchs of the continent had quite a different conception of authority and government, one that even British Tories deplored. This fact was hard to miss. "The shift in British foreign policy was noted even in Anglophobic America," as the historian Robert Kagan pointed out.[2]

The result was a more rational appraisal of Great Britain and its place in the world, even from politicians who had supported the War of 1812, like Secretary of State John Quincy Adams (son of John Adams) and President James Monroe. Britain was now opposed to the principles advanced by its allies, "which this country abhorred," Adams wrote in 1823. "This coincidence of principle, connected to the great changes in the world passing before us" might be "a suitable occasion for the United States and Great Britain to compare their ideas and purposes together, with a view to the accommodation of great interests upon which they had heretofore differed."[3] In 1823 Canning made such a proposal—an explicit alliance between the two countries, aimed at Spain and France. Most remarkably, Thomas Jefferson, in retirement, greeted the British approach with great enthusiasm, as did Madison. Jefferson had to swallow his previous comments on the nature of British government and with Madison greeted "co-operation" with the British as a foundation for a new American foreign policy.

In both Great Britain and the United States there was a public opinion on foreign affairs. This was not new and what it meant was that governments had to pay some attention to what the people around them might be saying. National revolutions, uprisings against tyrannical governments, these things excited individuals—most spectacularly Lord Byron, the very liberal aristocrat and poet—who could inspire others to take up their cause.[4]

There are a number of points that should be made here. First there is the existence of a transnational public opinion, sometimes amounting to a public obsession, on an issue that had sufficient romantic significance to attract and keep attention. It was not limited to English-speaking countries or even to those countries with some freedom of the press. In the case of Greece, a particularly moving or compelling cause, the catalyst was Turkish atrocities against the Christian Greeks.[5] Ideology and systems of government weighed heavily in American notions of foreign interest and foreign connection or "co-operation." Similarity of government was close to, perhaps identical to, similarity of interest in repelling the shadow of absolutism and despotism. Taken a bit further, this proposition leads to the theory of the "democratic peace," the idea that democratic countries, or *truly* democratic countries, do not go to war with one another.[6] To comment that this proposition is historically dubious is not to say that it is not attractive, or that it has not from time to time had great power over international events. There is another point to be made, which would become even more apparent in the next forty years: the United States and Great Britain (and Britain's colony, Canada) were part of the same moral universe. A moral issue that resonated in one country would resonate in another. A democratic peace may thus involve overlapping politics if a moral issue made the leap from good will and high principles into politics.

The British government was willing to go to some length, as it had been doing since 1815, to coexist in a friendly way with the United States. Furthermore, it wanted actively to seek an alliance with the Americans that would pit the two English-speaking nations against most of the powers of Europe. The British colonies in America and still more the British-Canadian colonists had nothing to say in these great matters. That is not to say that their interests were not considered and "virtually represented" by Canning, because in its details the British alliance project proposed to freeze acquisitions of territory by both countries in the Americas, a point that would have guaranteed the British provinces as much as the republics of Latin America.

It was on the point of territorial expansion that John Quincy Adams demurred. There would be no alliance, but there would be parallel policies, with Adams drafting a statement for President Monroe in December 1823, a paper that became known as the Monroe Doctrine. The Monroe Doctrine disapproved any further European expansion into or in the New World, but it did not limit American expansion. The United States, it is true, did not have the power to give effect to the Monroe Doctrine; for that, and for guarding the Atlantic Ocean against the Europeans, it relied on Great Britain. The unacknowledged nature of this relationship did not make it any the less real.

The United States had its own political struggles, but by and large they were not about the great issues of liberalism as liberalism was understood (except for slavery). In the postwar period they centered on the proper role of the federal government in directing an economic progress that was broadly agreed. Government levied tariffs, gave direct subsidies to industry, and built roads and canals at public expense either directly or indirectly. Of course this involved a great deal of money, and there was much debate over how it should be spent, and by what level of government—states or the federal government. As a result, American politics in the 1820s were fiercely partisan, producing a kaleidoscope of parties on both the federal and state level. The question of voting rights—the analogy to "reform" in Great Britain—might be controversial, but it did not occupy the same central place in American politics as in Britain and Europe. And behind the political eruptions of the 1820s there lurked a much more explosive question, slavery. But slavery as a political issue would only begin to come into its own in the 1830s.

It could be argued that much of the government's expenditure in the colonies was the result of "largesse" from the British taxpayer—the great forts at Quebec and Halifax, or the smaller forts defending Kingston and Montreal and points in between, or, especially, the Rideau Canal, built between 1825 and 1832 under the direction of the Royal Engineers, at the time the single most expensive public work in any British jurisdiction.[7] There is much truth in the notion of largesse; it is also a virtual certainty that local taxation could never have supported works of such cost. Whether the money was well spent or not, it was spent in pursuit of the defense of the Empire as a whole, against a foreign power with the capacity to harm much more than the local frontier of empire in British North America. But the American taxpayer paid, cheerfully or not, for forts and for canals too, either directly (the Erie Canal) or indirectly, through public subsidies of private companies; in directly parallel projects, so did the Canadian taxpayer. Later on, railways in both British North America and the United States also received public money, often many times over.

It is hard to see these activities, sponsored by liberal states both north and south of the border, as examples of rugged individualism or of the ability of private enterprise to provide for national needs through a cumulative but undirected process of assertive investment. The frontier of monarchy looked very similar to the republican frontier to the south. Certainly the inhabitants of the British provinces believed that to be so or, if they thought it was not, devoutly hoped they could follow the American example.

Politics in the provinces of British North America were in many respects close to those of Great Britain and those of the United States. Though both Canada and the United States early acquired the reputation of democracies, in both property qualifications of a rather mild but effective kind persisted well into the nineteenth century and in some cases, even later. It was not so much the right to vote but the right to govern that was at issue in the various provinces; and because it was an issue that had been settled in the United States forty years earlier, the question attracted interest and sympathy in that country. "Reform" meant altering the distribution of powers in the colonial constitutions, mainly in the direction of popular rule and democracy.

The British government might have learned the lesson, from the experience of Massachusetts in 1775, that making a general into a governor was not necessarily good politics. The generals of the eighteenth century had to get along with the colonial elites, a task they often botched, but the generals of the nineteenth century had to adapt to the imminence of democracy. Though generals are political creatures, theirs was and is a somewhat different kind of politics, modified by the habits of command and obedience. Votes and elections are seldom primary considerations for generals, though forts, supplies, and discipline, their stock in trade, often bring them into close contact with politicians. British North America had very recently been a theater of war, and defense was very much on the British government's mind, and so a procession of generals were named to the governor-generalship as well as the various lieutenant-governorships. With opportunities for military employment shrinking with the size of the army, appointing generals as governors must have seemed an expedient solution.

The remote colonial capitals to which the generals were assigned were limited and claustrophobic. "We have here a petty colonial oligarchy," a British immigrant wrote, "based on nothing real, nor even upon any thing imaginary." What struck Anna Jameson was that the local establishment's emotional identity was not Canadian. "Their love, their pride, are not for poor Canada, but for high and happy England; but a few more generations must change all this."[8] Placemen, place seekers, and Anglican clergymen, who could be both, dominated life, both official and social. The tone was reactionary, and the effect was to exclude from favor subjects belonging to the wrong religion, born in the wrong place (the United States), and supporting the wrong thing (Reform, however interpreted). John Strachan, the Anglican archdeacon and later bishop of Toronto, spoke for the reactionary establishment in Upper Canada, and there were analogous representatives and groups in the other provinces. Strachan and his contemporaries did not take a relaxed or accommodating view of relations with the United States or with Americans, and they were free with their opinions. In local politics, those opinions mattered, but in international affairs they did not.

Sometimes local politics spilled over into international matters. Discrimination against American-born immigrants would be noticed and remarked upon in the United States. Quarrels between British governors and their appointed advisers and the legislative assemblies of the provinces were also noticed and reported in the American press in the 1820s and 1830s. But it was only in 1837 that colonial discontent threatened to become an international matter and a diplomatic problem along the border.

By 1837 the "Reform" and "Patriote" opposition in Upper and Lower Canada respectively had decided to force the departure of the British and to establish republican governments in the respective provinces. Such a policy could hardly be obnoxious to Americans—the whole affair was close enough to what Americans knew of the history of the 1770s to excite some sympathy. As it turned out, the sympathy was restrained, when present, and balanced by other concerns.[9] Nevertheless the Reformers/Patriotes exaggerated, to others and to themselves, the kind of support their cause would attract south of the border. Except along the frontier, it had few supporters, and none of those was important in politics, government, or business.[10] The American federal government and the state governments remained aloof. The violent clashes between government troops and rebels around Montreal and north of Toronto (renamed from York in 1834) and the flight of rebel leaders to the safety of the United States provoked only official warnings to American citizens not to become involved. President Martin Van Buren issued a proclamation urging neutrality and threatening to withhold official help from any American with the misfortune to be caught by the British while aiding the rebels.[11] The British government appreciated American restraint. Queen Victoria recorded in her diary her prime minister's comment that "the Americans were behaving well and not countenancing the Rebels."[12]

The American reaction to the rebellions was complicated by the capture of Navy Island, British territory, by the rebels. Situated in the middle of the Niagara River, it became a rebel base (also called "The Republic of Canada"), supplied by the American steamer *Caroline* from the American side. The *Caroline*'s activities were definitely an un-neutral act, but so was the British response. Some Canadian militia, led by Colonel Allan MacNab, crossed the river, seized the *Caroline*, killing one American in the process, set the ship ablaze, and sent it over Niagara Falls. The US government protested at the time, and local opinion was aroused against the British, but the American government took the issue no further. Unluckily, some years later one of the British party talked loosely and drunkenly of his role in the affair, and even more unluckily he was in an American tavern. Alexander McLeod was arrested for murder, referring to the American casualty during the capture of the *Caroline* in 1837. The McLeod case occupied the British and American governments for six months in 1840–1. Tried in New York state, McLeod was acquitted, thereby averting yet another crisis in Anglo-American relations.[13]

The *Caroline* affair has had a long afterlife. Colonel MacNab, the British commander, got a baronetcy for his efforts and went on to become premier of the province of Canada in the 1850s. He could not have anticipated what else would follow. The British-Canadian seizure of the *Caroline* was claimed at the time and since to be anticipatory self-defense. As a British note put the case, in 1842, "Her Majesty's Government . . . are of opinion, that the transaction, which terminated in the destruction of the 'Caroline,' was a justifiable employment of force, for the purpose of defending the British Territory from the unprovoked attack of a band of British rebels and American pirates, who, having been 'permitted' to arm and organize themselves within the territory of the United States, had actually invaded a portion of the territory of Her Majesty." The American government at the time disagreed, but not very forcefully, and negotiators in 1842, with more important matters to resolve, let the matter drop.[14] In twenty-first-century terms, this was an example of "pre-emption" and was cited as justification for the American (and British) attack on Iraq in March 2003, and for similar transborder enterprises undertaken by one aggrieved state—often the United States—against another.

The American administrations of the 1837–1842 period were, on the whole, rather pacific in their inclinations. Van Buren, for example, refused a request from the newly independent republic of Texas for admission to the Union in 1837—a move that would certainly have meant war with Mexico, which was trying to reclaim Texas, its former territory. A boundary dispute between Maine and New Brunswick, a question that definitely involved the interests of the United States, was settled rationally and peaceably, and favorably from the British point of view, and the boundary defined ultimately by arbitration. (The boundary from Lake Superior to Lake of the Woods was also finally clarified.)[15] In negotiating the Webster–Ashburton Treaty of 1842, which regulated a series of Anglo-American disputes, the American government was not unaware of British interest in Texas; there was the possibility that good relations with Great Britain in the north were being exchanged for British passivity in whatever might arise between the United States and temporarily independent Texas.[16]

In 1844 the relatively peaceable Whigs (a Whig party existed in the United States between the 1830s and 1850s) lost the presidential election to the more populist Democrats, a considerable change, but nothing in comparison to the change that was overcoming American politics.[17] The Whigs were more conservative, but also more favorable to spending government money on economic development and commerce; the Democrats were associated with a more populist approach to politics.[18] Increasingly the country was divided between "slave states," the South, where slavery was not merely tolerated but enshrined as a first principle of economics and politics, and "free states," the North, where slavery had been abolished. The South dreaded being outnumbered in national institutions and fought tenaciously for the admission of new slave states to the Union, while the North increasingly—but not as yet exclusively—sought the opposite. The Democratic platform of 1844 sought to straddle the issue by demanding the annexation of a northern territory, the Oregon condominium (the slogan was "Fifty-four forty or fight," referring to Oregon's northern border), and Texas. And so, as with the settlement of the New Brunswick border and the *Caroline* case, there was a whiff of slavery behind what a contemporary Democratic journalist called "the manifest destiny" of the United States to expand across the whole continent of North America.[19]

The "manifest destiny" took the form of the annexation of Texas in 1845 and the Mexican War in 1846. Hostilities had already begun when President James K. Polk, the victor of the election of 1844, accepted a British proposal that had been current for some for some years, to extend the forty-ninth parallel boundary to the Strait of Juan de Fuca, and then bring the line along the middle of the Strait to the open ocean, meaning that all of Vancouver Island would remain in British possession. As the northern frontier was composed, the southern was expanding—not just Texas, but California, New Mexico, and the other future southwestern states were detached from Mexico and added to the United States.

## Liberalism and the Colonies

It was fortunate that the government of the United States had little interest in or desire to intervene in Upper and Lower Canada—the only two

colonies where political and constitutional extremism had produced actual violence. (The Maritime provinces had solved their problems peacefully, and on the whole sensibly, while Newfoundland's politics had not yet
developed to the point of battling for the control of government.) It was
fortunate too that the insurgent leaders in Upper and Lower Canada were
incompetent if not actually ridiculous. William Lyon Mackenzie in Upper
Canada and Louis-Joseph Papineau both escaped to the United States
within days of the commencement of their uprisings, to the great disgust
of many of their followers, who remained behind to risk death in battle or
death by hanging after their arrest. In a final piece of good luck, the government in London was Whig if not actually Liberal in coloration (British
Whigs were turning into Liberals in nomenclature and political attitudes)
and far less obdurate in examining colonial problems than Lord North's
administration had been in the 1770s. Finally, the British and British-
Canadians were fortunate in having a competent general on the ground in
Lower Canada, capable of organizing loyal forces and the regular army, and
implementing the suppression of the rebellion. It also helped that French
Canadians were divided, geographically, socially, and politically, with, once
again, the higher clergy endorsing authority and the government. Once
suppressed, the revolutionary spirit both lapsed and collapsed. Having
been granted a respite by the rebels' failure, what would the British do to
regroup their colonies and reorganize their colonial experiment?

The government in power in London was headed by Lord Melbourne,
who had the distinction of being the eighteen-year-old Queen Victoria's
first prime minister. "The news are, I grieve to say, very bad from Canada,"
the queen wrote in her diary on December 22, 1837, "that is to say rumours
and reports by the Papers, though we have no Official Reports. But Lord
Melbourne hopes it may not be so bad as it is rumoured. There certainly
is open Rebellion." When the cabinet met to consider what should be
done, it initially agreed only on sending troops. Eventually, it also agreed
that the Constitution of 1791 would be abolished, as far as Lower Canada
was concerned, and the 1774 Constitution reinstated (in effect, not literally), which meant a reversion to an authoritarian style of government.[20]
Melbourne found an inconveniently prominent Liberal peer, Lord Durham,
to become governor general of Canada, with a mandate to govern, investi-
gate what had happened, and decide what should now be done, and on
that point the more liberally inclined members of the cabinet agreed.[21]
They were also agreed that Lord Durham was better three thousand miles
away than at home, making trouble for his fellow Liberals.

Durham's nickname was "Radical Jack," and in his brief mandate in Canada—he stayed only six months in the single year 1838—he lived up to it. Melbourne's ploy in sending Durham three thousand miles away exploded when Durham spectacularly resigned and returned to London to make as much trouble as he could for the prime minister. Yet Durham's importance was less in what he actually did than in the views he brought to North America, the impressions he carried away, and the expression he gave to a more liberal and tolerant relationship between the mother country and its North American colonies. Durham's Report recommended many things, some durable, some not. He famously described Canada as "two nations warring within the bosom of a single state," encapsulating a major part of Canada's political dilemma. There was more: Durham "believed that English Canadians and Americans shared a strong commitment to individual enterprise and material progress, and felt that the French of Lower Canada would be best served by assimilating to the same values."[22] His solution, absorption of the French Canadiens into the British-Canadian majority, proved chimerical, but in his basic approach Durham broke the constitutional logjam that had paralyzed colonial politics in the Canadas (and Nova Scotia too) since the 1820s. In a long aftermath to Durham and the Report he produced for the British government in 1839, the old colonial model of government was swept away, Upper and Lower Canada were reunited into a single province of Canada, and "responsible government" was instituted. In effect, the Canadian subject was freed, through his vote and his legislature, to determine his own government (bearing in mind that at the time these were all male attributes). This settlement took a decade fully to implement, for there were many backings and fillings, and was completed during the governorship of another Liberal peer, Lord Elgin.

The significance of the changes made to the government of Canada and the other North American provinces meant a divergence in structure from the monarchical-republican model adopted in the United States in 1787, where the head of state was (and is) also the head of government. Canada's new style of government was the replication of the British form of government as it existed in Great Britain itself in the 1840s, which was a very considerable advance from the conventions of government in the 1780s and 1790s. Most of George III's governments had depended on the co-operation and support of the king, although George III did once have to accept a government that he entirely disliked, in 1783. He worked hard to get rid of it and succeeded, but the principle was established, and confirmed by the experience of his son, William IV, and granddaughter,

Victoria, that a politician who could command the support of a majority of the House of Commons was thereby entitled to become prime minister, whatever the monarch's preferences might be.[23] By Victoria's time, elections rather than the monarch determined the political coloration of a government and, except in very unusual circumstances, who the prime minister should be. The office of prime minister was stabilized and enhanced, almost to its present dimensions.

Out of the disturbances of 1837–8, therefore, what can be called a "liberal empire" was born. Durham and his successors, and his colleagues back in London, were brought to recognize local self-determination, the necessity of giving colonists the ability to rule themselves, as far as they wanted. There was a contradiction here, for the North American provinces were still British colonies and subordinate members of the British Empire. If the colonials wanted to take responsibility for government, it followed that they should pay for it—in effect, "no representation without taxation." In cash or in credit, that is what the colonial governments of the 1840s and 1850s did, and what the colonial secretary in London (effectively, the minister for the colonies), Lord Grey, implemented in 1846. Grey, not coincidentally, was a relative of Durham's.

Simultaneously in the 1840s there was an ideological sea-change in British politics. Political reform had won the day in a Reform Act of 1832 that extended the franchise and abolished some of the worst electoral abuses of the past. The next question was economic—changing British tariff and trade policy so as to implement free trade. The Navigation Acts and the Corn Law had to go, and with them the preference in the British market for colonial products. Great Britain could get food cheaper elsewhere than in the British Isles or the Canadian colonies. In some respects this was a generational transformation. Memories of the Great War were fading. Great Britain was no longer an imperiled, isolated island facing a united absolutist continent. The restrictive policies that had encouraged domestic production under British political control were deemed no longer necessary safeguards for national security but an unjustifiable cost.

The loosening of political ties was therefore accompanied by a loosening of the economic bonds of empire. It would be an understatement to say that this change of policy stimulated fear and rage among Canadian Tories. They did have something to complain about—at a stroke the guaranteed market for Canadian products was lost, and a sharp commercial depression settled over British North America. The Canadian Parliament building, then located in Montreal, was burned down by an angry mob, the governor general's carriage was stoned, and conservative merchants sponsored a manifesto demanding annexation to the United States. In its employment of mob violence it was an unconscious mimicry of the revolutionary process of the 1770s, but it was so restricted in support that it did not survive the year 1849. Perhaps in other years, or other decades, the Americans would have taken notice, but in 1849 the United States had more important things to consider.

## Trade, Morality, and Slavery

The American political system was beginning to come apart under the strain of the slavery issue. National politics increasingly became a theater for confrontation, and the ability of politicians to reach a compromise between North and South steadily diminished. Each concession designed to appease the South stimulated more rage in the free states, a prominent example being the Fugitive Slave Act of 1850, which allowed slaveholders the facilities of the federal government to pursue and arrest their escaped property. Like the British colonial measures of the 1770s, the Fugitive Slave Act could be applied only by force, and each confrontation fed resistance.

The Canadian colonies figured in the slavery drama, because slavery had been abolished in the British Empire as a whole in 1833 and was restricted rather earlier in British North America.[24] Escaping slaves might find shelter in the northern free states but secured immunity from pursuit only by crossing into British Canada. Escaping slaves found their way facilitated by an organized network called the Underground Railroad, leading them from the Ohio River to the Canadian border; upward of thirty thousand ex-slaves are estimated to have crossed into Canada by this means. As in Great Britain and the northern states, slavery became a liberal cause in Canada; indeed, anti-slavery was a defining issue for Canadian liberals, as for liberals elsewhere in the English-speaking world.

An Anti-Slavery Society was constituted in Toronto in 1851, and from its origins it was directly linked to the American anti-slavery movement. The first meeting of the Society was addressed by the African-American anti-slavery leader, Frederick Douglass; helping to constitute the society were local eminences like George Brown, publisher of the Liberal newspaper, the Toronto *Globe*, and Oliver Mowat, a future premier of the future province of Ontario. It was neither the first time nor the last that Canada would be a refuge from American politics, and as on previous and future occasions, the Canadian anti-slavery movement was part of a larger international phenomenon.[25]

Not all British North Americans took an active interest in events in the United States. Canada as such had no foreign policy and no foreign relations. Britain gave it political security and paid for defense, as it had ever since 1776, but no longer provided a positive economic context. The governor general of the day, Lord Elgin, concluded in 1848 that Canada's political stability and its attachment to the Empire depended on a paradox. Writing to the colonial secretary, Lord Grey, Elgin argued, "The true policy in [trade] according to my judgment, is—to secure for Her Majesty's subjects in Canada, free access to the markets of the States.... You must then trust to [the Canadian's] affection for his own Institutions... to induce him to remain steady, and to resist the blandishments of the 'Stars & Stripes.' "[26]

Elgin proposed to replace the preferential relationship to Great Britain with one to the United States. He had the co-operation of the Canadian government, which by itself would have been unable to conceive, much less implement, a serious trade policy. The idea was not unique to Elgin; it had already been raised by several local politicians, and Elgin was assured of support among some, or even many, of his colonial subjects. Lord Elgin, as a senior British official, could employ the services of the British legation in Washington; as a lord—properly, the Earl of Elgin—he could attract the attention of American society. As a politician, he understood how to run a political campaign and to take advantage of the divisions and weaknesses of his American counterparts. He also understood a cardinal point of American trade policy that under the constitution trade was controlled by Congress. Although technically the executive (that is, the president) had to conclude treaties, they were dead letters without congressional consent. The executive was happy to let Elgin do the running on the trade issue, and he did. Elgin therefore directed his abundant hospitality—an open bar at his hotel—at members of Congress and senators.

The interest of the southern slave states was to maintain the balance of power in Washington, the equal division between free and slave states in the Senate. If British North America collapsed or fragmented because of its economic problems and sought admission to the Union, it could hardly be resisted, and the effect would be to add two million new citizens and three or four new states, with representatives and senators to match. The reconstituted United States would in that case have a clear anti-slavery majority, not only numerically, which was already true, but politically. One solution would be to favor British North America with economic concessions, so as to maintain its economic viability and political separation. Lord Elgin accordingly plied southern politicians with wine, whiskey, and blandishments.

The interest of the northern states was just the opposite. Canada was an economic competitor in many areas, but that could be overcome if Canada was ultimately destined to join the Union: political similarity and anti-slavery would add to the strength of the country, and particularly of the North. If the Canadians could be conciliated and made to feel that the United States was not a hostile or alien force, then concessions today would win the great political prize tomorrow, or at any rate next week. And so the North consented to a deal that permitted free trade in natural products—from fishery, farm, and forest, and minerals too—but allowed both parties to maintain tariffs on manufactured goods. Reciprocal concessions, mirror images, furnished the title for the treaty—Reciprocity. It might seem that American manufacturers were at a disadvantage in terms of the Canadian market, but on the other hand, they got cheaper raw materials from British North America. There was one further, favorable, factor: the United States in the 1850s was in a low-tariff phase. The United States' new manufacturing interests were not politically powerful enough in the equally balanced Congress to implement a thoroughgoing policy of protection, for the South was insistent on low, or lower, tariffs, and not enough northerners were willing to defy southern opinion.[27]

As a result of Elgin's efforts, the Reciprocity Treaty was concluded. It should be underlined what an unusual achievement this was. Between the foundation of the republic in 1789 and 1933—eighty years after Elgin—the United States concluded and ratified precisely three trade treaties, and Elgin's was one. A great deal of credit should therefore go to the earl, whose political talents were fully equal to the challenge of democracy. Elgin had pandered to the respective illusions of the North and South and, appropriately enough, the effects of the treaty were mostly illusory too. The illusion consisted in how statistics were interpreted. British North America and the United States were just getting into the business of adding up trade, and as far as statistics are concerned 1849 was the year zero. If 1850 is compared with, say, 1858 or 1864 there is no doubt: trade increased hugely. That would be enough for any politician, whether in the nineteenth or in the twenty-first century—the Reciprocity Treaty must have done it. This is a case of *post hoc, propter hoc*: an event, preferably a simple event, causes another, later event. Post hoc is a logical fallacy, and so is the conclusion that improvements in the economies of the two reciprocal partners after 1854 must derive from the treaty. Economics is undoubtedly a powerful factor in politics, but economic reality does not always coincide with political phenomena.

In the case of Canada, it is clear that the economy was recovering by the time Elgin packed his trunks and set out for Washington. There he and Congress laid their golden egg in the nest of Reciprocity, and trade grew forthwith. Happily for the citizens of the 1850s, but unhappily for the legend of Reciprocity, trade was already increasing. As economic historians have pointed out, trade had as much to do with the availability of the new technology of railways to transport goods as did the Reciprocity Treaty. Hauling freight on a railway bridge was much more efficient than ferrying it across the St. Lawrence or Niagara Rivers, or driving it in a wagon across the land frontier. Given access where before there had been little or none, trade flourished.[28]

## Receding Horizons

Illusions were not restricted to the economy. In the aftermath of the War of 1812, both the United States and British North America believed, and had reason to believe, that they had been the victors in the war. Sea battles and land victories seemed to be equally balanced. The British blockade was forgotten, and with it the economic aspects of the war that had almost brought the United States to financial ruin. For these and many other reasons, American self-confidence flourished in the years after the war and was remarked upon by visitors to the United States, as well as by the North American neighbors. A steady flow of immigrants to American shores, drawn by economic opportunity and the prospect of betterment, raised the population until, in the 1850s, as many people lived in the United States as in Great Britain itself (thirty-one million Americans to twenty-eight million British and Irish by 1860). At the same time, the relative populations of British North America assumed a steady ratio: there were, roughly, and at all times, about ten times as many Americans as British North Americans or, later, Canadians.[29] As population grew, so did wealth. By the middle of the nineteenth century Americans were, per capita, about 30 percent (and sometimes more) wealthier than their northern cousins, although they still lagged considerably behind the inhabitants of Great Britain.[30]

Comparisons were inevitable, and they were not always flattering to the northern colonies, either demographically or economically. Forty years after John Graves Simcoe, it was clear that his fantasy of an orderly British province of Upper Canada providing a model to the neighboring states had not come to pass, nor did New Brunswick or Nova Scotia seem anything more than a backwater to New England. "The United States are increasing in population and power beyond all former calculations and experience," an Upper Canadian agricultural society claimed in 1828. Perhaps the republic would eventually grow "to eclipse the present glory and splendour of Great Britain." This was an inversion of the future, as Simcoe had envisioned it.[31] In an important sense, however, Simcoe had been right: the population was more "British"—that is, British-born. The large majority of the European-derived population in the Maritime provinces spoke English, with an admixture of Gaelic in Cape Breton Island, which in 1820 was reunited with mainland Nova Scotia. In Lower Canada, British (including Irish) immigration raised the English-speaking part of the population, especially in the cities, so that even Quebec City for a time had 40 percent of its population English-speaking and Montreal a majority of English speakers. Most immigrants passed through Montreal, proceeding either to Upper Canada or onward to the United States. Sixty-six thousand came from the British Isles in 1832 alone, and 110,000 in 1847.

"British" immigrants included Irish, since the country of origin had been, since 1801, the United Kingdom of Great Britain *and* Ireland. The Irish were both Catholic and Protestant, and in fact in this period the majority of the Irish immigrants to Canada were Protestant; as a consequence, the Protestant Orange Order became an important player in the politics of British North America, much to the dismay of the British governors and their political masters in London, for whom it was a disorderly if not actually subversive phenomenon.[32] As for the Catholic Irish, many had arrived in British North America before the Irish potato famine of the mid-1840s drove hundreds of thousands from the island. Despite proximity to the United States, the history of the Catholic Irish in Canada was to prove rather different from the American experience. The Irish-Canadian Catholics tended to follow the counsel of a reformed Irish revolutionary, Thomas D'Arcy McGee, to adapt and join in Canadian society, including Canadian politics. Though McGee was assassinated in 1868 for his views, the Catholic Irish became enthusiastic and influential participants in a Canada that was and remained a part of the British Empire—a point of difference, if one were searching for it, between the two North American countries.[33]

Is it possible, looking at British North America in the mid-nineteenth century, to discern major differences between British North Americans and Americans? Seymour Martin Lipset argued that the difference had begun with the Revolution; by the 1840s the differences should have widened, and become even more apparent. There were some differences:

monarchy versus republic, independence versus empire, the beginning of government and politics in two languages rather than one—these are indisputable. As for the subject matter of politics, canals, railways, subsidies—broadly speaking, collective action for the collective good—it is hard to see the distinction. What the British colonies had certainly not become, or in the case of French Canada had remained, is traditional or feudal or even semi-feudal. Indeed the last vestiges of feudalism were erased by legislation appropriately entitled An Act for the Abolition of Feudal Rights and Duties in Lower Canada, passed in 1854 and duly signed by Lord Elgin, who could thereby consider his work in Canada complete.[34]

Americans coming north in the 1820s and 1830s saw the English-speaking provinces of British America as a continuation of their cultural universe. As early as the 1780s and 1790s, a sense of "equality" and "insubordination" was remarked on in Upper Canada, as it had been in New Brunswick.[35] A later visitor, William Henry Seward, former governor of New York and soon to be Secretary of State in Abraham Lincoln's administration, found English Canadians to be an "ingenious, enterprising, and ambitious people," qualities much like those of the Americans across the Great Lakes.[36] Seward's admiration was not necessarily altruistic: the Canadians were "building states to be hereafter admitted to the American union," he said in 1853.[37]

Alexis de Tocqueville, then a traveling French magistrate, found in 1832 that the English Canadians were "identical with that of the United States," both being part of "the British race," which was "not confined within the frontiers of the Union." "I myself saw in Canada," he wrote, "that the English are the masters of commerce and manufacture," like their counterparts in the United States.[38] Tocqueville might not have described the Canadiens as Henry David Thoreau did, as "a rather poor looking race clad in grey homespun," distinct from the better-clad British-Canadians and Americans, but his conclusion was the same.[39] As for differences among anglophones, most travelers agreed that they were matters of degree rather than kind. Sited on a smaller, poorer territory, limited in its ability to sustain a sizable population, British North America was, from the time of the Louisiana Purchase, destined to be smaller and poorer than the United States. But, in another sign of the interchangeability of the North American population, it would soon become a major source of immigrants to the United States.

Similarity was not everything. Embedded in the relations between the British Empire and the United States was political dissonance. The United

States existed in opposition to the British Empire, even as culture, economics, and history drew the two together. The result was an odd Anglo-Saxon anglophobia, in which the United States uniquely embodied the best qualities of its British ancestor. As historian Peter Onuf put it, "American exceptionalism, in all its varieties, bears the imprint of its British imperial pedigree, perhaps most tellingly—if inadvertently—in the anglophobic assertion of a fundamental, world-changing difference between mother country and new nation."[40] Perhaps as a result, non-Americans meeting the citizens of the republic in the early nineteenth century considered exaggeration and boastfulness to be fundamental American characteristics. Americans would reply that there was much to boast about, in progress, expansion, and industry, in the activity that visitors noted in American towns and cities. More abstractly, there was liberty (except where slaves were concerned), contrasted with the lack of liberty elsewhere.

Not surprisingly, the British, and British-Canadians, reciprocated. Sometimes the portrait of the American resonated with Americans themselves, as in the Nova Scotian Thomas Chandler Haliburton's "Sam Slick," the story of a fictional Yankee clock peddler, who prowled around the Maritime provinces taking advantage of the slow-witted and slow-moving provincials. Sam Slick caught on not only in the small provincial market, but also in the United States and Great Britain. Agile, sly, indefatigable, the Sam Slick character was also boastful and vulgar, but the mixture of good and bad characteristics was obviously sufficiently appealing to overcome American sensitivities.[41] Less affectionate were the depictions of the United States and Americans by the British authors Tom Moore, Frances Trollope, Charles Dickens, Harriet Martineau, and Frederick Marryat. Violence, slavery, boastfulness, and anglophobia were frequent themes. The South, according to the Earl of Carlisle, was "the Ireland of America," hardly flattering to either party.[42] Dickens wrote that he could not bear to visit the South beyond Virginia, because of the practice of slavery. Dickens, being Dickens, was forgiven; but from his point of view the Americans kept re-offending.[43] Dickens, who was as close to a universal author as the nineteenth century produced, was read and appreciated in Canada as well as the United States. His comments on the Americans doubtless went down well in conservative Canadian households.

Dickens was not alone in finding the Americans persistently aggravating. Privately, British politicians, administrators, and generals were sorely tried by American threats, official and unofficial—during the Canadian rebellions, over the New Brunswick boundary dispute, and the Oregon question, not least because these threats all had implications for the British military budget. Should more troops be sent to North America, or not? Which fort was the most urgent to complete?

It was fortunate indeed that American energies were engaged elsewhere. The South and its need to defend slavery diverted a large part of American nationalism. As far as the South was concerned, Manifest Destiny meant Mexico, or Cuba, or Central America. As far as the North was concerned, "aggression" was not something that came from outside the country, but inside, from the South. Kansas, not Canada, filled American newspapers as the two sections drifted toward war. Since Americans' principal enemies were internal, there was no time and no occasion to pick a quarrel with the British or the British Americans. That would have to come later, if it ever came at all.

# 5

## A Colonial Nation, Its Neighbor, and Its Empire

"THAT THE CANADIANS hate the Americans," a young Englishman advised his countrymen in 1867, "can be no reason why we should spend blood and treasure in protecting them against the consequences of their hate." The British policy of maintaining a North American colony was flatly opposed to "the best interests of our race." As for the argument that "the Canadians are loyal," and thus could not be abandoned, it was a mere contrivance. "Our loyal colonists of Canada" levied exorbitant protective tariffs on British goods—no less than 20 percent!—just as Great Britain was "fighting China and conquering Japan," sacrificing itself on behalf of its ungrateful Empire. The twelve thousand British troops in Canada should be withdrawn from a colony they neither could nor should protect. Let the Canadians become independent forthwith, and protect themselves, if they wished to. Canada would then cease to be an encumbrance to Britain's relations with the United States, and vice versa: American grievances against the British would no longer endanger Canada.[1]

The youthful author Charles Dilke had been visiting North America in 1866, in the aftermath of the American Civil War, and like many British travelers he passed through Canada en route from one part of the United States to another, then on to the South Seas and back to Britain. Aged twenty-five, he enjoyed instant success with a book on his travels, *Greater Britain*. Dilke found many marvels on his voyage, but Canada was not one of them. Instead, he urged his readers that British affections toward the wayward colony should be conditional, arguing that the main attraction for Great Britain in North America was not the British colonies, but the American republic. Even a talented statesman like "Sir James Macdonald," as he called the Canadian premier, could hardly cope with the unpromising material of his nascent country.[2]

Dilke would prove to be the shooting star of British politics, moving from brilliant promise to youthful prominence in a Liberal cabinet, to personal disgrace and an aborted career, and finally to a very lengthy semi-retirement; he never got the chance to put his conception of Canada's proper place in or out of the Empire into practical effect. Yet Dilke had visited Canada at a prophetic moment: the American Civil War altered not only Canada's relations with the United States, but its connection to Great Britain. As Dilke proposed, the British garrison in Canada was soon al-most entirely withdrawn and coincidentally or not, Canadian relations with the United States settled down to a low, continuous, but peaceful grumble.

The United States that Dilke toured had just experienced a great civil war, and the war, in turn, had transformed the country and, incidentally, American relations with Canada. The United States of the 1850s was po-litically paralyzed, drifting toward disunion and possible collapse. The ques-tion of slavery, its existence or its spread, found its way into every political issue. Foreigners, including British North Americans, found slavery conven-ient in dealing with Americans, because it gave them the moral upper hand. Harriet Beecher Stowe's *Uncle Tom's Cabin* was a bestseller on two conti-nents, and it did not go unnoticed that British Canada was the promised land for the escaping slaves in the novel. Stowe largely based her book on the memoirs of Josiah Henson, an escaped slave who came to Canada in 1830 and subsequently became a Methodist preacher and an organizer of a fugitive slave community near Chatham in Upper Canada.[3] The arriving slaves discovered that their hosts might oppose slavery, but were not free of racial prejudice: segregated communities and segregated schools appeared in areas where escaped African-Americans made their homes.[4] Whatever the faults or deficiencies of the British colonies, slavery could not be held to their account, but it could be, and was, freely attributed to Americans.

Opposition to slavery was a point of difference with the United States as a whole, but increasingly it was a sentiment held in common with a majority of Americans in the northern states. Remarkably, George Brown, the editor of the *Globe* newspaper, and a leader among Upper Canadian Reformers or Liberals, reminded his followers in 1852 that "we too are Americans; on us, as well as on them, lies the duty of preserving the honour of the continent."[5] But there was a difference—absent slavery, absent too the political convulsions the Americans were enduring.

British North Americans could create their own problems. If they were not divided over slavery, they were divided by language and religion, and increas-ingly by constitutional deadlock in the province of Canada. Upper Canada was now almost fully settled and prosperous, with a population surpassing that of Lower Canada. Yet the Constitution gave Lower Canadians—mostly French and Catholic—the same number of seats in the legislature as Upper Canada, English-speaking and mainly Protestant. This imbalance in favor of Catholicism and French could not be allowed to endure. George Brown, as opposed to Catholicism as he was to slavery, led the agitation for representation by population, "rep by pop."

Canadian politicians barely paused to take note of the 1860 election in the United States, the election of the anti-slavery Republican politician Abraham Lincoln as president, and the secession of the southern states—eleven states gone out of thirty by the middle of April 1861. Lincoln did what he could to prevent conflict, assuring the South that he would do nothing to abolish or harm slavery where it existed and would merely prevent its further spread. His secretary of state, William Henry Seward of New York, toyed with the notion of compensating the northern states for the departure of the South through the acquisition of Canada. There were certainly others in the northern states—the New York *Herald* and Senator Charles Sumner of Massachusetts—who hankered after the British provinces, and who thought the colonials would make better Americans than the secessionist Southerners. It was an idea that some feared would lead Seward to seek a quarrel and then a war with Great Britain—suggesting that the pressure of events had temporarily unhinged Seward's judgment—and it was swiftly abandoned.[6] In any case the South was not to be appeased, and before long its government—the Confederate States of America—was doing its best to bring about British intervention in what swiftly became a Civil War.

The Civil War reversed the British and American positions on maritime rights and on the morality of war. In 1812, Great Britain fought for its independent existence, and even its survival, against the tyrant Napoleon; in 1861 the northern states—the Union—fought for their survival as a country, and (eventually) against the monstrous tyranny of slavery. In 1812 the British condemned Americans for obtuseness, if not worse (justified, as we have seen, in the case of Jefferson and his fellow anglophobes). In 1861 Americans found the same fault in the British. Some troops were sent out in the summer of 1861, causing the *New York Times* to editorialize, "The people of the United States do not feel any concern whatever in the act of the British Government in reinforcing Canada. . . . The Americans have not seriously entertained a thought of a war with England or an attack upon the Canadas; and if they had, they would hardly deny the perfect right and propriety of the British Government in reinforcing their adjacent colonies as largely as they might desire."[7]

Things were very different a few months later. Union infringement of British rights on the high seas brought the two countries close to war in December 1861. The US Navy stopped a British vessel traveling from Havana to Liverpool and removed two Confederate envoys. These were conveyed as prisoners to New York, and in a season lacking in Union victories, their capture seemed a huge triumph, not only over the South but over Britain as well. Let the British retaliate if they dared, a Philadelphia newspaper proclaimed. It would only furnish an excuse to complete the War of 1812 (as the War of 1812 had completed the Revolution) and "consolidate Canada with the Union."[8]

As events teetered, the British government mobilized such troops as it had to hand, 11,500 of them including the Grenadier Guards, and sent them to reinforce the province of Canada, the most vulnerable colony. Compared with 1775 or 1812, they came swiftly, and reached British North America by steamer to the Maritime provinces, by rail, and by marching, in mid-winter, from New Brunswick to Lower Canada. The British hoped the regulars would be reinforced by Canadian militia, optimistically estimated at 100,000 men, and together they could make a creditable defense of the line of the Great Lakes and St. Lawrence—for a while at least. Meanwhile the Royal Navy would blockade Union ports and if necessary bombard them into submission. The troops soon arrived, though the militia were not ready. Fortunately they were not needed, for the crisis had abated, though they were undoubtedly a useful symbol that Great Britain still felt a connection to its loyal subjects in America.

British North Americans divided during the war into pro-Union and anti-Union factions.[9] Liberal newspapers like the Montreal *Herald* and the Toronto *Globe* printed Union dispatches and shaped their content to please those citizens who preferred to contemplate the victory of the Union. Conservative newspapers, preferring American disunion, did the reverse. Readers of the differing papers might as well have dwelt in separate universes.[10]

Numbers of Canadians joined the Union army, and some were even said to have enlisted in the Confederate forces. The numbers of Canadians in the war have fluctuated over the past 150 years according to the taste of the various historians who chronicled the phenomenon. It is possible, even probable, that tens of thousands of Canadian-born served in the Union Army—perhaps thirty thousand out of a total Union force of two million. But many of these "Canadians" were already living in the United States, and their numbers are much smaller than those of German- or

British-born American soldiers. No doubt some of these Canadians were moved by anti-slavery ideology or a devotion to democracy, but the numbers of the ideologically motivated at best would have been in the low thousands.[11]

It was hard not to notice that the war was definitely good for trade. "[The] Province [of Canada] was overrun by Americans who bought up cattle, poultry, eggs and other staple articles of food, in enormous quantities....[M]oney flowed into the country in a steady stream. Our farmers... had never enjoyed such a golden opportunity."[12] British-American exports soared, more than replacing the trade lost with the blockaded South, and since the war lasted four years, so did prosperity. In retrospect, the prosperity of the war years would be ascribed to the workings of reciprocity, but it is obvious that treaty or no, the supplies to the North were going to flow.

Confederate agents found sympathizers in the British provinces and in Great Britain itself. Some Loyalist descendants saw the cause of the South as the cause of their ancestors—persecuted aristocrats.[13] Others merely rejoiced in the prospect that the mighty Yankee would be humbled and that North America would be more conveniently in balance if there were three rather than two countries occupying it.[14] The Confederates naturally agreed, but as the war went on and Confederate prospects declined, the Southern government decided that more active measures had to be taken. Agents were sent to Canada to do what they could. There followed a series of annoying incidents along the border, culminating in October 1864 in a Confederate raid on St. Albans, Vermont.

The St. Albans raid was not very serious, compared with the desperate fighting going on in Georgia or Virginia, but it took the life of a local citizen, and it was destructive and annoying, as well as a violation of British neutrality. The raiders returned to Montreal with bags full of money— $170,000 worth. They were arrested and brought before a witless Montreal magistrate, who found that they had not committed an extraditable offense—and evidently no offense at all. They were released, handed their loot, and allowed to disappear.

If the raid had stimulated American anger, the release of the Confederate raiders momentarily rendered the Americans incandescent. The Canadian government now hastily bolted the barn door after the Confederate horse had fled. They fired the magistrate and out of government funds compensated the Americans for the St. Albans losses. They hired detectives and sought out further Confederate plotters. It was not enough. Lincoln "denounced" (gave notice to terminate) the Rush–Bagot Treaty of 1817, providing for disarmament on the Great Lakes. The general commanding Union forces along the northern frontier proclaimed that he would pursue any raiders across the international boundary. The government in Washington imposed a requirement for passports along the frontier, to the dismay of American consuls north of the border, who suddenly had to cope with hundreds of passport-less American travelers marooned in Canada. The House of Representatives passed a resolution terminating the Reciprocity Treaty of 1854, which would therefore expire in March 1866.

By March 1865 tempers had cooled. Lincoln terminated the requirement for passports on receipt of compensation for the money taken from St. Albans' banks, and Seward rescinded the denunciation of the Rush–Bagot agreement.[15] Naturally the governor general, Lord Monck, took a strong interest in appeasing the Americans, but the Canadian cabinet was equally anxious, and effective, in making amends.[16]

The war soon came to an end. The American government no longer had to worry about Confederate raiders, for the South's surrender was complete. Slavery had already been mostly abolished, and a constitutional amendment freed any remaining slaves. Defeated, the Confederates did not rise again. The Southern states were occupied by the Union army, and the government in Washington tried to induce the formerly seceded states to recognize a world in which slavery was no more. Eventually, however, the North and South reconciled themselves to a world in which African-Americans were technically free, but in practice unequal, a situation that would forcibly be maintained, legally or illegally, into the late twentieth century.

## The Aftermath of the Civil War

Relations between British North America and the United States soon subsided to a new normalcy. There was no longer a Northern army patrolling the northern border; the army, such as it was, occupied the South or fought natives in the West. Some Canadian veterans of the war returned home, while others, probably the majority, stayed in the United States. Some Irish-born Union veterans, members of the Fenians, a revolutionary society favoring the achievement of an independent Irish republic free of Great Britain, sought to advance their cause by invading Canada from the adjacent states. They even fought a minor battle at Ridgeway in the Niagara Peninsula, in which the defending Canadian troops quite sensibly ran away: they were raw, disorganized, and untrained, and the Irishmen were not. As a result, casualties were relatively light.[17] The Fenian danger lasted some years, and the Canadian government spent millions of dollars keeping troops mobilized along the border; but eventually, for reasons that had little to do with Canada, Fenianism subsided, and the danger, such as it was, passed. The frontier disturbances encouraged a sense of solidarity among Canadians and gave them a war that was entirely their own to commemorate.

The American government enforced its neutrality on the Fenians, who on returning to the United States were disarmed and sent on their way. The Canadian government counted its expenditures in guarding the border and wondered where to present the bill, while the American government totted up the cost to the United States of the many violations of British neutrality during the war—especially by the British-built Confederate warship *Alabama*—much of which could be ascribed to the negligence of the British government in preventing Confederate-bought but British-built ships from leaving British harbors. The US government also picked up the cost of the defense in Canadian courts of captured Fenians, though it did not add that sum to its total demands for a British indemnity.

Many of the American politicians and publicists who had favored annexing Canada at the beginning of the Civil War returned to the idea now that the war was over. Seward, still secretary of state, wanted to purchase Alaska from Russia, and to crown his purchase with the acquisition of the sparsely populated colony of British Columbia, which would give the United States the entire Pacific coast. It would be a mere matter of accounting, since by ceding the Pacific colony the British could pay off the *Alabama* claims.[18] Seward's ambition paled beside that of Senator Sumner, who would accept nothing less than the whole of British North America in return for dropping the *Alabama* claims. It was Sumner, much more than Seward, who had contrived American retaliation for Confederate activity in and from Canada, and after 1865 Sumner took full advantage of his position as a senior senator and chairman of the Senate's foreign relations committee. Arguing that British aid to the Confederates had actually prolonged the war, Sumner claimed hundreds of millions of dollars in compensation, which the British could avoid paying by handing over British America.

Seen from the perspective of American acquisitiveness, the federation of the British North American colonies, creating the Dominion of Canada, occurred just in time. True, the original "Canada" that came into existence on July 1, 1867, comprised only Ontario, Quebec, New Brunswick, and Nova Scotia, but in and behind the negotiation for colonial union there was always the prospect that the western British territories, Rupert's Land, belonging to the Hudson's Bay Company, plus British Columbia, would be joined to the new dominion. Speculation did not stop with the West: because Nova Scotia was a very unwilling participant in the Canadian federation, and Prince Edward Island and Newfoundland had not joined at all, some American politicians floated the idea that at least those two provinces—and later all the rest, when they came to their senses—should join the American union. To help them on their way, President Ulysses Grant suggested in 1869 that Canada hold a referendum on independence from Great Britain, as a first step to a subsequent loss of independence to be achieved by joining the United States. Grant also had in mind access to Canada's east coast inshore fishery, granted under Reciprocity and rescinded when Reciprocity ended, which had resulted in clashes between Canadian and American fishers, and the seizure of American ships by Canadian authorities.[19]

The government of Canada, headed by Sir John A. Macdonald, moved quickly. Rupert's Land was bought from the Hudson's Bay Company in 1869, and the province of Manitoba created in 1870. British Columbia agreed to join Canada in 1871, in return for the promise of a transcontinental railway within ten years, and Prince Edward Island joined the dominion in 1873, in return for the payment of its debts. These political actions, backed up by British loans, blocked the way of American would-be annexationists, but what was also needed was American acceptance of the facts on the ground—a settlement of outstanding Anglo-American disputes that would put an end to opportunistic American expansionism. It would not do to leave the matter to President Grant, who in addition to his referendum idea told his cabinet, "I wish Congress would declare war upon Great Britain, when we would take Canada, and wipe out her commerce as she has done ours, and then we would start fair." Grant did add a qualifier to his Canadian musings—it would be a wonderful idea, he said, "Were it not for our [national] debt."[20] Grant's ideas of the effect of Canadian policy on American economic interests were large, as well as bizarre, but since he was president, they had to be taken seriously. The British colonial secretary advised caution: "When you have to deal with a powerful and most unreasonable nation such as [the United States]...the first requisite is to keep one's temper. We shall do the best we can for Canada but the Canadian Gov[ernmen]t must make some allowance for the inherent difficulties of the case."[21]

The British considered themselves lucky eventually to secure American agreement to a negotiation on outstanding differences—and lucky too to overcome the misgivings of a suspicious Canadian government, which had become convinced that the British would sacrifice specific Canadian desiderata in the larger interest of Great Britain and the British Empire. The Canadian prime minister, Macdonald, agreed to serve on the negotiation team. Macdonald's main objective was the return of the Reciprocity Treaty, dead since 1866, which by giving mutual access to the fisheries on both sides of the border would solve the fisheries disputes at the same time.

Macdonald did not get what he wanted, and a recent examination of the history of the negotiations convincingly argues that he knew he would not get it. Nevertheless he made an issue of Canadian co-operation with the British, proved a complaining and uncooperative colleague for his fellow British commissioners during the negotiation, and at one point turned down an American offer that was arguably better than the one he ultimately accepted—as he knew he must. By the Treaty of Washington of May 8, 1871, the *Alabama* claims and all they represented were satisfied. They and other contentious issues, like the international boundary in the San Juan Islands off Vancouver Island, were sent to arbitration. The Atlantic fisheries were to be rented to the United States, for an amount to be determined, also by arbitration. Canadian claims for damages in the Fenian raids were ignored, but contributed to a later financial settlement by Great Britain that featured a £2.5 million loan to build a transcontinental railway.[22]

Despite Macdonald's theatrics, Canada gained considerably from the Treaty of Washington. The most significant gain was intangible: the American recognition that the dominion was a legitimate political entity, and during the treaty negotiations the US government made a serious attempt to come to terms with Canada's negotiating position. The British government took the position that only Canada could dispose of what was Canada's property, the inshore fishery. On that, Macdonald held a veto, which, in the end, he traded for other considerations. He lost nothing, in reality, from the abandonment of his goal of American reciprocity: reciprocity's positive economic impact had been greatly exaggerated (and would be again). More to the point, reciprocity could simply not be achieved in the existing state of American politics.

The proposition that Canada or parts of Canada might be transferred to the United States was not mentioned in the Washington negotiations, and Canada's ability to choose its own form of government, monarchical and British, was tacitly accepted.[23] The one significant border dispute, over the San Juan Islands with the United States, was put to rest by the arbitration of the German emperor in 1872, accepting the American claim to the islands. An arbitral tribunal met all summer and most of the fall of 1877 at Halifax, sifting through evidence on the conduct of the fishery in order to determine the compensation due Canada from American use of Canadian waters. The Atlantic fisheries proved to be worth more in compensation than either the Canadian or the American government had expected—$5.5 million, a large sum for the time, which was grudgingly voted by an irritated Congress.[24]

The fisheries question was hardly settled: it was too important a continuing interest for fishers in both countries. Negotiations followed arbitrations, and every decade brought some variation to the basic issue of the ownership of fishing grounds and the exploitation of fish stocks. The British continued to be involved in negotiations, either directly or as backstops for the Canadians, for the rest of the nineteenth and on into the twentieth century. Indeed, the fishery remained to plague diplomats well into the twenty-first.

Why, then, did the United States accept to get along where Canada was concerned? Possibly, arguably, the United States was distracted. Certainly the Americans had many other important matters internally and externally to keep them busy. Nor was Canada the only target for American rhetorical belligerence in the 1870s and 1880s. To take one example from the 1870s, there was Santo Domingo in the West Indies where, for a time, American annexationist attentions were focused. That project fell apart from its inherent absurdity, but also because the territorial acquisitiveness of some prominent politicians was balanced by the reluctance of others to embark on a never-ending imperial adventure. And after Santo Domingo, there was Cuba, which would in fact lead to a Spanish–American war in 1898.[25]

There was also a difference between American attitudes to Canada and attitudes toward Mexico and the Caribbean. Views of Mexicans and West Indians were heavily racially tinged. These were not Americans: their language, religion, skin color, society—all these things were different, and intractable. At worst, Canadians were slightly slow on the uptake, a less advanced kind of American—but, in the American imagination, Americans nevertheless. And if they were "British," what did that mean? They had elections, responsible government, and democracy, perhaps even a more advanced form of democracy than Britain itself. These were familiar things, as was language, or law, or the Protestant religion (in English Canada only to be sure). The foundation of Canadian–American relations was cultural; as a recent historian put it, "The idea that social connections matter, and can be thought of in networked terms, should startle few scholars."[26]

The various schemes to incorporate Canada into the United States presumed that by the stroke of a pen, Canadians would become Americans. After all, tens of thousands of Canadian-born immigrants to the United

States—the English-speaking ones anyway—disappeared without a trace into the general population. When Secretary of State Seward thought of acquiring Canada, and he often did, it would be through the voluntary action of its inhabitants. His successor as secretary of state, Hamilton Fish, like President Grant saw a referendum as a vehicle for Canada's political transformation, and at first assumed that holding a vote would be sufficient, since the result of that vote could scarcely be in doubt. When the facts as reported to Washington got in the way of this happy future, the effect was only to postpone the inevitable—if not now, then surely the day after, or next week, next year, or the next decade. But not forever.

## The Myth of Reciprocity and the Election of 1891

In the twenty years after the Treaty of Washington, Canada could concentrate on its own destiny. There was enough to grab the attention: two rebellions in the West, clerical agitation in Quebec, railways and railway politics and railway scandals, quarrels over the use of the English and French languages, and, in a federal system, disputes between the central government in Ottawa and the governments of the provinces. There was, above all, the tariff.

Sir John A. Macdonald got a new lease on his political life when, after surviving a scandal that would have ruined a lesser politician or a more sensitive man, he brought his Conservative party back to power in the election of 1878. Macdonald's government promptly implemented what he called the National Policy—high protective tariffs designed to encourage Canadian industry by discouraging cheaper imports from abroad. Canadian consumers would pay the price of high-cost, small-market manufactures, but grateful manufacturers and their workers could be counted on to vote Conservative, as they did in the next election, 1882, and the one after that, 1887. The National Policy was part of a Conservative trifecta—the other legs being a transcontinental railway, the Canadian Pacific, and the settlement of the western prairies.

The settlement of the prairies was painfully slow. In retrospect it is remarkable that any settlers came at all, even after the Canadian Pacific was completed in 1885. For most of the time the movement of population was in the other direction—out of the country. Perhaps the most notable fact about Canada in the 1870s and 1880s was how many Canadians left the country for the United States: 825,000 in those two decades; compare this figure with a population of just over 4.8 million in the 1891 census. Between 1870 and

1890 Canada was neither attracting nor holding new population. Settlement of the West went slowly compared to the United States—and in fact many of those moving to the American West in this period were Canadians who found more opportunity south of the border. West of Ontario, Canada had barely 350,000 inhabitants. If we look at a longer time frame, between 1820 and 1950, 4.3 million Canadians left for the United States; as the historian Michael Fellman pointed out, this figure matched the much more conspicuous Italian immigration to the United States over the same period.[27]

Many, perhaps most, Canadians faced economic diminution if not outright adversity. Canadian farmers—and the majority of Canadians lived in rural areas—were badly served by the National Policy and, of course, the American tariff. "Having paid extra for US goods," Christopher Pennington writes, "Canadian farmers then had to pay punishing tariffs on their own crops before exporting them into the US market. This extra expense made it almost impossible for them to compete with American farmers."[28] Five and a half million Canadians enjoyed on the average a 30 percent lower standard of living than the inhabitants of the United States, or, for that matter, the British or the Australians.[29] Few Canadians could afford to move to Australia, even in the unlikely case that they knew how much better off than Canada that colony was, but many could afford to leave for the United States, and many did.

There were compensations to being Canadian, to be sure, and politicians and publicists regularly directed attention to them. Canada was still a colony of the British Empire, though perhaps it is fairest to call it a "colonial nation," for its inhabitants viewed themselves as citizens or subjects of both the United Kingdom and the Dominion of Canada. As we have seen, their situation did not correspond to what many Britons understood to be the definition of a "colony," a possession operating for the immediate and direct benefit of the mother country, the lack of which so astonished Charles Dilke in 1866. The benefit to the Empire was that it enhanced the standing or importance of both colony and mother country—prestigious, bigger, stronger, and more impressive—"soft" connections as opposed to the "hard" links of direct taxation and rule from London that had proved so effective in provoking the American Revolution.

Their nationalism was a British Empire nationalism, which saw pride in the Empire and pride in Canada as complementary rather than contradictory. The British system of government was superior to the American, and to all others. Canadians might be materially deprived compared with their American neighbors, but they had by far the better constitution.[30] This was a sentiment difficult to convey to nationalistic Americans, though it could be recognized as a component in a British-Canadian national pride. Canadians told themselves they were part of a worldwide Empire, much larger than the United States, and certainly much grander.

Keeping up their spirits against the outward flow of Canadians across the border obliged Canadian nationalist-imperialists to depreciate the United States, the character of its people (often posed in racist terms), and the materialistic cast of its civilization. Neither point would have been unfamiliar to conservative Americans: their complaints about the decline of their own society and its Anglo-Saxon values furnished ammunition, unconsciously, to conservative and imperialist Canadians. Violence, lynchings, divorces, corruption of all kinds in the republic might even point to a society on the verge of dissolution: lucky Canada, to be insulated from these evils by its monarchical, parliamentary, and traditional institutions. This cast of mind even allowed English Canadians to take comfort in their conservative and traditionally minded fellow subjects, the French Canadians, and, unusually, to rejoice in the steadying power of Quebec as a bulwark against the madly materialistic United States.[31] This appreciation balanced but did not displace more traditional Anglo-Saxon and Protestant views of Catholicism and tyranny and the power of the Pope, the fear of which was also very much in evidence in Canada in this period.[32]

Monarchy and the Empire were fixed stars in the constellation of Canadian nationalist thought, but beside them, waxing in the late 1880s, was the full moon of American prosperity and the memory that for a brief time Canada was prosperous and linked to the United States by the Reciprocity Treaty. The American market was huge and ever-enlarging: the forty million Americans of 1870 became the sixty-three million Americans of 1890. It followed that a renewed reciprocity with the United States would work even better than the last one. That the prosperity of earlier decades could be attributed to other and extraneous factors was not an argument made by anyone (although as we have seen it was much closer to reality than the reciprocity-is-prosperity nostrum), and so two myths clashed over the destiny of Canada in 1890–1: the promise of wealth through trade, geography, and economic development, against the promise of monarchical stability and superiority. It was a dispute that might have been fought out under Simcoe in the 1790s; it would be fought out under Macdonald in the 1890s.

The Canadian general election of 1891 was a one-sided affair. Fought on the issue of an advantageous trade deal with the United States, it attracted little attention in that country outside the political class. In 1891,

Canada battled with itself over whether it would have very close trade ties with the United States; however, the decision as to whether it would have such ties or not was the business not of the Canadian Parliament or electorate, but of the Congress of the United States.

American politicians too had imbibed the "lessons" of reciprocity. Back in 1854—well within living political memory—reciprocity had been sold to northern politicians as a splendid way to encourage Canadians eventually—or not so eventually—to seek political union with the republic. Instead, the Canadians had raised their tariffs on American manufactures, which provoked the same kind of resentment in the United States as Canadian tariffs on British goods had in the United Kingdom. The conclusion was obvious: If Canadians wanted admission to the American market then it must be on American terms. Those terms would be such as to avoid any possibility of Canada drawing back. Political union must follow tariff union.

Canada's apparently unending economic depression furnished the spur to opposition politicians in Canada in 1887 to find a new and more effective vehicle to get rid of Sir John Macdonald. Complaints against the National Policy and its high tariffs were loud and getting louder in meetings across rural Ontario in the summer of 1887. Testing the wind, Liberal party politicians decided they must channel this obviously strong sense of grievance and that the vehicle to do it would be unrestricted reciprocity, UR for short. When reaching into one's political bag of tricks, the way to secure prosperity was obvious: trade. Trade would keep the population at home, happily producing for an export market that longed for their products, whatever those might be. The destination of trade, the United States, and the vehicle for trade, reciprocity, were also prescribed by recent history. Why not have reciprocity again—not to mention the right kind of reciprocity—in natural products, which would allow Canadians to keep out those bothersome, cheap, and competitive American manufactured goods?

That was not the only question confronting the Liberals. Their leader, Edward Blake, resigned after losing his second general election. As his successor, he recommended a youthful politician from Quebec, Wilfrid Laurier. This caused some misgivings, and the reasons were the traditional ones: Laurier was a Catholic and a Frenchman. Memories of 1688 promptly resurfaced, and Laurier was well aware of the difficulty. He repeatedly tried to pass the leadership to someone more suited, only to have it always handed back to him. Could someone be a true subject of Queen Victoria aspiring to Canada's highest elected office without also being a Protestant?

This was and is no idle question in English-speaking countries. Canada's first Catholic prime minister, Sir John Thompson (1892–4), suffered endless abuse and deep mistrust even among his Conservative party followers because not only was he a Catholic, but he had converted from Protestantism to Catholicism in marrying his wife. Even a hundred years on, in Great Britain, a Catholic-inclined prime minister, Tony Blair, postponed converting to Catholicism until he had retired from office; and in the United States no Catholic was elected president until 1960. Of course in Ireland thousands have died well into the twenty-first century in violence between, essentially, Protestant and Catholic factions. As if to remind Laurier, Canada was in 1888 and 1889 convulsed by the arcane question of compensating the Jesuit Order for estates that had fallen into the hands of the Crown when the Jesuits were temporarily extinguished almost a hundred years before. If anyone wished to confirm that anti-Catholicism was a deep and powerful force in Canada, two years of public bigotry and bitter rhetoric must have proved it. Canada was, in a manner of speaking, the test case. In the 1880s, the immigration of Catholic French Canadians into the New England states, the drift of French speakers over the border into Ontario, and the gradual displacement of English speakers in Quebec's Eastern Townships by *Canadiens* did underline the similarities in attitudes among subjects of the queen and citizens of the republic: it was those similarities that made the question of Canadian–American relations politically volatile in the 1880s.

Laurier's religion seemed to be irrelevant to the immediate question of securing the American market. In retrospect, it is hard to imagine anything that Laurier could have done that would have accomplished that object. He began by falling into the trap of imagining that if something is politically desirable domestically, then it must be achievable. To Laurier, "unrestricted reciprocity"—dropping tariffs on Canadian and American products crossing the border in either direction—did not imply anything more than a means to secure Canada's economic future while in other ways continuing on as an autonomous member of the British Empire.

That was not how the matter appeared to the dominant Republicans in the American Congress, or to the Republican secretary of state, James G. Blaine, in the administration of President Benjamin Harrison. It was not that these Washington politicians took no interest in Canada. They did. It was not that they did not recall the Reciprocity Treaty of 1854–66: they remembered it all too well. It should have led to Canada joining the

Union, especially the northern states, so similar in political, religious, and economic patterns to Canada; the Canadians would then have reinforced their cultural cousins south of the border. In fact, they still could. The unfinished business of one generation would be taken up by the next. Any replication of reciprocity would have to bind Canada permanently to the United States and should lead to the absorption of Canada by the United States. Far preferable to an exchange of tariff concessions was a treaty that would bring Canada inside the American customs frontier—"commercial union," which, given the disparity in size and prosperity between Canada and the United States, would situate all important decisions on tariffs and trade where they had always been—in the United States Congress.

American proponents of commercial union or CU—the intelligent ones anyway—understood that presenting Canadians with a bald proposal for annexation would not do: it would be rejected. But propagandists for commercial union received an overwhelmingly friendly reception in rural Ontario—torchlight parades greeted an Ohio Republican congressman who favored commercial union, and who arrived at a meeting in a carriage drawn by four white horses. Benjamin Butterworth's assurance to the crowds that it was all strictly business and had no political implications was rapturously received.[33]

That was hardly the case. Secretary of State Blaine proposed to squeeze the Canadians with high and higher tariffs until they surrendered and agreed to come where they belonged, as citizens and states of the American Union. He rejected overtures from the Conservative government in Ottawa that Canada would be delighted to have a reciprocity treaty of the old kind again. His public repudiation of what were originally intended to be private and unofficial conversations embarrassed the Ottawa government and gave Sir John Macdonald little choice but to call an election over the issue of patriotism—British-Canadian patriotism. Canada's soul, Canada's nature, was at stake, Macdonald proclaimed. Canada was established to be British. The Liberals had committed "veiled treason," and soon the treason was unveiled, for it was clear that some Liberals were all too willing to talk of annexation with the United States.

American pro-annexationist sentiment could not be suppressed. Senator John Sherman of Ohio, a very senior Republican, told his Senate colleagues, "I want Canada to be part of the United States." Butterworth, the apparently moderate congressman, confirmed in public that in his view commercial union was but "a stepping-stone to political union." Even Queen Victoria was brought, figuratively, into the election tumult. According to a

Boston newspaper, she was "an obese, beer-guzzling German woman who has no more claim on [Canadians] than has the Ameer of Afghanistan."[34]

The election was set for March 5, 1891. Macdonald and the Conservatives won decisively. Laurier, reflecting on his loss, and reasonably believing he had been the victim of false counsel, turned away from UR and CU, and waited on events. Those events, beginning with the death of Macdonald in June 1891, were not long in coming, and they would lead him more surely to power than would the ideology of free trade or the myth of reciprocity. The election of 1891 had its roots in economics, but as the politics evolved, the contest was only ostensibly about economics. As the historian Christopher Pennington has argued, it was a contest between two kinds of Canadian nationalism—between the confident kind that held that dropping tariff barriers along the border with the United States was simply a sensible and long-overdue economic measure, and the less-confident kind, which saw free trade, whatever it was called, as a fatal step toward inexorable union.[35]

The trouble was that free trade had to be negotiated with somebody; given the complexion of American politics, and more broadly the political culture of the United States, it would have to be negotiated with politicians who all believed that Canada should be absorbed into the United States. They were not hostile to Canadians as such—except possibly French Canadians. As Theodore Roosevelt said at the time, "The American regards the Canadian with the good-natured condescension always felt by the free man for the man who is not free."[36] But they were incredulous at Canada's incomprehensible insistence on remaining part of the British Empire. American incomprehension matched and fed Canadian fears of absorption. Under the circumstances, any negotiation with the United States for restricted reciprocity, free trade, unrestricted reciprocity, or commercial union would have failed.

The Americans liked Canadians too much, not too little. That liking was not entirely positive, for it included a tinge of racial prejudice—the Canadians were liked as much for what they were not, as for what they were. If asked, American annexationists might have pointed out that they would not have offered annexation—which after all meant equal political rights inside the United States—to the Mexicans or Cubans. A few years later, when the United States conquered Cuba, it did not make it a state but converted it into a semi-autonomous, if theoretically sovereign, country. The Philippines and Puerto Rico became, simply, colonies, and Hawaii, an acquisition of 1898, remained for sixty years a territorial dependency. As the historian Robert Kagan summarized Republican attitudes, "With its white, predominantly Anglo-Saxon and Protestant population, Canada could be absorbed without injecting a tropical, dark-skinned poison into the nation's bloodstream."[37]

If, unaccountably, and against their best interests, Canadians turned away from the republic, that could be borne. Like the previous generation, who had failed to absorb the Canadians in 1871, the generation of 1891 could console itself on the subject of the Canadians. They would surely be back.

# 6

## Siblings and Their Rivalries, 1891–1914

BY MOST REASONABLE standards, the Canada of 1891 could be described as a sturdy but stunted growth, surviving on drafts of political elixir in an adverse world economic climate that consisted of brief moments of speculative prosperity encased in a long, grinding depression. Canada was surviving, but unsuccessful for all that. The signs were worse than most Canadians realized. Canadians knew that their country was dwarfed by the United States in population and prosperity. That fact was reflected in the annual outflow of emigrants to the American states and the very slow growth in the population left behind—while the Americans increased by five million people between 1891 and 1896, Canada's gain was a mere 200,000. While Canada was more populous than distant Australia, Canadians would have been pained to learn that they were 40 percent beneath the Australians in average income—indeed, that 3.1 million Australians had a higher gross domestic product and consequently a higher standard of living than 4.83 million Canadians.[1]

None of this information came as a surprise to Toronto's resident public intellectual, Goldwin Smith. For Smith, who had come to Canada from Oxford University via the United States, Canada was an unfortunate hangover of the American Revolution and stood in the way of greater Anglo-Saxon harmony.[2] Indeed, Canada was handicapped from its inception by the significant presence of the French Canadians, who interfered with its Anglo-Saxon identity and destiny. English Canadians had more in common with other English speakers, most notably those south of the border. If proof were needed, it lay in Canada's fractious, sectional politics. Geography and economics had spoken, and the market had ratified their judgment. The Americans, in Smith's view, were at worst separated cousins, at best a vivid, vibrant, profitable (and much richer) society, and Canada's best bet would be to join them.[3] Smith had been a passionate supporter of unrestricted reciprocity in the 1891 election, as a way station on the road to Canada's complete absorption into the republic. For the time being, political corruption and appeals to a misguided patriotism had stymied progress. But that outcome was merely temporary. The British connection was not only antediluvian; it was completely at odds with the North American character of Canada, so remote from the "feudalism" of old Europe. The adverse result of the election was a mere political hiccup; sooner or later the great forces of rational political economy and the call of the Anglo-Saxon race would eliminate the border, and Canada.

Smith was not alone in dismissing Canada's future by invoking higher principles. A traveling American, Samuel Moffett, produced a book in 1907, entitled *The Americanization of Canada*.[4] Moffett noted that the lines of communication—above all the railways—in North America increasingly ran north and south. On those railways traveled Canadian emigrants—for example, the million or so Canadians from the Maritime provinces who had settled in the United States—more than still lived in the Maritimes. Back up came American ideas, fashions, and values. The small Canadian cities would inevitably be—in some senses already were—engulfed by the larger and livelier American metropolises, from Chicago to Detroit to Buffalo[5] to New York to Boston.

Yet between 1891 and 1910 circumstances had changed. Freight rates fell, grain prices climbed, and investment boomed. Emigration shrank between 1890 and 1900, and shrank further between 1900 and 1910.[6] The Canadian gross domestic product climbed above the Australian,[7] though for many years Australia on a per capita basis was still a far wealthier country. Money flowed into Canada, as did immigrants, with the population rising from 5.2 million in 1896, when the immigrant influx began, to just over eight million in 1914. Of course, the United States was still the natural comparison, and there a gap in per capita incomes remained but, again, it was a much smaller gap than in 1896.

As the existential question of Canada's economic viability receded, at least for the time being, the imperial pageant resumed. When people like Goldwin Smith and Charles Dilke moved populations and territories around on their racial chessboard and erased the Canadian–American frontier, they ignored or discounted questions of sentiment, allegiance, and symbolism. The United States, most obviously, had a highly developed civic culture, oriented around the republic's particular history, from which the British and British-Canadians were excluded or at best were remote onlookers.[8] The Civil War was an American event, and its martial celebrations and commemorations did not and could not include their Canadian cousins except for those who had actually fought in the war. Yet to the extent that the Civil War was a war against slavery it had a transnational appeal, even a kind of grandeur to which Canadians and Britons were not entirely indifferent.

Similarly, American nationalism in the post–Civil War era coexisted with ancestral longings, trips to England for the elite, and an interest in British history, culture, and politics. The nineteenth century in the United States was the "Victorian" era, not the age of presidents Jackson, Lincoln, or Grover Cleveland. Charles Dickens competed with, and out-sold, most American authors, as Sir Walter Scott had in the previous generation. When the queen died in January 1901, the American president William McKinley thought it worth a reflective comment in his next cabinet meeting, as if the queen's life and times had helped him define the age, an age that was passing with the old century.

McKinley was an appropriate conduit for sentimental anglophilia, expressed as a feeling of kinship and shared values. One thing that the United States and the British nations shared was an imperial impulse, for in McKinley's presidency the United States defeated Spain in war in 1898 and acquired a non-contiguous empire—Puerto Rico, the Philippines, and Hawaii—and then started up a genuine colonial war in the Philippines to subdue local discontent. The Spanish war nearly coincided with a simultaneous British war in South Africa, and the effect of the two conflicts was to remind citizens of the republic and subjects of the Empire that they had related missions. In some respects the United States had always been a projection of British imperial impulses dating from before independence; the American march across the continent might be taken as the fulfillment of the speculators and conquerors who had established the Empire and defeated the natives back in the seventeenth century. In that reading, the secession and civil war of 1776 were less decisive, and less conclusive, than the *longue durée* of English-speaking political culture. McKinley and his cabinet recognized as much when they met on January 22, 1901, and devoted part of the session to Queen Victoria.

If the two, or two and a half, or three nations resembled each other in imperialist enthusiasms, they also mimicked each other's anti-imperialism. In Canada, Goldwin Smith led the way although, ironically, the main support for the anti-imperial cause in the dominion came from French and Catholic Quebec. Smith eventually found this too big a stretch and maintained his disdain for French Quebec, its religion, and its politicians.

And in Quebec skepticism about the British Empire was matched by a fervent commitment to the spiritual Empire of the Pope. Indeed, lavish ceremonial commemorations of the Empire in Canada were matched by church parades of local militia units up and down Canadian streets—the most spectacular in Quebec, but elsewhere church parades for the troops were a regular, even embedded, feature of life. It followed that many of the same militia units marched in the several processions, secular and religious. Patriotism, national affiliation, loyalty—all found expression in what the historian David Cannadine has labeled *ornamentalism*; and admittedly of all nations, the British practiced a particularly spectacular and impressive form of public ceremonial.[9] Within limits, ornamentalism is a useful device for examining the North American end of Empire, since ornamentalism is itself a kind of vicarious experience, and the Empire was a phenomenon that allowed the distant subject, or the privileged spectator, to live in another, near-mythical space.

Queen Victoria was at the center of British commemorations—in person if these were in London and through her image in less central parts of the Empire. Her fiftieth year on the throne, 1887, became her Golden Jubilee, but that event was dwarfed when she became the longest-reigning British monarch after her sixtieth anniversary, in 1897.[10] Every dignitary the Empire could muster came to London; foreign monarchs, many of them close relatives, came too, and there were representatives from other governments as well, including the American. Canadian devotion to the Empire was reaffirmed—it was difficult for any contrary view to be expressed, even in Quebec. But the Empire, as it was meant to, impressed foreigners as well, especially Americans. Indeed, rich Americans, being richer than rich Canadians, could afford the cost of travel to and residence in London more than Canadians. Some rich and prominent Americans stayed, some as brides for impecunious British aristocrats, and others, like novelist Henry James or artists James McNeill Whistler and John Singer Sargent, because they preferred Britain and British society to their native United States.[11]

Canadians were eligible for some things that American citizens could not aspire to—mainly knighthoods plus the occasional barony—Sir Wilfrid Laurier, the prime minister, and Lord Strathcona (previously Donald Smith), the railway baron,[12] are examples. With the titles came plumes and uniforms, an entrée into the titled end of London society, and the attention, as Laurier found, of charming duchesses. The young William Lyon Mackenzie King, at the time deputy minister of labor in the Laurier government, found abounding hospitality when he visited London—tea with the foreign secretary, Christmas with the secretary of state for India, and, when he moved on to India, the hospitality of the viceroy.[13]

King, to be sure, had standing, and he had status, and most important he had a mission, which was to reconcile Canadian policy on oriental immigration with British policy for maintaining order and harmony in imperial India, as well as solidarity with the United States. In Washington, which he also visited, King had easy access to President Theodore Roosevelt and was privileged to listen to the president's schemes for holding the line on Asian immigrants to the Pacific Coast of North America. Later in life, King would get to know another President Roosevelt, Franklin, the cousin of Theodore, and would listen to him too, as he spun out his visions of worlds both real and imaginary. King would by then be prime minister of Canada, though unlike Laurier he was never knighted, receiving instead other prestigious imperial honors that were less perceptible—because not embodied in words or the hard print of newspapers—to his constituents back home. He did, however, acquire a court uniform, duly embroidered, and a hat with plumes, and he wore them proudly to ceremonies in London. It is a safe bet that his voters in Saskatchewan or Prince Edward Island or Ontario would never see Mackenzie King in his full imaginary role as an imperial grandee. In the end, this embodied the contradiction at the heart of the imperial romance. As King himself said, in words that one of his biographers enthusiastically adopted, he lived "a very double life" and never would the twin halves of his life meet—not if King could help it.[14]

There is a curious parallel between this late-Victorian ornamentalism and the world that John Graves Simcoe had imagined when he set out to organize and colonize Upper Canada in the 1790s. Simcoe's world, embodied in the Canada Act, also had titles, privileges, and a hierarchical society; and it too, rather more naturally in the extravagantly dressed eighteenth century, was a world of plumes, epaulets, and ribbons. But the real world was bogs and bugs, tree stumps and subsistence farming of a rock-strewn soil in Simcoe's day, and factories and fields and machinery in Mackenzie King's. Ever practical, King knew that knights and plumes did not mix well with plow horses and factory whistles—except, and it was a large and very real exception, as occasional entertainment. A mundane country like Canada needed its diversions, and its link to another world and the monarchy provided that.

But a monarchy in 1890 or 1900 need not be a traditional hierarchy, nor was the remaining monarchical part of North America a replica or even a descendant of feudalism. Ornamentalism took the place of wide-spread deference. Though Canadian public ceremonies—the opening of legislatures, the firing of artillery salutes, lieutenant-governor's levees and balls, and the parading of troops—could be ostentatious, their impact was limited. Ornaments were all very well in their place, but the peerage or even the gentry had difficulty planting roots in North America. John Graves Simcoe had found the swamps of Canada and its denizens singularly in-tractable back in 1795. Only the most eccentric gentry would settle in Canada while it was still a wilderness. Paradoxically, taming the wilder-ness in the mid-nineteenth century removed the romance of the forest, as well as the challenge of "roughing it in the bush." Few gentry and fewer nobles went west, when there were maharajahs and tigers and tea planta-tions to be had in the Indian empire, not to mention frontier wars and the temptation to become a minor autocrat as a district commissioner, col-lector, or éminence grise at the elbow of some submissive sultan.[15] As David Cannadine skillfully argues, such prospects were much more tempting to well-educated but conservative Britons who found county society at home stifling. There were some possibilities in the ranch country of Alberta and British Columbia for children of the gentry and even the aristocracy,[16] it is true, and there were the fabled "remittance men," young Englishmen sent abroad to both Western Canada and the Western United States with an allowance and the expectation that in return for their money their families would never have to see them again.[17]

The interchangeability of Canadian and American ranch country for the British (usually English) immigrant suggests another feature of Canadian–American relations, one that had not changed greatly over the previous hundred years. Passing the border did not mean crossing into another culture, except to or from the province of Quebec. Travelers encountered roughly the same accent, distinguishable from British accents, or from Australian or South African English. Canadian downtowns looked like American city centers, Canadian and American railways looked the same—and sometimes were the same, as in the Grand Trunk Western (a subsid-iary of the Canadian Grand Trunk Railway) that snaked across lower Michigan to Chicago, stopping at Canadian-type stations en route. Railways, telegraphs, telephones, and then electrical systems all spanned the border, linking north to south, conveying the cultural similarity between English Canada and the United States that had existed ever since the 1780s.

The "borderlands," areas immediately along the border, depended on frequent interchange, travel across the frontier, which, for Canadians, meant access to the greater variety of American life, and for Americans, access to the (relatively) unspoiled Canadian landscape. Crystal Beach, Ontario, was amusement park and playground for Buffalo, New York, from 1888 on, and even in the twenty-first century the place retains an American character. At Niagara Falls, Canadian and American entrepreneurs, and their thousands of willing customers, created and shared rituals around honeymoons.[18]

With the new century, for the first time in at least seventy years, Americans arriving in Canada outnumbered the Canadians departing for the United States. American farmland was by the 1890s largely occupied: no more free land for immigrants. Canada, however, advertised itself as "The Last Best West," and would-be settlers responded. The number of American-born rose dramatically between the census years of 1901 and 1911, to more than 300,000; but that was only part of the flood from the United States. Canadians living in the United States were tempted back, and immigrants from other countries living in the United States saw no harm in moving on for better terms and better farms.[19] (It was, admittedly, dwarfed by comparison with the numbers arriving from the British Isles, contributing to the approximately 800,000 British-born residents of Canada in 1911.) As a historian of Saskatchewan matter of factly comments, "Given their affinity with Anglo-Canadian traditions and institutions, and their experience farming the open plains, Americans generally had little difficulty in blending into Saskatchewan society."[20] Socially and economically there was little they had to change. As for politics, in the world of 1900 or 1910 they were just exchanging one empire for another. And it was the idea of "empire," and not the particular nationality, American or British, that mattered.

## *"Small Matters"*

There was one difficulty with Anglo-Saxon inter-relations, and with the respective empires. Despite all the resemblances between Canada and the United States, and the hundreds of thousands of migrants moving from one to the other, Canada was the most likely point of difference between the British and the Americans. The British, as it turned out, had few problems with the Americans, and the Canadians many.

In the 1970s American secretary of state, Henry Kissinger, after a briefing on the outstanding issues between his country and Canada, waved his hand at his staff. "These are small matters," he exclaimed. "Solve them."[21]

But the small matters, if allowed to accumulate, could become large, and if large, there could be serious consequences. As for solving them, generations of negotiators, British, Canadian, and American, had been trying. Sometimes they succeeded in putting an issue to sleep, and very occasionally a problem dwindled away, never to return. But there were always new problems. For a variety of reasons, circumstances in the early twentieth century were favorable for devising transborder processes and finding solutions.

The coincidence of imperial enthusiasm in the British Empire (Canada) and the United States was not by itself enough to predict how Canadian–American relations would eventually turn out. As contemporary theorists like the British radical J.A. Hobson and the Russian Marxist Vladimir Lenin pointed out, empires often or probably or inevitably clashed—a good thing, in Lenin's view, since imperial wars and their consequences would lead to the collapse of capitalism and the arrival of the socialist millennium. It was all very scientific, a view of the world in which there was no place for ornamentalism, which Lenin in any case would have labeled false consciousness.[22]

For the British, however, the Empire continually and persistently offered alternative attractions. In the 1780s and 1790s the Empire had been re-founded elsewhere—expanding in India and Australia, as well as Canada. In the 1800s and 1810s, the war with Napoleonic France was enough to divert British attentions, to the extent that the different venues of empire had not already turned the trick. After the War of 1812 ended, there was never much more appetite in Great Britain for additional chunks of North America, and by the 1850s the British were consciously deferring to American expansionist notions in Central America—appeasement of the United States, in short, was becoming a fixed British policy. Occasionally, matters got more serious, as in disputes over the boundary of Venezuela and British Guiana in the 1890s, or the collection of debts from Caribbean countries around the beginning of the twentieth century. But in each case, the essential insignificance of the matters in dispute brought about peaceable outcomes, outcomes that were by no means always unfavorable to British interests.

By the 1890s official British interests in Canada had atrophied. The constitutional connection remained, and with the connection there came a governor general in Ottawa. Yet the governor general, like the queen in London, reigned but did not rule, and he often sat as a privileged but bemused spectator as his ministers quarreled among themselves over political patronage or sectarian rivalries, slicing up the diminishing pie of revenue. Sometimes the governor general's influence seemed to extend no further than his miniature colonial court on his estate in Ottawa, the grandly styled Rideau Hall. The vice-regal mansion was more impressive in name than in appearance—it was at best a middling English country house of undistinguished design.

There were otherwise only two obsolescent naval bases, one on each coast, and Britain's economic interests, which were very considerable in terms of investment and important when it came to trade. Yet in those fields, investment and trade, Canada contrasted with the United States, where British interests flourished without any need for an imperial or constitutional linkage. Ever since 1783, and continuously since 1815, Great Britain had been the United States' largest trading partner; Canada as a destination for British products and British money lagged behind. Great Britain was the largest foreign investor in the United States, and though the United States was itself becoming a significant foreign investor, it trailed behind Great Britain. Even in Canada, massive British investment in Canadian railways placed British interests far ahead of American. And when Canadian governments needed to borrow money, they went by preference to London, not New York. As one observer somewhat later commented, it was "infra dig"[23] not to go to what was both the imperial capital and the world's financial center.

There was one other familiar linkage between Canada and the Empire. Immigration, resuming on a large scale in the middle of the 1890s, came largely from Great Britain. Almost 60 percent of the 680,000 foreign-born in Canada in 1901, a census year, were born in the British Isles. (Nineteen percent came from the United States, meaning that more than three-quarters hailed from English-speaking homelands.) The British proportion declined to 49 percent over the next ten years, although in numbers it substantially increased, as the total number of immigrants, meaning persons born outside Canada, also rose to nearly 1.6 million. The proportion of immigrants from the United States remained the same, at 19 percent. The number of Canadian-born in the United States, on the other hand, had reached a plateau at around 1.2 million between 1900 and 1910. There is no doubt that the British-born influenced Canada's political culture, at least as voters, and on any question of Canada's relations with the British Empire they would be an affirmative force.

The Americans, on the other hand, had less to say about Canada's membership and participation in the British Empire, but they brought an awareness of public issues in their own country and stressed the similarity of daily life. On the prairies, American immigrants saw that their antagonists were the railways and the grain companies, and the high Canadian protective tariff that forced farmers to buy their supplies from Canadian manufacturers at protected prices, while selling their product abroad at the world price. In the United States, prairie discontent was a force, and in Canada that was also the case,. In the 1890s, widespread American dissatisfaction produced Populism, a short-lived political phenomenon. Populists were elected to office in various parts of the country. In one case, John W. Leedy, the Populist governor of Kansas, who had previously tried both the American major parties, would move on to Canada, where as a naturalized Canadian he would eventually run twice for office—and be defeated both times.[24] His experience shows that politics as well as people could cross the border, and not all of the politicians were as unsuccessful as Leedy.

Some of the immigrants recorded in 1901 had come because, in 1896, gold was discovered in Canada's North, in what in 1898 was hastily organized as the Yukon Territory. The Yukon abutted the American territory of Alaska, and to get to the Yukon, or for its gold to be exported, people and goods had to pass through American territory to reach the Pacific seacoast. (There were other routes but they were time-consuming and expensive, and effectively impractical.) The Canadian government used the occasion to assert, or re-assert, a claim to some inlets of that Alaskan seacoast, using a rather strained interpretation of the relevant treaty defining the border as its rationale and ignoring the fact that for years official British, as well as American, maps accepted that the whole coastline lay in American territory.

A Joint High Commission wrestled with the Alaska boundary in 1898 and at times came close to a solution that might have satisfied both sides, including the concession of an Alaskan harbor to Canada. When word of that offer leaked, opposition in the American Pacific Northwest was fierce and, ultimately, irresistible. The Joint High Commission adjourned without agreement.

Perhaps the Laurier government thought the Americans might agree to the same terms or even better ones, or that Great Britain would repay Canada's participation in the South African War of 1899–1902 with diplomatic support. But it was not to be. President Theodore Roosevelt, the United States' newly minted president after the assassination of President McKinley, construed most of the Canadian claim as "an outrage pure and simple," and it is hard to disagree with him. The Canadian claim to ports on the Alaska panhandle was a late-blooming phenomenon, appearing only after gold was discovered in the Yukon. (Roosevelt did, however, allow that the southern end of the disputed area, where it was a question of where a line should be drawn between various islands, was in fact a matter of genuine doubt, where a fair decision could go either way.)[25]

Roosevelt's attitude to Canada was, fortunately, conditioned by two things: his larger views of the British Empire, and his appreciation for the natural beauty of Canada and its resemblance to, and contiguity with the United States.[26] The United States and Great Britain, he believed, "ought to be in specially intimate relations," as he told a British friend.[27] As for the Canadians, Roosevelt had spent time in Canada researching a book,[28] he was very familiar with the wildlife of the prairies and the Rockies, and he knew they were the same north or south of the border. He saw Canadians as similar to Americans, but constitutionally misguided, and, like many Americans of his generation, he expected that they would eventually join the United States and throw over their incomprehensible wish to remain part of the British Empire. "I hope to see the Spanish flag and the English flag gone from the map of North America before I'm sixty," he declaimed to an astonished senator Mark Hanna early in 1898.[29]

Roosevelt did not mean to annex Canada by force. The Canadian—at least the English Canadian—was qualified by ancestry to a superior place in Roosevelt's race-bound thought[30]—sufficiently so as to be admitted forthwith to all the privileges of American citizenship. For the time being, it sufficed that Canada was a part of the British Empire, with its masterful and manly qualities expressed in its imperial domination over hundreds of millions of non-whites. To be fair, Roosevelt also admired the rule of law and orderly and progressive government that acted for the common good. Viewed through that optic, Canada was expected to be a good neighbor, at worst as a ward of Great Britain, a civilized and powerful country that certainly did not merit and did not receive the aggressive intervention that Roosevelt bestowed on the United States' Caribbean and Central American periphery.[31]

Like other, earlier boundary disputes, the Alaska boundary controversy proceeded to arbitration, but arbitration of a different kind. Convinced as he was that there was nothing to the Canadian contention, Roosevelt would not agree to a real arbitration in which the issue might be in doubt. Perhaps to save the Canadians face, and because it was a dispute with the British Empire, he agreed to what was in fact a sham tribunal, which solemnly and expensively and publicly met in London in the late summer and fall of 1903. The members of the arbitral tribunal were drawn equally from the United States and the British Empire, but of the British appointees only two were Canadian, the third being the British Lord Chief Justice. In the result, the Americans voted as expected, the Canadians voted as expected, and the Briton voted with the Americans, even on that portion of the question where the Canadians might actually have had a legitimate claim.

There were immediate cries of outrage from the Canadian government, especially Prime Minister Laurier, who should have known better and probably did, but who understood that he had to follow his supporters on this issue, for he and his party were supported by a patriotic if badly informed public opinion. Laurier did, however, understand part of what had happened and that he had no option but to accept the result because, as he said, the United States was a very large and powerful neighbor. However indignant, Laurier would have to argue for peace, and he did. The affair left a lasting scar on the prime minister, manifested in an increased reluctance to do any more bargaining with such an unequal partner.

Given the choice of supporting Canada and risking a serious deterioration of relations with the United States, and moreover endangering American relations for no good reason of law or principle, the British had chosen to appease the United States.[32] It was probably true that the British had gone overboard and that the small part of the Canadian claim that even Roosevelt had once conceded was negotiable or properly justifiable was gone with the rest.

## Cleaning the Slate

Canadian diplomacy, if it can be called that, not to mention the quality of Canadian political leadership that it displayed, did not show to good effect over Alaska. This should have been enough to alarm the British government about its large and wayward dominion. The damage had been limited over Alaska, but damage had been done, especially to Anglo-Canadian relations. It could happen again. And so after 1903 the British were duly alarmed. A three-thousand-mile border gave plenty of opportunity for friction, a possibility that worried the British and the Americans, if not the Laurier government. The long border also lent a certain character to Anglo-American relations, reducing them to minutiae over hunting accidents and water rights and the offshore purchase of herring. Nor were all disputes or differences Canadian in origin or cause: Massachusetts fishing interests, Michigan shipyards, Seattle sealers, and amateur naval enthusiasts on the Great Lakes all set in motion difficult and often impossible disputes, which were often solved only by steadily ignoring logic or precedent—and sometimes both.

An example was the Rush–Bagot agreement of 1817 that provided for naval disarmament on the Great Lakes. The problem was that when the United States government started a shipbuilding program for the navy, any American state with a shipyard wanted a part of the action and the contracts. Some of those shipyards were on the Great Lakes. The Rush–Bagot agreement and almost a hundred years of disarmament were of small account when compared with the needs of a Michigan shipbuilder. Then the US Navy wanted to place training ships to educate Great Lakes mariners in the crafts of the sea. Then there were surplus Spanish warships captured in the Spanish–American War, and what to do with them? Because Laurier did not wish to offend or be unreasonable, and because he was convinced that opposition would only cause the Americans to abrogate the agreement, he and the Canadian government connived at a series of exceptions that gradually allowed the Americans to create a small fleet on the Great Lakes.[33]

On the east coast, there was the unending problem of the fisheries, which had bedeviled successive generations of politicians and diplomats on each side of the border. The treaty that governed the fisheries dated from 1818; it had been superseded or supplemented by agreements in 1854 and 1871, but as these expired the governing rules always reverted to those of 1818. Fundamentally, the problem was that American fishers were not satisfied with the 1818 document; wanted more access to fish, including inside territorial waters (three miles out from shore, in those days), and facilities for supply and processing of their catch; and defied the efforts of British authorities to hold them to the letter of the 1818 convention. As for the British authorities, the responsibility of regulating the fisheries was passed on to the several colonies—after 1867 the dominion of Canada and the colony of Newfoundland, which was, like, Canada, self-governing.

The first flare-up occurred between Canadian authorities and American fishers from 1867 to 1871; it was resolved, for ten years, by the Americans effectively renting the Canadian fisheries. The expiration of that agreement led to more clashes and more conflict, during which New Englanders manifested anything but fraternal affection for their Maritime Canadian relatives. British and American commissioners (the British including Joseph

Chamberlain, a once and future minister in British governments) reached a modus vivendi—a means of getting by—in 1888 that gave American fishers largely what they wanted but maintained the fig leaf of Canadian jurisdiction.

The 1888 arrangement turned out to be both practical and workable until 1905, when the government of Newfoundland altered its fishing laws and regulations specifically to target American fishing boats out of Gloucester, Massachusetts, New England's major fishing port.[34] Newfoundland's objective was to bring reciprocity back to the negotiating table (for Newfoundland, like the rest of British North America, had been part of the reciprocity arrangements of 1854–66, and dreamed of its return; unlike Canada, Newfoundland had got to the stage of a draft treaty with the Americans a few years earlier). The Republican senior senator from Massachusetts, Henry Cabot Lodge, connected by political interest to the Gloucester fishing industry, saw no problem in forcefully representing its welfare, as any Massachusetts senator would. Lodge was more than an ordinary senator: he was a close friend of the president and was the dominant figure on the Senate Foreign Relations Committee. In the resulting quarrel, the Canadian government supported the Newfoundland government.

In supporting Newfoundland, the Laurier government raised the fisheries issue to a status that got the attention of the American government at the highest level. Two events set the ball rolling. The first was Theodore Roosevelt's conclusion that he could no longer bear the tedious Sir Mortimer Durand, the British ambassador in Washington. He wanted someone younger, livelier, and more intelligent. Word was conveyed to London through back channels, and Roosevelt's complaints struck a chord in London where they were seen to be both perceptive (as to Durand) and reasonable (in terms of the importance of having a better conduit for Anglo-American relations).[35]

The choice for ambassador was not what Roosevelt hoped for, but when it was proposed, he could hardly resist: James Bryce. Bryce had been appointed as a youthful Regius professor at Oxford about the time Goldwin Smith abandoned the place; like Smith, he had a fascination with the United States. Bryce was both a historian and a political scientist at a time when the difference between the two fields was indistinct and he wrote works on the Holy Roman Empire and American politics and government. The Liberal government in London had an intellectual side, well connected to Oxford, and Bryce was a very strong Liberal. He served in Parliament for more than twenty-five years as a Liberal MP, was a minister in three governments, and in 1907, when Washington became vacant, he was chief secretary for Ireland in the cabinet of Henry Campbell-Bannerman. His eminence, his character, and his politics all commended him, and he was appointed.

Americans could not help being flattered. It was as if the French king Louis Philippe had sent them Alexis de Tocqueville in the 1840s. Bryce was one of the few truly eminent foreign experts on the United States; his book *The American Commonwealth* was generally read by the educated classes and was assigned in American university classrooms. Bryce's main task was of course to deal with, and keep friendly, Roosevelt and his administration. Part of the job was to see if he could also remove Canada and erase Canadian–American disputes from the Anglo-American agenda. This was "cleaning the slate."[36]

Cleaning the slate of what exactly was the question. Secretary of State Elihu Root had already begun the process by visiting Ottawa in 1906 and 1907.[37] The visits were officially announced to be social, and Mrs. Root accompanied her husband to lend color to the story. But socializing in Governor General Lord Grey's conservatory was the last thing on Root's mind. Root was both an eminent and a very careful lawyer. He was not afraid of detail; he recognized the role of details in bolstering and winning a case. If dealing with Canada consisted of understanding detail, Root was the man for the task. In his first visit in early 1906, Root discussed what subjects needed attention with Laurier and afterward laid down the list for the British ambassador in Washington. They were:

1. Pelagic sealing;[38]
2. The North Atlantic fisheries;
3. The inland fisheries;
4. United States pecuniary claims;
5. Boundary waters.[39]

These were all complicated questions, with a hundred years or more of disputed history behind them. In the case of pelagic sealing, Root as early as 1906 had a proposal ready, based on an up-to-date appraisal of the actual state of the pelagic sealing industry; Laurier, who on this subject was intransigent and in any case still resented the 1903 Alaska boundary award, refused to contemplate it.[40] The trick, then, was finding a way of removing such questions from high-level discussions and relegating them to an uncontroversial, or less controversial, forum. This arbitration was the key.

The real purpose of his Ottawa visits was leaked before Root left Washington, and it is an interesting forerunner for later "spins" on information. The *New York Times* reported that Secretary Root had long contemplated repairing relations with Canada, following the Alaska boundary affair. He could act now because "the chief obstacle" to harmonious relations with Canada, British ambassador Sir Mortimer Durand, whose "hostility" to the project had blocked it, had been "removed."

Root was too intelligent to believe that Durand was the main obstacle; indeed in Canadian–American relations Durand was incidental, and the termination of his ambassadorship collateral damage. Ideally, Root wanted "a treaty with Great Britain that would serve to define the relations of Canada with the United States." To get it, he realized that not just Canadian resentment of the United States but Canadian distrust of Great Britain must be abated—another legacy of the Alaska episode. Visiting Ottawa, Root would be given cover by Governor General Lord Grey for the "social" side of things, but otherwise proposed to meet with the prime minister and members of the cabinet for some serious negotiation.[41]

Root understood how best to deal with Laurier—persistent, charming, and determined, he secured yet another arbitral tribunal, to consider the question of who had the right to do what, with which, and to whom in the fishing grounds off Newfoundland and the Maritimes. The tribunal had its high points, and they demonstrated Root's skill in deploying American resources to secure an outcome that would be satisfactory to both sides—a political solution via a judicial proceeding.

The result was a comedy of contradiction on the "British" side, against a cool, well-coordinated and well-briefed legal team of Americans. In the first place, the "British" side consisted of three jurisdictions: Canada, Newfoundland, and Great Britain. Newfoundland, though it had caused the problem in the first place by altering its fishing regulations, thereafter left things to the Canadians and did not participate even to the extent of issuing instructions to the "British" legal team. The team was led by the Canadian minister of justice, Allen Aylesworth, who would not listen to advice or receive information from others: he also literally could not hear, because he was deaf. The workhorse of the British team was a well-known Canadian nationalist, John Ewart, able enough, but afflicted with personality quirks. He would not speak to the other members of his delegation for months on end, as they sat in The Hague, in the Netherlands, painstakingly arguing out the law and the facts. The result was a judgment that awarded the Canadians the letter of the law, recognizing their sovereignty in principle, and handed the Americans the practical results. In virtually every respect of the preparation, the definition of the question to be arbitrated, and the argumentation, the Americans had the upper hand, while the Canadians seem to have had difficulty understanding what was happening.

Nevertheless, when the arbitration was over, and the decision handed down, both sides professed themselves satisfied, and the historians from the respective countries have echoed their respective satisfaction. In the opinion of the historian of these events, it was a pleasing result because it brought to an end a century's worth of fishing disputes around the 1818 treaty and produced a fishing regime in which the Canadians consulted the Americans about the fishing regulations they wished to impose.[42] The Canadian–British side was so pleased that Aylesworth was knighted for his supposed accomplishment. It is important to underline that it did not end all maritime or fishing disputes for all time: these persist even to the present day, but never again would the fishery ignite Canadian–American "fish wars" of the nineteenth-century kind.

The origins, narrative, and conclusion of this last episode of the fish wars took five years, 1907 to 1912, and it is a revealing example of what was meant at the time by the phrase "cleaning the slate." It is perhaps the last episode in Anglo–American–Canadian relations in which the presence and prestige of the British Empire were crucial and instrumental to Canada's relations with the United States. Newfoundland had been the occasion, even the instigation, but the main effect was on Canada. Although Root and Bryce were the two principals in getting the process going, they did so very much with the authority and even propulsion of the larger governments they served. In the background stood Theodore Roosevelt and Sir Wilfrid Laurier, and behind Laurier the British Colonial and Foreign Offices, sometimes encouraging, and sometimes deploring, his actions. Roosevelt's role was to utter encouraging words, set the context, and provide political cover; Laurier's was to delay as long as he could, sometimes maddening the much more efficient Bryce, and eventually to acquiesce to what he considered to be inevitable, while smoothing over any rough edges with his habitual good grace. It helped that in 1909 there was a change in presidents in Washington, with Roosevelt giving way to Taft, and Elihu Root to Philander C. Knox as secretary of state. As Alvin Gluek, the best historian of these events, wrote, "Both the [new] secretary and President Taft were more conciliatory than Root and Roosevelt and the men around them...took their cue from the top."[43]

There were two other important chapters in the story of cleaning the slate. One was pelagic sealing, the other, boundary waters. In something of a contrast to the Atlantic fishery, the Canadians secured the advantage and the money for pelagic sealing. The issue had dragged on far longer than it should have, and that most of the Canadians seemed to be ten years out of date when it came to the facts on the ground. The main fact was that pelagic sealing, and especially the Canadian end of it, had collapsed, and getting anything at all was probably more than the business was worth.[44] The boundary waters issues could have become bogged down in detail, mirroring the many north–south streams and lakes along the frontier. It did not do so, but instead concentrated on working out bodies and procedures under which any and all Canadian–American issues could be thrashed out.

In boundary waters, Canadian negotiators sought a regular and permanent mechanism for dealing with a myriad of issues, from sewage to irrigation to water levels on the St. Lawrence, and came away with a Boundary Waters Treaty, officially a treaty between the British Empire and the United States, but actually a Canadian–American product. It established a permanent International Joint Commission consisting only of Canadian and American members, three on each side. Its immediate purview was to examine and adjudicate disputes involving the many waters along the border, but it could, if desired by both governments, examine any Canadian–American issue whatsoever. In effect, it was a permanent arbitration commission.

Finally, in February 1909, the last month of his presidency, Roosevelt convened a North American conservation conference in Washington, to which he invited Canadian and Mexican delegates. His objective was to secure common policy over common ground. At an earlier stage of his life, Roosevelt had hoped to see the Canadians co-operating with their fellow Americans. Accepting that that was unlikely, Roosevelt sought co-operation between nations, as a prelude to a projected world conservation conference. But that conference had to be left to his successor who, as it turned out, had no interest in pursuing it.

The new American president, William Howard Taft, Theodore Roosevelt's chosen successor, was nevertheless very pleased with the state of Canadian–American relations. Taft was, possibly, the president most disposed to accommodating Canada in this or any other period. An eminent lawyer, Taft had imbibed the mythology of the common law, seeing it stretching back in a continuity unbroken by the American Revolution to Anglo-Saxon times. The links between Great Britain and the United States were important to Taft, as they had been to Roosevelt and McKinley before him. Taft was so taken by the connections of culture and history that he was willing to contemplate a universal arbitration treaty between the United States and the British Empire, putting their relations on an entirely new and fraternal basis, and where Canada was concerned, his sentiments were if possible even friendlier. Every summer, Taft and other privileged Americans made their way to Murray Bay (today La Malbaie) on the lower St. Lawrence; and from it Taft, already well disposed to Canada as a British dominion, derived a personally warm and friendly attitude. (Admittedly, Taft had to interrupt his annual trips from 1909 to 1912, inclusive, because of a now obsolete custom that the president of the United States must not leave American soil. For the four summers of his presidency he vacationed, rather unhappily, in Massachusetts.)

The International Joint Commission could be many things. Commissions could be investigative bodies, and they could also render judgment. Arbitration commissions presided over adversarial arguments, from opposing sides addressing pre-defined questions. The International Joint Commission could go beyond that, formulating its own questions, conducting its own investigations, and depending on fair play and camaraderie among its members to reach conclusions that would be acceptable to both sides. Taft was confident that under the law, and impelled by the law, Great Britain (and Canada) and the United States could find common ground, that turning international relations into a form of court proceeding would, as in the common law, make Anglo-American relations a matter of precedent and procedure. Accordingly, to show what he hoped for the International Joint Commission, he gave it a place in American official protocol, inviting its members to his annual levee for the Supreme Court and other eminent jurists.

The final episode in "cleaning the slate" was a logical consequence of the repeated and complicated discussions involving Canada and the United States, and the inconsistency and amateurishness of the Canadian response. Laurier was moved to establish an office dealing with "external" questions—"external" because it was dealing with the British Empire as well as the rest of the world, and since Canada was a British country, the British Empire was not "foreign." Laurier saw his new Department of External Affairs as a matter of process rather than principle. It would safeguard Canadian interests, certainly, but it was, he assured the House of Commons, nothing more than a means of organizing Canada's business, not a first step out of the British Empire. But by recognizing and then formalizing a Canadian capacity for external action, Laurier also created the possibility that it would, some day, be used.

## Excitable Impulses

Canadian–American relations came of age in 1910–11 so vividly as to govern political relations for the next half-century. It was a drama in three acts. First, positively, President Taft and Prime Minister Laurier reached an agreement that would lower tariffs between Canada and the United States. Trading concessions, they created a reciprocal trade deal that was far from abolishing the respective tariffs and could not be mistaken as any form of a free-trade deal, but that nevertheless recognized the similarity, and the complementarity, of Canadian and American interests. Certainly it lowered barriers to interchange and in particular allowed some American products freer access to the protected Canadian market. Second, the deal became the subject of a federal election in Canada that was notable for its extreme anti-American character. The Canadian government was removed by the election, and a year later Taft was also defeated. Finally, successive Canadian and American governments tacitly overlooked what had occurred and proceeded in public as if nothing had happened. In private, both governments recognized that something quite important had occurred and that Canadian nationalism was a factor that must in the future be taken into account.

Taft and Laurier had banked on the resemblances between Canada and the United States, and these were many. Both North American countries settled the West with an eye to economic expansion—the prairie settlers would absorb immigrants and surplus population and serve as an internal market for the manufactures of the Northeast and Midwest in the United States, and eastern Canada, respectively. The structure of the prairie economy in both countries centered on an export industry, wheat, shipped east by railways into a market dominated by private grain companies. It would be sold at a world price, determined by the market, and affected by wheat supplies from competing countries—the Russian Empire, or Australia, or Argentina. It could be, and usually was, a matter of low prices and high costs. All this led settlers to question the illusory promises of prosperity that had enticed them to the West in the first place.

There were, however, substantial interests on the other side—notably manufacturers and their workers, who quite plausibly owed their jobs to the Canadian or American tariff systems. The Liberal Party in Canada had accommodated itself to this reality, and though Liberals were not philosophically a high-tariff party, they showed little discomfort with Canada's high-tariff system. The Republicans, or at least the Republican leadership in Congress, had no doubts what they represented—industry, trade, and money. As for tariffs, the higher the better, except, perhaps, with Canada.

There had already been an abortive reciprocity pact with Newfoundland. Although it had come to nothing, the incident showed that the notion of reciprocity was not completely dead. Meanwhile, Canada was growing in importance. Recovered from the decades-long slump of the late nineteenth century, the Canadian economy was growing and pulling in American investment, which increased nearly 400 percent in the Roosevelt period. Despite very high tariffs, trade seemed to adjust and grow, to the point where exports to Canada exceeded those to Great Britain. Compared with the 1870s, Canada was actually economically significant to American business, and might become more so, as a potential source of raw materials and as a recipient of American exports.

In an imperial world, where empires created their own sprawling trade zones, it was only prudent to consider where American trade would fit and how it might avoid being excluded. In fact, the signs were not good. Canada in 1897 initiated a policy of lower tariffs for British goods ("Imperial Preference"); its reverse was non-preference for the United States. Canada, as Elihu Root recognized in 1907, was going to use exactly the same tariff policy as the United States, and that meant high tariffs levied on American goods.[45] The British were debating free trade versus imperial protection for the first time in sixty years, and if the debate came to some kind of change of policy, away from free trade, then Canada might well be lost to the United States. Could it be time to change policy where Canada was concerned, and seek to bind Canada more closely, economically speaking, to the United States and its destiny? These were arguments Hobson and Lenin might have read with interest because they showed that the natural state of empires was cutthroat competition, one with another.

While great thoughts about the future wafted behind closed doors, in the State Department or the Chamber of Commerce, politics up front was getting lively. Disillusion led to discontent, which led to political revolt. The revolt was more formidable in Canada, because the governing Liberal party not only used the settlement of the West to point to its great accomplishments, it also needed Western votes to keep power in a finely balanced political system, in which the movement of 3 or 4 percent of the popular vote could determine victory or defeat.[46] The United States simply had more people, more diversity, and more regions to consider. But since the governing Republicans were already a regional party, having been effectively excluded from the eleven states of the former Confederacy, they too needed prairie votes to dominate Congress and, until 1909 or 1910, they had them. The votes were channeled into the election of Republican representatives who sat in serried ranks behind the speaker of the House in a party system that, very much like the Canadian, rewarded loyalty and regularity.[47] Then in 1909 the Republican majority in Congress pushed through an even higher tariff, in the teeth of Western protests, but what did it matter? There had been protests before, and they had come to nothing.

This time was different. The Payne–Aldrich tariff of 1909 attempted to force exporters to the United States to grant "most-favored-nation" status to the United States—tariff rates as low as those granted to the nations that had bargained for them and had made concessions to get them. Canada, which charged the United States its highest ("general") tariff rate was abruptly exposed to an even higher American tariff unless it conceded lower rates on American imports in return for nothing at all. Laurier and his finance minister refused, and suddenly there was a possibility of a trade war between the two North American neighbors. This was definitely not what President Taft wanted.

At the same time the American political system began to fray, the speaker was deposed, and the Democrats, almost unthinkably, won the House of Representatives in the off-year elections of 1910. (A Socialist was elected for the first time to the House, which might, or might not, have suggested a different kind of political future.) The turnover was huge, and it got Taft's attention. In Canada, Western farmers staged a "Siege of Ottawa," marching onto Parliament Hill four abreast, and storming into the Parliament Building, the galleries, and even the floor of the House of Commons. Laurier and his colleagues had no choice but to listen to a flood of farmers' grievances and think of how limited their political future might be if they ignored them. On top of all that, there was concern among American businessmen to do something—not too much, but something—to secure Canada before it was too late.

Negotiations with Canada started in the fall of 1910 and were prolonged into the winter. The Americans offered both free and lower duties on natural products, not complete free trade in natural products as in the 1854 treaty, but enough, they hoped, to secure Canadian acceptance. To help secure congressional consent, Canadian duties on some items manufactured in the United States were to be lowered, to prove to suspicious Congress-folk that their government had got concessions. Of course, what was attractive to American congressmen was unattractive to Canadian manufacturers, and that was a risk. The Canadian negotiators decided to take that risk. An understanding gradually emerged, and it was soon time for the principals to seal the bargain. Taft and Laurier accordingly met in Albany, New York, in January 1911 and blithely signed the Reciprocity Agreement.

Conventional political wisdom in Canada said that Laurier had a winning issue. He could please his Western constituents with free access for their products to the American market and please them again by letting in American manufactures at a lower tariff rate. The Conservative opposition in the House of Commons agreed with him. But many Canadian businessmen, attached to protection, and despairing of their future in direct competition with American exports, decided to fight the thing. This gave hope to the Conservatives, who promised to obstruct reciprocity in Parliament, which was sufficient to bring Laurier to call a general election a year early, in the full expectation that he could crush the Conservatives at the polls.

The resulting election campaign, in the summer of 1911, was one of the fiercest in Canadian history. The opposition charged Laurier with selling out to the United States, betraying the British Empire, and abandoning Canada's fundamental, national, tariff policy. When the incoming Democratic speaker of the House of Representatives, Champ Clark, proclaimed that he wanted to see the American flag wave all the way to the North Pole, this was taken as proof positive. Attempts to paint Clark as an ignoramus (a fair case could be made for that) who did not speak for the Taft administration (true) or for the United States as a whole (debatable at best), were unsuccessful. And in any case, other American politicians chimed in, to the same effect.[48]

From coast to coast in Canada, the American flag was vigorously booed, Americans were insulted on the street, and the Conservative press told their readers that reciprocity was the first step to annexation, and with annexation all manner of horrors would be let loose, from Sunday newspapers to universal divorce. More positively, Union Jacks proliferated, and imperial paraphernalia were suddenly everywhere. It did not hurt that the coronation of George V occurred in 1911—another triumph of ornamental symbolism that was repeated, in miniature, in parades and celebrations from one end of Canada to the other. Laurier had proudly attended the coronation, which proved to be his last serious official function as prime minister. Returning home, he found that going to London to see the king crowned had won him no points among effusively loyal Canadian monarchists and certainly had not helped with newly awakened French-Canadian *nationalistes.* Pro- and anti-British-Canadians discovered that they had something in common—a desire to get rid of Sir Wilfrid and his compromising ways.

Laurier was trapped. The opposition used every argument to portray him as a traitor to the British cause and a pawn of the Yankees.[49] On September 7, the poet of empire, Rudyard Kipling, immensely popular in Canada as around the English-speaking world, encapsulated the opposition to reciprocity in a statement to a leading Conservative paper, the *Montreal Star*:

> It is her own soul that Canada risks today. Once that soul is pawned for any consideration Canada must inevitably confirm to the commercial, legal, financial, social and ethical standards, which will be imposed on her by the sheer admitted weight of the United States.

Not content with strategic considerations, Kipling pointed to the Americans' well-known ethical shortcomings: "She [Canada] might, for example, be compelled later on to admit reciprocity in the murder rate of the United States, which at present, I believe, is something over 150 per million per annum."[50]

Laurier desperately blamed the Americans for delaying reciprocity, but now that they had come round, with Taft not Laurier making the approach, it would be "a crime against civilization" to refuse "a bond of friendship and amity between the two countries."[51] These were feeble arguments, a sign that Laurier knew his cause was doomed.

So it was. On September 21, with a swing of about 3 percent of the electorate, the Liberals lost, the Conservatives won, and the 1911 version of reciprocity was dead. Canadians could sleep safe in their beds, unthreatened by the American murder rate. It was a defeat for Laurier, but it was also a defeat for Taft, who had gambled much of his political credibility to get the treaty ratified, even convening a special session of Congress to do it.[52]

The absurdity of many of the arguments used against the Reciprocity Treaty and by extension against the United States in 1911 has tended to color interpretations of the meaning of the treaty, which is usually presented as a benign instrument, an economic arrangement with no ulterior political significance. More recently, however, historians have glimpsed traces in the American archives that suggest that Champ Clark was not wholly wrong in his interpretation of the meaning of the treaty, and that some members of the Taft administration saw the treaty as a means of moving Canada out of the orbit of the British Empire and into the sphere of influence of the United States. As Taft himself confessed in a letter to Theodore Roosevelt, even before the treaty was signed, the advantages to the United States were so great that if the Canadians knew the real consequences they would surely vote the proposition down:

> Meantime, the amount of Canadian products we would take would produce a current of business between western Canada and the United States that would make Canada only an adjunct of the United States. It would transfer all their important business to Chicago and New York, with their bank credits and everything else, American links to Canada had not and it would increase greatly the demand of Canada for our manufactures. I see this as an argument against reciprocity made in Canada, and I think it is a good one....[53]

In confidence, a senior State Department official argued that Canada's east–west linkages would give way to the more natural north–south flow: Canada would not only be placed in the American orbit, but its various parts would adhere to their immediate, American neighbors rather than to the artificial ribbon of the Canadian economy and Canadian life. Canada, in this reading of the future, would join the United States, but if it did not, its parts would separate and accomplish the same end. Champ Clark had put it more crudely, but it was the same argument and the same conclusion, and it was, moreover, a conclusion that the American political class broadly shared.

Taft was disappointed, but he was relieved of the burden of defending the treaty to American voters, especially farmers, who would have faced free imports of Canadian agricultural products, like wheat. But Taft's political future was as dim as Laurier's, though like his Canadian colleague he did not know it until too late. In just over a year he would be defeated for re-election, and in eighteen months he would be gone.

It remained to be seen what the new Canadian and American governments would make of the defeat of reciprocity. The answer was not much. Obviously, Canada's links to the British Empire, economic, political, and emotional, remained intact. American links to Canada remained much as they had been. Ex-president Taft resumed his travels to Murray Bay. His daughter Helen took such a strong interest in Canada that she became a Canadian historian.[54] The fisheries and pelagic sealing disputes were settled, and worries over Great Lakes disarmament simply went away.

The incoming prime minister, Robert Borden (soon, by virtue of orna-mentalism, Sir Robert Borden), was not anti-American. He had lived in the United States, liked the place, and enjoyed his visits there. Borden saw no contradiction between friendly relations with the republic and enthusi-astic participation on the British Empire. Much more than Laurier, he saw Canada's external relations as an Atlantic triangle; and, better organized and more purposeful than Laurier, he was able to contemplate relations with the United States at greater leisure. There was, in 1913–14, no reason to hurry.

# 7

## *Relations Transformed by War*

ON JUNE 28, 1914, Serbian revolutionaries assassinated the heir to the Austrian throne and his wife in Sarajevo in Bosnia, then a part of the Austro-Hungarian empire. The news was of interest elsewhere in Europe and in North America: deplorable, certainly; important, no doubt; but at worst there might be another Balkan crisis, an innumerable category, or a Balkan War, the third in two years. That was a matter for distant concern, but undoubtedly the powers of Europe, with Great Britain as the foremost power, would step in and arrange matters.

The powers, however, had other matters to concern them, and, sometimes, serious matters. Great Britain had Ireland, and in June 1914 that island, and perhaps the entire British nation, seemed to be perched on the edge of civil war. It was the old story of Protestant–Catholic animosity, now focused on the British government's plan to give Ireland an autonomous Parliament, similar to the provincial and state legislatures in Australia, Canada, and the United States, with continued representation in the British Parliament for larger matters. The Protestant minority saw itself abandoned, and the minority was a majority in northeast Ireland, Ulster; incited by Conservative politicians, they threatened civil war rather than submit and began arming themselves, rather like the provincials in America in 1775. The Catholics in the south responded by arming themselves, while the British army, largely officered by Protestant Irishmen, indicated that it might not obey orders to suppress a rebellion in Ulster.

While these events were transpiring in Europe, the Canadian government was trying to ward off a ship full of Sikh immigrants from India. To protect the purity of a white Canada (about 98 percent white in 1914), the Canadian government did its best to prohibit settlers from India, China, and Japan, not to mention blacks from the United States, and tried to mask its policy under various forms of verbal and legal subterfuge. Japan, unfortunately for Canadian racial purity, was an ally of the British Empire, and so discrimination there took the form of an agreement with the Japanese government, which did not favor the emigration of its subjects. Japanese immigrants were restricted to four hundred males a year as a result.[1] As India was part of the Empire, it was not good policy to overtly discriminate against Indian subjects, which might cause them to question whether they really were better off as subjects of the King-Emperor in London. But white opinion in British Columbia was as unreasonable as that of the Protestants of Ulster, and the officials of Britain's Indian Empire stood aside.[2] Very disgruntled, the would-be immigrants were finally forced to sail away; by the time they reached India, the world would be engulfed in war, in which the Sikhs' services would be actively solicited.

## Autonomous and Imperial?

By 1914 Canada was no longer an active impediment in Anglo-American relations. British officials could be pardoned a certain complacency when they looked at the dominion as an international factor. A department of external affairs functioned in Ottawa, and most ordinary disputes could be dealt with rationally if sometimes slowly, using the British embassy in Washington as a representative facility. The departmental under-secretary, Sir Joseph Pope, had made friends in the new Democratic administration of Woodrow Wilson in Washington—he could drop in on the secretary of state and exchange cordialities with the departmental counselor.[3] The British ambassador, Sir Cecil Spring Rice, was instructed when he took office in 1913 that the embassy "has now for a long time been accustomed to report separately and directly to Canada on all matters which appear to be of interest to the Dominion." He copied his mandate to Ottawa, obviously in the expectation that it would cause no excitement, and it did not.[4]

Spring Rice made no reference to Canadian advice on Anglo-American relations. He would have considered it an absurdity, or an impossibility, and, in the world of 1913, he would have been right. Canada did not link Great Britain and the United States; it was not, as a common notion would have it, a "linchpin" between the two larger countries.[5] Borden, however, liked the idea that Canada should connect its two larger English-speaking associates.

Ottawa plainly expected no serious problem with the United States. Relations were continuous, but routine. They required nothing more than the occasional consultation among civil servants in either capital. What did the United States expect from the relationship? It is a question that is almost impossible to answer. The 1911 election did, however, shed considerable light on the subject. Liberal defeat and Conservative victory affirmed Canada's primary political connection to the British Empire. The British Empire was not a threat to the United States, either strategically or ideologically. This fact was generally sensed and, as far as the elite was concerned, consciously admitted.

It did not lead to a crisis in Canadian–American affairs. While Canada's rejection of reciprocity was noticed in American political circles, and in greater detail inside the US State Department, it was a lesson to be studied and learned from. Obviously there was such a thing as Canadian anti-Americanism, and attentive readers of American newspapers would occasionally find examples of it. There was, it appeared, such a thing as Canadian nationalism—distinct from British colonial status and contradicting the notion that Canadians were Americans in waiting. What the Canadians actually were, and what the components of Canadian nationalism might be, were questions that could be resolved later. For the time being, it was important to treat Canadians gently and to avoid offending them by untimely suggestions that Canada's true destiny was to join the United States. That time, they now realized, might never come.

But if Canada did not and would not formally become part of the United States, what about its informal position? Did Canada between 1890 and 1914 pass into the strategic sphere of the United States from that of Great Britain? More bluntly, did Canada become part of an expanding American empire at the beginning of the twentieth century? Was that the lesson administered by Theodore Roosevelt and learned by Sir Wilfrid Laurier in the Alaska boundary dispute of 1903? The answer is mixed, but on the whole negative.

Perception must have something to do with the answer. Canadians in 1900 or 1914 did not see themselves as subject to American imperial domination. They might or might not dislike Americans, but while the American government had been high-handed over the Alaska boundary issue, there had been no further negative consequences. The American government placed no demands on the Canadian government and made no requests that sought to bend Canadian policy to an American course, as opposed to a British or a Canadian direction. It may be argued that Canada unconsciously followed the American road, sleepwalking into subservience, but it is hard to write the history of oblivion. American officials might exchange memoranda and letters on the subject of Canada's eventual destiny and murmur about the dominion's place in an American scheme of things, but these considerations had no practical outlet. As a practical matter, American domination must be discarded as an explanation for Canadian politics or Canadian policies.[6] The fact of the matter was that the United States was not dominant in Canada.

It is well known that the years after 1896 were years of mass immigration to Canada. The popular image of Canadian immigration is of a minister—the Liberal Clifford Sifton—a broad-minded and imaginative politician, welcoming "men in sheepskin coats"—settlers from Eastern Europe, previously looked down upon as peasants if not barbarians, into Canada. The "sheepskin coats" phrase is a positive image, but it is also misleading. In the first place, it was a policy of relatively limited duration and was downplayed if not discontinued by Sifton's Liberal successor as minister in charge of immigration. This leads to a second image, in which a European-focused Canadian government kept out people of non-white races. And so non-white immigrants were few and marginalized by an overwhelmingly white and European-derived society.

What is omitted, and what is generally forgotten, is the overwhelmingly British nature of Canadian immigration in the fifteen years leading up to 1914. Between 1901 and 1920, more than 1.6 million voyagers arrived in Canada from the British Isles—the vast majority of them immigrants. Outpaced by Australia until an economic downturn in the early 1890s, Canada suddenly became a favored destination—favored, for many, because it was *British*.[7] Arriving immigrants went both to the farm and the city, and for all of Canada's larger cities, immigrants made their mark, sometimes reinforcing existing institutions, sometimes replicating those from home,[8] and sometimes creating their own. As recent historians have pointed out, the colonies were not "passive recipients of empire," for sometimes migrants beamed back their sense of what it was to be British to the mother country.[9] Churches and charities also began to send colonists and children out to the healthier climate (it was supposed) of the dominions—especially Canada, the easiest to get to. In a kind of reciprocation, stalwart (and usually manly) colonial figures began to appear in British fiction, often bucking up the confused or ineffectual inhabitants of the mother country and making their own distinctive—but British—contribution to its well-being.[10] Seen from this perspective, there was no contradiction between a certain kind of colonial nationalism and a British identity or loyalty.[11] On the other hand, given that there were more men than women in the colonies, especially on the frontier, young women were also encouraged to migrate. In some respects, it was no different from the situation of eighteenth-century American colonists; but, as in the eighteenth century, the quest for appreciation was an argument that needed to be fed with constant dollops of respect.

Arguably the Empire figured more prominently in British life in 1910 than in 1760. As in 1760, there were economic connections, which tended to reinforce, rather than contradict, imperial links and thus bolstered the electoral verdict of 1911. The connections began with the shipping lines that carried immigrants and commerce, and carried on through enterprising British merchants seeking out customers, professional connections, transnational societies—all contributed to what recent historians have dubbed the "British World." "Information, trust and reciprocity" fueled the imperial engine and facilitated the expansion of imperial trade.[12] The connections went both ways, as Canadians (and other colonials) promoted their goods and organized themselves into chambers of commerce to secure their entrée into the overseas imperial world. And of that world, Canada was definitely a part.

A distinction should be made between the "British World" that was defined by British sovereignty and loyalty and the larger "Anglo-world" (what is today often called the "Anglosphere") that included the United States.[13] Canadians were familiar with this notion in practice—where it was usually treated as either benign or inescapable—and, if they were politically attuned, in theory. The two were not compatible. The Anglo-world treated Great Britain and the United States as equivalent and so mixed in blood and in destiny that they should be treated as one. This was, after all, the point of view of the late annexationist Goldwin Smith, whose posthumous approval made it obnoxious to most Canadians of 1911. Practically, the resemblances and influences were obvious between the two North American neighbors, making Canada a partial exception to the patterns of colonial consumption of British products.

Finally, Great Britain was not exactly a passive witness to the development of Canada, but an active participant and a very interested party. The existence of an empire of settlement, complete with British laws and British institutions, was important to more than imperial enthusiasts, remittance men, and ornamentalists. To many Britons, it had financial significance as a haven for safe investments, often guaranteed by the British government, which would yield a regular income. To the dominions, and around 1900 that meant especially Canada, it meant that raising funds was easier and cheaper than for competing, non-British jurisdictions. Given the fact that the money was being placed in infrastructure projects, very expensive and with a very slow payback, this was extraordinarily important.

British investors, banks and individuals, consciously accepted a lower rate of return for their money because it was safer and more predictable when housed in Canada.[14]

## The Early Anglosphere

Borden was anything but a revolutionary in politics, but he was neither reactionary nor unimaginative. He had something of an American background, not especially indicative, but it did not predispose him to hostility to the United States. His ancestors were pre-Loyalists, who had moved to Nova Scotia from colonial Massachusetts in the 1760s, and for Borden as for other Nova Scotians, the United States did not seem especially foreign. In 1911 Borden quickly told the American consul general that the excitement of the election was no indication of his real policy, and as far as Canadian–American relations needed policy, that proved correct.[15] Like Laurier, Borden had great respect for James Bryce, still British ambassador, and much later, after Bryce had retired and become a lord and a world war had intervened, he still consulted him on the great issues of the day. Bryce's policy of conciliation and harmony with the United States caused Borden no difficulties, either practically or philosophically.

Indeed Borden can be partly understood in American terms. His preoccupations as prime minister would have seemed familiar to American observers—establishing a "scientific" tariff, marketing grain through a government elevator system, bolstering an impartial and expert civil service, and broadly using the power of government to rein in private enterprise—all of which were ideas and policies that echoed American politics at the same time.[16]

In terms of political foreign policy, however, Canada diverged, which, as a member of the British Empire, it had to, in terms of Canadians' self-identification. In 1911 the most emotional issues in Canadian politics had to do with the British Empire and with a financial contribution from Canada to the Royal Navy. Borden broadly expressed Canadians' sense of British identification, one that was more than the sentimental and anachronistic imperialism or anti-Americanism that later generations of Canadians associated with the generation of 1911. Once the issue of relations with the Americans was framed in imperial terms, it is hard to see how English Canadians could not have been carried along with Borden and his anti-reciprocity followers. When Borden proposed to build up British naval strength with contributions of money from the dominion, it seemed like the most natural act of self-defense—again, as the issue was publicly understood.

But there was a difference between Canada and the other members of the Anglo-world. Borden did not, in 1911 or later, carry most French Canadians with him or his imperial policies, a significant point of weakness politically. French Canadians made up 80 percent of the population of the province of Quebec and almost 30 percent of the population of the dominion. In 1911 Borden made inroads into Quebec, but Laurier still carried the majority of the French-speaking vote in the province and elsewhere. It was a reminder that Canada was in some respects only a partial and, for French Canadians, a conditional, member of the Anglo-world.

## Canadians and Americans

The Anglo-world was therefore incomplete as far as Canadian–American relations were concerned. The existence of the British Empire was a barrier to some kinds of formal connections—sharing political space, for example, or erecting a common judiciary. Nevertheless the actual government-to-government contacts between the dominion and the republic just before 1914 indicate a fairly harmonious approach to sharing the common space of North America. The approach was sinuous and sometimes internally contradictory, but it contributed to a growing good feeling. The International Joint Commission (IJC) created by the Boundary Waters Treaty of 1909 was never given a chance to function precisely as President Taft and his fellow legalists would have wished. Taft had wanted a kind of joint international court, founded on a common legal ideology. Before it could begin functioning as such, Taft had disappeared from the political scene. On the Canadian side, it fell into the hands of C.A. Magrath, a Borden appointee, who helped direct it onto a path of negotiation rather than arbitration. The IJC became more of an investigative body, eliciting facts, soliciting expert opinion, and using consensus to reach its decisions. Ideologically, it was "Progressive" in its views and its practices, relying on "fact-based" materials, and assuming that Canadians and Americans could be convinced and motivated by the same evidence that would point to the same conclusions. Thus it encouraged conciliation and agreement, thereby helping to establish an instant tradition of trans-boundary cooperation.

The existence and early actions of the IJC fell into the category of contributions to Anglo-American harmony, but they pointed as well in a different direction. The IJC was entirely North American in its composition.

It reported to governments in Ottawa and Washington without passing by the British embassy or through the British Foreign Office. The Canadians on the commission did not represent British interests and had no need to seek British instructions. Without planning a political result, or intending one, the IJC was a precursor in disentangling Canadian interests from British, to Canada's advantage—itself a very new and radical concept. Instead of a handicap, Canada's unintended separation from Great Britain could be an advantage, especially in dealing with American interests that were not as pro-imperial or pro-British as those of the New England or New York elites. There were not only Anglo-Americans, but also Irish-Americans and German-Americans, and in some sections of the country—even in parts of Boston—anglophobia was more apparent than anglophilia. (And, it should be underlined, not all ethnic Anglo-Americans were well disposed to the British.)

What was intended to be a celebration of good relations between Great Britain and the United States helped to illuminate the limits of the Anglo-American relationship as well. When an American Peace Centenary Committee was established in 1912 to commemorate the hundredth anniversary of the Treaty of Ghent in December 1914, and thus a hundred years of Anglo-American peace, it found its efforts challenged and even condemned in the House of Representatives, which declined to endorse any official remembrance or memorial. The would-be American commemorators accordingly denounced "the persistent campaign of a most inconsiderate minority of the American population against anything and everything pertaining to Great Britain."[17] Not for the first or last time, it was a question of *whose* history was to be celebrated and whose would be submerged. If Canada had ceased to play a negative part in Anglo-American relations, there remained a host of hostile immigrant nationalities in the United States ready to take a whack at the British and their empire. Perhaps fortunately, the celebrations would be aborted by the outbreak of war in Europe; by December 1914 celebrating what had become an exceptional Anglo-American or North American peace during a war in Europe seemed somehow inappropriate.

Canadian–American relations, on the other hand, were unexceptional. Americans continued to travel to Canada for cool air and pine trees in the summer. American investors reached behind the Canadian tariff wall—so similar to their own—and erected factories to supply the Canadian market. Singer Sewing Machine, Edison Electric, Swift's (meatpackers), Parke Davis pharmaceuticals, and Coca-Cola all established northern branches.

Canadian department stores, like their American counterparts, went into the mail-order business, selling mass merchandise of American origin or American design, homogenizing tastes and habits across the border.[18]

Canada had a more serious problem than worrying about relations with the United States or American influences on Canada. There was in North America and especially Canada a sharp economic depression that reduced gross domestic product between 1913 and 1914 by more than 6 percent, with the effect of sharply raising Canada's rate of unemployment.[19] The unemployed were mainly male, and in the nature of things, many were immigrants, and the largest source of immigration was, as it almost always had been, Great Britain. Canada was not alone in sliding into depression: the United States and Australia also declined in economic output, although European countries, including Great Britain, did not. In any case, economics prescribed waiting out the depression, letting interest rates fall, until, at some point, demand once again stimulated supply. In the summer of 1914, Canadians and Americans were still waiting for that magic moment.

## The Great War of 1914–1918

On August 4, 1914, Canadians learned, rather to their surprise, that the Empire had gone to war against Germany. The powers had not after all resolved the Balkan crisis, and one after another they had declared war, with Great Britain, France, and Russia (plus Serbia) on one side ("the Allies") and Germany and Austria-Hungary on the other ("the Central Powers"). Germany had invaded neutral Belgium, en route to attack France, which gave Great Britain a justification for declaring war—"the rights of small nations." Soon Japan would join in, as an Ally, and Turkey would join the Central Powers. (The Japanese navy would patrol Canada's Pacific coast to ward off German raiders, much to the discomfort of racist British Columbians.) The war, when it acquired a name, became "The Great War"—like the preceding Great War of 1793–1815. Luckily, it would not last as long; unluckily, and unlike the previous war, its results as far as Great Britain and its empire were concerned were mostly negative.

As the war spread around the world, one major power abstained; the United States declared itself neutral. There is an incomplete parallel with the American Civil War, when Great Britain declared neutrality at the beginning of the war, to the irritation and resentment of the American government, which had expected more and better from the British. For the time being, however, all the belligerents had confidence in the outcome of the war, and thus direct military help and political alignment were not needed. The British government hoped merely that the Americans would sell requisite quantities of food, ammunition, and money to the Allies; and on that score the United States did not disappoint. As for that other parallel with the Civil War, the thousands of Canadians who served in the Union army, there was no real comparison. Some Americans did sign up, and at one point Canadian recruiters hoped to form an "American Legion," but in the end only one battalion (eight hundred to a thousand men) was formed, and it was broken up to replace casualties in other units already at the front.[20]

Controversy over whether the United States should enter the war was initially confined to the United States, where it pitted the president, Woodrow Wilson, who had defeated the hapless Taft in 1912, against Theodore Roosevelt, whom he had also defeated, in one of the rare three-party contests in American political history. Roosevelt did not take kindly to defeat, or to Wilson. It was only a matter of time until his resentment burst forth, and it did so over the question of whether America should go to war.

The two men were unlikely soulmates, personal rivalry aside. Though both Roosevelt and Wilson were closely connected to British culture, Roosevelt was fixated on the Empire and enjoyed being the guest of the king and assorted other British ornaments. Wilson's preference was for the rather unornamental Liberal politician and prime minister William Ewart Gladstone. "That is Gladstone," the sixteen-year-old Wilson explained to a cousin who was sitting under the great man's portrait, "the greatest statesman that ever lived. I intend to be a statesman too."[21] There was a whiff of pacifism and moralism about Gladstone that appealed to Wilson as it repelled individuals like Roosevelt, who preferred action to talk and delay, both of which were characteristic of Gladstone—and Wilson. Perhaps that was why Gladstone had an exceptionally long political career—more than sixty years—and was four times prime minister. The great cause that ended his career, home rule for Ireland, inspired English-speaking liberals the world around; that Gladstone had not succeeded in that task was a spur to complete his mission, if not over Ireland, then over equality of opportunity and the beginnings of a social welfare state.

Gladstone had stood, however imperfectly, for a world in which international law and a common standard of good behavior should prevail. International law was much on the public mind in the years before 1914, and several serious efforts were made to codify proper international behavior. For Sir Robert Borden, the Canadian prime minister, the war was both an automatic requirement of British citizenship and a justified response to the breaking of international law. Canada belonged to the British Empire, he reasoned. The Empire was at war, and therefore Canada was at war. He knew that if he ever forgot that basic principle, Canadians would remind him of it. And of Canada's 7.2 million inhabitants, more than 10 percent (785,000) were born in the British Isles, and for many, perhaps most, of them ties to the mother country remained strong; and this does not begin to count the millions of Canadians of British descent—54 percent of the total population in the 1911 census. On the other hand, Borden argued the case for war as a response to Germany's violation of international law by invading Belgium—"the rights of small nations." That should concern Canadians as full citizens of the Empire, and, by extension, as citizens of the world. It is doubtful that Borden thought of Canada at the time as a "small nation" in an international context; Canada was after all part of the British Empire.

Borden's case was strengthened by the behavior of the German army as it passed through Belgium and invaded France. Civilian hostages were freely shot, evidently with the intention of terrorizing the population and deterring any possibility of popular resistance. German troops doing the shooting were well aware that the individuals they were executing had not themselves done anything, but were put to death as an example to others. In Leuven, the beautiful fourteenth-century building housing the university library was torched, along with all its contents. These facts were soon widely known and even more widely disseminated by Allied propaganda, and in the retelling, of course the facts became less factual. By themselves, the German atrocities of August 1914 were enough to turn public opinion against Germany and to underpin the view that the Germans instinctively behaved like the Huns of old. For Borden, these events justified his case for war at home; even more, they gave him a text to use with Canada's American neighbors.[22]

The atrocity stories were too recent to have played much of a role in stimulating a rush to join the army in the first months of the war. Canada's largely British immigrant composition was ready-made for a war in which the old country was in danger. The enlistments reflected some of the dominion's recent arrivals, which combined with the unemployment rate helped ensure that Canada could send a first contingent of thirty-three thousand troops, mainly British-born, to Europe in October 1914. More followed, allowing the creation of a "Canadian Corps" of four divisions, which, by

1918, was thought to be one of the strongest units in the British army. Eventually 600,000 Canadian recruits would go to war in one capacity or another, out of a population of 8.3 million in 1918;[23] they would fight in France and Belgium (and also Russia), or on the high seas in between North America and Europe. Some would become stars in the sky as well, as part of the British Royal Flying Corps. The army would remain in Europe for the next five years, and sixty thousand of its soldiers would be buried in imperial military cemeteries in France, Belgium, and the United Kingdom.

To Roosevelt, the Great War of 1914–1918 was a clash of both empires and principles, in which Great Britain and its values were plainly his favorites. Roosevelt associated politics and policy with morality and was shocked both by the German invasion of Belgium and by German atrocities in the first months of the conflict.[24] For Wilson the war made sense— if it could make sense—only as a contest between good and evil, the great principle around which he believed Gladstone had organized his life. It would not be too much to say that to Wilson war was an evil and thus required absolutely incontrovertible justification. For him, the war only slowly came into focus, and he resisted attempts to use German acts of war to draw the United States into the conflict. His patience was sorely tried by a German submarine's sinking of the British ocean liner *Lusitania* in May 1915, in which more than one hundred American passengers were drowned, among the ship's twelve hundred fatalities, as a reason for declaring war.[25] It was on the sinking of the *Lusitania* that Wilson and Theodore Roosevelt finally came apart. For Roosevelt, it was an unforgivable barbarity; for Wilson it was a spur to demand that the Germans cease submarine warfare. He temporarily got his way, but submarines were, in the final analysis, too effective and too convenient for the Germans to forego.

The sheer size of Canada's military effort was matched, eventually, by economic contributions. It took a while: the government, the banks, and the country's opinion-makers had no idea what the potential of the economy might be. Canada's prosperity was believed to hinge on its ability to produce primary products for export—wheat, wood, and minerals. Canadians saw the dominion as a developing country, requiring constant infusions of immigrants and foreign capital—the poorer, younger cousin of the United States. Replicating the political colonial relationship, the money flowed from London into Canada. To the great regret of British investors, much of it never flowed back, at least to the share- or bondholders. It was lost mainly in Canadian railway promotions, but also in mining schemes and fruitless agricultural colonies.

The war furnished the occasion for some of the greatest investments to go to the wall and, paradoxically, to prove their worth; the Canadian Northern Railway and the Grand Trunk Railway, two of the largest corporations in Canada, were effectively bankrupt and had to be nationalized by the government during and just after the war. And yet all was not lost. The railways carried wheat to the Atlantic ports and soldiers and munitions to Quebec or Halifax, the first stage of their voyage to the war in Europe. It was, in a sense, the ultimate justification of a great imperial investment.

The economy grew, certainly, from 1914 to 1918; using the economic historian Angus Maddison's calculations, the gross domestic product grew in constant dollars by about a seventh during the war—rather less, proportionately, than the American economy in the same period.[26] Nevertheless, Canadian prosperity advanced, until in 1917 it finally surpassed Australia's on a per capita basis and seemed to be closing in on the United States. In terms of exports, it grew remarkably, after a brief disruption in 1914, especially when one takes into account the absence of many able-bodied young men who ordinarily would have kept the woods, fields, and mines producing. The significant facts were that Canada's gross domestic product was large, that it had a large amount of American investment, and that it was both a source of raw materials for the United States and an obvious export market.

In the meantime, Sir Robert Borden discovered that for some purposes he was the senior political representative of the British Empire in North America.[27] British politicians, and certainly British cabinet ministers, did not usually transport themselves to North America, which required a commitment of at least three to four weeks of travel. For Borden, a speech in the northeastern states was at most an overnight trip, in the comfort of the prime-ministerial railway carriage. To be sure, the British ambassador signified more real power than Borden could ever hope to wield, but Borden was definitely a prime minister, a successful politician, and someone who could explain, from a North American perspective and in a flat Nova Scotia accent, why a British victory mattered in the European war. It was helpful that Borden was not obviously a direct representative of the British upper class and that he occupied a middle position—British without actually being British—in American eyes and to American ears.

Soon Borden was traveling to Boston or New York and addressing bodies like the distinctly anglophile and upper-crust Pilgrims Society, whose purpose was to celebrate the common roots and shared interests of the United States and Great Britain and, by not much of an extension, the

British Empire.[28] It was obviously ready-made to be a vehicle for propaganda and influence. As a result, Borden did form an impression of the neutral United States in the un-neutral and pro-British atmosphere of the American Northeast. As most of his hosts and interlocutors were Republicans, the establishment party of the day, he also imbibed a view of Woodrow Wilson and his Democrats that was neither especially helpful nor realistic.[29]

From Borden and from the daily press Americans would have imbibed a tale of Canadian sacrifice—a grim war undertaken for noble principles, carried on as a matter of duty. Undoubtedly Canada's reputation improved, at least among Borden's chosen audiences, and when Borden spoke, as he made plain, he was a representative of the British Empire as well. Not surprisingly, the unity of the English-speaking peoples was standard fare on these occasions—to slightly paraphrase the historian Peter Clarke, Borden was speaking in a common language about the values created by a common culture.[30] Where culture led, surely policy—bringing the United States into the war—must follow.

Those Americans who wanted to be convinced were convinced. Theodore Roosevelt was already convinced—had been since the *Lusitania*—and later conveyed where he believed Canada stood, and what its participation in the war signified. Colonel Roosevelt spoke in Toronto on November 26, 1917, in support of a "Victory Loan"—a war bond campaign. This could be construed as a non-partisan event—everyone except the farthest political fringe approved the Victory Loan. But a federal election was only three weeks away, and Canadian politics were unusually fierce. The prime minister, Borden, made a point of greeting Roosevelt at the train station, and the finance minister, a Toronto MP, chaired the colonel's meeting. Introducing Roosevelt, Sir Thomas White described him as "a statesman, a gallant soldier, as a humanitarian, and, above all, as a man, for he is every inch a man."[31] Roosevelt told the cheering crowd ("you men and women of the north") that the cause of the British Empire was the cause of all humanity, and that the Empire's "free commonwealths"—Canada, Australia, New Zealand, "the Ocean Islands,"[32] and South Africa—had played "a part of extraordinary significance," which would allow "your children's children, for generation after generation, shall hold their heads high." Once "our nations" were victorious, a new era would dawn. The new era, as Roosevelt described it, bore traces of an older era, the era of 1911 or 1891, perhaps, when the two kindred countries would come closer, much closer, together. "As regards Canada and the United States," he declaimed, "I think the time has come when we should declare that no possible question can arise which cannot be determined substantially as questions between the various states and provinces are determined, at Washington or Ottawa."[33] The devil as always was in the details, and Roosevelt did not specify how, exactly, provincial or state questions were dealt with, or how they should be dealt with. It was one of those phrases that masked raw politics with a harmonious smile—"like lipstick on a pig," as a later American politician would say.[34]

It was not surprising that, given stimuli like Roosevelt's speech, Borden might believe that Canada now had a larger role to play. But what role was that? Canada had no regular representation in the United States, merely agents to promote Canadian trade and Canadian products, of a peacetime kind. Accordingly Borden sent a "War Mission" headed by a prominent businessman to Washington, where it busied itself with contracts and supplies, along lines discussed in Borden–Wilson meetings in February 1918. Washington was unfamiliar territory, but it was now crucial. Canada depended on the United States not only for vital supplies, but also for loans to carry on the war. The war had closed up the British capital market, centered in London, and the British themselves were petitioning the Americans for loans to allow them to carry on the war. And not just the Americans—the Canadian Victory Loans, for which Roosevelt had been speaking, went to pay for British munitions, manufactured in Canada, or supplies of Canadian wheat to the mother country and the other Allies. For Canadians it was a revelation: nobody had dreamed, before 1917, how much money could be raised domestically. Although the money was spent on behalf of the Empire, it was a sign that the close relation between Canada and the City of London, as the source of almost all money, might be diminished after the war.

So the War Mission had work to do, work that the British themselves could not pay for. The War Mission came under the general aegis of the British embassy, which itself in 1918 was having convulsions as the British searched for the right ambassador to deal with the United States and Woodrow Wilson, finally settling on the Lord Chief Justice of England, Lord Reading, who in an earlier life had been a very active politician.[35] Reading was obviously not sent to Washington to busy himself with Canadian affairs, a subject in which he had no training, interest, or experience. Not surprisingly, the Borden government began to consider whether it should permanently appoint its own representatives to Washington, to serve in a senior and distinctive role within the British mission.

Plainly the British embassy was pleased to have Borden contribute to friendly atmospherics, but it would have reacted differently had he tried to insert a Canadian point of view into the larger questions of Anglo-American relations. Those questions were very large, and for the most part the British government believed they were none of Canada's or Borden's business. While Canadian interests were very much involved in Anglo-American relations—more and more the case as the war went on—Canada's information on truly important matters and consequently Canadian inputs into policy were restricted to meetings in London. In one sense, that was just as well, because on a high political level Borden, and the Canadian government, had nothing much and certainly nothing positive to contribute. Though members of the State Department knew and maintained cordial relations with officials like Sir Joseph Pope, they expected to deal with Pope and Canada on housekeeping matters that seldom required any intervention from a higher political authority. American entry into the war did little to change matters.

Nevertheless Borden believed that he had absorbed American opinion and, more, that he understood the United States. Impressed both by the similarity between Canada and the United States and by the overwhelming fact of American wealth and power, he came to believe and argue that the British Empire and the United States shared a deep common interest that should take precedence, in foreign affairs, over all other considerations.[36]

## War into Peace

The exigencies of the war kept Borden for many months in London as part of what was called the Imperial War Cabinet. The Imperial War Cabinet was a creation of the British prime minister, David Lloyd George, and it consisted of senior British ministers and senior representatives of the dominions. In 1918, as a result, Borden spent more time in London than he did in Ottawa; in return he sat in on high-level meetings that determined the most important military and diplomatic issues facing the Empire. Most importantly, he got his hands on the papers, the information, that fed the cabinet—though the British, on matters that might embarrass their relations with Canada, specifically withheld information.

Returning to Canada in August 1918 with the Empire's strategy for the 1919 campaign against Germany provided for, Borden was almost immediately told to turn around and return to London, since the war was suddenly and unexpectedly coming to an end. Victory, in November 1918, was in sight. The cabinet's agenda was no longer how to win the war, but how to win the peace. There would be a peace conference. It would be in Paris,

and everybody—that is, Woodrow Wilson—was coming. So were an assort-
ment of prime ministers, foreign ministers, sheikhs, pashas, and generals;
but Wilson was the one who counted. How should Wilson be handled?

Unwisely echoing the views of a rich Canadian businessman, Borden
told the British prime minister, Lloyd George, that many in the United
States thought President Wilson was "a Bolscheviek" [sic] who hated
Britain and the British class system.[37] Having delivered himself of this
insight, Borden let the matter rest. By then the war was over.

Borden and Wilson had met once during the war; at that point, early
1918, their business had mostly to do with arranging secure supplies of
American fuel and other raw materials to keep Canadian industry functioning and Canadian homes heated in the coal-scarce winter of 1918.
These measures to some extent integrated the American and Canadian
war economies—again, a sign, like the Victory Loans, of what could be
done, and would be done, should another wartime emergency demand it.
Borden was present to witness Wilson's triumphant reception in London
in December 1918, and they met again when the Paris Peace Conference
met in January 1919 to draft a treaty to end the war with Germany.

Borden's main concern at the conference was to secure recognition
and hence validation for Canada's role in the war. The dominion had spent
sixty thousand lives and billions of dollars—dollars the Canadian government had not imagined existed in Canada—to secure victory for the
British Empire, and in return Borden demanded a place for Canada at the
conference table in Paris, as well as membership in Woodrow Wilson's
projected League of Nations. The British government was acquiescent:
Lloyd George did see that Canada and the other dominions had made an
essential contribution to keeping the British armies in being, in the last
two years of the war, and he knew that the British Empire was by that
token more powerful, more significant, and more important in world affairs. Ever expedient, always on the alert for a means of smoothing present
difficulties, but perhaps, in this case, with an eye to an uncertain future,
the British prime minister therefore supported the Canadian request for
delegates at the conference.

Now the consent of the senior Allies had to be obtained, and, of the
Allies, only two really mattered. The chair of the peace conference was
French premier Georges Clemenceau, who on being apprised of the pres-
ence of the dominions, cheerily told Lloyd George to bring on his "sav-
ages."[38] The Japanese and Italians did not raise objections, which left the
Americans. Wilson had not been thinking of the dominions when he came

to Paris. As the leader of the most powerful nation at the conference, he had many other things on his mind—principally the creation of a league of nations that would avoid war by enforcing peace. But first there had to be a peace, and the terms of peace were bought and sold over and over again in Paris over the first six months of 1919. As for the dominions, and Canada, after a puzzled discussion with his confidant, Colonel House, Wilson agreed that the dominions could be autonomously represented at the conference. He knew that this was not without risk back in the United States, where it could be misrepresented as conceding the over-representation of Great Britain and the British Empire, but Wilson knew, as did Lloyd George and even Borden, that giving Canada separate delegates at Paris had no functional importance. If Borden wanted the symbolism, he could have it.

At Paris the Canadian delegates were part of the British mission, headed by Lloyd George. Canadians were assigned to conference committees as representing Great Britain or the British Empire, and they received their instructions from the continuation of the Imperial War Cabinet, relabeled in Paris as "the British Empire Delegation." As such they had some significance or importance and became a factor in some of the more intractable issues before the conference, such as an affirmation of racial equality to be embodied in the treaty and in the founding document, the Covenant, of the League of Nations (important, for opposite reasons, to the Japanese and the Australians). Apart from peace with Germany, the conference's main business was Wilson's League of Peace or, as it became known, the League of Nations. On that subject, Borden differed with Wilson on two fundamental points. A league of many nations of differing histories and cultures, Borden feared, was impractical. What he wanted was what Taft wanted and Roosevelt might have accepted, a league that would bind together the English-speaking peoples, the British Empire and the United States. Cultural compatibility, in Borden's view, was the foundation of peace, and because of the combined power of the British Empire and the United States, they would actually have the ability to impose their will on a quarrelsome and untrustworthy world.[39]

Such a restricted league was no more practicable in terms of American politics than Wilson's all-encompassing League of Nations. American nationalism combined with Irish-American nationalism and German-American nationalism would have united to suffocate any such privileged scheme—to snuff out what would have been a "special relationship" on steroids. It should not be forgotten that in 1919 Ireland was in a state of rebellion against the British—a guarantee that (Catholic) Irish-American opinion in the United States would have been strongly and negatively engaged against any special bilateral deal.

The Great War of 1914–1918, eventually renamed the First World War, was the first time that Canada and the United States fought on the same side in a real war. Actual contact was limited. Economic co-operation was probably the most significant aspect of the joint war effort; in France, the American and Canadian troops were in very different parts of the front, and had few common experiences. Only in Russia did Canadian and American troops serve together—in a "cold war" in Siberia, where little fighting was done, and in a very hot war in northern Russia, around Murmansk. Canadian and American soldiers celebrated Christmas 1918 fighting off Bolshevik attacks—real Bolsheviks this time, and not just figments of Borden's imagination. It was a harbinger of contacts to come.

## *The Linchpin that Failed*

Having survived the war, the Anglo-world had to deal with the peace. Woodrow Wilson's League of Nations should have been enough to bring the British Empire and the United States together, and, had it done so, it is quite possible that the Empire and the republic (and Canada) might have discovered and developed real habits of co-operation. But the League succumbed to a case of constitutional deadlock in the United States, in part because the League of Nations was to count Canada, Australia, New Zealand, South Africa, and India as full voting members. By the arithmetic of suspicious nationalists in the US Senate, that gave Great Britain six votes to the United States's one. The real sum was probably two, because India was not self-governing and on foreign policy matters was subject to British authority: but six was more outrageous in stimulating negative American opinion than two.

Wilson had a stroke while trying to persuade his fellow citizens not to abandon the League that their president had created, but his efforts were unavailing. The wreckage of the League passed from the American political scene along with the wreckage of Wilson, and a new Republican administration took power under Warren G. Harding, a senator from Ohio, in 1921. The Republicans had not only the presidency, but also a majority in both houses of Congress, which they used to jack up the American protective tariff. This Congress periodically did, treating the tariff as just another piece of domestic legislation, and the result can be seen in Canadian–American trade figures, where the sharpest dips in Canadian exports south of the border are usually associated with a new American tariff—always higher.

Borden, like Wilson, ended the war exhausted. Like Wilson, he spent the summer of 1919 preparing to get the Treaty of Versailles and with it the League of Nations ratified—Wilson by the US Senate, Borden by the Canadian Parliament. Unlike Wilson, he knew he could do it—he had a solid parliamentary majority, and that was enough. But just as Parliament met, Borden suffered a nervous breakdown. Instead of presiding over Canada's postwar government, he cruised around the West Indies on a British battle-ship, ostensibly studying naval defense for the future, while hoping to re-cover his health and his nerves. But it was not to be: Borden decided he did not want to be in active politics any longer, and in July 1920 he retired. Having retired, Borden speedily recovered his health and passed from one imperial assignment to another. Appropriately, he became a director of the British Barclay's Bank and ended up embodying Canada's imperial eco-nomic connection as well as its imperial political linkages.

During the war, Borden had given thought to Canada's present and fu-ture linkages. The United States loomed large in his mind, but mainly because it was big, it was rich, it was English-speaking, and it was there. Moreover, Great Britain, as Borden knew very well from his wartime expe-rience, was not as rich as it once had been, nor as powerful. Strengthening the Empire, in Borden's view, meant securing and keeping American friendship and co-operation. It was not a choice between the Empire and the United States, or putting one before the other. If pressed, Borden would certainly have identified himself as British, but it was obvious to him that he would remain British with a great deal more certainty if Great Britain were closely linked to the United States.

The question of Anglo-American relations arose during the brief ad-ministration of Borden's Conservative successor as prime minister, Arthur Meighen. Meighen, like Borden, saw himself as a British stalwart. But even as a senior cabinet minister in Borden's government, he had had lit-tle to do with external affairs or imperial matters. The Empire to Meighen was a happy abstraction, but, like Borden, he could see well enough that the United States was richer and more powerful than Great Britain and that it was populated by people whose basic view of the world, of politics, morality, even daily events, closely resembled the views held by Canadians and, for that matter, Britons from the British Isles.

Great Britain, as part of its rivalry with Germany before 1914, had signed an alliance with the Japanese empire. The alliance had come in handy during the Great War, because Japan promptly declared war on Germany and scooped up German colonies and shipping around the Pacific. Not everything about the Japanese alliance was positive, because the Japanese used the war as an occasion to bully concessions out of China—the beginning of thirty years of aggression and war against their neighbor. The Americans, the other naval power in the Pacific, accepted the situation as long as Germany was a factor, and for the duration of the war. But when, in 1921, it became known that the British government wished to extend the alliance, prolonging it for another term, it was not clear against whom the pact was directed, or what military purpose it served.

Meighen and his foreign policy adviser Loring Christie picked up the evident signs of American uneasiness. Christie, a graduate of Harvard Law School and, though a Canadian, a one-time appointee in the Taft administration, was very well connected in Washington, and what he learned there made him very uneasy. The Republican victory of 1920 had been a vote against Woodrow Wilson's too interventionist, too co-operative foreign policy, but it was also a victory for a more self-regarding and self-contained American nationalism. A Japanese alliance with Great Britain would not be, could not be, tolerated.

British justifications for dealing softly with Japan were not entirely irrational. Japan had been a (mostly) good ally and should not be insulted. Who knew what might happen if the Japanese were allowed to drift away, isolated and aggrieved? Japan had a large navy and was a Pacific power. Australia and New Zealand, big British islands, were closer to Japan than to Great Britain. Britain had large and valuable commercial interests in China and had important investments in its colonies in Southeast Asia. The British were not as rich as they had been and needed to pay off the war, yet worsening relations with Japan might force Great Britain to spend more money, not less, building up the defenses of the British Empire in Asia. What would the United States do to protect that empire, and especially vulnerable and under-populated Australia and New Zealand? In imperial terms, having good and privileged relations with Japan made eminent sense.

Lloyd George, still prime minister, faced a contradiction and resolved it in favor of Australia, New Zealand—and Japan. At an Imperial Conference in London in June 1921 he impatiently heard out Meighen's arguments for keeping on good terms with the United States as the Empire's primary foreign policy goal. And he heard out, too, Meighen's conclusion, which Borden would have echoed, that Canada, sitting as it was next door to the United States, could not afford to be on bad terms with its giant neighbor.

There was no reason to be on bad terms, as long as the Anglo-Japanese alliance was abrogated. But if it were not, relations with the Americans would take a turn for the worse and, under the circumstances, Canada would not be bound by the Japanese alliance. Lloyd George disbelieved that argument too and said so. Let Meighen go, he later told his mistress, who recorded it in her diary as another example of Lloyd George's genius.

Lloyd George was not a fool. He had based his rejection of Meighen and Canada on the best advice the Washington embassy could supply. In a reversal of custom and experience, the embassy was far worse-informed than the Canadians, and only belatedly did the ambassador realize that he had been feeding sunny claptrap back to London. He changed his opinion and his advice, and urged the prime minister to do the same. Suddenly the law officers of the Crown discovered legal difficulties in renewing the Anglo-Japanese alliance. Lloyd George made a heartfelt speech on the sanctity of treaties and the new order of international law, including the League of Nations that was dawning. The Americans wanted to have a conference, and a conference there must be.

This was apparently a happy outcome. But the process rather than the conclusion is of greater interest. Lloyd George had been confronted with the contradictions in the British Empire's strategic position—the interests of some dominions against the interests of one. He had chosen to favor Australia and New Zealand and to take the risk that Canada would effectively secede from the Empire on a very important foreign policy issue and publicly align itself with the United States. Lloyd George was forced, finally, to make a choice between unpleasant and very real alternatives, and he made it in the style of the Anglo-world, the harmony of English-speaking peoples, even though the world was divided against itself.

The promised conference met in Washington in November 1921, and Sir Robert Borden was one of the British delegates. (It thus became one of the many, many Washington conferences.) The conferees agreed on a new regime of peace in the Pacific, agreed to reduce their naval armaments, and agreed that they had no serious differences among themselves—as, in all probability, they did not at that moment. Everybody was short of money; navies were expensive; and the Washington naval treaty became one of the few genuinely effective disarmament agreements. It would last ten years and a bit.

Meighen was not in his office to receive the news that he had been right and that the Washington conference had been a success. He had taken his government to the polls in early December 1921 and had been thoroughly drubbed. Incredulous, the prime minister sat at his desk for several weeks until one of his staff told him it was time to go. Meighen reluctantly departed, and his successor, the Liberal William Lyon Mackenzie King, duly took his place, just in time to celebrate the New Year of 1922. Part of Meighen's reluctance to leave had been his disbelief that someone like Mackenzie King—whom he had known since they were undergraduates at the University of Toronto—could possibly beat him. Meighen was a man of principles—too many principles, and the wrong ones, most Canadians believed. Mackenzie King was a man of different principles—and a different, softer, way of applying them. But what were those principles? Canadians had voted for anyone but Meighen, but what had they voted for? It would end badly, Meighen murmured to himself.

\* \* \* \*

Between 1911 and 1921 Canadian–American relations were tested by the aftermath of the 1911 election, and by the First World War. Both Canada and the United States approached those relations in the context of the British Empire. Domestically and abroad, Canadians were too closely connected to Great Britain—to British interests, British culture, and the British political system—to contemplate a world in which they were not British. The Americans were slowly coming to treat Canada as more than lunchmeat on their political plate. Theodore Roosevelt, who actually paid attention to the issue, unlike Woodrow Wilson, made the transition via Canada's heroic and worthy war record, which to his mind and undoubtedly the mind of many others, showed that Canada had earned the right to be treated as a separate entity, with a future that was close to, but in the short and medium term separate from, that of the United States. As for the longer term, who knew? The forces of harmony would have to do their work and notify the politicians of a future generation of the result.

Positively, that meant that officials in Washington, and in the US consulate in Ottawa, were coming to grips with the phenomenon of Canadian nationalism. Negatively, it meant that Congress could cheerfully pass the Fordney–McCumber tariff of 1921 that raised duties on Canadian imports and, one more time, diverted the channels of American trade. But with the war over, with normalcy—Harding's word—prevailing, and with peace on the indefinite horizon, that was probably as much as could be expected.

# 8

## The Great Thaw, 1921–1939

WHEN, IN 1927, Canada and the United States established permanent diplomatic missions in their respective capitals, the Americans placed theirs in a new and impressive building on Ottawa's Wellington Street, facing the Canadian Parliament buildings under a canopy of dignified elms. The Americans sent a senior professional diplomat to Canada, William Phillips, previously the ambassador to Belgium and before that under-secretary of state. In diplomatic protocol, Phillips took a technical demotion in rank by moving to Ottawa, for Canada rated only a "minister," who headed a "legation" rather than an embassy. Phillips's appointment was a sign that the United States government, at least, took Canada seriously. The Americans put up a brass plaque reading "American Legation" on their new building and waited for signs of local interest.

The interest was not long in coming, but it was not quite what the diplomats had expected. A local newspaper took up the name of the new building. Canadians were Americans too, the editorialist argued. Geographically, he had a point—there were plenty of Americans and plenty of American countries outside the United States. But the real point was cultural and historical: Canadians were Americans too, even if not republicans, or citizens of the United States. Americans had been, could still be, monarchists. The plaque was hastily taken down, and a new one—Legation of the United States of America—replaced it.

Canada reciprocated with its own legation in Washington and appointed the well-born and well-placed Vincent Massey to head it. Massey was also well educated, and had been a businessman who was, unusually, also a Liberal; he had served briefly in Prime Minister William Lyon Mackenzie King's cabinet. Of at least equal importance, he was rich and could supplement government entertainment allowances from his own funds. He was also an anglophile, which as we have seen was a quality he shared with many northeastern Americans of the kind he was likely to meet in Washington. (To be sure, Washington also boasted non-anglophile, midwestern or prairie

Americans who were definitely not Massey's type.) Massey chose a building on "embassy row," on Massachusetts Avenue, close enough to downtown, the State Department, and the men's clubs where so much of the American capital's business was transacted. The Department of External Affairs' under-secretary, Dr. O.D. Skelton, sent a sprinkling of fledgling professionals to serve under Massey: they included Lester B. Pearson and Hume Wrong, who like Massey had been educated at the University of Toronto and at Oxford and counted among Canada's small educated elite.[1]

Massey, Wrong, and Pearson had more in common with their American counterparts than cultural formation. Wrong and Pearson as well had less in common where genuine anglophiles were concerned: Wrong had been through the First World War and had returned with a skeptical approach to the British Empire, a point of view that Pearson, another veteran, generally shared. The Canadian legation's objective was to do more than simply represent the Canadian government on the thousand-and-one border minutiae that had overburdened the British embassy. Like the British diplomats they were supplanting, the young Canadians in Washington were professionals, for Dr. Skelton had modeled their fledgling service mainly on the American Foreign Service, though with a nod to the British too. This gave them something in common with other diplomats—very much including their American counterparts. The Canadian envoys also had to project a Canadian identity in Washington and beyond: one distinct from but not hostile to Great Britain, and distinct from but also friendly to the United States.

Today we describe the twenty years after the Great War as the "interwar" period, an interlude broken down into two very distinct decades: the 1920s, an extravagant period characterized by frantic expansion and construction, growing prosperity with a rising standard of living, and a general loosening of the cultural controls that had bound up Victorian and Edwardian society; and the 1930s, a grim and impoverished ten-year ordeal that ground inexorably toward a disastrous denouement in the outbreak of the Second World War in 1939. The 1920s are sometimes described as the first modern decade, and, in terms of rising incomes and the appearance of a mass consumer society, that is true. Women had the vote, almost universally, except in Quebec, France, and Switzerland, and were considered "emancipated," which in some respects was true; the higher the class or the income, the more likely it was to be true. (Income differentials between rich and poor in the 1920s were extreme, and would not be matched until the 2000s.) Yet the lifestyle of the rich and famous did not indicate much more than a distant glamour; if Canadians truly wanted and could afford to experience the true high life, they did what their mothers and fathers had done, and went to London or New York or even Paris. Some moved there permanently.

Yet the foundations of society had not shifted as much as people believed at the time or recollected afterward. Churches and religion, for example, were strong, vital, and growing. There might be skeptics with access to publicity, but they were, as always, a minority, and probably not much different from the "village atheist" of rural folklore in the nineteenth century. The canons of respectability were more complicated than before but were enforced with stringency and a sharpness that would surprise later generations. The politics of the 1920s were conservative, if you were lucky, or anachronistic if you were not, as Canada, the United States, and the British Isles strove to recover a certainty and predictability in their respective identities, and the politics that reflected the identities.

"I . . . enthusiastically imbibed Canadian (read *English, Protestant*) patriotism at school in Toronto," in the 1920s, the historian William H. McNeill later wrote,[2] and the same would have been true in any English-speaking school across the dominion of Canada. Canada was British, by right of conquest, certainly (which disposed of the French Canadians), but also by the superiority and continuity of British institutions. Arguably—and it certainly was argued—Canada's British identity was confirmed, not undermined, by the achievements of the Great War, like the Canadian victory at Vimy Ridge in 1917. The war was Canadian, but it was also and inescapably imperial. Thus, when the Vimy Ridge monument was inaugurated in 1936, the occasion was presided by the empire's highest authority, King Edward VIII, while Canadian politicians—Liberals, and members of Mackenzie King's cabinet—stood respectfully by. They all knew—even the Catholics and French Canadians among them—that Canada was "English, Protestant," in McNeill's words. Mackenzie King, who did not attend the Vimy ceremony, understood that English, Protestant Canadians were very much British. King's practice of politics reflected that fact—even as he also bore in mind that for French Canadians this was an unpalatable if inescapable fact.[3]

Retrospectively, the 1920s do not seem to have been a time of Anglo-American mistrust and disharmony, but at the time relations were not especially comfortable. At American insistence, the British had abandoned the Anglo-Japanese alliance in 1921: the episode was an unpleasant reminder that the United States was economically superior to Great Britain and had threatened to outbuild the Royal Navy if the alliance was not abandoned. The British swallowed the humiliation of shaping their foreign policy to meet American demands, but it was not easy. Worse still was the recognition that Britain's standing as the world's number-one naval power depended on American sufferance, a point that the United States used to insist on British concessions in subsequent naval negotiations. There was also continuing dissonance over war debts, owing from Great Britain to the United States for the prosecution of the First World War. From the American point of view, Britain and other European debtors were simply deadbeats, and it was politically advantageous in the United States to stress the fact. American carping was greatly resented in Britain and elsewhere, as the British and other Europeans struggled to emerge from the financial hole into which the war had plunged them.

Consequently, during the 1920s, Anglo-American relations on the political level passed from the unhappy to the acerbic and back again. British military staffs toyed, half-seriously, with the possibilities and consequences of a war with the United States. (Their studies were admittedly rather discouraging.) The chancellor of the exchequer, Winston Churchill, fulminated, "It always seems to be assumed that it is our duty to humour the United States and minister to their vanity."[4] While some pundits still trumpeted the notion of Anglo-Saxon solidarity, they were matched and perhaps outweighed by critics of American policy, or critics of the United States *tout court*. The Americans, it should be said, were not especially careful to avoid provoking the British. Duly provoked at a naval disarmament conference, the British foreign secretary even called the head of the American delegation a "dirty dog," which must be a high-water mark in official vituperation.[5] Although Canadians have, and have had, a sometimes deserved reputation for anti-Americanism, it can pale beside the sentiments of other countries. Such was the case in the 1920s.

A young Canadian studying in England drew a contrast between the views he heard there and those he had experienced at home in Tory Toronto. In Toronto, anti-Americanism was formulaic and almost quaint, a ritual like complaining about the weather. "When I went to England in 1927," Charles Stacey wrote, "I encountered real anti-Americanism, with nothing funny about it....One met bitterness and resentment on every side....[To] my utter amazement [,] I found myself defending the Americans."[6] Many would have agreed with him, including the British foreign secretary, who in August 1927 wrote, "English opinion about America is more sore than I have ever known it," but even so, "the thought of war does not enter into anyone's calculations."[7]

In terms of power politics, Canadians could not afford the luxury of anti-Americanism—or, at least, their government couldn't. Nor, ultimately, could the British government. The proposition of an Anglo-American war was "a crime," in the foreign secretary's opinion in 1927. That was true in general, and it was especially true if Canada was brought into the equation. Canada served as a control on British behavior, as the British ambassador to the United States explained, confidentially, to his superior, the foreign secretary: "A war between the British Empire and the United States is, I believe, physically impossible." Impossible for the British, he meant, since there was no way the British army could arrive on the Canadian frontier before the Americans overran it. The US Navy had the strength to blockade Canada's east and west coasts, negating even the faint hope that imperial reinforcements could arrive in time, or arrive at all. The Americans obviously would have a much easier time of it. Canada's three-thousand-mile frontier was "utterly indefended [sic] and indefendable [sic]." Canada would have no choice but neutrality, the other dominions might follow Canada's lead, and the British Empire would collapse.[8]

Nevertheless, anti-Americanism seemed to contemporary observers to be a dominant fact in Canada too. Prime Minister Mackenzie King noted the phenomenon in his diary in 1929, along with anti-Catholicism and anti-French sentiment, as real political dangers to his government and to his Liberal party.[9] While King's perceptions of peril were often exaggerated, there was always a kernel of realism in his analysis.

American tariff policy continually added fuel to smoldering Canadian resentments: a savage emergency tariff passed Congress in 1921, followed by the Fordney–McCumber tariff of 1922, passed just as soon as the Republican majority were able to manage it; it jacked up tariffs to protect the American market and American jobs, in response to the economic depression of 1920–1. The new Republican president, Warren Harding, happily signed the tariff act. A particular target of the emergency tariff was foreign agricultural imports, largely from Canada. Fordney–McCumber repeated the same formula across the board; it conformed to Republican economic doctrine and, better still, was popular at home. Most consumers then as now were unable to recognize what was raising their prices and so, like the farmers, were politically neutered, while foreigners who might be affected did not vote—a classic recipe for political success. (The farm vote—for farmers were consumers too—was defused by sky-high tariffs on such items as imported wheat, which virtually destroyed the market for the Canadian product in the United States and enhanced the sales of the domestic variety.) The foreigners eventually retaliated, raising their own tariffs and cutting off American exports. Canadian trade with the United States was clearly adversely affected, with both imports and exports falling. Exports to the United States fell noticeably, and for the whole of the 1920s did not recover to 1921 levels; with the Great Depression they fell again, much more sharply, and only in 1941 did their dollar value return to the level of 1921.[10] Imports to Canada from the United States also suffered, but a decline in American exports was not enough to sway Congress from its assigned task of protecting American special interests.

Not all transborder contacts were matters of trade. The growth of an automobile industry centered on Detroit, and the availability of affordable transport produced a demand for roads leading to the border, and tunnels and bridges crossing it. A Peace Bridge, inaugurated by the Prince of Wales in 1927, crossed the Niagara River from Fort Erie to Buffalo,[11] and an Ambassador Bridge did the same for Detroit and Windsor. Tourists flowed across the bridges in both directions, contributing to a significant American summer presence in cooler Canada, in those days before widespread air-conditioning.

If tourist traffic was bi-directional, other human traffic moved in one direction only, south. Here the auto industry was also a factor, since large American factories required large numbers of workers, and to get them Henry Ford and other industrialists offered decent pay. Southwestern Ontario helped supply the autoworkers, who, as John Kenneth Galbraith, who came from the area, reported, "were profound admirers of Henry Ford."[12] The Maritime provinces similarly supplied New England. French-speaking Quebecers were not immune and had been flowing south for generations: the 1920s gave a final fillip to the descent of French speakers into New England, bearing identifiably Quebec names unpronounceable to their descendants. The numbers were significant, especially when put in the context of the numbers of French Canadians remaining in Canada. All told, 320,000 French Canadians immigrated to the United States between 1900 and 1930; in the Canadian census of 1931, French Canadians numbered 2.8 million, in a total Canadian population of 10.4 million. Their presence or absence would not have made much difference to the proportion of French speakers in Canada, however, given the very large numbers of English speakers who had also taken the road or the railway south to higher wages and greater opportunity.[13]

Canada lost more than would-be industrial workers. The kinds of opportunities Canada afforded were not enough to keep ambitious young people at home. There were only so many professional posts, so many executive jobs, or so many university professorships—meaning so few. There were so many more of these right next door. According to a 1927 survey—the art of the survey was just beginning—13 percent of the living graduates of eight Canadian universities had gone south. It was the obvious lure of a country right next door where the standard of living was at least 25 percent higher than in Canada—to say the least. An émigré Canadian doctor in Detroit explained, "In five years' time [since leaving Canada] I am making more than the eminent practitioners in Toronto, men who have been there twenty-five years or more."[14]

At certain levels, the standard of living was more than 25 percent higher. Very rich Canadians did not compare to very rich Americans or Britons. The summit of luxury and extravagance and culture could only be achieved in New York and London—real opera, a symphony orchestra, flashy night-clubs, the mansions of Newport or the townhouses of Fifth Avenue, or Mayfair or Belgravia. Traveling Canadians—by definition, those who could afford to pay for ocean voyages, or railway trips, or fashionable hotels—not surprisingly kept discovering the need for more travel.

There was also American investment, circumventing the Canadian tariff wall to find a safe haven in the dominion. As far as investment was concerned, the 1920s were an expansive decade. Money poured into pulp and paper mills, so as to feed American newspapers, and into minerals, so as to supply American factories. To be fair, much of the inflow of money passed into the mysterious realms of speculation, justifying the definition of a Canadian mine as "a hole in the ground with a liar on top." The Toronto stock exchange had a particularly bad reputation among investors, but in the 1920s, with so much money available, losing money there almost seemed like the price of doing business. Not every investor was happy: the collapse of the Grand Trunk and Canadian Northern railways showed that even apparently solid imperial enterprises were no more than speculation. Partly as a result of the devaluation of British investment in the Grand Trunk fiasco, American investment in Canada surpassed British investment in the early 1920s.[15] In manufacturing sectors like automobiles, American ownership was just about complete, while in other areas, like mining, it grew steadily more significant.

Not only was American business competitive with British investors in Canada in the 1920s; for the first time the American government had entered the lists, with the opening of its legation in Ottawa. This was a logical consequence of the devolution of British authority to the self-governing "dominions," and of the unwillingness of the British government to cope with the strain of a common Imperial foreign policy; it followed that the various parts of the Empire would do what they considered best on matters that directly affected them. All was for the best in the best of all possible worlds, imperial rhetoric proclaimed.

Some historians, using the insight provided by hindsight, have taken the sugary official pronouncements of the 1920s at less than face value, as words designed to conceal a dwindling reality. It was true that with the dominions placed ornamentally to the side, Great Britain could pursue an active policy in Europe in the later 1920s and sign treaties with no thought that they would bind the dominions, or ever need to. Yet, as the historian John Darwin later pointed out, there turned out to be considerable force behind the words, as the 1930s would show. It was admittedly based on an intangible, what John Darwin called "the cultural and racial sympathy that was supposed to exist between Britain and the dominions and which derived from the 'British' character of their populations." Great Britain continued to be important to Canada, and when the final crisis arrived in the summer of 1939, the rhetorical assumptions made in 1926 turned out to be reality, and not fancy.[16]

Devolution was also in some respects a recognition that British power was no longer what it once had been, a painful fact. The governor general, Lord Willingdon, was profoundly disturbed. He urged the British government to establish its own very prominent Ottawa mission—a big high commission with a prominent public figure at its head; it had to be called a high commission rather than a legation, because Great Britain and Canada were not "foreign" to one another. On consideration, the British government opted for a more modest office in Canada, reasoning that the United States was bigger, richer, and closer, and that attempts to counter these factors would be both expensive and futile.[17]

The American diplomatic approach to Canada was cautious and diffident—wisely, as it turned out. The American consul general in Ottawa, John G. Foster, had stayed at his post for a remarkable twenty-four years, from 1903 to 1927; he had watched the Canadian general election of 1911, with its anti-American theme, with a horrified fascination. Canadian nationalism, Foster concluded, was not something to be trifled with. Fortunately the worst anti-American rhetoric had passed unnoticed south of the border, so there was no real danger of awakening American nationalism in response to the Canadian variety; the main task was to keep 1911 from ever happening again. Foster had been appointed in the old-fashioned way, through politics, but by the 1920s the Americans were developing a professional foreign service, and in 1925 a young Texan foreign service officer, John (Jack) Hickerson, was sent to frigid Ottawa directly from his previous post, at Pará in the Amazonian jungle.

Over the next several years, Hickerson changed his focus from Latin America to Canada, assisted by Foster's copious fund of Canadian stories and reflections. On one point, Foster convinced Hickerson absolutely: Canada and the United States could, would, and should get along, as long as Canadian nationalism was allowed to slumber undisturbed. The two countries in fact resembled each other and during the 1920s came to resemble each other even more. That was obvious; but it was a fact that should not be unduly emphasized in public. Returning to Washington in 1927, Hickerson exerted himself to ensure that American policy and public utterances did not slop over into overabundant and effusive affection toward Canada—affection of the kind that might suggest to Americans and, worse, to Canadians, that Canada's glorious and inevitable destiny was to join the United States.[18] Hickerson had something else in mind: he was present as Canada's career diplomats were hired and sent out to missions abroad. Professional diplomats, Hickerson understood, had much in common, and as the Canadian foreign service developed, its members discovered that they and their American counterparts enjoyed real common ground. It would be a special relationship, but of a different kind.

In the meantime, Canadians joined Canadian branches of American societies—service clubs like the Lions and Kiwanis—read American Sunday newspapers, read American magazines, watched American movies, and listened to the new medium of American radio. In the larger cities, Canadians could attend touring American vaudeville shows, and some of the next generation of American entertainers spent months at a time in Toronto or Montreal, honing their skills entertaining Canadian audiences.[19] Baseball, not cricket, was Canadians' summer pastime, and football and hockey were also familiar contacts across the border, increasing with the professionalization and commercialization of sports in the 1920s. Canadians' points of cultural reference were increasingly American ones, and when Canadians slipped across the border they were indistinguishable from their American colleagues. In movies, Mack Sennett (born in the Eastern Townships of Quebec) became the "king of comedy," while the actress Mary Pickford, born in Toronto, became "America's Sweetheart," gazing doe-eyed and virginal at American audiences. She reminded Americans of themselves, or at any rate of they would like to be. Many years later, the commentator

Richard Rodriguez reverted several times in his broadcast essays to the image of Mary Pickford, and its attraction for Americans, contrasting it with the smoldering Latina Dolores del Rio, or Pancho Villa, menacing, scowling, and unshaven, symbolizing the unattractive aspects of the United States' other neighbor, Mexico.[20] Anglo-Saxon Wholesomeness was contrasted with Mexican Temptation, or worse—and, in terms of American imagery, much worse.[21]

There were other points of visual convergence. Canadian cities had always resembled their American counterparts, and in the 1920s, as steel-framed buildings pointed up, Toronto and Montreal looked increasingly "American," and definitely not like London or other British cities. Toronto's new premier hotel, the Royal York, laid claim to being the tallest building in the British Empire (with twenty-eight floors), a distinction it held for about a year, and then moved on to be merely the tallest hotel in the Empire, which it remained for many years.[22] It was succeeded as the tallest building in the Empire by Toronto's nearby Bank of Commerce, thirty-four stories, completed in December 1930 and the Empire's tallest building until 1962. These Toronto buildings imported American urban style to the north, reminding onlookers that Canada was, after all, the North American component of the British Empire. But even so, the relative sizes of Canadian and American buildings said something more. The thirty-four stories of the Bank of Commerce were dwarfed by New York's Empire State Building, with its 102 floors, completed a year later, in 1931. (And the Empire State Building was merely the tallest New York skyscraper: where Toronto had only two tall buildings, New York had scores as tall or taller.) The Empire State Building was the tallest building in the world; perhaps the architecture more than anything else indicated the relative standing of Canada with the United States—and not just Canada, but the whole of the British Empire.

Canada in the 1920s and 1930s was simultaneously culturally similar to, dwarfed by, and politically apart from the United States. Canadian and American communities of comparable size had much the same institutions—baseball teams in the summer, public (Protestant) schools, similar churches with similar, socially conscious messages, service clubs, and so forth. Sometimes politics and culture converged, as when "North America" was contrasted with the rest of the world. Canada might be smaller, but it was the same species. English-Canadian nationalism faced in two directions, toward (and sometimes against) the United States, and toward (and also against) Great Britain. The British heritage in Canadian history could reinforce that variant of Canadian nationalism that proclaimed its distinction from the United States, but the American or North American strands reinforced a strong sense of difference from Great Britain.

There was the phenomenon of prohibition. Many Western societies had struggled against the demon rum, and opposition to alcohol and its effects is by no means confined to the West. There were significant anti-liquor movements in Great Britain, as well as in Canada and the United States, but it was in North America that the "Prohibition" of alcohol took its firmest root. In Canada, after an abortive federal plebiscite on the issue under Laurier, it was mainly a provincial matter, and the various provinces either regulated or banned alcoholic consumption as they saw fit. But in the United States a constitutional amendment was passed banning alcohol outright at the end of the First World War, and for the next decade and a half the American government seriously tried to enforce the ban—on manufacturing, sale, and consumption. Virtue and vice contended, and gradually vice undermined virtue. "Temperance" in alcohol reached its apogee in Canada around the end of the Great War; from 1920 onward, the various provinces made one exception after another. Canada had whiskey distilleries conveniently located right on the frontier, and making alcohol was not illegal in Canada even if, in many places, selling it for domestic consumption was strictly forbidden or closely regulated.

Even with the sanctimonious Mackenzie King in power—King was given to lamenting or denouncing liquor and its effects in his diary—Canada would not put Canadian distillers out of business or their Canadian workers on the unemployment lines just to please the United States. Canada made various appeasing gestures toward the Americans from time to time, and American Prohibition officers from time to time violated Canada's sovereignty in pursuit of the gangsters who had taken over the American liquor business. There was drama on the high seas too, when the Americans pursued, fired on, and seized smugglers' ships, and considerable work for international lawyers sorting through the rights and wrongs of national sovereignty as it applied to booze. The problem finally went away in 1933 with a new constitutional amendment in the United States that made liquor in most of its aspects respectably legal again.

The recent experience of the Great War had reinforced Canada's links and ties to Great Britain, but it worked in the opposite direction as well: for some it suggested that too close a British identity, or any British identity at all, could lead to pointless sacrifices in a war of no great interest to Canada. Undoubtedly most English Canadians fell into the first, imperially linked, camp, but, with almost as much certainty, most French Canadians fell into the second. Pro-British and pro-imperial or not, Canadians had discovered between 1914 and 1918 that they could do things together, and that Canada could make a difference in great international events. For many and perhaps most British-Canadians, Canada's main effort should be inside the Empire; but for others, it was time to stand back and show that Canada could stand on its own.

It came as a surprise to many Canadians—even well-informed ones—to discover that Canada qualified to sit on the governing body of the new International Labour Organization, as one of ten nations of "chief industrial importance." Most Canadians thought of their country as small, developing, and dependent; yet it appeared that development had led to economic maturity. Could economic maturity mean political maturity? And if it did, what did that imply for Canada's relations to and with the British Empire and the United States? Was Canada beginning to catch up to the United States in wealth and prosperity? Canada's expanding suburbs, paved roads with Ford cars driving along them, and its electricity networks and new electric home appliances brought Canada's style of life closer to the American.

All the more reason, then, for Canada to maintain its British links—political differences and distinct national symbols, including and perhaps especially the monarchy, were all that stood between Canada and absorption into the United States. So reasoned many British-Canadians, and so thought the prime minister, William Lyon Mackenzie King. But if Canada did not want a common political destiny in or inside the United States, Canadians definitely saw their proximity to the United States as an advantage and, up to a point, it reinforced their "North American" separate identity too.

Perhaps the most prominent "North American" in Ottawa was Mackenzie King's deputy minister, or under-secretary, in the external affairs department. Dr. O.D. Skelton was a political economist by training, and a historian and biographer by trade, and also a professor and dean of arts at Queen's University. He was a Liberal, a liberal, and a nationalist. He considered that Canada's recent experience in the Great War should not be repeated, and could not be repeated, without risking the foundations of the Canadian state by provoking disunity between English and French Canadians. The danger of war meant that Skelton viewed the British connection with alarm, and in doing so he contrasted the Anglo-Canadian relationship with the link to the United States. The United States was an admirable and desirable neighbor, in Skelton's opinion, and above all it did not threaten to draw Canada into another, fatal, war.[23] North America enjoyed the fruits of what political scientists would later call "the democratic peace"; to Skelton and others at the time, Britain should look to the peaceful Canadian–American continent as a model for their own relations, but, Skelton thought, they would not do so. Better for Canada, therefore, to accept a North American destiny. In so reasoning, Skelton accepted a Canadian variant of American exceptionalism, and, as a consequence, North American isolationism.

Senator Raoul Dandurand, a member of the Mackenzie King cabinet and Canada's almost perpetual delegate to the League of Nations in Geneva, expressed this point of view when he told the League assembly in 1924 that "we live in a fire-proof house, far from inflammable materials." "We" were Canadians, the fire-proof house was North America, and the inflammable materials were Europe, with, regrettbly, Great Britain inextricably linked by geography to its pyromaniac European neighbors.[24]

Dandurand did not pause to consider which room in the fire-proof house Canada occupied. He might, on reflection, have identified Canada's living space as America's attic, cold in winter, warmer and recreational in summer, but most of the time functional and forgotten. This was nothing new: American attention to Canada since the 1830s had been sporadic. As a nineteenth-century French savant observed, history sometimes consists of forgetting as well as remembering, and by the 1920s American historical consciousness had definitely forgotten most of the historical facts about Canada. Occasionally the Americans thought about altering the framework, as with the question of deepening the St. Lawrence River canals (the so-called St. Lawrence Seaway) to allow ocean-going ships to reach the Great Lakes. This was a case where the Americans were interested in and eager for progress. That was a bad sign, Mackenzie King decided. He remembered 1911, when the Americans had shown similar enthusiasm, and in discussions with the American government the prime minister urged caution and restraint. In fact, while King probably would have preferred total silence, he opted for inaction as equally effective.

It was a sign that the prime minister too was aware of sleeping political dogs—imperial or nationalist, or both, they were the enemies of stable Canadian–American relations. King may have been over-cautious, and in punting the seaway he passed over various American blandishments; but, admittedly, they may not have been very seriously meant. In any case, the various parts of the American government had their own priorities, and for the Republican majorities in Congress what was most important, in 1928–9, was another rise in the US tariff. That, King told the American minister in Ottawa, might make progress on canal reconstruction—the Seaway—difficult, and his words were duly reported to President Herbert Hoover. Hoover seems to have taken King at his word and hinted back to Ottawa that perhaps canals and tariffs could be linked, which seems to have alarmed King even more. It is in any case doubtful that Hoover could have traded lower tariffs for the Seaway project without bringing up, one more time, a larger, stronger, and politically unsalable linkage—which could be the beginnings of a special relationship between Canada and the United States. King knew, or thought he knew, where *that* would lead.[25] He would not court defeat by indulging in a special deal that would enhance relations with the United States at a time when links with Great Britain seemed in need of resuscitation. He need not have worried.

## *Parallel Depressions*

The Republicans overwhelmingly won the general election of 1928, emerging with a 100-seat majority in the House of Representatives, a twenty-seat spread in the Senate, and the presidency, won by Herbert Hoover. The new majority immediately set to work on crafting the legendary tariff of 1930, known because of its legislative sponsors as the Smoot–Hawley tariff. The legislation took more than a year to get through the complicated American legislative system, even though majorities in the House and Senate agreed on its basic principle, to send import duties ever higher, while Hoover had campaigned in particular on raising taxes on agricultural imports. No foreign protests would have mitigated the provisions of the Smoot–Hawley tariff; it is fair to say that any such foreign protests were completely disregarded, as were those of the industrialist Henry Ford and the banker Thomas Lamont, the head of the J.P. Morgan firm—not to mention a loud protesting squeak from more than a thousand academic economists. The economists were right, and the American political consensus was wrong, but that inconvenient fact would be noticed only some years later, when it was too late.

There had been no formal complaint from Canada: "A diplomatic protest," one official advised the government, "might serve merely to prove to United States legislators that in raising certain duties they are on the right track." In Canada, Mackenzie King knew that he had to do something, and in the spring of 1930 he had Parliament enact retaliatory duties: Canadian tariffs on American goods would rise in proportion to the new American tariffs, when they were passed (as they would be) and took effect.[26] The new Canadian duties covered 30 percent of American exports to Canada by value—a significant measure. Canada was therefore early in the field with retaliation, and, it was observed, Canada was the United States' biggest trading partner. Other countries followed—enough of them to be noticed—and, as sanctions mounted and trade shrank, some Americans began to discern a cycle of cause and effect. As two later commentators observed, "The United States obviously did not expect such heavy retaliation, but it was sharp and rapid."[27] And it was apparently effective, for American trade fell farther, faster, than any other country's.

Drastic as the immediate effects were, what was more important was the creation of the "lessons of history." The Smoot–Hawley tariff stuck in the public consciousness, because it associated easily and immediately with the worsening conditions of 1931, 1932, and 1933. If the Depression was awful, and never to be repeated, so was Smoot–Hawley a great mistake that must never be repeated. The last milestone on the protectionist road that led to the dead-end of the Depression, Smoot–Hawley was also the first monument on the new policy highway of trade liberalization, the economists' new yellow-brick road that would eventually lead to the emerald city of "globalization."

There was much mileage to cover before even moderate tariff reduction was reached. A Canadian election was close at hand by the time King passed his tariff retaliation in the spring of 1930, and it was duly held at the end of July 1930. King evidently thought he would win and was greatly surprised, and irritated, when he did not. In this period he communicated regularly, or so he thought, with the spirit world and received appropriate comfort and guidance from the dead, but this time his spiritualist beliefs failed to console him. The spirits had evidently not kept track of the economic decline, which by the summer of 1930 was generally labeled as a "depression." Things could have been worse, and they would be. King should have seen the hand of providence in the election results, for they meant that the leader of the Conservative party, R.B. Bennett, would be in power for the next five years—the worst years of the worst economic depression Canada and the world had ever seen.

Bennett was doubly unfortunate. Not only had he achieved power, he had done so by making a great many promises about the happy future of Canada and its economy under his wise guidance. There was no doubt that Bennett was a highly intelligent and capable man, but there was nothing in his education or experience that could have prepared him for what was already slowly beginning to happen. He had promised to blast a way into the markets of the world, but by the good old reliable means of raising Canada's tariffs so that other countries would be pressured to reduce theirs. This nostrum turned out not to work, under the circumstances; perhaps it would not have worked under any circumstances. Canada, as Bennett later pointed out in another context, was a country of only 11.5 million people, less than a tenth the size of the American population, with an economy that was on a good day merely a twelfth of its neighbor's.

He did not add that the causes of the Depression went beyond tariffs, and even beyond national boundaries and the power of elected governments to solve. There was, for example, over-supply, guaranteed to drive down international markets. In this case, world trade began to sag in 1929. Commodity prices softened and continued on down. Wheat, the chief Western Canadian product, was hard hit, but so were pulp and paper, minerals, and other Canadian staples. Canada had placed too many of its economic eggs in one basket. This phenomenon was unforeseen, at any rate by Bennett, but because he had phrased his election promises in colorful and memorable language, his words were remembered and duly held against him.

During the 1930s Canada and the United States continued on parallel tracks, as far as misfortune was concerned. Economists now recognize that the Depression occurred in two phases: a general decline that started in 1929 and lasted into 1931, when a banking crisis undermined confidence in international exchanges and the banking system. This combination of crises affected Canada, the United States, and Germany most severely. Canada's gross domestic product fell by 49 percent, the United States' by 53 percent. Canadians could easily associate their own experience with American images of breadlines, hoboes, and street beggars—the "forgotten men"[28] featured in American movies resonated across the border. So did pictures of the "Dust Bowl." The over-optimistic colonization of the North American prairie lasted only as long as there was rain to support it. When the rains stopped, in the early 1930s, drought and dust storms drove thousands from the land, north and south of the forty-ninth parallel, leaving, as the novelist Wallace Stegner put it, " a dehumanized waste," where once his family farm had been.[29] In both Canada and the United States, government policy ratified what nature had done. Farms were depopulated, groundcover was replanted, and the land was allowed to return to its natural, grassy, arid state—undisturbed in some areas until the arrival of oil extraction—"fracking"—in the twenty-first century. But that is a consideration for a later chapter.

The experience of the Depression is a textbook example of the transmission of American political ideas, policies, and events to Canada—and the limits of that transmission. There was, to begin with, the parallel of the election of protectionist Republicans to the presidency and Congress in 1928, and the election of a protectionist Conservative government in Canada in 1930—in both cases with a substantial majority and triumphalist expectations. In both cases the expectations were shattered as unemployment rose, poverty increased, and the respective economies plummeted, reaching their lowest point around the end of 1932 or the beginning of 1933. In the United States, as in Canada and elsewhere, the Depression spawned a full range of political activity, reinforcing communism at one end of the political spectrum, but also lending strength to various forms of right-wing populism. The Americans produced among others Huey Long, the rabidly populist governor and senator from Louisiana, and Canada produced the anti-establishment demagogues Mitch Hepburn in Ontario, Duff Pattullo in British Columbia, "Bible Bill" Aberhart in Alberta, and Maurice Duplessis in Quebec. In terms of solving the Depression, the populists were ineffective, and in any case their impact was limited by state or provincial boundaries.

On the national level, politics were more serious and more cautious. Canadians, like Americans, probably had no clear expectations of the new Democratic administration and Democratic Congress that replaced the Republicans in Washington in March 1933. Franklin D. Roosevelt, the incoming president, had been governor of neighboring New York state and had at least a passing knowledge of some Canadian–American issues, like the St. Lawrence Seaway and hydroelectric developments along boundary waters like the Niagara and St. Lawrence Rivers. But in the face of the Depression, these were peripheral if not downright trivial matters.

Roosevelt promised Americans a "New Deal," and he put promises into action. Some of the action, we can now see, was ill-advised, and some results were not what had been hoped for. The important point, however, was action and activity, and the provision of emergency aid through government activity, just when it was most needed.[30] Roosevelt's policies were backed up by his eloquent speeches and radio "fireside chats." Legislation followed, reforming the rights of trade unions, establishing a conservation corps, reforming the banks, bailing out the farmers, pillorying the bankers, and financing huge public works and even public art and culture, engaging talents across the nation. Movies and radio brought Roosevelt's "forgotten man"—a figure from his speeches—to Canadians and emphasized the idealism of his program and the possibility of principled action against entrenched and corrupt elites.

Obviously Roosevelt's policies could have no direct effect in Canada, but the impact on the public and on public opinion in Canada was immense. R.B. Bennett as prime minister had to deal with the uncomfortable fact that the American president was in all probability much more popular in Canada than Canada's official political leader. Elected as a conservative, with a traditional and orthodox definition of society's problems, Bennett was aware that his nostrums were not working. Through his brother-in-law, William (Bill) Herridge, Canadian minister in Washington, he received regular reports on the New Deal and its political effects. Herridge made his legation a center of New Deal socializing and then undertook the difficult, but, as it turned out, not impossible task of converting his brother-in-law to New Deal thought. Bennett, like Roosevelt, grasped that the endless economic misery was sapping the foundations of an orderly society. He accepted that society had to be rescued from itself, and to the amazement of Canadians, their prime minister took to the radio to bark out a version of Roosevelt's "fireside chats," announcing swift and decisive government action to deal with, to solve, the Depression. Mackenzie King, good Victorian Liberal as he was, listened carefully and told his diary that Bennett had gone mad and was adopting Franklin D. Roosevelt's fascist policies. Fortunately King kept these thoughts to himself, because in the fall of 1935, after a Canadian general election, he was on his way to Washington as prime minister to meet and greet Roosevelt, all thoughts of his host's "fascism" now forgotten.

Bennett's New Deal had failed, both as a political proposition and as a legislative one. Very little of Bennett's ambitious attempt to reform the Canadian economy, and to enhance the government's response to the Depression, endured. Mackenzie King, his successor, continued Bennett's very modest attempt to rehabilitate prairie agriculture and would later pass various measures intended to prop up prairie farmers; but taken together it was dwarfed by the scale of American farm legislation.[31] And that is perhaps the most important thing to note about the New Deal parallels between Canada and the United States in the 1930s. The United States had a New Deal, and Canada did not.[32] The rigidities of the Canadian Constitution and Mackenzie King's cautious style of politics guaranteed that Canada would not—could not—do what Roosevelt had done. Canada remained, essentially, a conservative country where the economy was concerned. Thus, the United States arrived in 1939 with the beginnings of a social safety net, with an advanced regulatory regime to oversee the economy and especially the banks, and with a government committed to intelligent spending on behalf of a much broader public than had previously enjoyed the benefits of government action. Canada did not, except where banks were concerned.[33] Canadians reflected that the United States was a richer country, despite the misery of the Depression, and now a more liberal country, concerned to provide for the economic security of its citizens. This was something Canadians could aspire to, but for the time being they were stymied as to how get it. Canada reached 1939 with a government desperately worried about war and how to pay for it.

But that is to anticipate. In one area of foreign policy and transborder relations, the times were right. Most importantly, the tide in American politics had swung decisively against the protectionism that had either contributed to or not helped avert the disastrous Depression. Roosevelt's popularity and authority did the rest. Congress in 1934 passed a Reciprocal Trade Agreements Act (RTAA) that did more than reverse existing policy— it also revolutionized the mechanism for making tariffs. Up to and including Smoot–Hawley, Congress conceived, drafted, and enacted American tariff policy, essentially as an aspect of domestic legislation. In 1934 Congress actually delegated this function to the president, reserving to itself only the power to ratify agreements the president might make. What these agreements could be was laid down in the RTAA, which provided for reciprocal concessions on tariffs—essentially, "I cut my tariff and you cut yours," and the cuts had to be equivalent. Moreover, they could not be across the board, but on an item-by-item basis.[34] Henceforth the United States would negotiate trade treaties in the same way as other countries, abandoning its unique or exceptional way of setting the terms of trade.

By the fall of 1935 Bennett had already paved the way for a Canadian–American trade agreement. His first step was an apparent contradiction, the holding of a conference in Ottawa in 1932, where the various parts of the British Empire had exchanged preferential trade concessions with each other—the preferential rates being in every case lower than those granted even under the most expansive trade treaties with other countries. Only British countries participated, and only British countries harvested the resulting trade benefits. The Ottawa Agreements, as they were called, did in fact substantially redirect trade within the Empire, but, as important, they also were a major stimulus to American politicians to change their existing beliefs and seek forms of better behavior—embodied in the RTAA. Thus Bennett had had a hand in creating the political framework under which, in 1934–5, his delegates negotiated trade with the Americans.

His government had negotiated most of the details of an agreement, on an item-by-item basis, which took time and care, until time ran out in the summer of 1935. A few months' delay ensued, while Bennett was defeated at the polls, and Mackenzie King elected. Mackenzie King and Roosevelt now iced the wedding cake, and in November 1935 the first effective reciprocal trade agreement between the two countries since 1854 was signed. It was an outward sign of a larger inward harmony—the acceptance that a reduction of trade barriers held more promise than the continual walling off of separate national economies—an intellectual, even cultural change that reversed the character of economic diplomacy, negated a whole set of problems, and eventually created new ones to take their place. The economists of 1930, whom Hoover had so blithely ignored, had finally had their way.

Canada was only one component, though an important one, in Roosevelt's trade schemes. There were other nations to be engaged, and under the RTAA the most-favored-nation doctrine applied—that is, concessions granted to one country would be granted to all. There was, for example, an Anglo-American trade agreement in prospect, a prospect complicated by Canada's preferential agreement with the British in 1932. King in this case proved to be a tough and insistent negotiator, seeking and securing British concessions that preserved Canada's relative advantage in the British market, while at the same time the British achieved what they had sought, a trade agreement with the Americans. For the British, this 1937–8 negotiation amounted to cleaning the slate, ridding the Anglo-American agenda of existing annoyances, so as to concentrate attention on the one large item still to come, the approaching war in Europe.

## Isolationism and Exceptionalism

Mackenzie King and his new Liberal government were sworn into office on October 23, 1935, and on October 24 he made the rounds of the foreign diplomatic missions in Ottawa. It was not a long trajectory, since there were only three, of which the most important was the American. King had met the American minister, Norman Armour, before, but he seized the moment to recall his long acquaintance with the United States and his American connections, which included the billionaire Rockefellers and the previous president Roosevelt, Theodore, Franklin's cousin. King added that in Canada some called him "the American," and that Conservatives generally considered him "too friendly" to the United States.[35]

Armour responded warmly, as did his master, President Franklin D. Roosevelt. The White House opened its doors, on November 8–9, and King hurried inside. There was much to discuss. The trade agreement was quickly signed, and King and Roosevelt settled down to discuss the state of the world. King was concerned that Canada, a member of the League of Nations, might clash with the United States, a non-member, over League sanctions on Italy for its recent invasion of Ethiopia. The United States, after all, was isolationist, and he assumed Roosevelt was too. He need not have worried: Roosevelt privately deplored Italian aggression, hoped it could be stopped, and, again in private, wished good luck to any international efforts to rein in Italy's fascist dictator, Benito Mussolini. Roosevelt also constructed a fanciful friendship between himself and King, which, he claimed, went back to a time when they were both students at Harvard. They had not been there at the same time, but it didn't really matter. What was important, however, is that Roosevelt seems to have felt at ease with King. "In King," Bruce Hutchison wrote, "Roosevelt found an unprejudiced consultant to whom he could talk freely as he could not talk to most of his colleagues."[36] It did not hurt that King had genuinely known cousin Theodore, and it is certainly true that King and Roosevelt had moved in similar social circles in the northeastern United States, even if they had not met until just now. King was not and had never been anti-American; now he became pro-Roosevelt.

King had in a sense rehearsed his relationship with Franklin Roosevelt in 1907 and 1908, when he served as a go-between for Theodore Roosevelt in the latter's complicated diplomacy over Asian immigration to North America. In the 1920s, he had occasionally uttered the hope that Canadians could be the "friendly interpreters of Britishers to Americans alike in a manner which may substitute good-will for ill-will."[37] In his meeting with minister Armour on October 24, 1935, he had suggested that Canada was a natural link or intermediary between Britain and the United States, and recalled his earlier experience. The 1920s had not afforded much occasion for King to practice his harmonious skills, but the world in 1935 was different—darker and more urgent. Perhaps the opportunity for Canada to be a linchpin had come again.[38]

As King's diplomacy over trade showed, he was not willing to sacrifice Canadian economic interests as part of the purchase price for Anglo-American harmony, but in a broader sense he understood that Canada could only gain from good relations in the English-speaking family. He had a bit of a row to hoe, as far as the British were concerned. The bitter quarrels of the 1920s, especially over war debts, had left their mark on

British politicians and diplomats. Neville Chamberlain, the powerful chancellor of the exchequer, was especially skeptical of American good faith, and, when it came to Mackenzie King, he and many of his colleagues, civil servants and political figures both, had their doubts.

The reason for the skepticism and doubt lies precisely in the resemblances, real and apparent, between Canada and the United States, especially as they were perceived in the 1930s. The reason also lies in a serious difference between the two countries: what was then, and had always been, a dissimilarity between Canada and the United States, namely the presence of a different language, French, and an ethnic identity that was separate from the English-speaking majority. Paradoxically, it was this non-American, non-English-speaking grouping that gave force to views and politics in Canada that coincided with those of isolationist Americans. Mackenzie King had founded his political career not merely in harmonizing British and American interests but in conciliating those of English and French Canadians. French Canadians, most of them anyway, wanted to be left alone by the British and not dragged into European quarrels for which they felt no interest or affinity.

Franklin D. Roosevelt sensed the foreign element in Canada. Most of Canada, he seems to have felt, was familiar and friendly, a point that Mackenzie King also sensed. "On returning from one of his Washington visits," Bruce Hutchison wrote, "King remarked to a friend that of course Roosevelt would like to annex Canada." King took this in good part, which is to say, not seriously. "I would too, if I were President," he commented at the time.[39] French and *the* French—language and people—complicated matters, but there was a solution: the French of New England had been assimilated, and, Roosevelt advised Mackenzie King in a letter in 1943, the French of Canada could be too. No more French, no more problem! Roosevelt overestimated the extent to which Franco-Americans had been assimilated, but in the long run he was right—scattered over the New England landscape, without serious political leadership, they nowhere cohered into a political force. Gradually the language would diminish and ultimately disappear. King did not trouble to argue with his friend Roosevelt, and the letter went without any response.[40] Nor did he reflect that the part of Canada that Roosevelt found familiar, and presumably comforting, was the part that still identified with Great Britain and the British Empire and not, except as a fallback, with the United States—like King himself.

Incomprehension from the British was, at the time, a more serious matter, since it could be linked to domestic politics in which, arguably, British interests and British identities were still involved. There was still a strong sentiment of Empire, recalling the glory of conquest and pride of possession: "Quebec and Lucknow," Sir John Simon, a prominent politician, wrote in 1932, "these are the cities in the Empire which give me the biggest thrill."[41] Both places, in Canada and India, had seen notable British victories, in 1759 and 1857 respectively, though their histories since then had diverged considerably. If even the chilly Simon's pulse quickened at the thought of Wolfe at Quebec, it is a safe bet that others shared his sentiments.

The Empire was more than a matter of sentiment. It had been extraordinarily important in defeating the Germans in 1918, and what had been done once might have to be done again. As the 1930s drew on and Adolf Hitler came to power in Germany and then embarked on rearmament, only the willfully blind did not see a danger. Mackenzie King was not usually among the blind, though he was from time to time guilty of wishful thinking. By 1936 he was beginning to consider what might happen if there were a war, and by 1937 he was concerned enough about a conflict that he did everything he could to discourage it, first by telling the British at an imperial conference that Canada could make no automatic commitments in the hypothetical case of war, and then telling the Germans that if they attacked Great Britain—which King knew was at least a possibility—Canadians would automatically swim the Atlantic to stand at Britain's side.[42] In talking to the British, King was also speaking to a domestic audience—not of the usual kind, thousands of citizens gathered to listen to one of his dull speeches, but to a set of ears attached to Ernest Lapointe, his principal French-Canadian minister, who was sitting beside him at the imperial conference table. Lapointe had to be reassured that King's heart did not leap to an imperial drumbeat, and that he, like Lapointe, would make up his mind listening only to Canada's own interest.

None of this communicated any kind of firm message to the British. Mackenzie King's reticence was to be expected, not merely from a Canadian liberal, but from any Canadian. A senior British official, Sir Maurice Hankey, visited Ottawa in 1934 while Bennett was still in power, wrote home of Canada's "calculating aloofness," observed that many Canadians counted on the United States, not Britain, to defend them, and noted, finally, "if we estrange the United States we shall estrange many people in Canada." As for the United States, there was nothing positive to hope for; the best that could be expected was that there would be nothing negative either.[43] When Hankey found "calculating aloofness," he may have been asking Canadians the wrong questions—and possibly he was even asking the wrong Canadians the wrong questions.

That would not have been surprising, because the British High Commission in Ottawa sat in the middle of a tight little social circle that was conservative even by the standards of the Canadian Conservative party. These were people who had little contact with Mackenzie King and his government, or even with the senior civil servants. As a result, British high commissioners in Ottawa in the late 1930s sent a stream of misinformation to London about the intentions of the Canadian government in case of war—a war that was increasingly likely to be with Germany. The high commission missed the fact that in the Czech crisis of September 1938 Mackenzie King, however reluctantly, was ready to follow Chamberlain into war. The issue was never put to the test, allowing Canada to muddle into 1939 in a state of political opacity, as far as the British government was concerned. In London, the Canadian misinformation was blended into analyses of "dominion opinion," combining Canada with Australia, New Zealand, and South Africa. If the dominion components were at all differentiated, Canada was categorized as either doubtful or indifferent.[44]

What is interesting in this extraction of information about Canada is what was missing. King and Roosevelt conferred periodically, a fact known at the time. But from their discussions there was no serious consequence for Anglo-Canadian relations or any serious recalibration of Canada's basic political identification with the British Empire over the United States. If anything, Roosevelt valued Canada's participation in the Empire and had no desire to disturb it. Going a step farther, it is clear that by 1938 Roosevelt saw the British Empire, and not just Canada, as the outworks of a defensive system whose object was, ultimately, to defend the United States. Visiting Canada in 1938, and exchanging pledges of mutual defense with Mackenzie King, Roosevelt was careful to recognize and even emphasize in a speech at Queen's University in August 1938 that, "The Dominion of Canada is part of the sisterhood of the British Empire. I give to you assurance that the people of the United States will not stand idly by if domination of Canadian soil is threatened by any other Empire."[45] There was no hint in British high commission reports that the governments of Canada and the United States were acting together to avoid going to war.

What governments wanted was only part of the story. Roosevelt's views were not those of the political class in general, or of the majority of the American people. Roosevelt believed in international order—he had gone down to defeat in 1920 as a vice-presidential candidate supporting Wilson's League of Nations. He believed that the United States could not avoid sustaining that order, but that it would take a great deal of time, and a change in circumstance, to get Americans in general to accept that. He had learned a lesson in 1920, as King had in 1911. Their lessons pointed in opposite directions in the shorter term. King understood the power of Canada's pro-imperial feelings, while Roosevelt understood isolationism in the United States. There were English-Canadian isolationists, as there were American internationalists, but those were minority tastes. The English-speaking isolationists were emotionally and perhaps ideologically linked to their American counterparts, expressing the sentiment that North America was, morally and culturally, a world unto itself, and that Europe was a hopeless mess that North Americans could not afford to involve themselves in. Certainly as Germany grew in power in 1938 and 1939, there was plenty of evidence of Europe's apparently intractable condition.[46]

There was, however, an argument to be made on the other side. Isolationists argued that all European countries were involved in creating that continent's chaos. But in 1938 and 1939 that was self-evidently not the case. The British and French governments, representing democracies, not always cordially but nevertheless repeatedly refused to take decisive or forceful measures. Provoked by Germany and Italy, Europe's leading fascist regimes, the British prime minister, Neville Chamberlain, turned the other cheek. It is clear that Chamberlain's optimistic assessment of German leadership and German intentions was fatuous, so much so as eventually to be quite implausible, even to his cabinet colleagues in London.[47] Indeed, Chamberlain's "take" on Hitler in many ways resembles Mackenzie King's, who met Hitler as part of a European journey in June 1937.[48] Chamberlain, believed that he had had a personal impact on Hitler, something that King probably did not believe of himself.[49] On the other hand, neither Chamberlain nor King completely neglected to build up their nations' defenses, which would provide the narrowest of margins for military survival when war came. Meanwhile Germany grew stronger, and the democracies grew strategically weaker, shedding allies and losing ground in the face of German rearmament.

Appeasement culminated in September 1938 in a refusal by Britain and France to help Czechoslovakia resist German aggression, and in the imposition of a settlement at Munich on that hapless nation, which fatally weakened its defenses and undermined its political stability. All this was characterized as "appeasement," giving a special meaning to an older word; the word has ever since carried a heavy and very negative moral freight.

But appeasement at the time had real and positive political significance, especially in the British Empire and, within the Empire, in Canada. No one could argue that Britain and its ally France were disturbing the peace of

Europe, or that they were rash or provocative in their policy toward Germany. They were self-evidently peaceful and peace-seeking, and politically, in Canada and eventually in the United States, that counted for much. Inversely, Germany and Italy were neither of these things, which also counted for a lot. Mackenzie King, whose political barometer was highly sensitive to political atmospherics, and especially to storm clouds over Quebec, was very satisfied with Chamberlain's appeasement practices. Ernest Lapointe was satisfied as well: he had been given a plausible political case to make in Quebec, that the war to come was not another imperialist adventure. Franklin Roosevelt may have deplored the military and strategic effects of appeasement, but he too would ultimately benefit from the effects of Chamberlain's policy. Appeasement tapped many of the same sentiments as nineteenth-century liberalism, and its appeal crossed national boundaries. Although militarily weakened, the democracies were growing politically stronger.

The continuing crises in Europe in the winter and spring of 1939, as Hitler completed his occupation of Czechoslovakia and annexed Memel from Lithuania, while threatening Poland, were overshadowed by the great event of a royal visit, in which King George VI and his consort, Queen Elizabeth, were to become the first reigning British monarchs to visit Canada—and the United States, for that matter.

The visit had been Mackenzie King's idea, and had been proposed back in 1937, with the idea that it would both strengthen Canada's monarchical ties and promote good Anglo-American relations, on which Canada greatly depended.[50] Circumstance gave the trip a much sharper purpose, for by May 1939, when the king and queen set sail for North America, few could doubt that war in Europe was very far off. King carefully arranged that on the American part of the trip he would accompany the royal couple, becoming the "minister in attendance," and taking the place of the British foreign secretary and the British ambassador in Washington when George VI stayed with Roosevelt at his estate at Hyde Park, New York. King definitely thought the publicity from the Canadian and American legs of the trip would do him no harm when he called a Canadian election in the fall of 1939, but that theory, plausible though it was, would never be tested.[51]

From London Lester Pearson, the second in command at the Canadian high commission, cynically wrote that there was, another political purpose to the trip, to shore up Canadian sentiment and confirm the dominion's British loyalties, in readiness for the approaching war. That was doubtless true, and no doubt the trip accomplished its purpose. But Pearson's comment came too late, for Mackenzie King and his Quebec lieutenant,

Lapointe, had carefully worked out the terms on which Canada would go to war. Lapointe knew the government would be overwhelmed by British-Canadian public opinion if Canada did not go to war, and he accepted the fact. In March 1939, King and Lapointe told the House of Commons that Canada would not go lightly to war (King) but that Canada would go to war united (Lapointe). After that it was a matter of waiting, and while waiting there was the royal interlude.

The king and queen arrived in May at Halifax and stayed into June, crossing the country by train in the meantime, and visiting President Roosevelt at his country estate at Hyde Park, New York. The visit was a phenomenon. Wherever the king and queen went, there were crowds—not just large crowds, immense crowds. There were crowds in Quebec City, where the nationalist but conservative premier Maurice Duplessis vied with Mackenzie King for exposure next to the royals. In drought-stricken Saskatchewan, farmers drove for miles to catch fifteen minutes of the royal presence waving from the back of a train. In the Saskatchewan capital, Regina, population 57,000, 100,000 people saw the monarchs. In tiny Melville, the crowd numbered an incredible 60,000, who came from as far away as North Dakota and Manitoba. And gazing out on the crowds, just conspic-uous enough beside the royal couple, was the prime minister, Mackenzie King. Even in Quebec City, King knew he would not lose by associating himself with the symbols of Canada's royal and British identity. Better still, he knew that Canada's British links enhanced his country's position in the eyes of the American government. Britain had always safeguarded America from a hostile Europe, and there was no doubt that the Europe of 1939 was, indeed, hostile. Roosevelt saw Great Britain, the Royal Navy, and the British Empire in highly traditional terms, as the first line of defense for North America, and if Canada strengthened that defense, so much the better.

# 9

## Convergences, 1939–1949

### Converging Politics

BETWEEN 1939 AND 1949 the world reversed itself. A vast worldwide war began in Europe with Germany's invasion of Poland and spread round the world. Poland's ally, Britain, joined in. Following Britain, Canada participated from the war's first days, in September 1939, and the war lasted almost exactly six years, until the surrender of Germany's ally Japan in September 1945. Canada joined the war when it did because it was a member of the British Empire, and the British Empire, more obviously than in 1914, needed Canada's help.[1] Canada and the British Empire were victorious in the war, but only thanks to the intervention of the United States in 1941 and the extraordinary sacrifices made by the Soviet Union in defeating the Germans. The war was immensely costly not only in human life—the Soviet Union alone lost thirty-two million people—but also in money and supplies. Britain survived, but it emerged from the conflict so economically weakened that it could no longer maintain its empire.

The reality and the revelation of British weakness in itself produced a fundamental shift in Canada's world and in how Canadians saw that world. Terminating the British Empire was hardly one of Canada's war aims; Canada had entered the war precisely because most Canadians saw the Empire as a bulwark of order and sanity, and Canada's shield against aggression. During and after the war the Canadian government did everything it could to assist Great Britain and avert the defeat and disappearance of the Empire, which it (and most of the Canadian political establishment) saw as a dreadful calamity.

The palpable decline of the Empire weakened the strand of English-Canadian nationalism that used the power, wealth, and symbolism of British institutions to define Canada against the United States. There were, however, other forms of nationalism in English Canada that used the North American experience—the similarity of the North American frontiers, in the nineteenth century, or Canada's participation in the world wars of the twentieth[2]—as evidence that Canadians could now show that they had outgrown British forms and had become a nation in their own right. Under some circumstances, this argument had the advantage that it could appeal to French Canadians as well, although, given the unpopularity of the memory of the Great War in French Canada, it had to be employed with some delicacy. For some, it was a simple matter of power—Britain could no longer fill the role of patron and protector, so it was time to look to the United States.

Diminishing but not severing the British tie did bind Canada more closely to the United States. Refocusing Canadian attention from London to Washington or New York involved rapprochement with American political culture, supplementing all the other forms of American culture that flowed over the border. The change affected the attitudes of Canadian nationalists, who were now coping with a new world in which the British connection was diminished but by no means absent.

Yet the Anglo-Canadian–American relationship was not merely a matter of power politics. In other ways the three countries changed radically between 1939 and 1945, growing closer while diverging. Support for the war was high and remarkably consistent through six years of combat. In all three, resources were mobilized for the war, most obviously manpower, but also materiel, grown, mined, sawn, and manufactured. To pay for it all, taxes rose, at the top end to near-confiscatory levels. For many, living standards fell. The more comfortable members of the middle class lost their servants and saw their incomes shrink; but on the other hand, the servants found employment in war industries or replaced soldiers going overseas, and in both cases increased their incomes, with a high propensity to spend what they earned. Others, who had not found a job in years, returned to the work force, and still others, who had reached maturity during the Depression, found their first employment.

Canada reached full employment in October 1941, according to the statistics generated in Ottawa. Wage and price controls promptly ground into action. Supplies were already rationed—"controlled"—and to soak up money that might have bid for scarce commodities, compulsory savings were instituted. Naturally a black market emerged, or rather submerged, in Canada as in Great Britain and the United States, but it never assumed the same monstrous proportions as it did in some of the countries of continental Europe.

The point is that high taxes and stringent government regulation were accepted in Canada and the United States and Great Britain with far less complaint, evasion, or resistance than might have been anticipated. They gained support because they were seen to be effective, that is, part of a world where unemployment had been eliminated, poverty reduced, and money redistributed to the lowest income earners, thus producing, by indirection, a markedly more egalitarian society. In Great Britain, under immediate threat and afflicted by German bombardment and besieged by German submarines, things went farther—the drain on wealth, supplies, and society was faster and greater than across the Atlantic, while the British Isles had to house and feed millions of military personnel waiting to be sent off to Africa, Italy, or France to fight the Germans. But it was accepted that against this totalitarian enemy, nothing less than total mobilization would suffice, providing a broad platform in public opinion for what the economist Karl Polanyi called "the great transformation." The transformation was real, and it would permeate society for the next half-century; but, as we shall see, it was less permanent than optimistic economists hoped.

## *What Kind of War, What Kind of Nation?*

Hitler invaded Poland on September 1, 1939, and the British and the French declared war on Germany on September 3. Canada, following Britain's lead but anxious to assert a formal independence, declared war on Germany on September 10, and, following the precedent set in 1914, organized an overseas army, which began to arrive in Britain in December 1939. It would remain until 1946, as hundreds of thousands of Canadian troops set a precedent for millions of Americans pouring through the British Isles en route to the war in Europe. Tens of thousands of Canadians joined the air war over Europe, first in the Battle of Britain, and then in the night bombing campaigns that reduced German cities to heaps of rubble, as the Americans were doing by day. Like the Great War, the conflict spread beyond Europe as the Axis countries, Germany, Italy, and Japan and their satellites, battled the Allies, who eventually included the British Empire, the Union of Soviet Socialist Republics (USSR), and the United States. Every continent and every ocean was involved; only the Americas, North and South, were spared invasion or serious bombing.[3]

At the end of the war, Mackenzie King reflected with some pride that only two national leaders in office in 1939 were still in the same position in 1945—Josef Stalin, the Soviet dictator, and King himself. Roosevelt was removed by death in April 1945 and Churchill by the British electorate three months later. Stalin, could (and did) order his domestic enemies shot or deported before, during, and after the war, while King had no such luxury. Whole ethnic groups vanished into Soviet central Asia, escorted by Stalin's secret police. This was not a subject King dwelt on, and it is possible that his mind rejected any hint that the Soviet Union could possibly be an unworthy ally. At the end of the war one of King's senior officials thought it useful to remind the prime minister that Soviet democracy was not like Canada's.

Very few Canadians would have bet on Mackenzie King, the quintessential civilian, as a successful war leader, or on Canada as a successful country. Indeed, some Canadians could not imagine that Canada could possibly emerge intact and united at the end of the war. The history of the Great War, brought forward and applied to the world of 1939 or 1940, would have suggested that Canada would dissolve into ethnic chaos and class warfare as the social and economic order failed to measure up to the war's demands on manpower and manufacturing. Worse still, Canada and the other democracies were emerging from ten years of economic depression that neither the unglamorous King nor the debonair Roosevelt had been able to solve.

King, unlike Roosevelt, had frequently met the man who would shortly, in May 1940, become Britain's prime minister.[4] Winston Churchill had toured Canada in 1900, selling himself and his writings to an adoring and imperially minded audience. Some years later, as parliamentary under-secretary for the colonies, he and King, by then a Canadian deputy minister, met again in London, and over time their careers brought them together again, King as prime minister, and Churchill as a prominent British politician in and out of office during the 1920s. When not officially employed, Churchill resorted to income-enhancing tours, including Canada in 1929 and 1932. As prime minister, King lavished attention on the touring Churchill in 1929, even hosting him for an afternoon at his Kingsmere estate. When Churchill told a banqueting audience that in the British Empire, "United we stand, divided we fall," King murmured to his diary, "very fine & very true."[5]

Did King really like Churchill, or did Churchill like King? The answer is mixed. On one occasion, chatting with King, Churchill is said to have mused that when he first visited Canada he might have made a considerable ass of himself. "There were many Canadians who thought so," King is said to have replied, "[and] I was one."[6] In the approach to the Second World War, King thought Churchill bellicose and dangerous,[7] only to revise his views as the crisis of May and June 1940 created a military disaster, to which Churchill seemed the only possible response.[8] Thus King's view of Churchill evolved and fluctuated over time, and in assessing it we should distinguish political friendship from personal attraction. As politicians and as fellow prime ministers, King and Churchill were professional friends, and not rivals or antagonists. They were more useful to one another as allies than as antagonists, and they governed their relations accordingly.

Canada had something that Churchill undoubtedly anticipated and appreciated—he remembered the money, supplies, and troops that had flowed from Canada to Britain in the Great War, and that was enough to make him pleasant and congenial to Mackenzie King in the interwar years, even to the point of agreeing when King was critical of Churchill's own past conduct. It was King and King's government that were sending more troops, money, munitions, and ships in the Second World War, and as a matter of practical politics, Churchill was more than prepared to make the necessary reciprocal gestures. "He needed King's help," C.P. Stacey cynically wrote, "and he flattered him accordingly."[9]

There was a bit more to the King–Roosevelt relationship. Part of it was geography: Ottawa was close to Washington, and King liked to travel south. Washington and Roosevelt were en route to Virginia or Florida, and by proximity and personal inclination the two men saw a great deal of each other. Roosevelt was fond of Canada, as we have seen (above, p. 199), but the fact that Canada was part of the British Empire added to the president's interest—as it had done for his cousin Theodore forty years earlier. And, like Theodore, he found he could talk easily to King, and without the usual risks in talking to American politicians. Conversations with Roosevelt rambled freely from questions of continental defense to gossip about Winston Churchill's drinking habits to unemployment and pensions, and onward to Roosevelt's political schemes.[10] Most confidential of all the subjects was Roosevelt's unabashed but very private belief that the United States must support the Allies, and the British in particular. There were many other Americans who held that view, in particular Mackenzie King's friend and patron, John D. Rockefeller, who in April 1940 told King of his hope that the United States would soon join the war.

And so it was Mackenzie King's fate to be Canada's war leader in an alliance where Franklin D. Roosevelt overshadowed him and in an empire where Winston Churchill had the same effect. It was a burden that King bore with only the odd complaint. Association with Churchill and Roosevelt, after all, bolstered King's own popularity at home, while comforting his ego abroad—though even Stacey concedes that Roosevelt may actually have liked Mackenzie King, to the extent that he liked anyone. If the senior Allied leaders showed King public deference, and allowed themselves to be photographed with him at great Allied events, it was a notable assist to King's prospects of re-election. And indeed, in the first postwar election in June 1945, King's Liberal party played up their leader's international prominence and experience—as demonstrated by photographic evidence—to the hilt. In a hard-fought and narrow election, the fact that King was Canada's international statesman may well have made a crucial difference.

Yet it was true that King participated in great events crucial to Canada's well-being. It was just that those events were not grand strategy, but rather particular to Canada and Canadian interests, notably less spectacular than directing the movements of fleets and armies, invading Europe, bombing Japan, and cornering Hitler in his Berlin bunker at the end of the war. Neville Chamberlain, British prime minister when the war began, did not think of inviting the British dominions to help guide British war strategy. His successor, Winston Churchill, did the same.[11] Undoubtedly he realized that King had nothing to add, though he probably appreciated the fact that King did not even ask to participate in strategic discussions. King learned of the German attacks on Norway or on Belgium and the Netherlands in 1940 the same way most Canadians did—from the radio. Later in the war, with Canadian troops actually involved, he learned of the Allied landings in Sicily and Normandy the same way. No Canadian officer sat at American general Dwight D. Eisenhower's right hand while "Ike" as supreme Allied commander plotted the liberation of Western Europe, or stood beside General MacArthur as the Americans island-hopped their way across the Pacific toward Japan in 1944–5. King protested only the appearance, not the substance, of lack of consultation.

## Converging Destinies

Seen from the perspective of the senior Allies, Canada was important, useful, and reliable—but there was a difference in emphasis among those terms. Politically, Canada really was useful and reliable. Economically, Canada really was important. Canadian war production came third among the Allies and in certain categories, for example, mining nickel, smelting aluminum, and manufacturing trucks, it was quite impressive. Canada also made ships, planes, and shells, grew wheat, and refined uranium—all useful activities, but none of them irreplaceable. Canada and its leader were reliable: it was inconceivable that Mackenzie King would make a public fuss about Allied strategy. It was bred into King's DNA that Canada should not, must not, get out of line. There would never, with King, be an occasion for public reproach. But how important was Canada in the end? It depended how you defined the word. If American war production was sixty out of one hundred, and Britain's thirty-five, Canada's was the remaining five. Among all the smaller Allies, Canada stood out, temporarily richer than France and with a larger army engaged in the final battles for Europe in 1945. But after all, France had four times the population of Canada and human and physical resources that dwarfed Canada's. It was only a matter of time, and not much time, before those factors came into play again.

These were all matters that Mackenzie King understood, either instinctively or intellectually—and sometimes both. His age, or his longevity informed the view he took of the world. Raised in Victorian Ontario, King lived in a world of British wealth and power. The war in which Canada engaged in September 1939 would, he expected, be horrible and possibly long, but like the Great War it would result in Allied, and obviously British, victory. Even the opening of the German offensive in Western Europe on May 10, 1940, did not seriously alter King's, and most Canadians', hopes. But British defeat in Flanders, the Dunkirk evacuation, Belgium's surrender, and the fall of Paris to the Germans on June 14 were stunning. France's capitulation soon followed, signed on June 24, and the British Empire was alone in the war.

For King, the sudden collapse of the Allied armies in France in June 1940 came as an immense shock. The prime minister was not alone in his distress. The cabinet was shaken, and as the assumption of a secure trans-Atlantic line of defense crumbled, Canada suddenly seemed exposed and vulnerable to German attack.[12]

Canadians did not exactly panic in June 1940, but the stress of events is obvious in the rapid transformation of public opinion. It is clear that opinion shifted in a very short time, changing political life and opening political possibilities that weeks, if not days, earlier would not have been conceivable. (Fortunately, Canadians were shielded by censorship, secrecy, and distance from the very real panic that swept segments of political and general society in Great Britain, and that produced a discussion in cabinet as to whether the British should not seek peace terms from the Germans.) Despite promises to the contrary made as recently as the March 1940 general election, Canada soon had conscription for military service within North America, something that cabinet ministers from Quebec, and most MPs from that province, quickly accepted.[13] Foreign events, foreign policy, imposed themselves on domestic reality and transformed it. Arguably, it was at this point that Canadian public opinion shifted its bases—from isolationism to engagement for many, from a secure British Empire patriotism to something far less certain, and less comforting, than the cocoon of Empire security. The Empire was no longer safe.

Next, King authorized defense co-operation with the United States in an agreement at Ogdensburg, New York, in August 1940, somewhat to Churchill's distress, since to Churchill it was a reflection on British strategic weakness. But Churchill had troubles enough of his own, with a possible German invasion looming and the aerial Battle of Britain about to begin. There were thus no public political eruptions, and within a few weeks or months the pressure of events made any objections from the British moot. As Britain mobilized all the resources it could produce, buy, or borrow, strains mounted on the British economy. Early in 1941, Mackenzie King learned that Britain's foreign exchange reserves and gold supply were on the verge of disappearance; he wonderingly noted the fact in his diary. Britain "is a bankrupt country," King wrote, adding that he was told that the British were being very slow to grasp the consequences.[14] King was not, nor were the civil servants and some of the ministers around him. Britain by itself could not and would not win the war, even after Hitler attacked the Soviet Union in June 1941. That was why, when Japan attacked the United States in December 1941, ordinarily staid Canadian civil servants at a Sunday lunch party marked the occasion by dancing around their host's dining room table. Only then was it certain that the war could now be won—through direct American help and participation.

But until then, as in May 1940, Canadians were to some extent insulated from the realities of a war that seemed to have no good outcome. The steady progression of defeats, spiced with a few victories, from April 1940 to May 1942 masked the fact that the Allied powers, the Anglo-Saxon ones anyway, were drawing closer in other and very important ways. Externally unified, Canada, Britain, and the United States (not to mention Australia and New Zealand) were prosecuting the war not merely for the same end, to defeat Germany and Japan, but in much the same way. The result would be a convergence of policies, institutions, and values that would not merely assist in winning the war, but that would long outlast it.

## Converging Policies

North America in the 1930s had featured differences as marked as its resemblances. The resemblances were obvious: economic depression, persistently high unemployment, the dust bowl on the prairies, and some of the politics they spawned—populist demagogues specializing in quack solutions, on the one hand, and utopian radicals on the other, ranging from fascists to socialists to communists. Canada and the United States could legitimately claim to have all of these—in Canada in two languages. The greatest difference was political: the United States had Roosevelt and the New Deal, and Canada did not. Canada had a monarchy and an official trans-Atlantic connection, while for the United States the connection was unofficial, even if, in the end, the British-European link was decisive for both. Most important, government in the United States was more effective, implementing the New Deal through public works.

Canadian–American contacts were plentiful, but usually at an unofficial level. Canadian tourists and immigrants flowed south, and American tourists flowed north. Many Canadian companies were branch plants of American firms, ranging from the giant automobile companies centered in Ontario, near Detroit, to ceramics, to pulp and paper. With ownership came management, and with management, standardization. American industry considered itself a model for the world, with its vast factories, mass production, and scientific management, a point on which even Vladimir Lenin agreed. Canadian factories were smaller and more limited than those in the United States, satisfying a much smaller market that had grown smaller still with the disappearance of overseas markets in 1939–40. Satisfying the American munitions and defense market was a gigantic task, requiring vast factories and mass production and a mass workforce, and within the limitations of the Canadian workforce, Canada ratcheted up its industry to meet the demand.

In 1938 and 1939 Canadian industry had begun a modest redirection to war production—Hurricane fighters and Bren sub-machine guns. In 1940, after the military disaster in France, war production was exponentially multiplied, regardless of whether there was the money to pay for it. Since the British army had left most of its equipment on the beaches of France, there was no doubt that the British could and would use almost everything Canada could manufacture for them. The resulting explosion of war production steadily soaked up the unemployed until, in the fall of 1941, there was no more unemployment. Munitions and supplies for Britain also soaked up Canada's available gold and foreign exchange reserves, because equipping Canadian factories meant going to the American source for machinery. By March 1941 there was no more money to keep the Canadian war production program going unless drastic action was taken. The British had run out of convertible funds too—so much so that when the Roosevelt administration offered to lend the British the money to buy what they needed in the United States, the British let the Canadians know that they would have to buy American in the future, unless the Canadians could match the American terms, embodied in the "Lend–Lease" program. Fortunately King's excellent relations with Roosevelt proved serviceable in the emergency, producing an agreement in April 1941 that allowed the Americans to buy war supplies in Canada, for the United States was now itself gearing up for a war that would not be long postponed. King traveled to Roosevelt's country estate to sign the "Hyde Park Declaration" on what Roosevelt termed "a grand Sunday in April."[15] King was thereafter careful to keep Roosevelt informed about the extent of the Canadian war effort so that the unusual economic relationship with the United States—easing the jealously guarded American border where war production was concerned, could be justified if necessary. And indeed, when criticism of Canada and Canada's sacrifices for the war arose, Roosevelt gave a spirited defense of Canada's material and manpower contribution to the Allied cause.[16]

The effect of Hyde Park was to erase the border as far as war supplies were concerned. The American government placed war-supply orders with firms in Canada on the same basis as it contracted with American companies. When the United States did join the war, in December 1941, Canadian production was assigned by an Inter-allied board in Washington, DC, on which Canada had no representation. American requests for Canadian war production often took precedence over those of the Canadian army. How could it have been otherwise, when Canada, like all the other minor Allies, had no input into the Allies' grand strategy? The Canadian government had to be satisfied with the proposition that its war production would be distributed in such a way as to arrive in the hands of the right Allied army at the right time and in the right place. But others would know where and when that was. Thus, a Mountie would shake Mackenzie King out of his slumber on June 6, 1944, to tell the prime minister that the Allies, including the Canadians, had just landed in France.

More than orders flowed north. Blueprints for war equipment arrived from Britain and the United States, along with instructions on how to go about producing the stuff. As the war progressed, British production specifications were either modified or discarded, while American models were increasingly copied. The Americans had, after all, perfected mass production, and the Canadians applied it to manufacture trucks (in American-owned automotive plants) and ships (copies of American Liberty ships).

The effect was to train a generation of Canadian managers in American industrial culture—a clear case of cultural convergence, justified by the absolute conviction that this was the most modern and most efficient industrial methodology in the world. In some cases, the Canadians found that they could produce cheaper and faster—as long as the war lasted, and the market was for all intents and purposes unlimited. Free trade with the United States, the goal of generations of Canadian politicians, had finally arrived as the by-product of the Second World War. If one consequence of free trade in war goods was the wholesale importation of American management assumptions and industrial techniques, so much the better. "American" was demonstrably best. Because the war was a desperate struggle with a formidable foe, nothing could be allowed to stand in the way. Nor could lingering British Empire sentiments obstruct something that was as much for Britain's benefit as for Canada's. And so there was acceptance, admiration, and even envy for American leadership and direction.

American officials traveling to Canada on war business were mildly surprised by what they found. Canada, one reported, was a very conservative place, its labor and social policies far behind those in the United States. Yet not everything was conservative, and certainly not everything was unfamiliar. Many Canadian officials, starting with the prime minister, had been educated in the United States or Great Britain. Their academic credentials were certainly as good as those of their American counterparts, and they applied them to policies that aimed at total economic mobilization for the war effort. A Canadian with a Massachusetts Institute of Technology (MIT) degree was instantly recognizable and could be fitted into the appropriate social or intellectual category by a comparable American.

An example was C.D. Howe, minister of munitions and supply (1940–6). Howe had a degree from MIT, and, better still, he had been born an American. Opportunity had called him to Canada,[17] while lack of opportunity during the Depression had translated him into politics. His American background helped particularly when he dealt with some less-informed Americans. In one notable instance, Howe got a call from General Leslie Groves, the man in charge of the American project to build an atomic bomb. Groves had been told that he had to ask permission if he wanted to conduct certain activities in Canada and, much puzzled, he took the train to Ottawa. Calling at Howe's spartan office, with linoleum floors in a drafty clapboard wartime building, he was delighted to find a fellow MIT graduate. All Groves's doubts were put to rest. Though equipped with an ample distrust of foreigners, he made an immediate exception for Howe, and, as it turned out, Canadians.[18] This helped greatly in establishing Canada's place in the super-secret Manhattan Project—which was to host a British atomic laboratory in Montreal and to refine all the uranium that eventually went into the American atomic bombs dropped on Japan in 1945. It helped, as well, to fend off the designs of a would-be American super-patriot (a scoundrel, like many patriots), who urged that Groves simply appropriate Canadian uranium resources rather than leave them in the control of an unreliable foreign entity.[19]

In the less sensitive but equally important area of agriculture and agricultural production, Canadian and American officials easily integrated their work. A Canadian office was set up inside the US Department of Agriculture in Washington to coordinate wheat policy, and for many if not most purposes the forty-ninth parallel was erased. The arrangement was so convenient and so comfortable that the office remained in place for some years after the war, until, finally, it was closed as Canadian and American agricultural policies once again began to diverge. While most Canadian–American arrangements were not as cozy as that in agriculture, they were remarkably informal, and frequent—a matter of a phone call or, if necessary, a quick personal visit to the relevant capital. It helped that American officials enjoyed coming to Canada, where steak was not among the foodstuffs rationed.

Whether by design or by accident, Canada and the United States adopted strikingly similar policies in directing civilian resources to the war effort. It could not have been an accident, to be sure, because the people who made policy shared much the same mental universe. However, they did not precisely coordinate their policies, arriving at similar results at slightly different times, governed by the fact that Canada entered the war more than two years before the United States, in September 1939 as opposed to December 1941. Canadian ministers and politicians, remembering the hard and divisive economic policies of the Great War, resolved that as far as possible the second war should proceed along pay-as-you-go lines. As a tax official later pointed out, Canada was remarkably successful in attaining that objective.[20] High taxes would reduce spending power and lower inflation, the curse of the home front in the previous war. Income tax rates rose steadily until they were practically confiscatory in the top income brackets—almost but not quite at British levels. For those with an income exceeding $100,000 the rate was 98 percent on every dollar above that figure. There were, to be sure, few at that level; what really bit was 49 percent on the portion of income above $2,000.[21] (The reader should remember that these are current dollars; rendering them into the dollars of the twenty-first century involves both multiplication by at least a factor of ten—and imagination in recreating a very different economic world.) Taxation at that rate allowed the Canadian government to finance its own war expenditures—the raising, training, and equipping of a million men and women in uniform between 1939 and 1945—and also to pay for British purchases in Canada after 1941. The effect on Anglo-Canadian relations was highly positive, so much so that the British official historian—official histories are not generally given to warmth—described Canadian financial policy toward Britain as "outstandingly large-minded."[22] Canadian achievements in the unglamorous world of war finance lingered in American and British minds.

Government spending drove the economies of all the belligerents, and the gross domestic products of Canada, the United States, Great Britain, and all the other combatants rose markedly from 1939 to 1945. Canada's per capita gross domestic product rose 50 percent between 1939 and 1945; the American figure went up by perhaps 80 percent.[23]

Conscription of wealth matched and justified conscription of manpower, and helped the public accept the heavy casualties that the war entailed. Rationing of civilian goods—except for steak in Canada, as we have seen—was strictly applied, and the Canadian government could easily piggyback on the United States' extensive and attractive propaganda effort, as well as deploy its own. Price and wage controls proved remarkably successful, backed up, as they were, by shock and fear—the shock of defeat in 1940 and the subsequent fear of a Nazi victory. The Americans had a similar stimulus with the Japanese attack on Pearl Harbor, as well as the fearful spectacle of Nazi rule over most of Europe.

Mass entertainment both boosted morale and spread the message that individual sacrifice was imperative in the interest of the war effort. Canada had radio, and it had a National Film Board to warn and inspire, but it lacked a large-scale commercial film industry. That had been supplied by the United States and Great Britain before the war, and American and British movies continued to fulfill that role. Canadian cinemas showed the British movies, the whimsical *Pimpernel Smith*, with Leslie Howard, and the heroic *In Which We Serve*, with both Howard and the actor–playwright Noel Coward, but also American movies which spread the word—from *Casablanca*, with Ingrid Bergman and Humphrey Bogart, at the high end to *Mission to Moscow*, depicting a humane and genial Stalin, at the low. Canada did not often appear, but in 1941 an all-star cast—Laurence Olivier, Howard, Coward, and the then famous Canadian actor Raymond Massey—combined in *The 49th Parallel*. Olivier unconvincingly playing a French-Canadian trapper on the track of villainous Nazis who had landed in Canada by submarine. (Naturally the Nazis were defeated.)[24] American actors and other entertainers toured Canada as part of their patriotic missionary work to promote the common war effort, adding a spark of life to dreary wartime Ottawa.[25]

The point of the propaganda was to create a sense of common endeavor and equality of sacrifice. And while the war period certainly did not erase social and economic differences, it tended to compress those differences and with them the possibility of grievance against unequal rewards and unequal sacrifice.

As Mackenzie King spoke to his old patron John D. Rockefeller and to Franklin Roosevelt, so his officials spoke to their intellectual cousins in Washington. Details of policies might differ, but they were relatively unimportant, and Canadian and American overall objectives, and the manner in which they were publicly justified, were certainly the same. As late as 1942 or 1943, the difference between Canada and the United States was apparently one of size, usually expressed in terms of the enviable standard of living south of the border, or the greater opportunity afforded by a larger and richer society; that size would matter in other ways would only become evident later.

The resemblance was quite marked given the relative size and wealth of Canada and the United States. Morale remained high throughout the war, with no politically significant opposition to the basic commitment to a victorious end of the war against Germany, Italy, and Japan. The commitment was common to all English-speaking societies, including Australia and New Zealand, with the exception of neutral Ireland.[26] There was a close connection to British policies, though admittedly the British had extra incentives to sacrifice for the common good. Great Britain was actually under attack from the air for almost the whole war, while surrounded by German U-boats that were attempting to starve out the British Isles. There, the combination of wartime damage with stringent economic controls made a more obvious visual and social impact on the 500,000 members of the Canadian army and the Royal Canadian Air Force stationed in Britain.[27]

The Canadian and American military experiences were much closer than might be imagined. True, the Americans coped with a war across two oceans, sending armies and air and sea fleets to virtually every part of the globe. Canada necessarily was more restricted, given its limitations of manpower and economic resources. But in some theaters, mainly in Europe,

Canadian and American troops did much the same things, and at roughly comparable times. The 500,000 Canadians in the British Isles were the precursors of the American army and army air force. When the Americans began to arrive in 1942, the Canadians had already been in residence for nearly three years, while the British, having adapted to one friendly occupying army, could begin to adapt to another. The Canadians, though worse paid than the Americans, were nevertheless far better off than British soldiers, a fact that stimulated some resentment in and around Canadian garrisons.[28]

On the other hand, the Canadians served ultimately under British command, wore British-style uniforms, and assumed British ranks—meaning, in the air force, there were squadron leaders and wing commanders and so on as opposed to the majors and lieutenant-colonels of the American air service, and in the army warrant officers instead of the many American versions of sergeants, and brigadiers instead of brigadier generals. It has been claimed that Canadian soldiers serving in England more closely resembled British soldiers in their habits and attitudes, while the Americans and—in other parts of the world—Australians and New Zealanders had more in common. The truth seems rather more nuanced. Some Canadian soldiers were stationed in Great Britain for more than four years before they saw combat, and in the meantime had to endure endless training exercises that seemed increasingly pointless as time went on. Nor did British winters, cold, damp, and uncomfortable, help. Thus there were, by early 1942, serious problems of morale in the Canadian army overseas—although it should be stressed that these are common to any army that is underemployed and without any obvious sense of mission.[29]

Making matters worse was the fact, mentioned above, that Canadian soldiers were better paid than their British counterparts. Greater resources made them at least competitive with British soldiers and civilians for female companionship. The solution was found in billeting Canadian troops with British civilians—and where that happened, relations and interaction startlingly improved. British women and Canadian soldiers married by the thousands, a contrast with the American soldiery, who were strongly discouraged from marriage by the US army. The Americans, better paid than the Canadians, formed the top of the social pecking order in dealing with needy British civilians.

One solution for boredom was combat, which Canadian generals actively sought, and the Canadian army got action in the disastrous raid on the French seaport of Dieppe on August 19, 1942, in which 68 percent of the Canadian troops engaged became casualties—killed, wounded, missing, or taken prisoner. Dieppe was badly planned by British officers, including the king's cousin, Lord Mountbatten, making a disaster of some kind on the French coast a virtual certainty. When the disaster duly occurred, there was both a hunt for scapegoats (the luckless Canadian divisional commander) and a flight from responsibility. That two of Britain's most prominent commanders, General Montgomery and Admiral Mountbatten, had been involved could not be admitted, then or later. Mountbatten both in 1942 and after the war was almost hysterical in disclaiming responsibility; he had good cause to fear for his reputation. Indeed, if anything like the truth had been known, the incident might well have damaged Anglo-Canadian relations and could have undermined Canadian enthusiasm for the British way of war. After the war Dieppe engaged the attention of no less a personage than Winston Churchill as he sought to massage the history of this wartime disaster into an inspirational parable of Anglo-Canadian relations for his memoirs.[30]

The Canadian military was less closely associated with the Americans, when they arrived in Great Britain starting in 1942. Nor, for the most part, did the Canadians and Americans serve closely together in battle. The Canadian army was under the overall command of the American general Dwight D. Eisenhower, first in the Sicilian and Italian campaigns, and then in northwest Europe in 1944–5. In the aerial war over Germany and in the North Atlantic, the Canadians fought primarily alongside the British, wore British uniforms, and ultimately served under British command. Some Canadian officers, significantly, did sense that the balance of power was shifting away from Great Britain toward the United States, and drew the conclusion that their country's future lay with the Americans—richer, better organized, more compatible than the British.[31] Symbolically, and realistically too, the actual fighting of the war cannot be said to have brought the Canadians and Americans closer together; but because of the common war effort, it did not move them further apart. So while it can be said that the Canadians noticed the Americans and were interested enough to draw some conclusions from their experience, the same was not true in reverse, as the historian David Reynolds has noted. The main exception was that some black Americans noticed that blacks were better treated—not segregated, among other things—in the Canadian army.[32]

What did change in Canadian–American relations was the particular and intense relationship the two countries had previously enjoyed. Canadian–American relations ranged from family connections through business linkages through educational experiences. Prominent Americans owned properties in Canada, and traveled there for pleasure or business—William Howard Taft, Franklin Roosevelt himself, and John Foster Dulles being prominent examples. Few world leaders had voyaged to Washington, and those few usually derived little benefit from the experience.[33]

Down to 1941, Mackenzie King was Franklin Roosevelt's most important personal contact among foreign leaders. No other foreign statesman had been to Washington as much as Mackenzie King; no other foreign politician was as familiar with Roosevelt's political problems as his Canadian friend. It was partly a consequence of proximity and partly the result of compatibility. From time to time, Roosevelt sought to use King to influence or sound out his British colleagues, thereby putting a strain on King. In the larger world of strategy King was out of his depth, as he convincingly demonstrated in June 1940 when Roosevelt attempted to use him to secure the British fleet in case of a British surrender. It was all beyond King, and wisely he chose not to meddle in affairs that were outside his grasp. So much, we may say, for Canada or King as the "linchpin" linking Great Britain and the United States. Churchill, King knew, would not stand for Canadian interference, and Roosevelt, as King may have guessed, was desperately grasping at straws until in the fullness of time—not much later, as it turned out—he and Churchill could establish their own relationship based on common British and American objectives.

It was not that Canada had changed, but that the United States had—moving from being a potential world power to the real thing. The kind of advice or assistance Roosevelt now needed was far beyond Canada's capacity or competence. King and his ministers kept to issues that directly affected Canada's well-being—the balance of payments, supply questions, and postwar planning. The main objective was not to allow American wealth and power to force the British to accept a new trading regime that would abrogate imperial preference or nullify the Ottawa Agreements of 1932—not without Canada having a say.[34]

Nor was Canada without resources. The Canadian GDP rose 60 percent during the war and, thanks to the wartime trading relations with the United States, Canadian foreign exchange reserves, mainly American dollars, rose steadily. The federal government expanded too, in the short term to meet wartime needs, but in the longer term acquiring a capability that had previously been missing. The results showed in a smoothly functioning administration and the ability to explain and justify what Canada was doing—not only to its own citizens, though that was important, but abroad as well. Canada was a small but useful cog in the international system. It could do certain things—not as many things as a Great Power, but more than lesser or poorer countries—more than Australia, or Portugal, or Brazil.

To take the most prominent example, Canada gave or lent billions of dollars to Great Britain from 1941 to 1945—less than the United States, certainly, but Canada's ability to do so allowed the British an alternative to total dependence on the United States, and relieved some of the pressure on the US treasury in serving as banker to its allies. Equally to the point, Canada refused American loans: the essential inflow of American cash derived from sales to that country—the supply of war materiel to Canada's giant ally. Psychologically, this point was crucial: in the minds of Canadian ministers and civil servants, it was essential to keep the Americans from seeing Canada as yet another dependent ally. Because Canada was so much closer to and smaller than the United States, the Canadian government did not want to encourage the Americans to see Canadians as anything other than equals—smaller equals, but equals nevertheless. "Belief in Canadian virtue is widespread, and there is much respect for the greater political efficiency of Canadian institutions." Canada was, after all, "the only completely dependable good neighbour possessed by [the United States]." Writing from the vantage point of the British embassy in Washington, the British wartime civil servant Isaiah Berlin, who penned these words, described Canada as "that apparently quiet pool of good government" late in 1944. Nobody could have said that about Sir Robert Borden's government thirty years before, or, indeed, about Mackenzie King's own Canadian government in the 1930s.[35]

## A Functional Country

Mackenzie King's diplomats appropriated a concept, and a word, to encapsulate what they were doing. It was *functionalism*, an idea worked out by a British political scientist, David Mitrany. It is important to observe that functionalism fitted Canada, and not the other way around. Canada's experience with the governmental end of international relations was of two kinds. Relations with the United States and with Great Britain involved working back from details to principles—solving one issue after another, often after extensive investigation and agreement on facts. This was the process that had evolved over the thirty years of experience with the International Joint Commission (see above, chapter 7). Even the vexed issues of tariff policy often turned on discovering and pointing out the larger mutual advantage that lay under the connivance of special interests. Trade negotiations, or discovering and tracking pollution, or apportioning the flow of water on the Milk River were all specialized tasks, the province of experts. It was the kind of thing that appealed to Mackenzie King, whose early career was built on proving that he was just such an expert. Without exactly intending to do so, King had presided over the emergence of a progressive professional class in government and embodied them in his nation's civil service. This development matched what was happening in other countries, but especially the United States and the United Kingdom, and it conformed to the personal though limited experience of Canada's small corps of professional diplomats. It was compatible, too, with a faith in international law and the development of a common system of enforcement that would be bound by courts and precedent.[36]

Functionalism is an optimistic creed (or theory, if you prefer), and it fits well with a liberal philosophy of life, in which progress is the keynote.[37] Conservatives, pessimists, and "realists" (in the political science sense of the term, for their views are often wildly unrealistic) are frequently impatient with functionalists and, by extension, with the many Canadians who, consciously or not, adopted functionalism as their modus operandi in the middle years of the twentieth century. Realists, on the other hand, characterized the world as a fearsome place, requiring constant vigilance and preparation for the worst. Sometimes, as in the Second World War, realists and functionalists could agree—as on Hitler and the Nazi regime. More generally, the fascist and communist dictatorships of the mid-twentieth century presented an almost irrefutable proof of the validity of realist thought. Functionalists liked the Nazis and Communists no more than did the realists, and, for functionalists, there was a distinct preference for better-behaving countries governed by laws and operating on democratic principles, with democracy and open government acting as a control not only on the wickedness of tyrants, but also on some of the wilder schemes of the realists.

Certainly if Canada was to find a home among nations, it would find it in the company of other like-minded states, temporarily associated as "the United Nations" during the Second World War. Roosevelt and King had assumed as much when they first discussed the shape of the postwar world over dinner at the White House in December 1942. The subject of the day was the recent appearance of a report on social welfare by the British Liberal economist, Lord Beveridge, which had made a sensation on both sides of the Atlantic. Almost nobody had read the report, for it was long and dense and dry, but virtually every member of the political classes had read a summary.

Afterward, King told his diary that "we had quite a talk about Beveridge's report. The President said that the Beveridge report has made a real impression in [the United States]. [The report proposed] the thought of insurance from the cradle to the grave. That seems to be a line that will appeal. You and I [said Roosevelt] ought to take that up strongly. It will help both of us politically as well as being on the right lines in the way of reform."[38]

Unfortunately not all members of the Allied coalition could be said to be democracies: the greatest exception was most obviously the Soviet Union, but there were also Portugal (a fascist dictatorship), various shades of authoritarian regimes in Latin America, and China, divided between nationalists and communists, neither of them democratic practitioners. Even some of the leading democratic powers, such as the United Kingdom and the United States, practiced colonialism to varying degrees and maintained empires.[39]

Canadians had an ambiguous relationship to the notion of empire, and the British Empire in particular. So, for that matter, did the Americans, who, like Canadians in the 1930s, cheered on Hollywood's recreation of the British cavalry charging to victory over malcontents (always sinister) in British India or in the Sudan, in movies such as *The Lives of a Bengal Lancer* or *The Four Feathers*. When one of Mackenzie King's staff, Harry Ferns, suggested that Canada take a sympathetic interest in the cause of Indian independence, his advice led to grave suspicions that Ferns held very unsound views and may have helped terminate his career as a Canadian civil servant.[40]

By 1945 it was becoming unlikely that British cavalry would ever again charge anywhere in the old style, and certainly not with the old results. Victory in Europe in May 1945 meant the disappearance of Hitler and the Nazis, and victory over Japan in four months later relieved the Allies of the necessity of a costly and bloody invasion of the Japanese home islands— but at the cost of the explosion of two atomic bombs, at Hiroshima and Nagasaki. The bomb was composed of radioactive materials (uranium and plutonium) refined in a factory in Canada, and so Canada had a ringside seat in the new world of atomic insecurity that immediately succeeded the just-vanquished Axis Powers.

The end of the war left other pockets of uncertainty. The biggest was the result of the contraction of British power, and the sense that the British Empire could not be as much of a factor in balancing Canada's relations with the United States. The old psychological prop of Empire was weakened in direct proportion to the diminution of British wealth and military strength. The Empire immediately began to contract, as the British gave independence to India, Pakistan, Ceylon, and Burma, and abandoned the British mandate in Palestine. The Canadian government did its best to shore up the British economy, granting a very large loan to Britain in 1946—only to discover that in the absence of a proportionate American loan, it merely postponed Britain's financial crisis, which was the direct consequence of a lack of convertible foreign exchange reserves.

Paradoxically, on a personal level, Canadian–British relations had never been better. The billeting experience during the war suggested that left to their own devices, Canadians and Britons got along very well. The connection was expressed in the eighty thousand war brides and children who accompanied their Canadian soldier-husbands back to Canada after 1945. It expanded the meaning of the Imperial Family.

Britain's need for Canadian money and Canadian supplies guaranteed that the British government would see Ottawa as a strategic partner in an entirely novel way. Intellectually, Canadian officials were more likely to understand their British counterparts[41] and sympathize with them, even when the immediate consequences of Britain's economic austerity policies apparently harmed Canadian interests—especially Canadian exports—in the short run. What the Canadian government collectively understood, with a couple of exceptions, was that with the best will in the world, the British could not afford to buy Canadian products, unless Canada lent them the money to buy them. This Canada duly did.

The United States did not need the same kind of attention, or help, from Canada. There was an American military incursion into Canada in 1942–3, as the US army built roads and airfields and pipelines in the Canadian North, designed to supply American troops in Alaska and establish a staging route for aircraft en route to supply the Soviet Union through Siberia. For a few months, the American engineering presence in Northwestern Canada was so large and obvious that it alarmed some observers; but it passed and was forgotten, though it did leave behind the Alaska Highway as a permanent land connection between Alaska and the lower forty-eight states.[42]

The American presence in Newfoundland and Labrador was perhaps more noticeable, was more economically significant, and certainly lasted longer. Because Newfoundland was a British colony, and not a Canadian province, arrangements were different, for the British conceded the Americans sovereign base rights under exclusively American control. After the war, the US Air Force could freely use Newfoundland bases for nuclear patrols and as regular points of call between American bases in Europe and in the United States. In the shorter term, the American presence was certainly not unwelcome to many if not most Newfoundlanders, and stimulated a brief enthusiasm in 1947–8 for an economic union with the United States, in preference to the confederation with Canada that actually occurred in 1949.

On the highest level, Canadian–American relations remained cordial. Mackenzie King visited his friend in Roosevelt in the White House in March 1945. The two men passed a fair amount of time together, including an amiable evening imagining what they would do after the end of the war, and in retirement. King was Roosevelt's last foreign visitor, and he was the only foreign head of government to attend the president's funeral, some weeks later.[43]

Canada and the United States pursued parallel policies in the years after the war. King actually made an effort to implement the spirit of the Beveridge report by proposing to the provinces a system of national insurance, including health, but it ran aground, as King expected (and had predicted to Roosevelt in 1942), on the shoals of provincial jurisdiction under the Canadian constitution. Roosevelt's successor as president, Harry Truman, had neither the prestige nor, in his cabinet, the competence to follow Roosevelt's path. Truman himself, a vice-president who became the accidental president in 1945, was thought to be incompetent and error-prone, and there was an element of snobbery in Americans' general attitudes toward their president, for unlike the patrician Roosevelt, Truman was a failed small businessman in his pre-political life, without the benefit of any kind of university education, much less the Harvard education of Franklin D. Roosevelt. Truman's low political standing mattered, as did the ineptitude of most of his cabinet, because it was not enough to devise theoretical policies for the postwar world; one had to actually implement them. Thanks to a very strong Canadian cabinet, this proved possible north of the border. To the south, despite the obviously greater number of experts, the administration of reconstruction (the term for converting the economy to peacetime) was poorly managed.[44]

On the other hand, Canadian superiority should not be thought to mean that Canada was more advanced or necessarily better governed than the United States. The United States was much more advanced in such areas as labor law, social security, and government-sponsored systems such as education. Canada had a baby bonus that helped to redistribute income, a bit, and it had meager old-age pensions, and, since 1941, unemployment insurance. But Canadians could only dream of the level of American government programs that enriched life south of the border.

The principal concern of governments in the English-speaking democracies was to bring the troops home and avoid the revolutionary discontent that had marred the aftermath of what was now called the First World War. Naturally, intellectuals thought in parallels to 1919; but fortunately, it was 1945 and not 1919. Beginning in 1929, the Depression had intervened, as well as the war, and the result was the build-up of sixteen years' worth of unfulfilled (because unaffordable) demand. Despite heavy taxes, the war had built up savings as well as demand, both on the civilian side and in the pay packets of the troops. There was deferred family formation—late marriage and low birth rates in the 1930s, and the absence of males during the war. Marriage, children, and deferred gratification all played a part in what followed, and in the origins of the baby boom, an explosion of children in the late 1940s and through the 1950s. Learning from 1919, governments were very careful to treat the veterans well, with generous bonuses, free education through university, and other forms of assistance.

There had been, as well, a kind of technological build-up in the 1930s and the war, with the result that new technologies were ready to be converted, cheaply, into consumer products. There was another aspect to the years after 1945. International trade was low, with the world divided into two orders of economic policy. On the one side, there were "hard currency countries"—countries whose money could theoretically be taken to a bank and exchanged for another currency. In 1945–6, this bloc consisted essentially of the United States and Canada, with the possible addition of gold-rich South Africa. Then there was the soft currency world, where the value of money was artificially propped up by rigid economic controls and stringent restrictions on what could be traded, and by whom. (There were also the countries of the Communist bloc, where the notion of trade had a different meaning, and countries like China, where the currency was in chaos.) Europe, in particular, had a dollar shortage, exported little to North America, and bought little in return. This problem led directly to various aid schemes by, first, the Canadian government, and then by the United States government, principally through the Marshall Plan, which transferred vast sums of American dollars to the Europeans to kick-start international trade and return the world to a more or less stable and rewarding system of international exchange. Canada's aid program was inevitably too small, and Canada, probably inevitably, ended up taking a loan from the American Export–Import Bank, while imposing controls on its currency. The Americans, in granting the loan, singled out Canada for preferment for the explicit reason that they did not wish to be the sole solvent economy in the world, and that Canada's currency problem (too few American dollars) would soon be remedied. As it was, though not through trade but through an inflow of

American investment—itself another testimony to American faith in Canada's prospects and conviction that Canada was a very safe place to trade. These American views most probably were based on the wartime experience of trade with Canada, and the close contacts between American and Canadian officials at the time, as well as between the two business communities.

There was also contact in the workforce. This was mainly through similarity, for although the pre-war patterns of emigration from Canada to the United States resumed after 1945, there was not as much need. Jobs were plentiful in Canada, and even if the pay was not what it was in the miraculous United States, it was for many Canadians close enough not to justify pulling up stakes and moving to the States. The labor forces of Canada and the United States swelled with returning veterans after the war, but for the time being there was little addition from immigration. This fact gave a unique character to the North American labor force—overwhelmingly English-speaking, imbued with English-language political and economic culture, and isolated. That does not mean that labor in the postwar period was docile—it was anything but. Labor was a scarce commodity, and employers' alternatives were few. Frequent mass strikes helped make the point, in case employers had not noticed it.

There was an indigenous and autonomous Canadian trade union movement dating back to the nineteenth century, but there was also the Canadian branch of American labor—organized through the so-called "international" unions, the prime example being the United Auto Workers (UAW) that dominated the automobile industry, which, in turn, was organized around three giant American auto companies, General Motors, Ford, and Chrysler. Those firms had been the stars of Canada's war production, and their management and their workers were deservedly self-confident: they made more cars and trucks; they were the best cars and trucks; and they needed to make more. Foreign automobiles were almost unknown on North American streets in the late 1940s—Rolls-Royce, perhaps, and some pre-war luxury items, but very few of the ordinary production of European factories. The streets of North (and South) America were an American-designed and American-made reservation—though in Canada tariffs kept out automobiles actually made in the United States, and Canadians became accustomed to buying from a smaller range of models, and at higher cost. But the wages were there to allow the workers to buy, and they bought not only cars but houses and appliances—again, on the American model. And so there were strikes at GM, Ford, and Chrysler, as the workers showed that only they could make this happen. Wages rose, and benefits, and the expectation was created that this was a process that could go on forever, in a cyclical ritual of bargaining, followed by ritual strikes, followed by ritual but lucrative concessions; these not only made the North American industrial work force the best paid in the world, but created the expectation that this was some kind of natural phenomenon, like the seasons, or the flow of water over Niagara Falls.

The result was an economic boom, matching and making possible the baby boom. It was a consumption boom, and in Canada it was as well a foreign investment boom. Foreign investment in this period meant American investment, though there were some shreds of British investment that unaccountably survived the liquidation of Britain's overseas assets to pay for the war. But usually, in this period, when *boom* was mentioned, it was the baby boom. This was an American term,[45] and it characterized a birth rate much higher than the historical average. The number of births per annum rose steadily until, in Canada in 1960, it approached 500,000; the other English-speaking countries, but particularly the United States and Australia, experienced the same phenomenon.[46]

The boom was expressed in statistics. Canada's population rose steadily with the baby boom. The standard of living rose too, though income figures are complicated by a burst of inflation in 1947–9; the inflation helps to account for the number of strikes in the period. Wartime expenditure ended with the war, along with wage and price controls—rather more promptly and certainly less messily in Canada than in the United States. The highest marginal tax rate descended (on income earned over $500,000) from 97.8 percent to 84 percent. At the lowest end, 600,000 income earners were removed from the tax rolls through a large proportionate increase in personal exemptions.[47] These dull figures might not seem to merit comment, but they signify something rather important: taxation continued to work toward a compression of incomes, so that the richest citizens or taxpayers occupied a smaller proportion of the income pyramid than they did in 1939, and much smaller than they did in 1929. Another point is worth mentioning: on the whole, Canadian taxes were lower than American taxes, and, especially to business-minded American observers, Canada's government was more efficient and less costly than its American counterpart. Although the political left in Canada was lively and thriving, it was nowhere near dominant, and policies like those of Britain's Labour government remained the stuff of dreams. Thus the economic-political convergence that was a feature of North American life during the war continued into the postwar period. Though there was obvious and abounding prosperity, and although business was booming, so, on the whole, were the lower and middle classes.

Economics shaped politics. This was true in Canada and the United States, but also in Great Britain. It does not mean that there were not significant disagreements among the political parties, Conservative, Liberal, Labour, Democratic, and Republican. There was a right wing, as there was a left, the right wing being more prominent and obvious in the United States and the left in Great Britain, with Canada somewhere in between. The British election of 1945 did mark a caesura between British politics of the 1930s and those of the 1940s, and guaranteed a political outcome that nationalized much of the British economy and created the state-financed National Health Service. Winston Churchill and his political imp, the Anglo-Canadian Lord Beaverbrook, might well have prevented Labour's nationalizations, but they could not have done very much about British tax rates, nor could they have altered Labour's abandonment of large chunks of the British Empire. Being defeated in 1945 meant that Churchill himself did not have to concede independence to India and the other Asian jewels in Britain's imperial crown; and when he came back to power, he found that after all it did not matter. British life and politics went on.

Virtually nobody in Canada or the United States wanted to imitate Labour's nationalization policy, although Canada's democratic socialists, organized in a party called the Co-operative Commonwealth Federation (CCF) mumbled about it to themselves when they gathered in conclaves to wonder why they were not more successful electorally. Even the CCF had one success to its credit, and that was the election of a socialist government in Saskatchewan in 1944 under an attractive and plausible young leader, the Reverend Tommy Douglas.

This was quite a contrast with the United States, though the contrast is more one of phase or generation than of fundamental principle. It was not in Canada but in the United States where a socialist government was first elected, in Saskatchewan's southern neighbor, North Dakota, in 1918. And it was a true socialist government as it set about converting to state ownership parts of the North Dakotan economy. In 1945 Minnesota still had a Farmer–Labor Party whose platform, as its name suggests, was not oriented toward the encouragement or reward of big business. And the charismatic leader of the United Automobile Workers union, Walter Reuther, was a member of the American Socialist party (though he did eventually join Franklin Roosevelt's Democratic party).

To observers in the late 1940s Canada and the United States seemed to be on converging paths, especially when compared with the disorderly world outside North America. When Canada faced an exchange crisis in late

1947, the State Department urged support. As Isaiah Berlin had noted in December 1944, Canada's reputation in Washington was so high that Canada was regarded as a most exceptional country. That view continued into peacetime. "I am authorized to take the position for the State Department," an American official wrote in 1945, "that to treat Canada like any other foreign Government would be contrary to our policy. It is their view that the Canadian economy should be treated as nearly as possible like our own in peacetime as well as in war, based always on mutual reciprocity."[48] And so Canadian economic problems—problems of foreign exchange—were treated with sympathy as well as concern. Canadian and American delegations discussed, with some seriousness, the possibility of a free trade area or commercial union (no internal tariffs and a common external tariff); friends of Canada urged support. The view of the Republican-leaning but internationalist popular magazine *Life* is illuminating on how some Americans saw Canada in an editorial on March 15, 1948. Its publisher, Henry Luce, began it thus:

> Canadians are the closest friends we have in the world, and they are in serious economic trouble. From the US they need, and deserve, considerably less apathy about their plight. More than that, they need complete and permanent *economic* union with the US. The US needs this too, and so does the future of a healthy world.

Luce argued that political union did not have to follow economic union, and pointed out that loose American rhetoric had helped sink reciprocity in 1911, while foolish American economic tariff policy between the wars had only alienated Canada. Nonetheless, Canada, for its own good, and the United States should now find common cause.[49]

It may well be true that Canada and the United States in 1948 were closer to finding common cause than ever before or since. That was not primarily because of the Cold War, as is often supposed (and which is the subject of the following chapter). It was because of the Second World War and what it brought about—parallel and very comparable war efforts, an integration of economic policies and structures during the war, and very similar approaches to the problems of peace and reconstruction. Above all, it created what has been called a "great compression" in society, bringing the top layer closer than ever before to the bottom economic class. It was with that social structure that North Americans faced together the problem of the Cold War.

# Exceptional North America and the Cold War, 1949–1979

IN 1949 CANADA, the United States, Great Britain, and most of Western Europe signed a treaty in Washington that created an alliance for mutual security and, if necessary, mutual defense. Watching the ceremony unfold, as ambassadors signed the document, Canada's external affairs minister, Lester B. Pearson, cynically reflected that it was April 1, April Fool's Day, and that the US Marine band in the background was playing a tune from the musical *Porgy and Bess*, "I got plenty of nothing, and nothing's plenty for me."[1]

Strictly speaking, this was not true, for the treaty bound its signatories to come to each other's defense in case of external attack, though any diplomat who had survived the 1930s, as Pearson had, was familiar with the history of broken promises and false starts that littered the diplomacy of the period. Would the postwar world be any different? Pearson hoped so, and the treaty embodied his hopes. He had helped draft the North Atlantic Treaty and had overseen months of negotiations in 1948–9 to arrive at its terms. It had been a complicated negotiation, first defining what territory was to be covered, and then debating how an automatic response to aggression could be squared with the US Constitution and an untrammeled American sovereignty. For most of that time, Prime Minister Mackenzie King had kept an eye on the discussions, for King considered a treaty that bound Canada, the United States, and Great Britain together highly satisfactory, though for a reason that would have surprised Canada's negotiating partners—he was worried not so much about Canada's physical security, its safety from attack, as about its psychological well-being, its self-respect, in the belief and the hope that Canada's future would not be as an abject dependency of the United States, or as the forty-ninth state.[2]

King was at the end of his political career and at the end of his mental tether, when in November 1948 he resigned as prime minister. He found the world of 1948, indeed the world since 1945, confusing and distressing. In part that was because he saw the world changing in a way that unmoored his country and left it drifting on a current that seemed to lead directly to Washington, leaving behind the familiar shores of the British Empire. King understood very well that the British economy was on the ropes and that the end of the British Empire was probably only a matter of time, and not much time at that. Great Britain would continue to exist, but it would be a diminished Britain, not the country whose wealth and power had preserved Canada in the 1780s and the 1810s. He understood the economic power of the United States, and understood too that Canada's own prosperity, even its performance in the war just past, had depended upon American goodwill and the sense of a common cause between the two countries.

During the war and after King was reluctant to hang Canada's political fate entirely on the Americans. It was not how he personally saw Canada and Canadians or where he wanted them to go. It was the old story: Canadians were related to the Americans, and close to them in many ways, certainly, but historically they were bound to Great Britain. A Canada focused entirely on the United States would not be able to resist the pull of American wealth, power, and culture. For that reason King had vetoed an economic union with the United States in March 1948, to the distress of his bureaucrats and the puzzlement of those few ministers who knew of this ultra-secret possibility. There had been good reason to do a deal with the Americans, for Canada's economic stability depended on a regular flow of American dollars, earned through trade or investment, and Canada's reserves of American dollars were perilously low. But the proposed treaty omitted Great Britain, and thus undermined, in King's view, Canada's historic political identity. So a North Atlantic Treaty that bound Canada both to the British and to the Americans (with the Western Europeans thrown in) was an ideal solution. In terms of short-term politics it would reassure Canadian public opinion, still strongly bound to Britain, as it reassured King himself.

The Treaty of Washington of 1949 created the North Atlantic Treaty Organization and bound its signatories to come to each other's aid if they were attacked by a foreign power. Everyone knew that only one foreign power could do that—the Soviet Union. The alliance would shore up the confidence of its signatories and counteract the notion that communism was the wave of the future, and that resistance was futile. The ideological drive behind the North Atlantic alliance was strong—free countries with liberal and democratic institutions wanted to preserve their freedom against the threat of communism. That threat was defined in traditional terms, as inter-state aggression, but the real danger was not so much external or international, as domestic.

That was a point the Canadians made in the course of the NATO negotiations in 1948. "The Canadians realized more clearly than anyone else that a truly military alliance, as important as it undoubtedly was and is, was not enough," a sympathetic American participant recalled. "What was really needed was a progressive development of a true Atlantic Community, with a capital "C"—progressively closer unity in all fields."[3] In the Canadian point of view, or rather the Canadian government's point of view, such a community would be stronger than a mere military alliance, and in the British Commonwealth Canada had immediate experience of just such a linkage. But in the opinion of senior American officials, such a system was impractical, because it implied a supra-national commitment on the part of the United States; it was doubly impractical, because they knew they could not get it past Congress. The United States had become leader of an alliance, a league of liberal democracies,[4] but it was an unequal alliance, in which one ally was more equal than the others.

## Parallel Lives: Canada, the United States, and Prosperity

The international entity, NATO, created by the North Atlantic allies relied on the United States, on its military power, and on its monopoly of the atomic bomb. The members of the North Atlantic alliance were all sovereign states, theoretically equal. Theoretically it also rested on American military power, but in 1949 that consisted mainly of the atomic bomb, whose utility had yet to be determined. NATO's real edge was economic, in a world where the United States and its allies accounted for well over half of the world's wealth. The military side of American power was useful for keeping the Russians out and for deterring a communist attack, while waiting for economic superiority to make its mark. Economics would ultimately de-fang and derail all but the blindest Soviet partisans.

For Canada the fact that Great Britain was now a lesser power was as important as the fact that the United States was now much greater. It was a point driven home to Mackenzie King when he visited Roosevelt's successor, Harry Truman, in Washington, in the fall of 1945. Dean Acheson, an assistant secretary of state at the time, but destined for greater things, drove King back to the Canadian embassy from the White House. Acheson was unusual in the American government for many reasons, but one was that his parents hailed from Toronto, and his clergyman father had moved to the United States as the Episcopalian (Anglican) bishop of Connecticut. His mother came from one of Toronto's most prominent and wealthiest families. In a reversal of the usual pattern, Acheson's rich relatives were Canadian and in his memoirs he recorded his mild resentment at the manner in which they dispensed their largesse to him.

With Mackenzie King sitting captive beside him, Acheson took the opportunity to tell the Canadian prime minister that things had changed, and that countries in the Western hemisphere—Canada and the United States—had to see things from a different point of view than the British.[5] King did not say so later to his diary, but he did not disagree that Canada and the United States had much in common. It could not be denied that Canada and the United States looked different than the British Isles. There was no war damage. There had been wear and tear on civilian life during the war—things looked shabbier than they had in 1939 because upkeep had been postponed—but there were new factories converted from making munitions, new workers' housing around the munitions plants, and plenty of demand in a civilian economy. There were pent-up savings, which thanks to government policy could now be released to their owners.

A consumer boom occurred in the context of overwhelming American and Western economic superiority. There was almost no economic category in which the United States did not stand first. American technology put American resources to work, making steel and building automobiles, fleets of aircraft, and an infinite variety of consumer products. In the great American cities there were more skyscrapers than anywhere else, and taller, and floods of workers to populate their offices. Mass organization was an American specialty, and the science of management had been invented in the United States. Behind the consumer goods, American laboratories were busy improving or even transcending the technology that built them.

Above all, the United States stood first in how it organized its society, reflected in its standard of living, in the sense of equal opportunity and almost unlimited prospects that it conferred on its citizens (blacks excepted).[6] Taken as a whole, the United States was unsurprisingly immensely attractive to Canadians. In the 1920s, that had meant a steady flow of English and French Canadians to the United States; but in the 1940s and 1950s, things were different. There were more factories in the cities, while the resource industries—Canada's traditional strength—were booming. There were jobs to be had in Canada; in fact there was a labor shortage. Some Canadians did indeed move to the United States, many of them highly skilled and talented into jobs or levels of work that did not exist in Canada—a phenomenon known as the "brain drain." But proportionately there were fewer who left, compared with the 1920s, because there was improved opportunity at home as well as across the border. The Canadian standard of living rose like the American, meaning that factory or office workers in Canada, like their counterparts in the United States, could expect and enjoy a middle-class standard of living, owning a house or a car and the labor-saving appliances ("the magic boxes of affluence," in Avner Offner's wonderful phrase) that made housekeeping bearable and that also conferred status and materially signified belonging.[7] Above all, as the press never tired of pointing out, Canada and the United States were an almost unique island of great prosperity, as Europe struggled to regain its feet. For Canadians and Americans the allure of communism, with its promise of modernity, rationality, and equality, was superfluous—these things had already been achieved, and without the pain of a revolution or the dictatorship of the proletariat. Even if one took seriously communism's promise of true equality, with benefits equally shared by all, it could be and was argued that the United States in particular (with Canada not far behind) "has had a greater measure of social equality and social mobility than any highly developed society in human history."[8]

A perceptive American historian once dubbed Americans a "People of Plenty," which in some senses they were and had been, as long as one forgot the Great Depression. And so were Canadians. It was an aspect of uniqueness, or exceptionalism—different from, better than, the Europeans. But collective memory is short, and the 1930s began to seem another era, even another planet. Even if one did remember the 1930s, there was a sense that now the key to prosperity had been discovered, a philosopher's stone, an economic formula, that would lead on to indefinite wealth—and John Maynard Keynes was the philosopher. Keynes's disciples sat in the Canadian Department of Finance and crafted budgets that would have met the approval of the master, had he been alive to examine them (Keynes died in 1946). Collectively, Canada's senior civil servants were a homogeneous group, known to their admirers and detractors both as "the mandarins." They had an unusual combination of political, academic, and international skills. At the time, this was assumed to be the Canadian norm, but as it turned out, the age of the mandarins spanned only a couple of generations, from about 1930 to about 1980.[9]

The statistics of the period are illuminating. Economically, Canada and the United States did move in the same direction, which may be the most important point, but did not move exactly in tandem, since according to a later OECD study US per capita GDP fell after 1944 and did not return to that level until the mid-1950s.[10] Canada's GDP, on the other hand, grew steadily, with a dip only in 1945–6, meaning that the disparity in income per capita between Canada and the United States shrank in the late 1940s and after.[11] The Canadian–American income gap did not disappear, but in shrinking it removed a large part of the incentives for Canadians to move south. So Canada remained considerably smaller and slightly poorer in per capita terms, but in most important respects its social and economic institutions, its way of life, and its urban geography resembled those of the United States, and were attractive enough to offer the overwhelming majority of Canadians a viable alternative to emigration. To an American visiting or working in Canada in the 1950s, Canada was still conservative, and a bit backward, especially where social security was concerned,[12] but essentially the same as the United States.

Not everybody did equally well out of the economic bonanza. Blacks and native Americans and Canadians remained, by and large, poorer—in many cases, miserably poor. At the bottom of the income scale, even in the prosperous cities, families scraped to get by. And yet, with close to full employment year after year, with a labor shortage and restricted immigration from outside North America, incomes rose steadily. From the United States, Canadians imported models of how to live, or live better, and then built or manufactured their own variant behind a high tariff wall. In the case of automobiles, for example, American manufacturers continued to dominate the market except at the highest end of luxury vehicles, and their Canadian subsidiaries produced a limited and less glamorous range of the cars available to American consumers.

But even in the United States, high income taxes meant that disposable income for a truly luxurious lifestyle of the kind enjoyed before the war was limited largely to those with inherited fortunes. At the same time universal employment meant that the standard of living at the bottom had actually gone up during the war. The distance between the top and the bottom had shrunk, in what the economist Paul Krugman would later label "the Great Compression" in society.[13]

The similarity with Canada was obvious—so obvious that it was assumed rather than articulated. At the top Canadians earned less, but everything was relative. Compared with the rest of the world, Canada was a star; alongside the United States, however, it was a junior partner in prosperity. Accordingly, the quantitative difference between life in Canada and life in the United States—fewer gadgets, less choice, lagging styles—was palpable. "They used to talk a lot about the quality of life back 25 years ago," an American observer commented, reflecting on the country he had moved to in 1958, "but it wasn't that great. Now [1988] it's good," he added.[14]

A poorer country, Canada was also a more conservative country. The 1940s was the age when sociology and polling combined to study the roots of society. For American sociologists on a tight budget, Canada was a foreign country made to order, since for the cash-strapped academic it was only a train ride or even a bus fare away. Not surprisingly, they usually found it more conservative, especially in its French-speaking part, and, in terms of the English-speaking provinces, small and somewhat parochial.[15] The huge exception was the election in 1944 of a democratic socialist[16] government in Saskatchewan, with all that that might imply for the future of the left in the United States, as well as in Canada. Canada's socialists pointed to the installation of a socialist government in Great Britain in 1945 and argued that Britain was the model for the future. But for most Canadians, newly impoverished Britain was no longer a model they would easily choose, at least not for its economic policy. It was more important to catch up to the adjacent United States, meaning that Canadian incomes had to rise toward American levels. If there was an income lag, there was also a time lag—what happened one year in the United States in terms of gadgets or technology would happen in Canada the next, or the year after. As for style, the high-end Canadian department stores were careful to keep their stock up to date, since their customers could and did easily slip away to New York or London or Paris. If that was not sufficient, they could move there themselves.

Canada and the United States also overlapped in the general health and life expectancy of the population—basically the same in 1950. Whatever the economic and social differences in society, the two countries were very close in health outcomes. However, from the late 1950s on a gap opened up between the two countries, which by the mid-1980s was quite noticeable and significant: Canadians could expect to live two years longer. Two social scientists studying the phenomenon explained that "a 2-year life expectancy gap may not sound like a lot, but during ages 25–64 it translates into mortality rates 30–50 percent per year higher in the USA compared to Canada. Socio-economic analyses show that the poorest 20 percent of Canadians enjoy the same life expectancy as Americans of average income."[17]

Further up the income and social scale, things were different—and may even be said to reverse. Twenty years earlier, in the 1920s, a journalist had described Canada as a "headless pyramid." In the United States one could go further and higher, achieving recognition and reward that small Canada simply could not offer. The ratio of ten-to-one between the two countries' populations was hard at work, and encouraged many talented Canadians to leave the "one" and move to the "ten." The larger US population meant more opportunities, more publishers, more symphony orchestras, more places in radio and television, more jobs as architects or clothes designers. This was the country to which the tenor Edward Johnson emigrated, to sing in opera, ending up as the general manager of New York's Metropolitan Opera. Opera as far as most Canadians were concerned was something broadcast from New York, though those who understood such things were duly boastful that it was Johnson who was broadcasting it.

A country of fourteen million people, of whom more than four million spoke another language, had to strain to offer the same opportunities in business, or in the arts, or in academia, as a neighbor ten times larger and with a much greater substratum of inherited wealth—and one speaking the same language. There remained as well the lure of Great Britain, impoverished by the war, certainly, but with an exciting new government and social vision, as well as a flourishing cultural world. Small wonder that Marie Dressler, Mary Pickford, Raymond Massey, Glenn Ford, Thomas B. Costain, Sydney Newman, Lorne Greene, Peter Jennings, and John Kenneth Galbraith moved south to the United States or east to London. Canada, by their standards, was a country of limitations, fortunately attached by language and culture to larger countries with greater opportunities. And culturally, economically, even politically, because of the importance of New York within the American system, and now as the seat of the United Nations, there was no place like New York City.

With eight million people, New York was almost the size of English-speaking Canada. It dwarfed London in wealth if not population. Its art galleries, its skyscrapers, its culture high and low, its publishing houses, not to mention its new television studios, gave it a greater concentration of cultural industries and the money to support them than any other place on earth. To an arriving Englishman in 1953, "I was disembarking at the City of Cities, the apex of all the continents. Everyone knew this was so, and New York knew it most certainly of all. The city's architecture was the most exciting, its culture the most vibrant, its music rang round the planet, its banks were the richest, its slang infected the way people talked across half the world."[18] Robert McNeil, a Canadian emigrant in the 1950s, chose first to go to Britain, and then the United States where he became a major figure in broadcasting; he compared leaving for the United States to moving from black and white into Technicolor. Other examples abound.[19]

It is a truism, but one that bears repeating, that such Canadians were easily accepted into the United States. Sometimes they brought skills that were in demand—desirable qualities that Americans could access without difficulty because they believed they were, essentially, the same as their own. How could this be? For an academic theory there is again the sociologist Seymour Martin Lipset who learnedly and repeatedly stressed the uniqueness of American culture—American Exceptionalism—to explain why American political and other forms of behavior are different. Yet time and again Americans found, and find, that Canadians are not dissimilar to themselves. Lipset originally came to Canada to examine the Saskatchewan phenomenon—socialism in one province—and to see if it had any application in the United States. He concluded that it did not. Citing various sociological and cultural authorities, Lipset argued that American history and American political culture made that country truly unique. In particular, he believed that Americans' individualism meant that socialism could never flourish in the United States. He devoted a book to the subject, and another to the differences between Canadians and Americans.[20] Yet he also had no problem conceding that the differences between Canadians and Americans were relatively few.

"[T]he two resemble each other more than either resembles any other nation.... Their differences," he added, "as we have seen from many public opinion polls, are often in the range of 5 to 10 percent."[21] Polls from the 1940s show that Lipset was correct. Early in 1946 Canadians and Americans were polled on their attitudes to "big business" and labor, and the influence these groups should have in public life. The results were nearly identical when it came to the desirability of labor influence, though Americans were more inclined to give some influence to big business. (In Canada, pro-labor views accounted for 50 percent of those polled; in the United States, 48 percent. The pro-business figures were 11 percent and 22 percent respectively.[22]) When asked—six months after the end of the war—whether any country wished to dominate the world, comparable numbers of Canadians and Americans replied affirmatively, 58 percent and 59 percent respectively. Many more Canadians than Americans identified the Soviet Union as the would-be dominator (50 and 25 percent); and more Americans than Canadians thought the British, alone or in combination, harbored that thought (16 and 3 percent).[23]

The most consistent (and accessible) set of American opinions on Canada, its relations to the United States, and Canadians' differences from or resemblances to Americans, comes from the United States foreign service. This is, of course, a specialized group, well educated and generally articulate. By definition, these Americans had a larger perspective than most, having traveled at least somewhere in the world, with the task of making foreign countries intelligible in Washington, and vice versa.

Speaking the same language, educated English, they also shared many of the assumptions about foreign relations and public policy as their Canadian counterparts; almost to a man or woman they rejected force or the use of threats as instruments of public policy. Canada was familiar in other ways. The Canadian foreign service was structurally similar to the American. It was similar, also, in the way that diplomatic professionals viewed their political masters, which ran the gamut from impatience to despair. An excellent example may be found in a discussion between two American diplomats specializing in economic affairs, reminiscing about the signing of a sectoral free-trade agreement in automobiles (commonly called the Autopact) by President Lyndon B. Johnson and Prime Minister Lester B. Pearson in January 1965:

[WILLIS C. ARMSTRONG] Q: Well, it's highly questionable whether Pearson ever understood the automobile agreement.

[PHILIP] TREZISE: Well, LBJ also. All that mattered was that Dillon [a former US treasury secretary] and [George] Ball [under-secretary of state] knew what it was and they wanted it.[24]

The ignorance of politicians was to be deplored, but not too much, for in the end the politicians did what the trade experts on both sides wanted them to do. And the trade experts functioned from a common understanding of economics and what was economically desirable. As well, Canada, it should be remembered, was well regarded by many in Washington, not merely for its policies but for the structure of its government—the efficient, majority-based parliamentary system, a functioning democracy but with no nonsense about division of powers.[25]

American views of Canada thus tended to be extremely positive.[26] George Vest, a junior officer at the American embassy in Ottawa in the early 1950s, had been nonplussed when he was transferred from the American mission in Quito, Ecuador, to chilly Ottawa, but his lack of Canadian background guaranteed that his views on Canada would be fresh. Many years later, remembering Ottawa, he told an interviewer:

Everybody was impressed with what Canada could do or would probably do, and this went all the way through. It wasn't a big embassy. It was a wonderful group. The military were impressed with what the Canadians were doing in the far north and what they were cooperating with our military on. The agriculture attaché thought Canada was one of the greatest things in the world and was going to be one of the breadbaskets of the future. They were building the trans-Canadian pipeline. It doesn't matter what area you were in, for those who worked with them, this was one of the great periods of Canada. I mean, the prime minister was Louis St. Laurent; the foreign minister, external affairs minister, was Mike Pearson; the man in charge of the economy was a great old man named C.D. Howe. These people were tremendous leaders, very important, and they knew everybody in Washington and in New York and in Chicago. It was a very interesting time.[27]

Vest worked in a context in which, in the United States, Canada and Canadians were favorably regarded:

If you went...to the other areas of the U.S. Government, to elsewhere in the country, there was a general attitude of, well, Canada is a splendid place and the Canadians are splendid people and they're particularly splendid because they're so nearly like us. And there was a considerable atmosphere of taking Canada for granted.

There were worse things than American approbation. When Canadians complained of being taken for granted, as they frequently did, their American interlocutors advised them to leave well enough alone. Consider what might happen if the United States really did pay attention to Canada. Would that be at all desirable or actually work in the Canadian interest?

It was better to let most Americans outside the diplomatic corps believe that Canadians were just like Americans and that, like Americans, they deserved a break. Meanwhile, the similarities spoke for themselves. The great issue of policy, however, was the Cold War, which affected almost every policy, foreign and domestic, for forty years.

## Fear and Insecurity

The communist danger derived from fear, and fear concentrated the public mind. Every time the fear showed some sign of abating, or mellowing, Stalin felt called upon to produce one foreign policy blunder after another—sponsoring a communist coup in Czechoslovakia in 1948; blockading the

Western powers' sectors of Berlin in 1948–9, defeated by airlifting supplies into the isolated city; authorizing the invasion of South Korea by North Korea in 1950–3. Stalin's actions stimulated the formation of NATO and a massive rearmament by the Western powers, including Canada; the creation of the Federal Republic of Germany, cobbled out of the Western powers' occupation zones; and the formation of a NATO army based mainly in West Germany.

The fear was real, and was compounded in September 1949 by the Soviet explosion of a test atomic bomb, ending the Americans' nuclear monopoly. In October, the communists under Mao Zedong celebrated their victory in the Chinese civil war by founding the People's Republic of China. Mao forthwith traveled to Moscow, where he pledged his country to an alliance with the Soviet Union. It was small wonder, therefore, that the Western powers in 1949–50 felt beleaguered and threatened from without. Many also felt threatened from within.

The result was a form of panic that swept over several Western countries, but principally the United States, in the early 1950s. The unease that accompanied the communization of Eastern Europe in 1947–8 was part of the cause. The Soviet atomic bomb was another stimulus, and in both these cases, communist activity was characterized by political subversion and espionage. The Korean War created further anxiety, partly because of the intervention of communist China in the war and the consequent defeat of the American army along the Korean–Chinese border in November–December 1950. Canada's external affairs minister, Lester Pearson, reported to cabinet in mid-December that "Many Americans were almost hysterical about the urgency of further defence measures, and there was no doubt there would be increasing US pressure on Canada in this connection. Some Americans, although not the more sober members of the Administration, accepted the inevitability of a war."[28]

What would it mean for Canada? According to Pearson and defense minister Brooke Claxton,

> the likelihood of war in the next 18 months was now much greater than estimated six months ago.... In the circumstances, the government's aim should be to prepare Canada against conditions of total war, and in the meantime build up "deterrent forces" in Canada and in Europe under NATO as quickly as possible.[29]

Army brigades were sent to Korea and Europe; the Royal Canadian Air Force was expanded, to the point where it supplied a substantial portion of

NATO's air strength in Europe; and the Royal Canadian Navy expanded as well, with a cruiser and an aircraft carrier. Had a general war broken out, Canada would have re-fought the Second World War, sending troops to Great Britain, and invading Europe with the same kind of mass army as in 1944.

The war did not come. Stalin did not intend a war, could not afford one, and would not willingly endanger his communist regime in such an uncertain enterprise. Yet several times he unwittingly pushed the West close to an armed response and by creating fear and uncertainty he increased the odds against the Soviet Union winning any resulting war. All the Western allies rearmed to some extent, but the Canadian effort was particularly strong, as befitted an ally with a strong economy, a cohesive political system, and a strong tax base. As a result of the war panic of 1950–1, Canada maintained a garrison under NATO in Europe for the next forty years, with ships and planes to match. Canada's defense effort was substantial—$5 billion (in the dollars of 1951) for rearmament, and a volunteer military force of more than 100,000. The 100,000 would have been the nucleus of a much larger force, which, if organized on Second World War lines, would have topped a million personnel.[30] It is true that Canada's mobilization was partial and preliminary, and accordingly its size did not compare to the American version, where the army alone consisted of a million and a half soldiers in the early 1950s.

The difference in size and military expenditure became more significant as time passed, but for the time being, in the 1950s, the fact that Canada could and would put together an all-volunteer and all-professional armed force, with up-to-date weapons, somewhat mitigated the disparity. And, in the generation after the Second World War, Canada's significance was judged by what it had put into the field in the Allied cause between 1939 and 1945. An American observer put it plainly, many years later:

> We saw and recalled that in both World War I and World War II Canadian military participation had been outstanding. In World War II, Canadians put over a million of their citizens into uniform out of a population of about 12 million, which was very directly comparable to the commitment that the United States made, which was about 12 million in uniform about of 140 million. As almost all of the Canadians who served were volunteers, it was even more remarkable. Canada didn't have conscription until almost the end of the war and virtually none of the people that went overseas were

draftees. So, Canadian participation in World War II was really quite striking. At the end of the war, I believe they had something like the fifth largest army, the fourth largest air force, the third largest navy, and they were well positioned to have been able to build nuclear weapons had they desired. They had a heavy bomber force. They were operating an aircraft carrier, at least one. This was a very, very capable military. Throughout the core of the Cold War, the Canadians put a very effective brigade into Europe that was there full-time. They had an air wing stationed in Germany. The brigade was a unit that I saw during a NATO Exercise Reforger [an annual NATO exercise] where I went to the field in Germany and saw various units, including the Canadian brigade. It was a very fine unit.[31]

The Cold War was not purely military, and panic was not confined to defense measures. American panic also stimulated a hunt for disloyalty. Between 1946 and 1950, one country after another had slipped under communist control, and then in 1949, China. It must be, reasoned right-wing critics, that the Truman administration not merely was guilty of stupidity or folly—it must have been led astray by spies and traitors. Such panics had happened before—most recently in the Red Scare of 1919 and in the relentless anti-communism of right-wing politicians in the United States and Canada (and elsewhere) during the 1920s and 1930s. While the Soviet Union was an indispensable ally during the Second World War, anti-communism was submerged and domestic communists in the United States and Canada enjoyed a brief vacation in the sun of publicity and public approval of the Soviet role in the war. That role was ambiguous—Stalin wished to defeat Hitler, but he also wanted to provide for Soviet security, to maintain his ruthless dictatorship at home, and to guard against what he considered a probable betrayal by his wartime allies—they were capitalists, after all, and expunging communism could never be far from their thoughts.

In the United States, the congressional system, largely free of executive control, and the custom of investigatory congressional committees guaranteed anti-communists full and free publicity, and their targets public shame in congressional hearings that operated, essentially, as kangaroo courts. Membership in the Communist Party of the United States was made illegal, and communists were subjected to various forms of legal disabilities. The phenomenon of extreme anti-communism in the United States soon became known as McCarthyism after its principal sponsor,

Senator Joe McCarthy of Wisconsin, but there were plenty of other politicians willing to jump on the bandwagon, notably the California congressman and later senator, Richard Nixon. It was in many senses an anti-elitist movement, with the well educated as particular targets. McCarthyism was widely reported and highly contentious in the United States; among Canadian elites, cousins to those being attacked in the United States, it seemed especially appalling. Nor were Canadians exempt. Lester Pearson, who had served at the Canadian embassy in Washington from 1942 to 1946, latterly as ambassador, was a target, a distinction he shared with many of his American friends, including the secretary of state, Dean Acheson, whom we have met earlier. When the Republicans took over the White House in 1953, under Dwight D. Eisenhower, it seemed that nothing now stood between McCarthy and a purge of the ideologically unfit in government and society. Great damage was inflicted on suspect institutions, such as the State Department, and as the purges proceeded, in government and out, some Americans pointed to the Canadian government's restraint. There were no congressional hearings, no public purges in Canada.[32]

As the bogus nature of the charges and the squalid morality of McCarthy and his associates became known, it provoked a reaction—what can be called anti-anti-communism, because anti-communism was so obviously the province of the unscrupulous. Outside the United States, anti-anti-communism could easily shade into anti-Americanism. In Canada, McCarthyism could easily be associated with and adopted by Canadian anti-communists, but after a spectacular failure by the main opposition party, the Progressive Conservatives, who used it in the federal election of 1949, anti-communism or McCarthyism, American style, retreated to the outer fringes of politics.

It was not that Canadian politicians or civil servants or intellectuals were "soft on communism," to use a phrase of the period. Canada prosecuted its own Cold War, matching its commitment abroad with security at home. There were loyalty investigations, discreet terminations of careers, and a public atmosphere of disapproval for supporters of the Soviet Union or advocates of the communist cause in China or elsewhere. The Canadian Communist party (known as the Labour-Progressive Party or LPP) was not, however, outlawed, and some communists continued to sit on city councils or in provincial legislatures. The RCMP kept the communists under surveillance, and it was commonly understood that a fair proportion of the party's members were actually police agents. The LPP was an increasingly pathetic spectacle, its main mission being to support the Soviet Union and lend its support to Soviet causes when called upon. Its obvious subservience to Soviet purposes eventually undermined its appeal, and its members who actually believed in communism or communist ideals either became disillusioned (and converted to capitalism) or drifted off to other left-wing sects.

The main causes of communist decline were thus internal to the movement, but it is certainly true that the Canadian government did its best to assist. A communist labor union was undermined with the full co-operation of the Canadian government. Canadian trade unions helped in that enterprise, and went on to destabilize another union: many of the fiercest opponents of communism in Canada came from the moderate left, which abroad had been one of the communists' major targets. Communism abroad was repaid with persecution of communists at home. And there was also the Korean War, which broke out in June 1950 when communist North Korea invaded non-communist South Korea. Mackenzie King had concluded that a third world war might originate in the Korean peninsula, and he had tried to avoid any Canadian involvement with that troubled country. When war did break out, however, Mackenzie King was no longer prime minister.

## *Consensus and Contradiction*

Politics shifted in Canada in 1948. Mackenzie King, for so long the center of Canadian political life, finally moved on and retired in November 1948. He had orchestrated the selection of his successor as Liberal leader in August: Louis St. Laurent, the senior minister from Quebec and since 1946 the minister for external affairs. St. Laurent was of mixed Irish and French descent, a corporate lawyer by trade, and a late-blooming and rather reluctant politician. St. Laurent extended the King era, inheriting his most effective ministers from King, adjusting well to the civil service that King had created, and perpetuating policies that had already worked well in converting the country from wartime prosperity to peacetime wealth. It was an unbeatable combination, and St. Laurent was rewarded with two majority governments. In setting his views on the world outside Canada his Irish element was probably the more important. He did not instinctively love Great Britain and the British tradition in Canada, but on the other hand he was a traditionalist and readily found that the British connection—the monarchy and the evolving British Commonwealth of Nations—suited Canada's interests.

It also suited Canadian sentiments. Canada celebrated its British heritage as well as its American links. While members of the political class and the bureaucrats in Washington and Ottawa could easily talk about the things they held in common, they knew that there was another, British, side to Canada. The political symbols were different, the political rituals were different, and the political institutions took some getting used to. George Washington and Thomas Jefferson were absent from Canadian coinage, even if Canadians might have been uncertain about who Washington's anti-revolutionary contemporaries, George III or the king's viceroy in Canada, Lord Dorchester, might have been. But Queen Victoria was for older Canadians a living memory, and the kings and queens since were real. *Maclean's Magazine*, English Canada's most influential periodical, ran a regular column keeping its readers abreast of events in Britain,[33] and British periodicals like the *Illustrated London News* or the lower-class *News of the World* had a regular Canadian readership, enhanced, of course, by heavy British immigration since 1945. Even to Americans familiar with Canada, through family connections, Canada was a different place. "We were very aware it was a different country and in [Southwestern Ontario] it was very, very British at that time," one American remembered.[34] The death of King George VI in February 1952 was followed by great public mourning in Canada; he was succeeded by his twenty-five-year-old daughter, Elizabeth II, who had toured Canada to considerable enthusiasm the year before. Naturally there was a coronation.

As with the coronations of 1902, 1911, and 1937, politicians and the merely rich contended for seats at the feast in London, while Canadians at home did their best to duplicate the hullabaloo. The mayor of Ottawa, Charlotte Whitton, took her cue from the medieval monarchs of England, dressed herself and her uncomfortable council in replicas of British civic costumes (robes, furs, and ceremonial chains), and led a barge procession through the heart of the city up the Rideau Canal. Bands played, troops marched, and a good time was had by all. "I arrived [in Ottawa] on Coronation Day [for] Queen Elizabeth II. You never saw a city looking more splendid, banners everywhere, magnificent," an American diplomat, Louise Armstrong, recalled. "It gave one a great lift."[35]

Not everything was a great lift. The 1950s saw a general restlessness in intellectual life, a sense that society had achieved stability and prosperity at the price of conformity or, more politely, consensus. The sentiment was widespread in the United States and Great Britain, but in Canada it was mixed with a sense that associated conformity and materialism, concluding that both were stifling American imports. There was a residual sense that British was better—meaning in the 1950s more progressive, more socialist, more non-conformist (which would have been news to British intellectuals). It was a world that read the *New Statesman* or *The Guardian*, and, further to the right, *The Economist* or *Punch*. These points of view (with the left side tending to predominate) found expression on the CBC, in newspapers, in university faculties that still recruited from British universities, and at annual conferences of academics and other thinkers, which were a feature of the period and, to American observers, a characteristic of life in Canada. On both left and right there was a tendency to sniff at the United States, as not quite civilized (Joe McCarthy was exhibit number one), or not up to British standards.[36]

This particular characteristic could grate. "Well there's a certain type of Canadian, yes, who's impossible," Louise Armstrong recalled:

We used to go to an annual summer conference at which these Anglo Canadian super intellectuals would gather and it was always very "loftier than thou" when it came to anything American. We were the uncultured barbarians. We got awfully tired of that. The *Globe and Mail* was must reading, but it was so full of anti-Americanisms. It's par for the course. I don't think it will ever change.[37]

It is certainly true that a comparable gathering of American intellectuals would not have sported the overt nationalist tinge of their Canadian counterparts that demanded attention and specific respect—things that were simply assumed in the United States. The few American academics who studied Canada—more of them in the 1950s than the 2010s—noted that the disparity in size and wealth created an automatic advantage for American cultural exports. That was especially noticeable in television, where over-the-air broadcasting from Buffalo or Detroit or Seattle, starting in 1948, wafted American programs across the border. Soon Canadian evenings were defined by *Alfred Hitchcock Presents, Four-Star Playhouse,* and, above all, *The Ed Sullivan Show.* Wanting an audience when it started television broadcasting in 1952, the CBC signed on to American programs and programming—which were, after all, an extension of the radio programs familiar to their Canadian audiences from the thirties and forties. True, there were some Canadian programs and British imports, the *BBC News Direct from London* at noon, and a half-hour of (mainly) British military marches and rousing songs in the morning, recalling to Canada's many veterans the sounds of their youth in camps in England; it also met CBC broadcast executives' conceptions of what Canadians were or should be. This kind of programming began to give Britain a comic-opera tinge in Canadian culture toward the end of the 1950s, and increasingly as the decade wore on it was replaced by a combination of Canadian-based and Canadian-themed programs. British cultural imports were not restricted—they did not have to be—but there were restrictions on certain American product. For example, the Canadian editions of *Time* and *Reader's Digest*, replicated cheaply with some editorial apparatus in Canada. Canadian publishers complained, and restrictions followed. When cable television arrived, the government decreed restrictions on American commercials carried on Canadian cable. American publishers and broadcasters complained vigorously. Louise Armstrong admitted that there was some reason for Canadian concern. "But honestly, you can see why they needed to do something like this. They can't control what comes in from Buffalo, over the radio and television."[38]

The great conundrum of the 1950s and early 1960s is when and how Canadian cultural, or political-cultural, polarities shifted. Arguably they did not move very much, except in the very important respect of Canada's ultimate national symbols—the monarchy, the monarch herself, and the connection to Britain. The authorities were anxious to encourage more frequent and closer contact between Canadians and their sovereign. There were major royal visits in 1951, 1957, and 1959. 1951 and 1957 were spectacularly successful: in 1957 the young queen, resplendent in the latest and best British fashion, opened the Canadian Parliament under its new Progressive Conservative government, led by John Diefenbaker. Even the weather cooperated by producing a spectacularly warm and sunny Indian summer. But by 1959 things had frayed a bit: there were complaints and exclamations about over-exposure, and even the first hints of creeping republicanism in the media.[39]

There was simultaneously a decompression of British power. It was possible in the early 1950s to see Great Britain as still a Great Power, and the term still had meaning. There was still an empire, although, in the mid-1950s, Britain was simultaneously fighting three colonial wars, in Cyprus, Kenya, and Malaya. British prime ministers strenuously tried to uphold Britain's status and where Canada was concerned made sure to include Ottawa when they traveled to North America—partly to prove to Canadians that Canada and Britain were still significant allies with a particular relationship. Increasingly Britain's "special relationship" was with the United States, by far the most powerful and the richest British ally. Canada could not replace the Americans in any balance of trans-Atlantic power, and to its credit Canada did not try.

When the Conservative British government strove to prove that Britain was still an independent actor in foreign affairs, in the Suez crisis of November 1956, they were brought up short by an American refusal to support them. The Canadians also refused, both because the Canadian government agreed with the Americans that the British attempt to reconquer the Suez Canal was quixotic and anachronistic, and also because they knew it exposed the real weakness of Great Britain's strategic position. A run on the British pound brought the British to heel, to the disgust of their French allies, and the invasion was terminated short of its objectives. Lester Pearson, representing Canada at the United Nations, worked out a face-saving device (based on an American draft) that replaced the British and French invaders with United Nations "peacekeepers" whom the countries in the area, Egypt and Israel, agreed to let patrol their mutual frontier.[40] Pearson's initiative pleased not only the Americans but also those officials and politicians in London who saw the Suez expedition as a lamentable and blindly sentimental throwback to the days when Britain ruled the Middle East—and could afford to. They knew, and told their Canadian friends, that Britain might retake Suez, but could not afford to keep it.

The St. Laurent government thus conformed to an occasional Canadian tradition of representing the British interest better than the British government of the day could—as in the Sudan in 1885, or Chanak in 1922, where Canadian governments resisted ill-advised British belligerence and refused to take part in imperial escapades. Not only did Canada secure passage of the peacekeeping scheme through the United Nations, but it sent troops to join the new UN force, specialized units that Canada's well-equipped military could provide. The peacekeepers went where the great powers, especially, for our purposes, the Americans, could not. They served both a global and a Western interest, placing potentially divisive controversies on ice, in the hope that, eventually, the quarrel that provoked peacekeeping would fade or be resolved. It was not exactly a heroic phenomenon, but it was indubitably useful and well within Canadian capacities—an example of functionalism,[41] in fact.

In retrospect, Pearson's diplomacy was skillful and realistic. It was rewarded with a Nobel Peace Prize, but it did not sit well in much of English Canada. The government took the decision not to support the

British with some misgivings, especially from ministers who represented traditionally minded parts of English Canada. Taken it was, and the following year the Progressive Conservative opposition under John Diefenbaker made the most of it. In English Canada, Liberal vote totals shrank enough in the election of June 1957 to hand the Conservatives a narrow electoral victory. Diefenbaker would be prime minister for not quite six years from 1957 to 1963.

## The Diefenbaker Era

The American embassy reported to Washington that the Diefenbaker government could be expected to be more nationalistic than its Liberal predecessor, and in some senses this was true. Some of Diefenbaker's ministers were suspicious of the United States, and many believed there was an automatic bond to Great Britain, more than to the United States. In his evangelical style Diefenbaker was certainly a change from his staid Liberal predecessors. Ideologically the Liberals and Progressive Conservatives were not that far apart, and no substantial changes in domestic policy occurred in the six years of Conservative rule. Diefenbaker's main distinction was to make Anglo-Canadian as well as Anglo-American relations more irritable than they had been under his predecessors.

Canada under Diefenbaker continued to be a faithful member of NATO, mildly co-operative in international trade policy through General Agreement on Tariffs and Trade (GATT) negotiations, and a stalwart supporter of the United Nations. Taxes continued high, to support a government budget in which military preparedness was a foremost consideration, and prosperity continued at an acceptable level as well.

In the Diefenbaker era Canada, like the United States and Great Britain, was preoccupied with the menace of nuclear weapons and what seemed to be the great danger that the world would be incinerated in a nuclear exchange. This was to some extent the result of the boastful and domineering rhetoric of the Soviet leader, Nikita Khrushchev. Khrushchev's bark was much louder than his bite, and his boasts shielded the deficiencies in the Soviet Union's weapons systems, but at the time his speechifying raised the level of public concern and stimulated anxiety if not outright panic.[42]

Western nuclear strategy was pre-eminently an American concern, although Great Britain had its own small nuclear weapons force. The fact of the North Atlantic alliance made little difference. Even after the North

Atlantic Treaty had been militarized in 1951 the United States kept its own defense arrangements out of NATO's purview. The Liberal government and particularly external affairs minister Pearson tried to secure information on what the Americans proposed to do with their nuclear weapons in the event of war, but with little success. The United States was unwilling to allow even a hint of foreign control over the American strategic deterrent, and Canada thus remained bound by American strategy but ignorant of all but the largest generalities of what the Americans proposed to do in the event of a nuclear exchange with the Soviet Union.

That fact was driven home during the Cuban missile crisis of October 1962, when the American government confronted the Soviet Union over the emplacement of Soviet missiles in Cuba. Only the British, obliquely, had any kind of special information as to what was going on. The other allies, including Canada, were expected to wait and hope. The crisis was resolved without resort to force, though in retrospect it was a very close thing. The Diefenbaker government in its own way and for its own reasons stumbled through the crisis, irritating the Americans without securing any advantage for Canada by doing so. It was, however, evident that on issues of war and peace, and nuclear weapons, Canada's large investment in its armed forces had not produced and probably could not have produced a seat at the table where real decisions were made. On the great issue of atomic war, Diefenbaker had little to offer; but on the other hand, the Americans did not want to listen. One American diplomat who served in Canada in this period put it this way, referring both to official pronouncements and media commentary:

> As you could imagine, we expected loyalty of allies in those days. It was the heart of the Cold War and we didn't like some of the Canadian rhetoric. We understood that the Canadians may have some gripes about our foreign policy and our actions, but when it came to defense and security arrangements, we thought that allies should be allies and it was exactly on nuclear issues that we had our biggest problems.[43]

The "nuclear issue" came to a head in 1962–3. Diefenbaker was not emotionally or instinctively anti-American, and had readily acquiesced in air defense arrangements between Canada and the United States. Diefenbaker had requested the emplacement of an American anti-aircraft missile system, the Bomarc, in Canada. The Americans obliged, thus extending that

aspect of North American air defense northward. There were several problems with this. In the first place, the Bomarc did not work very well, if at
all. Second, it could work only if equipped with nuclear warheads. Third,
a vigorous anti-nuclear movement had taken root in Canada as elsewhere
in the Western world, and while not a majority it was vocal and influential,
even among Conservatives.[44] Diefenbaker's external affairs minister, Howard
Green, and at least some Canadian diplomats sympathized with the idea
of reducing or abolishing the nuclear threat. The cabinet was split and unable to come to a decision on how, or whether, to equip the Bomarcs, as
well as Canadian forces in Europe, with nuclear weapons, which would be
kept under American control until actually needed. The Americans grew
impatient with the delay, and in the aftermath of the Cuban missile crisis
of 1962 made their discontent very evident. Canada's role as an American
ally was in question, not just in Washington but in Canada, where the
news of a Canadian–American quarrel over continental air defense seemed
to many Canadians to be counter-intuitive. But that was only part of
Diefenbaker's foreign policy dilemma.

If the Cuban missile crisis unhinged one standard Canadian assumption about foreign relations, simultaneous British negotiations with the
European Common Market negated the residual imperial connection. In
the early 1960s Canada and other Commonwealth members still enjoyed
tariff preferences in trading with one another. These were left over from
the Ottawa Agreements of 1932 and had been grandfathered when Western
countries adopted a regime of tariff reduction through the GATT in 1947.
The preferences could be continued, but not increased, and if diminished
or abolished, could never be replaced. When Great Britain finally decided,
very much with American support, that its destiny and prosperity lay in
making a deal with the European Common Market, it represented a significant potential loss for Canada and other Commonwealth countries, such as
Australia.

It did not help that the British, in presenting this new policy to their
Commonwealth trading partners, chose to obfuscate what was happening—if in fact the British government did not outright lie to them. In
part the British government (Conservative, under Harold Macmillan) was
motivated by concern that the countries of the Commonwealth—especially
the colonies of settlement like Canada—were still a factor in British politics, and that the government might be punished by conservatively minded
Britons if it was seen to be harming Canada or Australia or New Zealand.
Although there was by 1961 no formal participation by Commonwealth

countries in British politics or political institutions, there was still a real political connection.

It is an important point because there was no comparable relationship between Canada and the United States. Canada as such was not a political factor at all in the United States, and the diminishing Anglo-Canadian connection would have been impossible to imagine in Canadian–American relations. Canada had been and was still to be for a few more years an item in Britain's domestic life—and in British political culture. The United States would not compensate for that loss, and for many Americans it was not possible that the United States, exceptional and unique, could have any kind of automatic or axiomatic political relationship with any other country. When the prominent Canadian historian Donald Creighton lamented the loss of the British Empire as far as Canada was concerned, he was remarking on the end of a particular political link and thus the end of an ability to rely on the British. Canada, Creighton saw, was alone in the world, unless Canadians chose to join the United States.

This created a paradox, for in the 1950s and 1960s the power and influence of American culture encouraged foreigners all over the globe, and not just in Canada, to identify with the United States, or with the American experience—the American way of life and all that it brought with it, good and bad. Problems discovered or identified in the United States spread across the border through the prevalence if not ubiquity of American books, movies, television, and music. Books and movies, imported from the United States, depicted the *Organization Man*, whose destiny was to conform, follow rules, and meet expectations that others had set. The *Organization Man* was the conception of an American sociologist, William Whyte, and drew its examples from the United States, but Canadians could sense that their fate, though smaller, was much the same. Nor was it a bad fate, for it was coupled to a sense of belonging and community, on both the Canadian and American sides of the border, from a local level up to a national plateau.[45] Another sociologist, David Riesman, came up with the notion of a *Lonely Crowd*, the title of his book that depicted herds of conformists seeking approval from others—flexible though not supple, such people were bound to follow the herd.[46]

Homogeneity of style was mirrored by a relative homogeneity of income—high-income Canadians and Americans could live well, and high-income Americans lived better, but not on the same level as the robber capitalists of the late nineteenth century, or the almost untaxed millionaires of the world before 1939. High taxes seemed the new normal—by the end of the 1950s there had been twenty years of them, and life carried on. High taxes or not, the economy grew every year, and with it incomes, while what could be bought with after-tax income seemed to grow, as new gadgets began to appear in kitchens and living rooms.

But following, imitating, or paralleling American ways did not produce Americans, unless individuals so affected chose actually to move to the United States. This proved uncomfortable for many Canadians and puzzled at least some Americans, who in meeting Canadians or visiting Canada found a country and a people that sounded and behaved remarkably like themselves. One fairly senior member of the Eisenhower administration, Clarence B. Randall, suggested to the State Department that talks should begin for the merger of Canada with the United States. American diplomats, who knew about Canadian nationalism and understood what even the most pro-American Canadian politicians would say in response, derailed Randall's proposal, and left matters where they were.

The dream, however, did not die. It showed up from time to time, particularly among political appointees. Adolph Schmidt, an otherwise unremarkable American ambassador (1969–74), impressed one of his staff as "Charming, a really fine man who probably thought that Canada should be a state of the union but who realized that that was not on and that the best thing to do was to have the best relations with Canada that one could."[47] It revived in the mid-1960s in the thoughts of the American under-secretary of state, George Ball. Ball's focus was economic: like Randall, he was originally a midwestern businessman, and like Randall he reasoned that Canada should, logically, recognize where destiny had placed it, in North America with another and much larger country with the same culture and the same interests. Ball's tenure in office coincided with that of a new government in Canada, that of Lester B. Pearson (1963–8), and his Liberal party.

## The Shadow of Vietnam

The Liberals had exited office in 1957, defeated in an election in which their purported anti-British sentiments and pro-American behavior had been loudly condemned by John Diefenbaker and his Progressive Conservatives. Diefenbaker in his turn had been pilloried for his own purported anti-Americanism and defeated in the bitterly fought election of 1963. The John F. Kennedy administration had welcomed the return of the Liberals, and perhaps, had Kennedy lived, a new and even more than usually harmonious era might have dawned in Canadian–American relations. But Kennedy was assassinated in Dallas in November 1963, and the Liberal government had to deal with a new president with a very different personality and background compared to his predecessor—and, as it turned out, compared with Pearson.

Lyndon B. Johnson had little choice but to carry on with many of Kennedy's appointees, including Ball, and he inherited a basketful of issues from his predecessor. These ranged from Vietnam, where the United States was struggling to preserve an anti-communist government in the face of communist subversion and insurrection, to Canada, where there was a dispute over the Canadian government's policy of subsidizing the manufacture of cars and trucks in Canada. Johnson had no idea how to deal with Vietnam then or later, but he was able to manage the Canadian issue through a group of able bureaucrats under the leadership of George Ball. On the Canadian side, the principal figure was or should have been Pearson's finance minister, the very nationalistic Walter Gordon. It was Gordon who subsidized an American manufacturer, Studebaker, to move its factory to Canada, and Gordon who whenever he could, tried to reduce American influence over the Canadian economy and enhance the standing and importance of Canadian-owned companies.

The American ambassador, W.W. Butterworth, emphatically disapproved of Gordon and all his works. He disapproved of most Canadian politicians, whom he saw as unscrupulous opportunists, willing to play the anti-American card whenever they could, merely for political advantage. Butterworth also shared American impatience with allies so obtuse as not to recognize the bargain their countries had made, by trading strategic security for support, unquestioning support, of American foreign policy. American power and wealth made Canada, like Western Europe, safe. If the United States for its own good reasons—and Butterworth was certain they were good—wished to fight in Vietnam to keep communism at bay, it ill behooved an ally to question American actions. Canadians had a psychological problem, Butterworth told his superiors in Washington—they feared that they were merely second-rate Americans, and naturally were jealous of the genuine article. Fortunately for Canada and Pearson, Butterworth managed to irritate his colleagues in Washington as much as he did his hosts in Canada.[48] Finding nowhere else to put him, the State Department kept him on ice in Ottawa for almost six years—a very long posting by any of the customary diplomatic standards.[49] Presumably that was because he did no absolute harm even if he did no real good either—he could fulminate to his heart's content, and nobody would listen because nobody had to listen, and fortunately, in a world that did not know the internet, there was no temptation to broadcast Butterworth's grumblings. On that point, it was best to remain silent, as far as knowledgeable Canadians and Americans were concerned.

The timing was good for a recalibration of Canadian–American economic relations. The world looked good, a few blemishes like atomic weapons and the Vietnam War apart; the Vietnam War had yet to draw in American ground forces and had not yet become a major issue in either American international relations or American domestic politics. There were no serious political difficulties at all between Canada and the United States, nothing to cloud the horizon but economic diplomacy. The United States was prospering mightily. American corporations were the largest, richest, and most advanced in the world. Per capita income was soaring, and Americans put their faith in unions to manage ritual bargaining sessions at the end of which there was always more money and more benefits to go round. Houses—individually owned—and cars and appliances abounded. What Americans had today Canadians would have tomorrow, or the day after. As for the British—perhaps next week, or possibly in five years or so. The difference there, in the 1960s, was that the French and the Dutch and the Germans might have them sooner, as the European economies organized in the Common Market whizzed by the British on the highway to affluence. The British consoled themselves that the Italians also still lagged behind.

American diplomats and trade experts believed as articles of faith, first, that the Canadians too would always lag behind themselves, and that it would be a good idea if the gap in incomes and affluence could be diminished between the two countries. In 1964–5 an agreement for free trade in automobiles and automobile parts was negotiated—soon universally known as the Autopact. In January 1965 it was formally signed by the American president, Lyndon B. Johnson (always known by his initials as LBJ) and the Canadian prime minister, Lester B. Pearson, at Johnson's Texas ranch. At the time, the Autopact's virtues were negative ones—it prevented a potentially fierce trade dispute and disruption to the business of the three great American automobile companies that dominated the North American market. According to one of the American negotiators, "LBJ presented the agreement to the press down in Austin,[50] what he stressed was that we had avoided a confrontation and a political dispute with Canada. As far as the automobile agreement itself was concerned, it was entirely political from his point of view. I've forgotten what Pearson said in reply, but I'm sure it was in the same vein."[51]

Perhaps, in Pearson's view, taking care of an economic grievance now would prevent worse political trouble later. He knew that automobiles had been a source of trouble in Canadian–American relations, and he knew too that his own economic expertise was limited. He was a political diplomat (and politician), not an economic one. As in 1948, he followed the advice of the trade experts—in this case the Canadian deputy minister of industry, the formidable and abrasive Simon Reisman.[52] The Autopact conformed to a predisposition to free trade that was well-nigh universal among economists, including those who served the Canadian and American governments. There was a contradiction in Canadian policy between protecting industry in a small country, Canada's traditional policy, and increasing world trade by dropping trade barriers—subsidies and tariffs. "The Canadians had this somewhat contradictory policy of being basically supportive of free trade, but were concerned about whether this would permit them to gain sufficient investment to build their own industries,"[53] said Julius Katz, one of the main American trade negotiators. Though the Canadian negotiators were tough and tenacious, at bottom there was a philosophical agreement as to what was desirable—lower tariffs, an end to economic distortions, and free competition. Katz continued: "The thing about negotiating with the Canadians is that, at least in those days, you have two parties that are speaking the same language, I mean literally and figuratively. There are some minor cultural differences, but for the most part the negotiations are between people who think pretty much alike."

There seems to have been nothing in the Autopact that rang any alarm bells in Pearson's mind, and perhaps he recalled, favorably, the aborted economic agreement with the United States in 1948. It just didn't make sense to have economic barriers at the border in the auto industry. The Americans were careful to let sleeping dogs lie and to scratch the ears of the slumbering Canadian beast by agreeing to safeguards in the pact that directed investment to Canada and guaranteed the investment that was already there. As Julius Katz put it, "But there was the Canadian sensitivity about absorption—being the 51st State. So one had to be sensitive about this. The idea of free trade, complete free trade as we have now, would not have washed at that point in time."[54] Both sides knew it and said so to one another, bluntly. "Negotiations with the Canadians can be pretty wild swinging affairs. They are not quite as structured, or as diplomatic, as they are with other countries." It was one agreement at a time—advancing either one step toward eventual global free trade, or one step toward Canadian–American free trade. In the form of negotiations, there was already a special relationship—could it be broadened, or extended? Time would tell.

The Autopact passed the Canadian cabinet with barely a peep in mid-January 1965. It was presented to cabinet by Walter Gordon's brother-in-law, the minister of industry, as a kind of economic marvel that would bolster employment and investment, which was true and gratifying to his colleagues, who concerned themselves only with how this achievement might best be presented to the public.[55] Later in the month, Pearson and his external affairs minister, Paul Martin, flew south to Texas to sign the treaty with Johnson. The most notable event of that visit, as far as the media was concerned, was that Johnson in introducing his guest identified him as Harold Wilson, the British prime minister.

It was a mere slip of the tongue, although in fact Johnson did not particularly like either prime minister. Already in January 1965 the president's main preoccupation was the war in Vietnam—up to that point a civil war, with deep American involvement on the government's side. In 1964 it was increasingly clear that the anti-communist government, which seemed to change with the phases of the moon, was losing. But in the winter and spring of 1965 Johnson sent in the marines and the army, and transformed the Southeast Asian conflict into a trial of strength between the United States and (Johnson thought) the communist world. Johnson overestimated American abilities in fighting a war in Southeast Asia, and he underestimated the strain that fighting a distant war on behalf of an unfamiliar people and with a conscript army would place on American society.

Pearson differed with him on all these points. American power was great, he knew, but it was not unlimited. He knew as well that many Americans, including the vice-president, Hubert Humphrey, believed the United States should not get more involved in Vietnam—with the logical conclusion that if the South Vietnamese government fell to the communists, that was a cost that would have to be borne. The Canadian prime minister dreaded becoming caught in a land war in Asia, with its huge populations. It would entrap the United States and other Western countries, and there would be no way out. In April 1965 Pearson unwisely gave vent to his feelings in a speech at Temple University in Philadelphia. American motives in Vietnam were good, Pearson conceded, but peace would be better. He proposed a pause in the bombing of Vietnam and a search for a negotiated settlement. For Johnson this constituted rank betrayal on the part of someone he had just helped out on the Autopact. Thereafter he saw Pearson as infrequently as possible, and he never took him or his advice seriously again.[56]

The Canadians found every possible reason not to join the United States in the Vietnam War. Luckily Canada was a member of the international truce supervisory commission in Vietnam, established at the end of the French Vietnam War in 1954, whose role Pearson interpreted as mandating a duty to be impartial, ever ready to rush in with a solution when and if the warring parties decided they needed one. Pearson may also have been skeptical as to what a Vietnamese involvement would do for or to his country. There was a comparison at hand in Australia, which interpreted its relationship with the United States to require Australian participation. The Australians sent a brigade, suffered casualties and political disruption—and in return harvested virtually no influence over the conduct of the war, or more than ceremonial appreciation in Washington.

The only direct consequence that Canada suffered from the US government was via Butterworth's secret fulminations in his reports to Washington, and a smoldering resentment from Johnson when Canada, Canadians, or Pearson were mentioned. Offending the president, even on an issue as important and crucial to his political future as Vietnam, did not cause him to cancel the Autopact, or seek to retaliate in some other sphere. Professionals engaged in Canadian–American relations—the diplomats—rejected connecting different issues, a tactic known as "linkage."[57]

On a bilateral level Canadian–American relations did not suffer greatly as a result of Pearson's incautious diplomacy with Lyndon Johnson. Johnson understood that the Vietnam War was unpopular with most of his allies, especially in NATO, and he chose not to make an issue of it, even with governments such as Charles de Gaulle's in Paris, that were much more vocal and critical than Pearson ever was. Opposition from the allies was the least of his worries: right from the beginning of the war there was increasing dissent at home in the United States. The quick victory that Johnson must have hoped for proved elusive, and in fact illusory. The North Vietnamese did not fade or abandon the conflict, and with crucial supplies from the Soviet Union and aid from China, they kept the war going.

Johnson poured more and more troops into Vietnam—more than 500,000 by late 1968—only to find that his generals kept asking for more. The United States for twenty years had used conscription, the draft, to fill up its armed services with necessary bodies, and the draft fell most heavily on poorer and less-educated citizens—all men, of course. For many of these life in the military with its benefits was actually an improvement, and so although the draft occasionally harvested the unwilling, in a time of peace they lost merely time, and were not expected to go into danger. College students could easily get a deferment, and did. And so the conscription system ambled along, until conscripts (draftees) were actually needed for fighting.

This happened in 1965. The conscription system had to produce more and more recruits, and that could only be done by restricting deferments. This immediately affected students in the universities. It soon became apparent that potential draftees did not see Vietnam as a necessary war, certainly not as one that they should be fighting. Dissent at first centered in the universities, among students, but as casualties rose it became more widespread, affecting chiefly the class of people who usually voted Democratic.

Vietnam scarred the Johnson administration and obscured (and sometimes diverted) its efforts in domestic policy. Johnson had been an unusually effective president, passing revolutionary civil rights legislation, in effect enfranchising large numbers of blacks in the south for the first time since the 1870s. A New Dealer, and himself from an impoverished background, Johnson also moved to complete Franklin Roosevelt's and Harry Truman's agenda by ramming a government-funded, single-payer health insurance system through Congress in 1965. It covered only part of the population—people over sixty-five and those with severe disabilities—those most unlikely to qualify for private insurance. And it came with a subtext. "We all saw insurance for the elderly as a fallback position, which we advocated solely because it seemed to have the best chance politically," according to Robert Ball, who helped design the system. "Although the public record contains some explicit denials, we expected Medicare to be a first step toward universal national health insurance, perhaps with 'Kiddicare' as another step."[58]

There was already a medicare program in existence in North America —in socialist Saskatchewan. It had begun as provincial hospital insurance in 1946 (imitated by Alberta in 1950), which was then adopted and implemented nationally in 1957. The next step was *universal* medical insurance, which was implemented by the New Democratic Party (NDP) government in 1962, to the fury of organized medicine in that province, expressed in a doctors' strike. The government did not give way, and the doctors, most of them, subsided. It was a precedent and a foundation for a national health insurance scheme, passed by the Liberal Pearson government in 1965, and finally implemented in 1968. The terms of medicare were sufficiently tempting for every province to sign on, thus overcoming some of the pitfalls of Canada's federal–provincial distribution of powers.

The appearance of medicare under the same name, though in two forms, in Canada and the United States is more important as a coincidence than for any obvious causation. In both countries it fulfilled a social security policy agenda that had been on the governments' table since the New Deal and the Beveridge Report, over which Roosevelt and Mackenzie King had clinked glasses in 1942. What it suggests, to revert to Lipset's observation that Canada and the United States resembled each other far more than they differed, is that the two countries (plus Great Britain, Australia, and New Zealand) were at this time in the same policy and political (and social and intellectual) universe as far as domestic affairs were concerned. As already noted, Canada and the United States shared the same assumptions on economic policy, taxing high to finance an interventionist state.

The assumptions flowed from the fact and the expectation that Canada and the United States, liberal capitalist societies, were lands of equality and opportunity. That had been so since the New Deal and the Second World War, and with the flowering in the 1960s of Canadian health insurance and an expanded pension system, and the foundations of what was hoped to be an expanding American medicare system, the two countries seemed more than ever to be on the same path as far as domestic affairs were concerned. But in terms of relations between the United-States-as-superpower and Canada-as-ally, things were far different.

## *Noises Off*

In Canada the advent of advanced social programs considerably affected the government's pattern of expenditures as compared to the United States. Canada never matched, proportionately, American defense spending even in the 1950s, but the military budget was considerable for a country of Canada's size. The result could be seen in Canada's up-to-date air force and well-equipped army, as well as its military bases in Germany. At the climax of the Cold War, around the time of the Cuban missile crisis, almost a quarter of the federal budget went toward defense. In a sense, Canada's military effort helped define the country's image and certainly gave it some prestige abroad—an intangible benefit, and sometimes an illusory one, as we have seen with regard to the Cuban missile crisis. A decade later, in the early 1970s, spending on social programs was twice what was spent on defense, and the size of the armed forces had declined by about a quarter. Canada's shrinking military now defined Canada in a different way and led to raised eyebrows among the allies.

What the military expenditure could not do was to affect the overall conduct of American policy or the way the United States government and most Americans saw the world. The United States' role as a superpower, leader of the Western alliance and policeman of the Western world meant that American presidents began to travel—to Western Europe, Asia, and Latin America. In return presidents, prime ministers and other political potentates beat a path to Washington, where power and money resided. As the British and French empires contracted, the United States took their place in Asia and Africa. Difference in size, difference in responsibility, produced difference in outlook.

A case in point is the Cuban revolution of 1959 that brought Fidel Castro to power. The American government early became alarmed about Castro's policies and intentions, at least in part because of the size of American investment in the island. The Canadian government, which had diplomatic representation in Havana, had its own, less alarmed view of the situation. The Eisenhower administration had good relations with the Diefenbaker government in Canada; the prime minister deeply admired the American president and certainly did not seek to steer Canada's Cuban policy in a direction hostile to American interests. On the other hand, Canada had its own interests in Cuba, in banking and insurance, and the Diefenbaker government very much wanted to increase trade, with Cuba and with anyone else. "Patient forbearance" was the right policy toward Cuba, Canadian ministers told their American counterparts. In the American view, Canada's understanding of the Cuban situation was sadly deficient. The Canadians on this issue should leave policy to those who understood it. It was axiomatic that the allies' job was to be allied—to give tangible aid if they could, but at least not to be seen disrupting the alliance's family photo-ops.

Being next door to a superpower inevitably muted Canada's pretensions to being a linchpin between the United States and Great Britain. The superpower had its own foreign service, underpinned by its universities and think tanks, and its own expertise. It had its own interests, which usually dwarfed any interests its allies might have. The same, obviously, was true of Great Britain, and as the Empire disappeared and the Commonwealth receded—remarkably quickly, in the 1960s—British national interests took precedence over a shrinking Commonwealth linkage. It did not mean that

Canada had no uses—peacekeeping, first in Egypt, then in the Congo, and then in Cyprus during the 1960s, was a constructive exercise on behalf of the Western alliance generally, and for the United States and the United Kingdom especially. Canada was not irreplaceable, for other Western countries could do the same thing, and did, but it was definitely useful. But Canada was useful primarily as a member of an alliance, and the American understanding of the nature of that alliance was, on the great issues of war and peace, not a relationship of equals. When Canada signed the North Atlantic Treaty in April 1949, it got what it wanted, a multilateral linkage; but in relations with the United States, it got rather more than the "nothing" of Pearson's cynical subtext from 1949.

# II

## Unexpected Destinations

THE COLD WAR seemed as if it would go on forever. Yet in the space of two years, 1989–91, the Cold War ended. Almost no academic, no general, no politician in 1969 or 1979 or 1988 would have thought it possible, without some form of nuclear cataclysm. In 1969 the Cold War was the polar star of international affairs. Two superpowers, the United States and the Soviet Union, two alliances, the West's NATO, the East's Warsaw Pact, with their constellations of bases, weapons systems, ideologies, clients, and complete mythologies that justified each side's position—it seemed as if it would go on forever. Nuclear weapons kept the peace, but made it unstable. The doctrine of "Mutual Assured Destruction" ensured that in a war between the Soviet Union and the United States, both sides, the liberal capitalist "First World" and the communist "Second World," could have both victory and obliteration.

Getting to victory without obliteration was the tricky part. By 1969 the two superpowers had concluded that armed conflict in Europe was an impossibility. Though both the US and the USSR and their respective allies maintained large and expensive armies in the center of Europe, actually using them would swiftly bring nuclear weapons into use, and the "nukes" would lay waste the territory that was being fought over. That became even more of a certainty when the Soviet Union in the late 1960s acquired nuclear parity with the United States. Nuclear weapons still could be used, might be used, but it was clear that the American and Soviet governments did not want to use them.

Victory in the Cold War, if it was ever to be achieved, would have to be found somewhere else. For that there was a communist theory, even a doctrine, dating from the early 1920s, that argued that the Third World, the nations of Asia, Africa, and Latin America, had a natural interest in resisting their oppressors, the empires of Western Europe, plus their surrogate, the United States. After the Second World War, with the European empires unwittingly on their last legs, it seemed that the theory was right after all. The British wisely scuttled the Asian part of their empire, including India, their most important overseas possession, in 1947, and Palestine in 1948, leaving their problems to their successors, India and Pakistan, Burma, Ceylon, and Israel. In none of those places was communism a serious political factor, but in French Indochina, where a rebellion broke out in 1946, it was. Communists led the struggle against the French in Indochina, and communists secured the defeat of France's army at Dien Bien Phu in 1954. Defeated, the French reluctantly abandoned Indochina, but not before dragging the hypersensitive Americans into their war "against communism" (and "for empire"). The Americans, though doctrinally anti-empire were even more strongly anti-communist. Rather like the American Revolution, though nobody at the time drew a parallel, the Indochina war was a civil war as well as a colonial conflict. Anti-communist, but nationalist, Vietnamese fought alongside the French against the local communists. When the French left, they drew the United States into the conflict, for the communist victory in 1954 was not total, but left an anti-communist fragment, South Vietnam, to its own devices, pending what most people took to be impending unification under communist rule. So the United States could still make a difference and save millions of people from communist rule. And why not? There were North Korea and South Korea, East and West Germany, so North and South Vietnam did not seem like such an impossibility. But North Vietnam had other ideas and resumed the war, and the South Vietnamese government proved unable to defend itself, even with literally tons of annual American military aid and the assistance of US military advisers.

In 1965, as we have seen, the United States entered the war and poured hundreds of thousands of conscript troops into the resulting battles. American leaders justified their actions by arguing to themselves that otherwise their allies would lose confidence in American determination to resist communism. And so, in some sense, this incredible war was fought to preserve American credibility to the world at large. It had precisely the opposite effect. Like the British in the Revolutionary War, the Americans won most of the actual battles, but like the British, they lost this distant war. Like the British in the 1770s, the Americans performed logistical marvels, keeping a war going on land, at sea, and in the air for eight years; but against an enemy that refused to admit defeat the United States simply could not muster the right kind of power, or resolution, to take the war to a victorious conclusion.

Most of the United States' allies stayed clear of the war. The Europeans and the Canadians—the NATO countries—saw Vietnam as a peripheral theater. They also differed from the Americans as to the essential character of the conflict, seeing it not as a war of national resistance against communism, but as yet another futile conflict. The Canadians had accepted a truce supervisory role in Indochina in 1954, and were still there in 1965, and 1969, and indeed until the end of the American phase of the war in 1973.[1] Canada used its membership on this commission as one of its excuses to avoid joining in the war. Other European empires had disappeared, or were about to: British, French, and (soon) Portuguese populations had refused to support distant expeditions against unfamiliar peoples who posed little if any threat to the home country. The Americans, in effect, contended that that kind of history had come to an end, and that they were exempt from its precedents. The Europeans on the whole thought not, and so, at the governmental level, did the Canadians. There is no doubt, for example, that this was Lester Pearson's line of thought. But denying the Americans their exceptional character might undermine the exceptional commitment the Americans had made, for more than twenty years, to defend those same allies who now criticized their commitment to Vietnam.

As in earlier wars, sizable numbers of Americans, when they thought about it, refused to follow where their politicians and generals were leading. As in the Civil War, the First and Second World Wars, and Korea, the American military was fueled by conscription, the draft. During the First and Second World Wars, there was nowhere for conscripts to go, except to war, to jail, or possibly into some form of compulsory non-combatant service. During Vietnam there was. American soldiers in Europe could opt to go to Sweden, not a member of NATO, or to some other neutral haven. In North America, they could go to Latin America or to Canada. Canada it was for some twenty-five thousand male draft resisters (usually called at the time draft dodgers), or deserters. The deserters were in a gray area, legally, in Canada, and were advised not to advertise their status and to hope that the authorities would not take the trouble to return them to the United States. But since Canada did not have conscription, simple draft resisters could not be extradited or deported unless they committed some offense in Canada. Nor was the refugee flow confined to men—at least as many women as men moved north of the border to show their disapproval of the war.

Not all Canadians were against "Johnson's war," as it was called until he left office in 1969. A fair number of Canadians—the son of Jacques

Dextraze, the chief of defense staff, for example—enlisted in the American armed forces, and a certain number were killed, including Dextraze's son. But relatively few Canadian politicians overtly supported the American cause (one, ironically, was John Diefenbaker) and surveys at the time showed there was relatively little difference in attitudes over Vietnam between Liberals and Conservatives, although the NDP was more overt, and more vocal, in its criticism of the United States.

Johnson did not allow the Vietnam War to sidetrack one item of his domestic agenda, the extension of civil rights to American blacks in the southern states. Progress was crucial and progress was achieved, but at the same time there were serious riots by blacks in many of the northern cities such as New York and Washington. Canadians in Windsor could watch the smoke rising from Detroit across the river. The combination of racial conflict and the Vietnam War in the United States lowered its standing abroad, including in Canada—suddenly the United States was seen as chaotic, warlike, and having somehow lost its way. And in Canada this coincided with an explosion of Canadian nationalism. One of nationalism's causes, perhaps its defining concern, was keeping Canada, described in pure and sometimes arcadian terms, out of the maw of the United States, which in this context was always negatively described.

The uproar around the riots and the war caused Canadians, even intelligent ones, to lose sight of other developments in the United States. They knew that Johnson's Vietnam War had caused his party, the Democrats, to fall in popularity as crucial Democratic supporters deserted the president. But it was really the civil rights legislation that transformed American politics, as white southerners, traditionally Democrats since the Civil War, transferred en masse to the Republicans. Now the Democrats became the party of the North, and the Republicans the party of the South—not uniformly, but nevertheless in such a way as eventually to give the Republicans by the 1990s predominance in most states south of Washington, DC.

The first fruit of the electoral turnabout was to give a narrow victory to Richard Nixon, a former vice-president and the Republican candidate for president in the election of 1968. Nixon already had an unsavory reputation, which later events fully justified, but obviously he would not have won had he not also been a canny and persistent politician. Nixon had no clear strategy for winning in Vietnam, except to wear down the enemy in the field, while negotiating with the North Vietnamese communists in interminable discussions in Paris supervised by his foreign policy adviser, Henry Kissinger. The war therefore continued, to the accompaniment of escalating protests and riots at home, an air-raid campaign over North Vietnam, and intervention in neighboring Cambodia. The Americans pinned their military hopes on a policy of "Vietnamization," bringing the South Vietnamese army up to a level where it could face the North Vietnamese with some hope of winning. As the training proceeded, American ground troops steadily left for home. Numbers of Americans captured by the North Vietnamese meanwhile languished in jails in Hanoi, and their release became another American objective. The North Vietnamese objective was simple: to get the Americans to leave Vietnam unconditionally, which would have meant abandoning the South Vietnamese government. Eventually, early in 1973, the Americans agreed to leave conditionally. There was a ceasefire, the North Vietnamese released their American prisoners, and the Americans pulled out their remaining troops.

The Canadians performed the same function for the Americans in 1973 as they had for the French in 1954, supervising the release of American prisoners and overseeing the ceasefire between the armies of the two Vietnams, as part of a new international truce commission.[2] Its main function was to serve as a fig leaf to give the American withdrawal some dignity. But the Canadians had learned their lesson from twenty years' futile service on the first commission and pulled out of the commission in the summer of 1973.

Nixon meanwhile had become entangled in a squalid comic-opera scandal, called Watergate after its first incident, a botched burglary of the Democratic party offices in Washington in the building of the same name. Nixon then tried to hide his tracks, so as to win the 1972 election. He did, but the scandal had legs and galloped past all his efforts to contain it. Eventually, threatened with the certainty of impeachment and removal from office by Congress, Nixon resigned in August 1974, the only American president to date to suffer that fate. His vice-president had also left after being convicted of income tax evasion (the real charge was that he had taken bribes as a politician in his native Maryland). Meanwhile two of Nixon's cabinet went to jail. Nixon's expletive-laden conversations in the White House, which he had taped for history, meanwhile became public property, including one in which he called Canadian prime minister Pierre Elliott Trudeau "that bastard Trudeau" among other titles.[3]

"I've been called worse things by better people," Trudeau shrugged. Prime minister since April 1968, Trudeau had been selected by a Liberal party convention to succeed Lester Pearson. He promptly called a general election, which he handily won, with a secure parliamentary majority.

Trudeau was Canadian prime minister for all of Nixon's term of office, visited him several times at the White House, and hosted him for an official visit to Ottawa in April 1972.

Dealing face to face, the two men overcame their dissimilarities and managed Canadian–American disputes as best they could. Trudeau meanwhile conceived an admiration for Henry Kissinger, Nixon's national security adviser, a former Harvard professor, political scientist, and historian of nineteenth-century diplomacy, whose lessons he endeavored to apply to the world of the 1970s—and not without success.[4] Trudeau enjoyed Kissinger's witty *tours d'horizon* of world affairs, and while the two men were hardly intimates, there was enough good will to survive into Kissinger's term as secretary of state under Nixon and Nixon's successor, his replacement vice-president, Gerald Ford.

This was all quite spectacular. Nixon appealed to many of the baser themes in American history—notably class resentment,[5] real Americans wearing hard hats, the "silent majority" who had had enough of "effete snobs," as the vice-president memorably phrased it, and the privileged, radical students rioting on campuses while securing credentials that would last them the rest of their lives, at the top end of the social and economic pyramid. Yet though Nixon arguably hated the American liberal elite, on many subjects he and they were in broad agreement. In many of his internal policies, Nixon can be seen as a continuation of Johnson and all the other presidents back to Franklin D. Roosevelt.

Political debate during Nixon's presidency centered on proposals that retrospectively were remarkably liberal—universal health care, a guaranteed annual income, progress on environmental policies, and experiments in wage and price controls. There was even a Great Lakes Water Quality Agreement, amicably negotiated between two governments that were roughly on the same page in terms of environmental protection. Plainly, Nixon continued a tradition of activist government—government as a solution for public problems. "Overall," David Greenberg wrote, "domestic expenditures jumped 44 percent between the 1968–69 and 1971–72 federal budgets, while defense spending ebbed—a reversal of the priorities of every other postwar president."[6] Nixon confessed to being a Keynesian, and used counter-cyclical budgeting to combat an economic downturn. Put in academese, liberalism was "the dominant discourse of the times," and in that sense Nixon's actions were perceived as being to the right—they were, however, right-liberal, not right-conservative.[7] But supporters of such measures were so repulsed by the president's character and conduct that they failed to seize the opportunity when it was offered. There would always be another occasion, they seem to have reasoned, under a better president. Some may even have thought that getting a positive accomplishment on the statute books might save Nixon—and Nixon may well have used the same reasoning. Crippled politically by the Watergate scandal from the summer of 1973 on, Nixon could not muster either the personal concentration or the political credibility that were necessary to get universal health care passed in 1974.

It is true that Nixon's successor, Ford, resurrected health care as an issue, but with even less success. And so the United States lumbered on with the same system of health insurance bequeathed by Johnson—part public and single-payer, what had come to be called Medicare, for over-sixty-fives, part single-payer for the truly impoverished, or Medicaid, part private insurance through employers or other private resources, and part nothing at all.

At the time, in the early 1970s, the United States was, as it had been since the Second World War, the world's model in providing a steadily increasing standard of living for its citizens. Almost every year, Americans on the average earned more than they had the year before, in constant, uninflated, dollars. More and more Americans worked for large corporations that seemed to incarnate power and stability and progress. General Motors, General Electric, and Bell Telephone issued gold-plated stock that gave their lucky owners steady annual incomes. The corporations in turn gave their employees not just their wages, but pensions, health benefits, and stability. These were the pay-offs for being an "Organization Man" and wandering around in a "Lonely Crowd." At the managerial level, the Organization Man wore a "Gray Flannel Suit"—all these phrases being titles of popular books during the 1950s. It could be called a kind of corporate feudalism, but feudalism, we should remember, was organized around the principle of protection against potential (and sometimes very well-known) dangers, on the principle of mutual security. Though the corporations were the bugaboos of the left and the intellectual elite, they actually shared some of their values, for all their hierarchical ways.

Canada had its own miniature corporate structure that functioned in much the same way—department stores like Eaton's or Simpson's, Canadian General Electric (actually Canadian-owned, though associated with its erstwhile parent, GE), Alcan, and Stelco. In the 1950s and 1960s, Canadian governments took over health-care costs, though there were still employer-financed supplemental health benefits for such items as semi-private rooms in hospitals. But in general terms, the benefits and pensions system worked much the same way in both countries, and in Canada, like the United States, it was financed by apparently endless prosperity and rising living standards.

At the time, it seemed that the corporations paid their executives vast sums. In the 1960s, for example, the chief executive officer of a large company could expect to make forty times more than the lowest-paid employee in his (it was always his) firm. In Canada, the gap was less, and the largest salaries were definitely lower than across the border, but the principle was the same, and in both countries progressive income taxes on high incomes narrowed the difference still more. Tales were told of the days of the "Robber Barons," the Goulds, the Rockefellers, and the like, or of the millionaires of the 1920s and their lavish lifestyles—but those days could never come again, surely. The Depression and the war had taught an enduring lesson, and scientific economics, Keynesianism, furnished a formula for enlightened government. And certainly those who had lived through the 1930s and 1940s had absorbed the lesson of their experience. So although it was worrisome, and certainly unfortunate, that the United States had not stitched up the gaps in its social safety net—a later term— prosperity could prevent and, if it could not prevent, absorb many of society's misfortunes.

Such, at any rate, was the general perspective at the beginning of the 1970s. It cast a hopeful glow over Canada's new leader, Pierre Elliott Trudeau, and his promise that his generation—Trudeau was forty-eight when he became prime minister—would do things differently, and better than the generation they were displacing: Great War veterans like Pearson and Diefenbaker.[8] Trudeau promised a "Just Society" that echoed and to some extent parodied Lyndon Johnson's promise of a "Great Society." Neither delivered, and their contemporaries judged them (and Nixon) harshly, and, in fact, more harshly than they deserved.

## *Problems, Real and Imaginary, in the 1970s*

In 1981 three Canadian historians, looking back on the decade just concluded, described the national mood of the 1970s as "an ear-splitting whine."[9] The judgment was perhaps unfair, though the character of much public discussion in the 1970s was certainly repetitive and tiresome. Canada had no Watergate, there was no huge, convulsive scandal but rather a slow decompression as the decade wore on and it became clear that Trudeau was, after all, a politician and not a savior. It was the decade that enjoyed both inflation and higher unemployment, previously considered to be an impossibility. There was an oil price crisis, as the price of oil rocketed from less than $3 a barrel to more than $30 and transferred power over prices from the Western (mainly American) oil companies to the governments of the Middle East, Africa, and Latin America. Meanwhile, some of the United States' large corporations began to show signs of distress—steel, chemicals, manufacturing generally, especially around the Great Lakes—precisely the region with the strongest economic connections to Canada. The American manufacturing hub became, instead, "the Rustbelt," and the gold-plated industries of the 1950s began flirting with bankruptcy. Chrysler, one of the "Big Three" automakers—the others were Ford and General Motors—had to be bailed out in 1979 with government-guaranteed loans. And because Chrysler's business straddled the border and employed many Canadians, the Canadian government was one of the guarantors. The population on the American side of the Great Lakes began to move along, as Detroit, Pittsburgh, Cleveland, and Buffalo massively lost population. Many of the factories were simply abandoned, though some of the disappearing businesses left a poisonous legacy in polluted earth and water, as in the Love Canal near Buffalo—close to the Niagara River. Settlement went into reverse, with some parts of cities reverting to agriculture, while other parts were simply laid to waste. By 2013, Detroit had less than a third as many people as it had had in 1950; Buffalo had lost more than half its population, and Pittsburgh not quite half. All this could be easily seen by day-tripping Canadians.

The population transferred from the Rustbelt to the Sunbelt, the American South and Southwest, regions distant from Canada, though not entirely unconnected because of the annual flood of Canadian vacationers—the "snowbirds," who began to be seriously noticed, and courted, during the 1970s. As the southern states gained, the northern states lost political power in a political system that was ultimately based on population statistics. Put in political terms, more liberal northern states lost influence, and more conservative southern ones gained it, just at the point that Canadians had put one of their more liberal (and Liberal) governments into office.

Though trained as a political economist, Pierre Trudeau had no game-changing answers to Canada's economic problems, which were many, and which grew over time. With perspective, we can see that the Canadian economy was still growing in the 1970s; but inflation was also growing, interest rates were rising, and the number of unemployed was higher than what Canadians had recently been used to. Politicians, national and provincial, regardless of party, operated in a fairly small intellectual box. Personally flamboyant but cautious when it came to policy, Trudeau's default mode was to study a problem and then discuss it, in some cases until the problem went away on its own. There was one exception to this rule: when it came to his home province of Quebec, Trudeau knew what his policy was and must be, and it was up to his ministers and officials to adjust to his conception of reality. That conception of reality was founded on the fact that in Canada ever since the 1790s French and English had been official languages.

## *Bilingual Today, French Tomorrow?*

It was the characteristic that Canada did not share with the United States: bilingualism, the policy that bridged the division between the English and the French that dated from the country's colonial origins. Admittedly, down to the 1960s it was not much of a bridge. French was very much Canada's second language, and Americans visiting nine of the ten provinces would have felt that linguistically nothing had changed when they crossed the international border.

A sense of inferiority or subordination caused by the limited status of French bred resentment and fed discontent, and the predominance of English in downtown Montreal and in Montreal-based corporations made things worse. In the 1960s the resentment broke out in a movement demanding the displacement of English and the predominance of French, which, it was argued, could only be achieved in an independent Quebec, the only majority-French province. Many and, at the beginning, probably most, French Canadians did not agree with independence, and hoped that a solution could be found short of separation.

Unlike the Loyalists in the British colonies of the 1770s, the Canadian or federalist cause in Quebec found a leader. Pierre Trudeau, a Montreal intellectual, became through an unusual and probably unique set of circumstances a Liberal member of Parliament, cabinet minister, and then prime minister. Trudeau and his allies from Quebec brought "French power" to Ottawa, determined to make the Canadian capital the center of French- as well as English-Canadian politics and policy. It was a matter of urgency. In the 1970s, caught up in the groundswell of anti-colonialism, the disappearance of empires, and the apparent liberation of peoples, it was tempting for Quebecers to opt for pulling out of Canada and founding their own independent state on the banks of the St. Lawrence—promoting, as it were, the existing province of Quebec to sovereign status. The political ideology that accompanied this was called separatism, although separatism could have a variety of meanings, from "sovereignty-association," in which Quebec maintained strong economic ties with the rest of Canada, after choosing that option in a referendum and not in an ordinary election, to a unilateral declaration of independence with or without any continuing link to the rest of Canada.

Trudeau had once been a Quebec nationalist and perhaps would have been a separatist had the movement existed when he was in his early twenties. Instead, Trudeau had become an anti-nationalist before settling down and accepting that Canadian federalism was after all the best that the inhabitants of northern North America could hope for. In that belief, Trudeau even encouraged Canadian nationalism, both in terms of a pan-Canadian identity, and as an identity separate from the American. Thus, the anti-nationalist Trudeau became his country's most prominent advocate.

Trudeau had little sense of the United States, something that both Americans and Canadians who met him perceived. And so he approached Canadian–American relations in terms of *realpolitik*. The United States was the dominant power in the region; American investment and American trade were crucial for Canada; and the Americans expected and needed a friendly, allied, state to the north. Trudeau was aware of American exceptionalism and had a fair knowledge of American political culture. He was, on the whole, uninterested in its literary culture, nor did he admire American nationalism. He liked individual Americans—he wanted to marry Barbra Streisand, who fortunately had the good sense to refuse—and he appreciated others, like Kissinger or American ambassador Thomas Enders. But he was not close to any. Of the four American presidents he dealt with, he was cool and correct with Nixon, friendly and cordial with Gerald Ford and Jimmy Carter, and incredulous when it came to Ronald Reagan. We shall deal with Reagan later.

The great Canadian issue for almost all of Trudeau's time in office was Quebec separatism. As prime minister, it was his job to frustrate separatism, and he set about the task with gusto. His attitude was caught on television in June 1968 when he held his ground in front of a riotous, missile-throwing, separatist mob in Montreal, and again in October 1970 when he used draconian emergency powers to suppress a short-lived terrorist movement in Quebec. "Just watch me," he quipped when asked how far he would go in combating terrorism. Some observers, especially on the left, were outraged, and constructed elaborate and generally fanciful explanations of Trudeau's conduct—all hostile. On the other hand, terrorism vanished, though separatism did not.

Quebec separatism was an existential question for Canada. Without Quebec Canada would be broken in two, the Atlantic provinces on one side, and Ontario and the Western provinces on the other. Its communications and institutions would be disrupted. Its national pride would obviously suffer a blow, for what kind of country was Canada, if some six or seven million of its population preferred to go elsewhere? For that, the separatists had an answer, expressed by one of their leaders, Lucien Bouchard, in 1996: "Canada is not a real country," he explained,[10] and therefore there was no loss if it disappeared, either from Quebec, or from the world.

Canada did have a very real function where the United States was concerned: it stabilized, even demilitarized, the northern border. Americans thought of Canada positively, although usually they thought of it very little. But on November 15, 1976, a legal and democratic separatist party, the Parti Québécois (PQ), defeated the Liberal party and secured a majority in the Quebec legislature. The PQ would use its majority to hold a referendum on Quebec's future, which was eventually scheduled for May 1980. In setting the date, the PQ premier of Quebec, René Lévesque, may have hoped he was taking advantage of the temporary disappearance of Trudeau from federal politics, for Trudeau had suffered an election defeat in May 1979 and subsequently resigned as Liberal party leader. His successor, the Progressive Conservative Joe Clark, was young and inexperienced, and though he was bilingual, French was obviously very much his second language. Lévesque anticipated an easy time steamrolling Clark and his allies in the referendum.

Unluckily for Lévesque, and for Clark, the Progressive Conservatives did not have a majority in the federal Parliament. They lost a key vote, called an election for February 1980, and lost—to Trudeau, who had returned from the political wilderness to save his party and his country. Trudeau and Lévesque knew one another well, disliked each other, and were only too happy to fight it out on the hustings. With a referendum scheduled for May 1980, separatism became a matter of concern for the United States.

The terrorist crisis of October 1970 had caught American attention. William Rogers, the secretary of state, was leading a senior cabinet delegation to Ottawa just after, and reported to Nixon that "Canadian ministers and officials spoke freely in private conversations about the possibility of a

break-up of the country, even speculating about what choices might then
be made by the different regions and provinces."[11] It is reasonable to sup-
pose that the "choices" mentioned might have included a petition to join
the United States on the part of some provinces.

What were the American attitude and the American interest in such a
circumstance? The answer is, alas, that the Americans were not sure.
Most though not all American diplomats and politicians were caught by
surprise.[12] The president, Ford, liked Canada: it was adjacent to his home
state of Michigan, he had visited, and he was aware of the booming auto
trade. Moreover, he liked Trudeau. If and when Canada reached his attention, he was disposed to be friendly and, if possible, obliging. The secretary of state after 1973, Henry Kissinger, was likewise prepared to be
friendly and obliging, though Canada occupied a very limited space on his
foreign policy horizon. Badgered by his staff into an "analytic" discussion
of Canada, its problems, and American policy, Kissinger discovered that
his diplomats thought that the pursuit of the status quo was the optimal
American policy. Canada was important economically, as the United
States' largest trading partner. It was not particularly important politically,
though in a modest way it was helpful, as with peacekeeping. The Canadians
had their sensitivities, and could occasionally be annoying, but basically
there was nothing to worry about.

And who knew? If matters muddled along amicably, perhaps, just perhaps, things could get a lot closer. There were three possibilities—closer
relations, greater distance, or muddling through. "There is a natural trend
moving towards greater integration of the two societies," Kissinger was
told—essentially George Ball's vision from 1968. That meant "you could...try
to speed that along, and move towards a relationship in which Canada
really becomes more and more a part of an American complex, and let it
proceed naturally." Admittedly, that option would have to result in "a constitutional convention—offer them statehood." Kissinger must have rolled
his eyes. "You know damn well this cannot be done." Even trying it would
produce the opposite result to the one desired. After a further half-hour of
fruitless discussion, Kissinger summed up:

> Well, I didn't ask for a meeting on Canada. I would not feel unful-
> filled tonight if it was my destiny that we didn't have a meeting on
> Canada. But if we have a meeting on Canada, or any other subject,
> the question I would like to have an answer to is what am I trying
> to accomplish.

Since there was no crisis, no urgency, nothing to be gained by a change in policy, then why bother discussing Canada?[13]

If a crisis was what was required, Quebec supplied it. On November 15, 1976, the PQ and René Lévesque came to power. He had won a provincial election by promising not to secede until after a process of referendum, negotiation, and, if all else failed, a second referendum to take Quebec out of Canada once and for all. Trudeau, his cabinet, and Canada generally were shocked—stunned. They did have some time—as it turned out, over three years—before the PQ was ready for its referendum. It suddenly became very important for the United States to have a Canadian policy, and it had to be the right one—unequivocal support for Canadian unity. Trudeau was by no means certain that that would be the American policy, and candidly ventilated his fears to the American ambassador, Thomas Enders, two days after the Quebec election.

Enders tried to formulate where American interests truly lay.[14] In doing so, he had to report both to the current administration in Washington, Republican, and the incoming administration, Democrat. Jimmy Carter had defeated Gerald Ford in the US presidential poll earlier in November, and any serious reaction to the Canadian separatism issue had to come from him. Enders had already been the recipient of views from prominent Canadian politicians and business leaders, including Trudeau himself. In the circumstances it mattered very much what the United States would say and do, and in Enders' recollection, the Canadians were genuinely uncertain what that might be.[15]

Enders later claimed that his view was clear. Canada and the United States were similar countries in more ways than one. Canada's disappearance or alteration would have an impact on the United States, not merely in material terms—trade and investment—or as a factor in national security, but symbolically and politically. Canada and the United States were liberal democracies that actually functioned. Moreover, they were both federal states, with remarkably similar institutions, and the failure of federalism in Canada might have an impact, sooner or later, on federalism in the United States.[16] In addressing Carter, a southerner, there was a residual memory that the last time federalism failed in the United States; in the 1860s, there had been a bloody Civil War, and it was the American South that suffered devastation and disruption as a consequence.

American reaction mattered very much to Quebec. Québécois attitudes to the United States were not so much ambivalent as contradictory. Religious difference and rural isolation had been no bar to French-Canadian emigration to the mill-towns of New England. American investment was welcomed by a church and state fearful of losing more people to the United States: at least at home the structure of society could be maintained with the tithes of the faithful employed by English-speaking capitalists, whether they were English Canadian or American. American material culture spread to Quebec, as to the rest of North America and the Western world, and Quebecers enthusiastically adopted it. In the prosperity of the 1950s, they could travel to the Maine seacoast, more congenial and picturesque than Quebec's own muddy tidal estuary. American music—rock, naturally, and country-and-western—and American styles proliferated. On the other hand, it was fashionable in intellectual circles to deplore American habits, and in the 1960s, as Quebec moved to the left and the grip of the Catholic Church weakened, the American capitalist menace replaced the Protestant threat. (Mainstream Protestantism was weakening too, at about the same time and at the same rate as Catholicism.)

The Vietnam War focused left-wing Quebeckers on the United States, and separatism in the 1960s had a strongly anti-American and left-wing tinge. When, in the 1970s, separatism grew as a political force and it began to seem that the separatists could come to power, the main separatist political formation, the Parti Québécois, modified its anti-Americanism and made sure to let the American government know it. An independent Quebec would be a firm American ally, would join NATO, and would maintain at the very least existing Canadian–American defense relationships. René Lévesque, the PQ leader, was genuinely and strongly pro-American, and would have been delighted to replace the English Canadians with the Americans. As it turned out, Lévesque's understanding of the United States was not as accurate or as reliable as he believed. A speech in January 1977 to the Economic Club of New York, important for reassuring investors, flopped.

Meanwhile the American government, now headed by Jimmy Carter, had made up its mind. It favored a united Canada, and its representatives said as much publicly while stressing that the outcome was for Canadians to decide by themselves. Trudeau was invited to the White House and afforded the platform of an address to Congress in February. In private, the administration made it clear to the Canadians that the very distinct American preference was for a united Canada. Canadian officials suspected, and had reason to suspect, that Carter's national security adviser, Zbigniew Brzezinski, was much more lukewarm on the subject than his chief. Polish-born and Montreal-raised, Brzezinski was not enamored of Montreal anglophone society or its prejudices and, perhaps because of his Polish background, he favored national independence as a general principle.

Indeed, American assessments of Canada's prospects were gloomier than Canadians would have wished to believe. In considering Canada's and Quebec's recent history, the State Department concluded that a continuation of the status quo was unlikely, although it posed the fewest problems for the United States. An independent Quebec would be imponderable, an economic association would be difficult, and the disintegration of Canada was a clear possibility. That would mean all kinds of problems— including "new responsibilities and opportunities"—in dealing with a collection of weak states on the northern frontier. For the time being, there should be no public change, but in private, with the Canadian government, the United States government could offer to be "helpful."[17] What "helpful" could mean, under the circumstances, was never tested.[18]

In fact the outcome that the Americans judged very unlikely—the continuation of the status quo—occurred. Trudeau fought and won the Quebec referendum of 1980. He did not have to devolve powers to Quebec alone or to all the provinces. Canada continued to have a strong central government—perhaps the stronger because Trudeau pushed through a revision of the Constitution that provided for a charter of rights and a process for constitutional amendment. The US government made its preference for a united Canada clear, but the margin of victory for the federalists in the referendum (60 percent to 40 percent) makes it doubtful that the "American factor" was decisive in securing the federalist victory. But it is possible that an ambiguous and ostentatiously neutral American position might have tipped the balance the other way or made the result narrower.

In analyzing the Canadian situation, the State Department observed that, ironically, since the eruption of the separatist threat, the Canadian government had been more conciliatory toward the United States and less stridently nationalist in its policies. That had been a relief, but the gratification did not outweigh the benefit of having a stable entity to the north, even if it was occasionally erratic in terms of American interests. The "quiet pool of good government" that Isaiah Berlin had praised in 1944 was still in evidence, and its existence was beneficial to the United States.

Besides the failure of the Quebec separatist movement in 1976–80 to achieve its objective, it is important to underline the sentiment evidently held by many Canadians, that their country could easily break up, and if it did, its pieces would want to join the United States. It brings to mind

Lucien Bouchard's later observation, "Canada is not a real country." It might also mean that to Canadians in 1980 and later, Canada was not a real country without Quebec. To Trudeau, it also meant that without a strong central government (and Quebec), Canada was not a real country. Trudeau therefore made sure that the government survived, and with it, the country.

## *Word from Abroad*

Outside Canada, it looked as if Trudeau had popped the separatist bubble. "Welcome to the 1980s," he quipped after his electoral victory in February 1980. But the 1980s turned out to be not quite as advertised. Three events had already occurred that would alter the character of the decade, and another was on the way. The first was the decision by the Soviet Union to alter the strategic balance against NATO by placing advanced SS-20 missiles in Eastern and Central Europe. The second was the Soviet decision to bring to power a communist government in neighboring Afghanistan, and to use the Red Army to do it. The third was the election in May 1979 of a Conservative government in Great Britain after a decade of runaway inflation, union militancy, and civil disorder. The new prime minister, Margaret Thatcher, promised she would change all that, and she did. Finally, eight months after Trudeau's election victory, the Republican Ronald Reagan was elected president of the United States. These events were accompanied by a new and extravagant round of oil price increases, which boosted the power of petroleum producers, such as the Soviet Union, and a sharp economic recession that depressed Western demand—along with incomes and GDP. The 1980s looked as if they might be a very uncomfortable decade.

The leaders of the Soviet Union thought they had history on their side, as a result of the American defeat in Vietnam, when what they had was the petroleum market and an Islamist revolution in oil-producing Iran. But the market could be foe as well as friend, and as demand declined, so did prices, and the Soviet Union's aggressive foreign policies turned out to be a bust. Soviet illusions of power fed Western perceptions of weakness in the face of an expanding Soviet Union. Western strategists saw missiles and aircraft carriers but they should have paid more attention to the true markers of history—bad housing and declining living standards in the Warsaw Pact nations, and consequent social unrest. The power of illusion was great, and the habit of distrust of the Soviet Union greater still—and apparently it was justified as the Soviet leadership made one clanging mistake after another in the late 1970s and early 1980s, raising fears in the West that a cataclysmic nuclear war might after all be imminent. The Soviet leaders for their part took Reagan's election as a sign that the Cold War was icing over again, and that an American nuclear attack was possible, and even probable.

In the circumstances of this later Cold War, Canada's external policy, even its self-image, came under scrutiny and some hostile criticism. It is apparent from American and British comments on Canada and Trudeau that they were not seen as fully engaged either in Western defense, because of the much-diminished size of the Canadian defense budget and armed forces, and that consequently Canada had less weight with its two most important allies, or in the NATO forum. Thatcher, using the term of denigration she applied to the soft-headed or weak-kneed at home and abroad, saw Trudeau himself as "wet." On the other hand, Canada did not break with overall NATO policy responding to Soviet missile deployment, and gave some incidental help, at some political cost at home, to American cruise missile weapons testing programs.[19]

What Canadians saw, and by and large approved, was a foreign policy less belligerent and confrontational than Reagan's, and less ideological than viewing the Soviet Union as an "evil empire." Canada's policy of deploying troops in support of United Nations peacekeeping and assisting generally in avoiding or smoothing over East–West confrontations, while paying attention and giving aid to the Third World, was thought both desirable and distinctive from American policy. But, as we have seen, some American opinion saw "alliance" as a straight trade-off, exchanging American protection for allied support. If the protection was unconditional (which is debatable) then the support should be unconditional too.

It did not help that Trudeau was personally alarmed by Reagan's strident anti-Sovietism, and that he barely concealed his contempt for the American president's intellect. "Grade Two," he muttered to his external affairs minister after listening to Reagan at a Group of Seven meeting, "Grade Two." Reagan, on the other hand, had read (and presumably absorbed) a denunciation of Trudeau by a Canadian right-wing journalist in the American conservative magazine *National Review*. Reagan's entourage were not charmed by Trudeau's National Energy Program, which sought to favor Canadian-owned energy producers over foreign ones—principally American. They did not like Trudeau's legislation that sought to limit foreign investment in Canada.[20] There was also Canada's defense shortfall, which always lurked in the background, though it seldom came up for dispute. A bitter confrontation over energy policy ensued in 1981–2, rising to the presidential level when a meeting was convened in Washington to determine whether the United States should retaliate against Canada for its discriminatory practices. The conclusion, urged by the American ambassador in Ottawa, a Reagan political appointee, was to do nothing. In the ambassador's opinion, Canadians' innate sense of "fairness" would win out, and Trudeau's discriminatory policies would eventually go away. There were too many American interests in Canada to begin juggling with retaliation, so that linking one subject with another through retaliation could produce incalculable—and incalculably bad—effects. It would be better to wait for events to take their course.[21] In the view of an officer at the US embassy in Ottawa, there was really little to be concerned about. "The relationship, in fact, between the Reagan administration and the government of Canada was a very good one," he argued. "It's a truism to say the countries' relationships are determined by their interests, and the interests don't change when a new administration changes."[22]

Events did, indeed, take their course. Trudeau retired from office in June 1984, and the Progressive Conservatives under Brian Mulroney vanquished the short-lived government of his successor, John Turner, in the federal election of September 1984. In the election, Mulroney promised to restore relations with the United States that, he claimed, the Liberals had worsened. He also stated that free trade with the United States was the furthest thing from his mind.

As often happens when a long-entrenched federal government is swept from power, Mulroney harvested the grievances of the provinces and the regions and used them to overwhelm the Liberals, achieving the largest majority in Canadian history up to that date. He could put together a competent and regionally balanced cabinet, which could also draw on newfound strength in Quebec. There, the separatist Lévesque government was on its last legs and would soon be replaced by the federalist Liberals under Robert Bourassa. This was important, because Quebec would play a crucial role in Mulroney's American policy over the next eight years, and Mulroney benefited from Bourassa's reluctance to support the federal Liberals.

At the time the Mulroney government was thought to be part of the same wave of conservatism that had brought Thatcher and Reagan to power. While true up to a point, the conservatism of the early 1980s has to be qualified. Thatcher headed an omnibus party, many of whose members accepted the welfare state with its pensions and, especially, national health care; indeed, Thatcher kept clear of seriously altering the British National Health Service. It took time for Thatcher to assert her ideology and her leadership, and in this enemies both external and internal assisted her. Externally, there was the Argentine military dictatorship that sought to distract its people's attention from their murderous misgovernment by picking off the low-hanging, lingering fruit of colonialism, the (far) off-shore Falkland Islands, a British colony since 1833. Mustering her limited military resources, Thatcher sent them eight thousand miles on a campaign to retake the islands and restore British dignity, and succeeded. The squalid Argentine government shortly fell, although that country's claims on the Falklands did not lapse and periodically resurfaced during times of domestic misfortune.

In recovering the Falklands, American aid was crucial, and, after a division of opinion in the American government, Reagan provided it.[23] Canada had already supported the British in their undeclared conflict with Guatemala over British Honduras (now Belize), so Canada's backing could be taken for granted, but Trudeau gave it publicity nevertheless.[24] The enraged Argentines promptly declared the Canadian ambassador in Buenos Aires persona non grata, forcing him to decamp to Montevideo in neighboring Uruguay until he judged the Argentine government had forgotten about him (about a week), at which point he returned to his embassy.[25] It is not hard to detect intimations of an Anglosphere in these maneuverings, although some Latin American states, notably Chile, did not assist the Buenos Aires regime.

Domestically for Thatcher, there were the trade unions, which had successfully brought down several governments during the 1970s. In 1979 the overweening power of the unions and their propensity to go on perpetual strikes had undermined the Labour government after a winter in which everyone, including the gravediggers, seemed to be on the picket line. The coal miners in particular clung to their right to bring the country to a halt whenever their obsolescent industry was threatened. Thatcher met them, essentially, with force, and by 1985 had broken their power. "Never forget," she told her audiences, "how near this country came to government by picket."[26] She considered politics to be a contest between good and evil, and regarded consensus and compromise with an unelected power like the miners' union as immoral. She took the same view of the war against the Irish Republican Army, which had been going on since the late 1960s; in riposte, the IRA nearly succeeded in blowing her up along with most of her cabinet. In public finance, she argued for a pay-as-you-go system based on the principles she had learned in her father's small-town shop in the 1930s.[27] Under Thatcher, the reign of Keynes was definitely over. Standing firm in the Falklands, standing firm against radical trade unions,[28] and standing firm against IRA terrorism made Thatcher a heroic figure and enhanced her reputation not only in Britain but overseas—including in Canada.

She did not like Trudeau or his policies, but curiously there was one point of similarity. When Trudeau confronted revolutionary, violent separatism in October 1970, he refused any compromise with violence or blackmail, and on that point distinguished himself from many other politicians, particularly in Quebec. It was, for Trudeau, a question of good versus evil, and in the event he rallied public opinion behind his clear policy of no compromise with terrorism. Moreover, his principled stand did not do him any disservice at the time or later in his home province—for the next four elections he won stronger and stronger majorities in Quebec, ending up with every seat in the province bar one.

Thatcher was fervently pro-American, the more because Ronald Reagan was in power. Reagan had set his face against the economic policies of the 1960s and 1970s, had confronted the public service unions, and fundamentally changed American fiscal policy—lowering taxes in a manner that was guaranteed to alter the shape of American society. There is a clear division between the shape of American government and American public policy before and after Reagan; arguably Reagan also changed the shape of American politics, moving his Republican party out of consensus and perceptibly to the right. All these factors appealed to Thatcher. In the annual meetings of the Group of Seven leaders she defended Reagan and denounced Trudeau's compromising ways when it came to the Third World or the East Bloc. She had made Trudeau "stand in a corner," she boasted. In return, Reagan deeply admired his British counterpart, who was the only British politician since Churchill to make an impact, not only on the president, but on the American imagination.[29]

Brian Mulroney was in many respects Trudeau's opposite in terms of personality—but while that did not make him especially resemble Thatcher, she is known on excellent authority to have liked him personally. Mulroney's charm and fellow feeling made him a welcome presence in Reagan's White House,[30] and in George H.W. Bush's thereafter; and it was the same with Thatcher. Perhaps in Thatcher's case opposites attracted.

Mulroney was not ideological, and maintained the tradition of the Progressive Conservatives as an omnibus party in which differing points of view contended and compromised. It is true that Mulroney began with a standard conservative flourish, promising to seek and destroy the "waste" that was held to be inherent in government, and with the savings pay for the rest of his policies. But failing to find enough waste, he decided instead to contribute to it, raising taxes and deficits through the later 1980s—but also maintaining Canada's social safety net and the bases of the country's welfare state. In foreign policy, apart from cleaving to the United States on East–West issues, Mulroney and his external affairs minister Joe Clark continued Canada's peacekeeping policies, and on North–South (or Third World) issues Canada was in much the same place as it had been under Trudeau and Pearson. And, ironically, the Americans continued to grumble that Canada was taking its defense partnership with its neighbor too lightly.

Mulroney is and will be remembered as the prime minister who brought free trade with the United States to fruition, an objective for virtually every Canadian prime minister since the abrogation of the reciprocity treaty in 1866. It was not his first choice of policy—as we have seen, he dismissed it out of hand during the 1984 election. Yet Canada's trade policy by 1984 was at an impasse, and Canada, officials and politicians knew, was increasingly isolated, a trading area of just over twenty-seven million compared with the hundreds of millions living in the United States, or Europe, or East Asia. In a world where trade blocs were becoming the fashion, Canada needed a partner, and none was on offer except the United States. Worse still, as American economic predominance faded, there was the possibility that the United States might turn to protectionism or opt for measures that would damage Canadian trade.

Ronald Reagan seemed heaven-sent as a negotiating partner. He had once talked of a "North American Accord," which, as a Californian, he naturally thought should include Mexico. To Reagan and his conservative contemporaries, Canada was still an attractive and congenial conception, despite the Liberal Trudeau government. After 1984 Trudeau was a bad memory, but one that Mulroney found he could use to his benefit. Mulroney began by establishing himself as the Canadian of American dreams—utterly pro-American, friendly, supportive, and, like Mackenzie King, undemanding except when he needed help. King had not been above seeking help from his fellow politicians Churchill and Roosevelt; and Mulroney—like King, a labor negotiator and compromiser by profession—asked his new American friends the question, What if Trudeau (or the Liberals) came back?

Paradoxically, therefore, the weaker Mulroney's political position at home appeared to be, the more the Americans were inclined to help him out. Reagan was often, if not usually, the catalyst for action. On a visit by Mulroney in February 1986, Reagan wrote, "He's had some bad times and we will need to send him home with some good news for his people." In this case, it was on the question of acid rain, a lively issue in Canada where over time Mulroney moved Reagan, who was not a strong believer in climate change, pollution, or other disturbing phenomena, into action.[31] Seen from below, presidential involvement was an incalculable boon. According to the American ambassador, Thomas Niles, "This interchange at the top cannot be overestimated in terms of its beneficial impact on the relationship because it forces our system to focus on the issues. It gives you a reason to say to all these recalcitrant bureaus and agencies in the United States that the President is involved, therefore, they need to get with it. It really helped."[32]

Negotiations with the Americans for free trade were difficult. Trading on the notion that Canada was dependent—at least for negotiating purposes—and on the necessity for Congress to ratify any trade deal, the Americans refused to give Mulroney what he most wanted—a treaty whose terms would not, could not, be altered by Congress. In the recent past, when the established trading rules on items like softwood lumber had not favored the Americans, Congress had changed the rules. Congress declined to give up this power. In September 1987 the Canadian negotiating team broke off talks and returned to Canada. Back in Washington, the American negotiators waited for the Canadians to return.

In Canada, the free-trade negotiations had been highly publicized, not least by Mulroney, who expected a triumph that would take him through the next federal election. They also had a time limit, fixed under American trade legislation. If an agreement were not reached by early October 1987, the negotiations would come to an end, and the free(r) trade project would fail, as it had in 1891, 1911, and 1948. Negotiations were moved up the line, involving the US treasury secretary personally, and a team of cabinet ministers and high officials on the Canadian side. The difficult question of unfair trade practices, subsidies and the like, was left unanswered and undefined—left in fact to each country's own laws. How national legislation was interpreted and applied could be referred to bi-national panels for a decision—and they would have plenty to do. The result was a partial free-trade system, not a merger of the two economies behind a single common tariff, with common trade rules, as in Europe.

Free trade became the central issue of a wild and wooly election in Canada in November 1988. The opposition Liberals under ex-prime minister John

Turner appealed to nationalist sentiment and to very commonly held beliefs in Canada—the contrast between the giant United States and tiny Canada, the certainty that Canada would be swallowed up by the United States, and that east–west links among Canadians would be severed. The election is remembered for a leaders' debate in which Turner overwhelmed the spluttering Mulroney. But Mulroney had politics on his side, the certainty of a treaty, the prospect that something worse would follow if the treaty were not ratified, and the effective support of the Liberal government of Quebec, which tied Turner's hands in appealing to the electorate in that crucial province. Mulroney seemed to be appealing to hope and to positive values, while Turner seemed to be appealing to the past and to fear. The reality was somewhat different. In the opinion of one of the treaty negotiators on the Canadian side, the best arguments for the treaty were all negative, keeping open the door for Canadian trade to the United States in the face of a greater American sense of economic vulnerability and the possibility—the probability if there was no treaty—of protectionist legislation. The Autopact of 1965 was highly vulnerable to American politics, and a collapse of the free-trade project might well have entailed the collapse of the special automobile arrangements. There was fear, in other words, and it is hard to say that it was unjustified.[33]

Certainly the Free Trade Treaty and its supplement, the trilateral North American Free Trade Agreement including Mexico (NAFTA) in 1993 were important markers in Canadian–American trade relations. It was a sign that relations with Canada were good and would remain so. Tariffs were indeed abolished, but trade barriers, the inventive and infinite subsidies and special arrangements in each country, were not. The dispute resolution mechanism worked well, but not perfectly. There were points at which some of the erstwhile supporters of free trade were reduced to apoplexy as they contemplated the latest American trade tactics in blocking imports of Canadian products, most notably softwood lumber.[34]

As free-trade proponents had successfully argued, Canadian culture did not disappear or drown in a tide of American mass cultural consumption. Canadians watched American movies before free trade, and they watched them after. They may even have watched more Canadian movies after free trade than before, because the quality of Canadian cinematic productions was actually improving, and its product therefore more worth watching. The Canadian wine industry, the object of worried solicitation before the election, did better than before because it too had a product that was worth buying and consuming. Had free trade occurred in 1950 or 1970, the result might have been different: the colored, foxy alcohol that Canadian wineries produced in the mid-twentieth century might very well have been overwhelmed by its American counterparts[35] and have disappeared without notice or lamentation.

These examples may be exceptions, and it is virtually certain that some Canadian industries were negatively affected by free trade, that some, perhaps many, Canadians became unemployed as a result, but as of this writing there is no comprehensive historical examination of the actual impact of free trade on specific industries or localities. While trade went up, it should be noted that the dollar went down, and that Canada's exchange rate policy in the mid to late 1990s priced Canadian products low on the export market. We might reasonably expect Canadian exports to do well, and do better, and they did. The same had happened under the Autopact: as the Canadian dollar fell in value after 1976, so Canadian production rose.

## The End of the Cold War

The election of 1988 in Canada was fought over the question of foreign policy, but it was not fought over the Cold War, which most Canadians, if asked, would have said was the foundation for the country's entire foreign relations. The Cold War did not rumble along in a uniform manner over its forty or so years. It had moments of high tension and rigid preparedness down to the Cuban missile crisis in 1962; but from that point on, despite the Vietnam War, and despite the very active (and quite justified) tremors of potential nuclear war in the early 1980s, it never again reached the same intensity. It is interesting to compare the abortive 1948 trade negotiations between Canada and the United States with those forty years on. In 1948, there was no doubt that the negotiations for a trade and economic arrangement were spurred by the fear that North America might soon have to gather its resources, as in the Second World War, to fight a third. Getting the continent's economy in order was therefore a high strategic priority. In 1988 there was no such compulsion; if the free-trade negotiations resembled anything, they were like trade talks in the 1930s, or even 1911 or earlier.

The Cold War had a positive and negative impact on Canada's relations with the United States. It meant that Canada and the United States were allies, formally and informally, throughout the whole period. In the earlier years, from 1948 to 1963, the two countries meant more or less the same thing when they used the term *allies* or *alliance*. Apart from the peculiar episode of John Diefenbaker's quarrels with John F. Kennedy, there was no real difference of opinion, and arguably many of Diefenbaker's Conservative supporters, including many of his ministers, agreed more with Kennedy than with the Canadian prime minister.

In the 1950s McCarthyism and in the 1960s the Vietnam War created dissonance, but it was against a background in which Canada was still spending more on defense, and hence alliance support, than on any other governmental objective. Similarly, Canada's early peacekeeping commitments, to the Sinai, or the Congo, or Cyprus, were for definably Western objectives and undertaken in harmony with American as well as NATO strategy. Even the Cuban missile crisis, when the world brushed against nuclear war, had not seriously shaken the allies, and in particular Canada. But over the twenty years after 1962 the danger receded, and the prospect of nuclear war seemed more and more remote. Even when nuclear war became, briefly, a real possibility around 1982–3, the Western public for the most part refused to believe it. The appearance of a "peace movement" in the late 1970s and early 1980s, on which the Soviets pinned their hopes of getting the West to accept their missile deployment in Europe, produced the exact opposite effect: in West Germany, it helped precipitate the fall of a socialist government and brought into office a much more conservative one. In Canada, governments Liberal and Conservative remained committed to NATO strategy, including both the deployment of new weapons and the pursuit of arms reduction in Europe.

Partly for domestic reasons, and partly because of the decompression of international tensions after 1963, the Canadian government cut its defense budget in the 1960s, as we have seen, moving in the Trudeau period to an eighty-thousand–strong military, reducing Canada's garrison in Europe, and altering its mission. There were no direct consequences of these actions, undertaken under both Pearson and Trudeau, but after 1968 appraisals of Canada's defense policy by Canadian allies took on a negative tone. (It should however also be clear that Canada was not alone in reducing its defense budget and cutting some of its commitments—the British government was a notorious sinner in all these areas, and the US government had in the 1960s seriously weakened its garrison in Europe to feed its army in Vietnam.)

The decompression allowed the reallocation of resources. In Canada, that meant moving toward the welfare state; in the United States it seems to have weakened the commitment to a higher-tax regime and permitted the cutting of taxes in the early 1980s, although simultaneously the

American government fervently and expensively rearmed under both Jimmy Carter and (even more) Ronald Reagan. The result was that Reagan's tax cutting helped create a massive American deficit, something that did not become the stuff of Reagan's political legend over the next thirty years.[36]

Peacekeeping, however, continued to find favor with the Ottawa government and with Canadian public opinion at large. So did initiatives aimed at reducing European apprehensions through agreements with the Soviet Union recognizing existing boundaries, a major Soviet objective, in return for commitments to human rights on the continent, including, the East Bloc. True Cold Warriors did not take these initiatives seriously, expecting them to be null and void in the face of Soviet power. But the Soviet government was looking for international legitimacy at a time when its ability to cope with internal problems, economic and social, in the Soviet Union and in its satellites, was coming into question. The Soviet Union was weaker than many in the West thought.

The Mulroney government (and the Reagan administration, and Margaret Thatcher and her disciples) accepted the common right-wing view that Trudeau had been too soft and too ready to accept Soviet assurances or policies at face value. But in some senses Trudeau was better informed than his prime-ministerial and presidential colleagues in NATO: he had formed a friendship with the very intelligent Soviet ambassador in Ottawa, Aleksandr Yakovlev; and Yakovlev in turn represented a different strain of Soviet thought than what usually emerged from the decaying minds of the Soviet politburo.[37]

This became apparent when Yakovlev's friend and patron, Mikhail Gorbachev, became Soviet leader in 1985. Yakovlev had brought Gorbachev, then the Soviet agriculture minister, to Canada for a tour of Canadian agriculture in 1983, and helped convert his friend to the view that Western prosperity was no figment of the capitalist imagination but was, on the contrary, widely distributed and accessible to most Western citizens. Gorbachev began to draw conclusions about what forty years of expensive confrontation had brought the Soviet Union and began to work to strengthen, as he saw it, Soviet society by opening it up and, after some initial hesitation, seeking an accommodation with the West. He found a ready partner in Reagan, who contrary to popular views, and contrary to some of his own rhetoric, was deeply concerned to lessen the danger of nuclear war.

Many Western specialists, in the United States but also in Canada, remained suspicious. There had been many false dawns in Western–Soviet relations. More to the point, most Western observers seriously overestimated the economies of the Soviet Union and its satellites, believing them to be far stronger than they really were. The evidence to the contrary was all around: the West German government was propping up the East German government through loans and other special economic relations, while the Eastern European countries survived on a diet of capitalist money infusions. Nobody in power seems to have added up the sums and come to the inescapable conclusion that the Soviet Union and its system were bankrupt, economically, socially, and politically.

Mulroney was late to the feast, but by 1988 he had joined the parade of Westerners who converted to the belief that Gorbachev was the Soviet savior. (The phenomenon was called "Gorby-mania.") Gorbachev in 1989 took the fundamental decision that the communist (and Soviet-imposed) governments of Eastern Europe would have to stand—or fall—on their own. The Soviet army would not help them. One after another they fell, until by early 1990 they were all gone. The Soviet Union was next, as its suppressed nationalities demanded first autonomy and then independence; after an aborted coup in Moscow, Gorbachev gave up the struggle. The red flag was hauled down from the Kremlin at Christmas, 1991, and the Soviet Union passed into history.

Not surprisingly, the Soviet collapse was hailed as the triumph of the West and liberal democracy—which arguably was true—and as the end of ideological struggle, which arguably was false.[38] If we see the Cold War period as an ideological deep freeze in the East Bloc, and as the persistence of a wartime model of government and society in the West, inside a kind of political refrigeration short of freezing, then the end of the Cold War soon set political temperatures boiling. Former communist countries, from China in the east to Albania in the west, wanted prosperity, interpreted as riches, but they did not necessarily want democracy, except to ratify and legitimate the political factions who happened to be in power when communism officially departed the political scene.

What was happening was not the end of history, but the release of history, as resentments and doctrines suppressed in the 1940s came back to life—especially when associated with extreme nationalism. The effect was neither liberal nor democratic. In the West, the effect was muted, as countries turned their focus inward and concentrated on more parochial problems. And yet, in the collapse of the Soviet Union and communism, there was one superpower still standing. It was America's moment.

# Something Old, Something New

## The Economic Anglosphere

The end of the Cold War allowed older patterns of Canadian–American relations to come to the fore. In many respects, they had never gone away—patterns of trade, investment, and cultural influence. Railways, pipelines, and electric transmission lines snaked across the border. The Internet extended into both countries, creating new contacts and new ways of doing bilateral business. American companies moved north, and Canadian companies moved south. In 1992, Canada, the United States, and Mexico signed the North American Free Trade Agreement, NAFTA, and ratified it after a change of governments in the two northern partners. The new American president, the Democrat Bill Clinton, was, like his predecessor, the Republican George H.W. Bush, strongly committed to freer trade and "globalization," the doctrine of universal economic interchange, under rules largely designed by Americans and embodied in the brand-new World Trade Organization (WTO) that replaced the cumbersome General Agreement on Tariffs and Trade, which had grown ever more complicated, cumbersome, and time-consuming. The WTO would be a fresh start. Canada naturally belonged.

These changes occurred regardless of the party in power in Canada or the United States. And the parties in power reflected the zeitgeist of the nineties, the belief that "the market" would now regulate all things and solve all problems. Some politicians believed more in the market, and some less. Most of them felt they had no choice. Communism had been a possibility, "wicked and unrealizable" though it might have been, in the words of John Maynard Keynes's biographer, Robert Skidelsky. But after 1990, he continued, "There suddenly seemed no alternative to money as a way of organising society."[1]

Skidelsky was right when he pointed to the question of alternatives, but wrong in his chronology. When Margaret Thatcher came to power in

1979 it was because the alternative, not communism but labor-socialism, had failed.[2] The trend in Great Britain under Margaret Thatcher and her Conservative successor, John Major, had been toward privatization of state enterprises and formerly public functions. Railways, electricity, even water supplies came under private ownership, although ostensibly (and sometimes really) they continued to be regulated by a much-diminished state. These developments were noted on the west side of the Atlantic, where they inspired a new generation of right-wing politicians.

A sharp recession in 1990–2 concentrated political thought and spurred on new political trends. This was particularly the case because of the election in 1990 of an NDP government in Ontario. The economy contracted, revenues shrank, and expenditures rose as the NDP tried to spend its way through the recession, only to come firmly up against the new market orthodoxy, which dictated lower expenditures, lower deficits, smaller debts, lower taxes, and higher returns on private investment. The Ontario NDP ran out the electoral clock and were defeated in 1995, making way for a much more radical right-wing government in the province, the Progressive Conservatives under Mike Harris.

Ontario's Progressive Conservatives had once justified both parts of their name, providing moderate, middle-of-the-road government at a time when the provincial economy was performing well and an expansive government seemed amply justified, as well as amply funded. They even presided over a huge public power corporation, Ontario Hydro, founded by their political ancestors (Conservatives, that is), at the beginning of the twentieth century. In that respect these earlier Progressive Conservatives resembled their cousins in Great Britain in the 1960s and 1970s, or their Progressive Republican counterparts in the United States at various points in the twentieth century.[3] The right wings of these several parties had for years been kept under sedation, lest they frighten off centrist voters. It was the ultra-conservative Barry Goldwater, Republican candidate for president in 1964, who pointed in another direction, exclaiming that "extremism in the defense of liberty is no vice." But Goldwater was nearly obliterated in the 1964 election, and for the next fifteen years Republicans hewed to the middle of the road, with Nixon and Ford. And then, suddenly, Thatcher and Reagan seemed to demonstrate that the contrary was true, and it was the moderates' turn to head for the exit. Tony Clement, a cabinet minister in the Mike Harris government in Ontario (1995–2003) and in the Harper government in Ottawa (2006–), summed up the reasoning, and gave credit to Margaret Thatcher, the new conservative role model. "In the 1970s, conservatism was just a poor, pale imitation of liberalism. Why would anyone vote for it? And here was a woman who said, 'No, we stand for something very different.'"[4]

Clement was right, up to a point, and he was certainly right about Thatcher's symbolic appeal. Young conservatives like Clement secured a leader of the right stamp (in all respects) in Mike Harris; under his leadership, and preaching the low-tax, limited government dogma of Thatcher and Reagan, the Harrisites swept to power in Ontario in 1995. They called it the "common-sense revolution," a not-so-subtle anti-elitist message aimed at populist voters. At bottom, the thesis was that private enterprise, working through "the market," was invariably more efficient and cheaper than any public-sector contrivance. Employees in the public sector, therefore, were by definition privileged and, while purporting to work in the public interest, were actually feathering their own nest.

And yet the common-sense revolution (and its contemporary counterparts in Michigan, Wisconsin, and Ohio) owed something to Keynes, or at any rate to one of Keynes's perceptions. Keynes was surely right when he quipped that even the most practical, hard-headed businessman was in terms of his (almost always his) economic assumptions the slave of some defunct economist. There was a considerable intellectual pedigree behind Harris's apparently anti-intellectual policies, and at all points, in Canada, the United States, and Great Britain there were numbers of intellectuals who lent themselves and their voices to the conservative cause.[5]

Stephen Harper had his own connections to right-wing think-tanks and pressure groups in the United States. More intellectual than Harris, he seems to have formed his conservative philosophy while in university.[6] As a politician, he sought out persons holding similar views, and the money to spread them. As a politician concerned with winning elections and keeping power, he was attentive to the techniques the American right found most effective.

This remained true even in the 2010s, when the Progressive Conservative leader in Ontario, Tim Hudak, was toured around right-wing think tanks in Washington by his host, David Frum.[7] The expedition may have encouraged Hudak to take a hard-right position in the Ontario general election of 2014, promoting austerity, low taxes, and a diminished public sector. This particular electoral concoction did not go over well with the Ontario public, and Hudak lost the election and his job as party leader.

There were many reasons for this tendency. One was a reaction against the suffocating piety of the dominant group of liberals in government and (especially) academia. This was not all that surprising, since much of the professoriate had assumed many of the functions of the clergy in earlier times. It was no stretch to take on some of the incantatory function of the clergy, chanting out nostrums and dogma that could be parroted by the faithful. (Of course, the same is true of any dominant system of belief, and the right on that score is no different from the left.) Another reason was a response to the disorder on Canadian and American campuses in the 1960s and 1970s, as left-wing revolutionaries pursued their various social-ist and communist utopias. Yet another reason was a response to the defi-cits, inflation, strikes, unemployment, and high interest rates of the late 1970s and early 1980s, which seemed to show that the state's performance in managing the economy (in Britain especially) was a failure.[8]

The ascendancy of right-wing conservatives was helped immeasurably by the disintegration of the Mulroney Progressive Conservatives in the early 1990s. Mulroney had become fatally entangled in the problems of the Canadian Constitution. Intending to revise the constitution in a way that would meet the demands of the federalist Quebec Liberals (who were despite their name in fact his political allies) then governing in Quebec City, and thus secure a document that was acceptable and legitimate in all parts of the country, Mulroney managed the opposite, alienating both English and French Canada over three years of almost constant constitu-tional crisis. He then passed a useful and necessary tax reform, which created a highly visible federal sales tax, to take the place of the invisible one that had existed before. Federal finances improved drastically as a result, but many on the Canadian right would not forgive Mulroney. The prime minister's resignation in 1993 did not improve matters, and his successor, Kim Campbell, was swept from office in the October 1993 fed-eral election.

The Liberals under Jean Chrétien were the immediate beneficiaries. The Liberals of the 1990s were a somewhat factionalized bunch, ranging from the moderate right to the moderate left—the standard major party model in Canada, up to that time—but they were united in their determi-nation to secure and retain power. Canadian conservatives, on the other hand, were disunited, split between the continuation of the Mulroney party (still called "Progressive Conservatives") and a populist right wing centered mainly in the West, called the Reform Party. There was as well a strong separatist party, the Bloc Québécois, which picked up most of the parliamentary seats in Quebec and which formed the official opposition to Chrétien. What was left over supported the NDP, which in this period had

a very limited appeal. Chrétien rode this fortunate combination of a disunited opposition to victory in three elections, 1993, 1997, and 2000, and
remained in office as prime minister for just over ten years, until December
2003.

The Chrétien government and especially its minister of finance, Paul
Martin, faced serious problems of financial credibility. The dominant
opinion in the business community, and among bankers in New York
City, was that Canada had become over-indebted through many years of
deficit finance. The *Wall Street Journal* nominated Canada to be an hon-
orary member of the socialist Third World, and not the solvent, orderly
First World, where responsible people arranged things properly, paid
down debt, reduced taxes, and kept expenditures to a minimum. The
irony of this position would not be apparent until fifteen years later, when
the crash of 2008 revealed how Wall Street and the world business community actually arranged their affairs. In the face of a kind of panic ema-
nating from the business community and such organs as the *Globe and
Mail*, the Chrétien government rearranged its budget, cut expenditures
drastically, though not across the board, and eventually produced a surplus, Canada's first in more than twenty years, and having produced one,
it brought forth another, and another.[9] The debt contracted.

Chrétien and Martin had that necessary political skill, luck, for the
economy bounced back from the recession of the early 1990s. Interest
rates dropped, lessening the amount that had to be paid to service the
debt, oil prices fell, the exchange rate dropped, revenues rose, and manufacturing and exports boomed. Many Canadians felt the pain that this
budgetary contraction entailed, especially in health care, but the basic features of the health-care system remained intact. That in turn meant that
the followers of the *Wall Street Journal* and the inhabitants of the newly
flourishing right-wing think tanks in the United States, and their counterparts in Canada, were not appeased.

The Chrétien government got along well enough with its British and
American counterparts in the 1990s, the "New" Democratic administration of Bill Clinton, and the British "New Labour" government (after 1997)
under Tony Blair. Both men were highly intelligent, and Clinton was a
brilliant orator who could and did deliver some of his major speeches
without notes or the universal electronic aids that handicap speakers in
the twenty-first century. Although Clinton tended to seek his economic
advice and direction from individuals closely connected to Wall Street, he
retained enough of the Democratic heritage to make achieving a universal

health-care system the main plank of his first administration. So while Clinton was cheerfully deregulating the financial system with one hand and preparing a smooth road that would lead directly to the Wall Street crash of 2008, he also did his best to follow Truman and Nixon to try to expand the United States' social safety net in a truly significant way. Unfortunately for his legislative legacy, Clinton could not manage the task; he did, however, succeed in mobilizing the American right wing, and the failure of his health scheme contributed directly to the triumph of right-wing Republicans in the congressional elections of 1994.[10]

Blair, though a skilled public performer, seemed to rely on spin-doctors to get his message across, causing observers to parse the spin in his speeches, trying to discern the real message. He did in fact manage some major changes in British public policy, creating a kind of British federal system that gave autonomy to Scotland, in particular, with its own legislature sitting in the old Scottish capital of Edinburgh.[11] There were, obviously, similarities between Britain's newly discovered federalism and Canada's, and many Canadian observers would have been inclined to advise Blair to leave well enough alone; but then, as later, Blair had no strong interest in securing Canadian advice or contemplating the Canadian experience. Certainly the grant of a local assembly whetted the appetite of the separatist Scottish Nationalists for more, and the local weakness of the London-centered British political parties provided an opening for the Nationalists to come to power in Edinburgh, with results that might have been predicted, not from Canada's distant past, but from the immediate present of the 1990s.

Quebec was not always the dominant political issue in Canada over the fifty years after 1960, but it was the most continuous and probably the most important. The failure of Mulroney's attempt to reform the Constitution raised, one more time, the specter of separatism. This was the more so because Mulroney, to get his revisions through, had denounced the inequities of Trudeau's (that is, the existing) Constitution. He helped discredit what was in force, using it as a symbol of injustice to Quebec, and then was unable to put anything in its place.[12] As we have seen, Mulroney's party and also the federal Liberals split on the issue, and Mulroney's Quebec remnant, with a few dangling Liberals, became the Bloc Québécois, while the Parti Québécois chased the provincial Liberals from power in Quebec City in 1994. For the second time in a generation the United States had to contemplate what kind of neighbor it wanted on its northern frontier.

## Clinton and Quebec

Bill Clinton was the third southerner in a generation to occupy the White House. All three were Democrats; all three overcame the intangible barrier of the Mason-Dixon Line to reclaim for the South some of the political prominence it had lost in the Civil War; and all three, situated on American history's losing side, conceivably had absorbed a sense that political division and sovereigntist politics were intrinsically risky if not outright bad. The first, Lyndon Johnson, had no feeling for Canada, disliked its prime minister (Pearson), and visited it as little as possible.[13] The second, Jimmy Carter, liked the prime minister (Trudeau) and generally approved of the country and Trudeau's policies; Trudeau reciprocated his sentiments.[14] Carter had been to Canada before and after he was president, but never managed a visit while in office. The third, Clinton of Arkansas, had no obvious Canadian connection, and he faced a prime minister, Chrétien, who believed that his predecessor, Mulroney, had multiplied his unpopularity by seeming entirely too close to the Americans. Nevertheless Clinton managed a successful Ottawa visit in 1995, impressed the locals (who anyway preferred Democrats like Clinton to the Republicans like Reagan and the two Bushes), and thereafter chummed around with Chrétien as occasion offered or circumstances required. "Good—and not too cozy," Chrétien said of the relationship.[15] American perspectives on Chrétien varied. One senior diplomat who served in Ottawa in the period remarked that the prime minister was simply not very interested in foreign affairs. From the perspective of 2001, he added, "The foreign affairs ignorance has persisted. It has been consistent. He has little or no interest in foreign affairs and less competence in it."[16]

Curiously, despite the size of Canadian–American trade and investment, the relationship on the economic side was neither good nor cozy, with frequent confrontations over such items as wheat marketing. Clinton's trade representative, Mickey Kantor, did not have a natural interest in nor sympathy for Canada, in the view of Canadian trade diplomats. It is not surprising that on the trade file, Canadian triumphs were few, and setbacks relatively frequent. That it did not affect a generally sunny connection may be an indication of both Clinton's and Chrétien's real interests and priorities.

By the 1990s Canadian feelings of anti-Americanism had also decompressed, easing the two leaders' tasks. It was a nice change, in the view of some American diplomats. "French and the English could go after each other on Canadian politics, but they weren't going after us in the same broad way. The Canadians, French and English, felt comfortable in the United States and they wanted us to feel that they were open for business and that meant attracting Americans to go there." It did not mean that differences were not there, but they were amiable differences in the opinion of liberal Americans and no threat to the United States. "There was a certain desire on the part of many Canadians to try and demonstrate that they were not Americans," according to the State Department desk officer for Canada. "They would stress their general liberal socialist traditions, or their being more 'European' than the United States."[17]

Economics and politics were very much on the mind of the American ambassador in Ottawa, James Blanchard. He had been the Democratic governor of car-producing Michigan, and connections between Michigan and car-producing Ontario were close, intertwined, and not to be interrupted. Like many (though not all) Michiganders, Blanchard felt some geographical and cultural affinity to neighboring Canada, and what Clinton lacked in knowledge of Canada, Blanchard was ready to supply. Chrétien understood, as his foreign affairs department put it, that Blanchard was "a close confidante [sic] of the President," and had "ready entrée to the highest levels of the White House and with US cabinet ministers, many of whom he knows personally."[18] Political appointments to the Canadian job were not the highest rung of political reward in Washington, and many of them passed practically unnoticed and unremembered in Ottawa society; but Blanchard's role proved to be crucial, both in his sense of the importance of Canadian–American relations, and in his political judgment, which, in 1995, proved to be superior to Chrétien's.

In contrast to the atmosphere in Ottawa in 1976–80, the mood in 1995 was almost serene. A Quebec referendum was imminent, but the prime minister believed the federal side would easily win it. (The subject was not even included in Chrétien's briefing book for Clinton's official visit in February 1995.) In part that was because the Quebec government's position was much more hard-line in 1995 than in 1980, with no "soft" option of an economic association in contemplation. The Quebec premier, Jacques Parizeau, wanted sovereignty pure and simple. Once that was achieved, other questions could be negotiated. For the separatists, that created a bit of a problem, politically. As in 1980 the Quebec electorate, even the French-speaking part, where a majority favored separation, wanted some reassurance that the economy would not immediately go into the tank. No wonder Chrétien and his advisers felt no need to highlight separatism and the referendum for their talks with Clinton. To this separatist dilemma, there could be only one response: fudge the question. As in 1980, the separatists and the not-quite-separatists worked out a question that was so complicated and convoluted its meaning was not readily apparent. Speaking from inside a cloud of obfuscation, not his natural habitat, Parizeau set the referendum date for October 30, 1995.

At first it seemed that his quest for independence was doomed. Many, perhaps most, French-speaking Quebeckers did not care for Parizeau's upper-class airs, or his appearance, which mimicked that of a British banker (he bought his suits in London, it was said, and the visual evidence suggested the story was true). Independence needed a man of the people, and the separatist leader in the federal Parliament, Lucien Bouchard, who like Chrétien came from a genuinely humble background, supplied that need. In 1995, however, Bouchard, an accomplished orator and charismatic leader, spoke for most French Quebeckers and the prime minister, as he painfully learned, did not.

Halfway through the referendum campaign, with only weeks to go, Chrétien learned that polls showed he was going to lose the referendum. He did not know, but may have suspected, that if that happened, even by a single vote, Parizeau would immediately proclaim victory and with victory, independence, unilaterally. A shaken Chrétien appealed to the American ambassador, Blanchard, for help. In 1980 tacit American support for Canada had not made the difference in a decisively pro-federal result, but in 1995 the Canadian government was willing to try anything.

Both in 1980 and 1995 the separatist government of Quebec (the PQ) had grasped the importance of the United States both in winning a referendum and afterward, in securing independence. In 1995, as in the late 1970s, senior PQ figures made reassuring noises as to what the future would hold, with an independent Quebec. "Quebecers in particular wanted the United States to understand exactly what it wanted, exactly what it was trying to do, exactly how it was going to go about it, and to emphasize that it could do so without being a security, economic, or political concern to the United States," recalled the minister-counselor at the American embassy in Ottawa.[19] As in 1980 the PQ did its best to derail American governmental support for Canada, and both times it was unsuccessful—rather more dramatically in 1995 than in 1980. Clinton spoke not once but twice of American preferences, leaving no doubt that his administration strongly preferred to have a single and stable neighbor north of the border. And it may have made a difference because of the exceedingly narrow margin in the referendum—50.4 percent for Canada, 49.6 for an independent Quebec.

The United States never did have to decide exactly what it would do in the event that Quebec actually separated. The PQ government would have declared independence, and it would have been recognized as a sovereign state by France, and in all probability by various Latin American countries—or so the rumor at the time had it. In the view of former US officials, the United States would certainly not have followed the French lead and would have needed time to adjust its thinking to whatever the new reality north of the border might be.[20] One of the embassy officials, David Jones, later published an article in the *Washington Quarterly*,[21] suggesting that the trend seemed to be setting in for a separatist victory and that the United States should be trying to prepare itself for such an eventuality. It was not an unreasonable proposition, although at the time it jangled nerves in Canada. In the immediate aftermath of the narrow federalist victory in the referendum, it was probably more logical than not to believe, first, that there would be another referendum, and second, that the separatists would win it. But in the medium term, it did not happen.

Bill Clinton once again did his bit. He gave a speech to a conference on federalism at Mont Tremblant, Quebec, in 1999 that lauded federalism as a governmental system and drew obvious comparisons between Canada and the United States. As a testament to shared political values, it could hardly have been bettered,[22] and it was given on Quebec soil with the separatist premier, Lucien Bouchard, fluttering around the periphery. Stability, solidarity, compatibility, democracy, and similarity once again carried the day.

As Pierre Trudeau said in 1987, in testimony before the Canadian Senate, no country lasts forever: that includes Canada, and by extension it includes the United States as well. Trudeau took the long view.[23]

## *The Return of the Whig*

Canadian external policy in the 1980s was remarkably consistent. Canada supported the United Nations, hoped for the best in the Cold War, and tried to disentangle potentially messy problems in the Third World. There were differences of emphasis, but it was more a matter of application of agreed principles on most matters. Despite its rhetorical fierceness on the subject of communism, the Reagan and Bush Sr. administrations gave Canada some leeway over the anti-communist wars in Central America and in relations with Cuba. The same applied to the question of South

Africa, where generally the Mulroney government—meaning both the prime minister and the external affairs minister Joe Clark—was active and encouraging in bringing about the peaceful of white minority rule in that country.

On all these issues it is difficult to imagine the Liberals doing much that was different, although the presentation, the public face of Canadian policy, veered between Mulroney's notable charm and Trudeau's notable intellect. As we have seen, Chrétien was less interested in the United Nations, and more in trade and trade promotion. His first foreign minister (the title changed in 1993), André Ouellet, took the post because it was senior and prestigious, but he had no strong interest in the subject, and vanished shortly after the Quebec referendum into a patronage job. That did not halt the course of events outside Canada, where there were crises to deal with and policies to formulate or apply; and several of these were of considerable importance.

The best-remembered were a United Nations intervention in Somalia, a failed state in the horn of Africa without even a government, and an attempt to restore order in what had been Yugoslavia, which had broken up into warring republics in 1991–2. Somalia was the crisis du jour of late 1992—and after the relatively easy victory in the war with Iraq in 1991, the great powers led by the United States assumed that this country without an army would be ripe for occupation and reorganization under enlightened international auspices. Canada sent a battalion of paratroopers, supporting both the UN and the United States in what was hoped would be a model for international behavior in the 1990s.

Unfortunately, Somalia did provide a template for events later on in the decade, because occupying the country and defeating its various bandit gangs proved to be much more difficult than the Americans or the rest of the UN had counted on. The Americans withdrew after suffering some spectacularly bloody casualties, to no good purpose; and the Canadians also withdrew, humiliated by the behavior of Canadian soldiers—also to no good purpose. There were Canadian soldiers in ex-Yugoslavia too, peacekeepers, conveniently transferred from Canada's NATO garrison in Germany, which was being wound up with the end of the Cold War. The Canadian force in the Balkans was fairly large, in terms of Canada's available resources, but it did not secure Canada a place in the direction or even the conception of peacekeeping policy there.

Of course, the fundamental requirement of peacekeeping is that there should be a peace to keep. Because there was peace between Israel and

Egypt from 1956 to 1967, the peacekeepers along their mutual frontier could be said to be fulfilling a function or were at least symbolic of the fact that there was no war. When war did break out, the peacekeepers had to get out. At least the Canadians were lucky, leaving a day or two before the actual shooting war began. A Canadian peacekeeping force in Cyprus was less lucky and suffered some casualties—but those were casualties over a thirty-year span. The international community was willing to let the Canadian peacekeepers stay in Cyprus indefinitely, but eventually the Ottawa government had had enough, withdrawing the troops against American cries and whispers to the contrary.

Ex-Yugoslavia was, on the whole, a zone of war—in some respects a repetition (but not a continuation) of wars that dated back to the fourteenth century.[24] The unhappy and very bloody history of the Balkans encouraged some Western observers to believe that war in that region was both infinite and inevitable. On the other hand, it was the twentieth century—almost the twenty-first. Surely humanity had lost some of its primitive propensities, or enough of them to make peace possible? There had been forty-five years of communist peace after the Second World War, and during that period there were many developments—migration from one region to another, intermarriage between ethnicities and religions, and an educational system that strongly discouraged ethnic hatreds most of the time.

Whatever the origins of Western and Canadian visions of ex-Yugoslavia, the various bandits of the Balkans had a view of the Canadians and the other troops operating on behalf of the UN: they were like plump poultry in uniform who had made themselves available to traveling foxes. And so from time to time the various factions bullied, surrounded, or took captive UN troops who were usually unable to defend themselves properly and were for most of the time forbidden do so. There is no doubt that just by being there, UN troops prevented the Bosnian Serbs, in particular, from achieving some of their gruesome war aims, which included "ethnic cleansing" by whatever means.[25] The means included the notorious Srebrenica massacre of 1995, in which thousands of Bosnian Muslims (Bosniaks) were murdered after surrendering to Serb forces. There was an exception when the Croat army tried to roll over Canadian troops, in this case a well-equipped and well-trained unit, on one of their offensives, and received a sharp lesson as a result. (This was the battle of the Medak pocket in 1993.)

The conflict in ex-Yugoslavia occurred at the same time as a spectacular atrocity in the central African country of Rwanda, again with a Canadian component, in this case Canadian general Roméo Dallaire, who commanded an inadequate UN force supposedly designed to keep contending Tutsi and Hutu at peace. The UN proved completely and spectacularly impotent in the face of an impending massacre of Tutsi; UN headquarters in New York ignored Dallaire's warnings. This was because the United States, the UN's most powerful member, without which no intervention in Rwanda could work, did not want a second Somalia, and instead it got much worse, a genocidal rampage that killed roughly 800,000 Tutsi. Even so, the French, who had their own interests to pursue even after Tutsi rebels drove the Rwandan government from power and across the border into the Congo, sustained the génocidaires. Dallaire became the visible symbol of the inability of the international community, working through the United Nations, to achieve results compatible with even a basic standard of morality.

If Somalia led to Rwanda, Srebrenica led to a revival of the old Whig doctrines in foreign affairs. In Canada that was assisted by the replacement of Ouellet by Lloyd Axworthy as foreign minister, in the United States by the arrival of Madeleine Albright as secretary of state in the second Clinton term, and in Great Britain by the defeat of the Tories who were pushed out by (New) Labour in the general election of 1997, bringing the enthronement of Tony Blair as prime minister and the appointment of Robin Cook as foreign secretary. All three were throwbacks to an age of moral interventionism—a tendency that in spirit had existed for centuries but that had been constrained since 1945 by the Cold War and the jockeying for relative advantage between the superpowers assisted by their respective alliances. With the removal of the crude Cold War pandering for any allies available, no matter how obnoxious they might be, it was time to judge international issues on the basis of universal standards of morality. For some, the great frustration of the Cold War was that moral causes had been forced to make too many compromises with "practicality"—accepting dictatorship in distant, lesser countries as the price of preserving democracy at home, or at least keeping out communism. Moreover, the term *international* was undergoing a redefinition.

*International* meant crossing borders, with weapons, armies, or some other kind of official and deliberate intervention in the politics of another sovereign state. Historically sovereignty was not watertight. Facts and ideas traveled, sentiments were universal, and people in one jurisdiction experienced fellow feeling for people in another. The religious wars of the sixteenth and seventeenth centuries can be seen in no other light; the appeal by the American revolutionaries to the good opinion of humankind is of the same variety. The French Revolution found sympathizers in every country in Europe and in the Americas. Gladstone made the domestic behavior of foreign tyrants a major issue in British politics and inspired a generation of liberal activists, mainly in the English-speaking countries. More recently, the alliances of the First and Second World Wars and the Cold War had turned on a conception of ideological compatibility—democracy versus autocracy, democracy versus tyranny, and the deeds of the dictators, fascist and communist, weighed heavily in mobilizing opinion against them, often long before disapproval gave way to armed conflict. On the other hand, ideological compatibility implied greater understanding, and a common purpose, and therefore a "democratic peace."[26] Before the Second World War politicians and intellectuals argued that it was not geography alone but ideology, or a shared belief in democracy, which isolated North America from the European propensity for war. St. Laurent's and Pearson's promotion of Article 2 in the North Atlantic Treaty of 1949 followed the same reasoning.[27]

In the same vein, the memory of appeasement embodied in the Munich conference of 1938 ("Peace in our Time") exercised an irresistible influence over policy-makers. Munich became an axiom, to the effect that compromise or coexistence with dictators was impossible and indeed dangerous. The link between tolerating domestic atrocious behavior, protected behind the veil of sovereignty, and risking an ultimate threat to one's own country, one's own values, was made. Dangerous behavior in another country could and would spill over national boundaries: tyranny was indivisible. There should be an international collective response, though until 1990, given the Cold War and the paralysis of the UN, that was wishful thinking. Briefly, the Soviet collapse mitigated the paralysis, though it did not remove the Russian veto, freeing the UN for a time to be an instrument of world order, operating under chapters six and seven of the UN Charter.

The UN under American leadership made war on the Iraqi dictator Saddam Hussein in 1991 because Saddam had invaded the neighboring country (and UN member) Kuwait. In the course of the build-up to war and its brief duration Western audiences learned from television and other media that Saddam was a transcendental villain and an existential threat. Canada under Mulroney threw its support to the war: the war was legal, because UN-authorized; it was American-led, and Mulroney was devoted to the American alliance; and it was short, with minimal UN casualties—though there were many more on the Iraqi side.

The horrific events in Rwanda and ex-Yugoslavia overcame the memory of the unsuccessful intervention in Somalia and primed Western opinion to be on the alert for the next villainy of the Serbian leader, Slobodan Milošević, which he duly furnished through the oppression of the Albanian majority in the Serbian province of Kosovo in 1998-9. This time, however, Russia was not co-operative; there was a Russian veto in the UN Security Council; and the Americans, Clinton and Albright, and the British prime minister, Blair, with his foreign secretary Robin Cook, used NATO instead. It was an aerial campaign, though conducted with the threat of intervention on the ground lurking in the background. The Kosovo operation was crowned with apparent success. Effectively Kosovo secured its independence, the Russians accepted the fait accompli, though, with considerable bitterness, and Slobodan Milosevic was ultimately overthrown as Serbian president and sent to confront a war crimes tribunal in The Hague, where he died during his lengthy trial.

Kosovo was a dry run for a policy championed by Lloyd Axworthy that became known as "Responsibility to Protect," R2P for short. R2P held that domestic tyranny—bad behavior by sovereign tyrants—was a threat to world peace and hence actionable by international authority.[28] R2P was not Axworthy's only notable initiative, however. There were two other notable causes—a ban on the use of land mines, and the constitution of an international criminal court—in the context of the larger issue, the Responsibility to Protect.

In the conduct of foreign policy Axworthy was a change from his predecessors. He had no hesitation in getting out in front on issues, without worrying unduly whether he was exposing Canada to criticism from the United States.[29] He had been partly educated in the United States and understood that there were all kinds of Americans, with widely differing views. Some he sympathized with, some he scorned. He gave voice to ideas that might or might not have been particularly Canadian in origin, but, like Trudeau on his peace mission in 1983-4, traipsing from New Delhi to Washington to Beijing, he could at least get a hearing, even if sometimes not a very attentive one, for the concepts he was promoting. If Axworthy could make a positive impression among progressive Americans and other nationalities, the reverse was also true. Americans who were not especially liberal, or were not liberal internationalists, saw Axworthy as an ally of their adversaries at home. David T. Jones, who served at the US embassy in Ottawa in the 1990s, saw Axworthy in a different light: "So, knowing what his general policies were because he was a left-wing liberal from the Vietnam era who had a Ph.D. from Princeton and his issues and interests were those of people that graduated from liberal schools in the 1960s, one could anticipate problems."[30]

Land mines had become a lively issue in the aftermath of the post-colonial wars in Africa, and in the wake of the wars in the Middle East. Destruction and loss of life went on and on, because no one picked up war-waste, including hundreds of thousands of land mines. The casualties—dead, missing, and victims missing limbs—were very visible, and in the United States and Western Europe a strong and emotional campaign was under way to get the weapons banned. But land mines undeniably had a function in inhibiting movement along or across front lines, taking the place of active and expensive garrisons, and the United States in Korea, and Israel along its borders, found them particularly useful.

As with earlier humanitarian movements, what worked in the United States worked in Canada too. "This came about, basically through NGOs, not governments originally," an American diplomat recalled. "Canada [was lobbied by] NGOs who are Canadian–American in nature, like everything else [—] an integrated kind of peace movement. Canada picked up on it much more rapidly than the United States because it was one of the issues that Canada is into: soft power and conventions and multilateralism...."[31]

The Democratic Clinton administration was sympathetic to the idea of a ban and made some moves to promote an international land mines treaty. But then the momentum stalled, and the American military panicked at the thought of an American garrison confronting North Korea across an un-mined border. At this point Axworthy stepped in. Karl Inderfurth, a senior official in the Clinton administration,[32] described what he did, noting the direct connection to earlier American efforts:

> The Canadians had a very activist foreign minister, Lloyd Axworthy, who had taken up this cause and skilfully. He worked with others, including the Norwegians. They basically took the language from the resolutions we had proposed in New York and put them into treaty language and then called on the international community to sign it. At a meeting in Oslo, there were efforts made to see if certain American exceptions could be made to the treaty. The Canadians and others were adamant that there could not be exceptions, that this was a universal treaty and that if the U.S. had its Korean exception [allowing the US to maintain minefields along the Korean

armistice line], Russia would have its Chechnya exception, and China would have its exceptions, etc. I'm sure Madeleine Albright, who by this time had become Secretary of State, had many conversations with Axworthy on this, and not always ones where they agreed![33]

Axworthy and Albright were in frequent contact. According to a historian who interviewed the participants, "Axworthy met often with Madeleine Albright, the new American secretary of state, who told him she personally supported the ban but had to find a way to accommodate American military interests."[34]

Axworthy gave sovereign representation to the non-governmental organizations promoting an end to land mines. His diplomacy and their public pressure put him and the government of Canada at the head of a "good cause" similar to anti-slavery in the nineteenth century. Mr. Gladstone would have approved. The result was the Ottawa Treaty of 1997, eventually signed by (at last count) 122 states. The count did not include the United States, or for that matter China and Russia, but there is no doubt that the treaty represented the point of view of many Americans. Karl Inderfurth continued:

> But I will say that I believe the Canadians deserve a great deal of credit for picking up the leadership on this issue when it became clear that the U.S. was not going to be able to reconcile our military and humanitarian imperatives and sign the treaty. This wasn't cost free in a military sense for the Canadians either. As a member of NATO and as an important UN peacekeeping nation, they had to make certain adjustments as well, although certainly not of the magnitude of dealing with the Korean problem as we had. But still, I think that they exercised very important leadership and I commend them for it.[35]

Another American diplomat, replying to a question about Canada's conduct of the Ottawa negotiations, disagreed with the questioner's premise that the Canadians, and Axworthy, were being anti-American in framing the treaty, by not excluding American minefields in Korea: "No, I wouldn't agree with that assessment at all." The US government's desire for a Korean exception was not feasible, and it was foolish to believe that it was.

There were remarkable similarities between Axworthy's diplomacy and the Canadian management of the Suez crisis in 1956. Taking an agreeable American initiative, which the United States was unwilling or unable to see through to completion, the Canadian government represented an American opinion that was unable to prevail in its own country. The same might be said of Suez, where Pearson and Canada represented that part of the British political and diplomatic establishment that had been unable to influence its own government. Pearson had tried to do the same thing in 1965 over Vietnam, but circumstances were against him: impacting the American political system was more difficult and more politically dangerous than working on or in the British one. Unlike Pearson, Axworthy did not win the Nobel Peace Prize, a political setback, but his cause did: two NGOs working for a land mines ban got the Nobel Prize in 1998. Lloyd Axworthy retired as foreign minister in 2000 and never secured the party leadership or the prime minister's office. Though less successful than Pearson in terms of his political career, his diplomacy in style and content replicated his predecessor's, and in terms of securing results, he was possibly the most successful, and certainly the most noticed, Canadian foreign minister since Pearson.[36]

Adjusting international law to enforce norms of justice was at least equally as challenging as and perhaps even more daring than banning land mines. It had for centuries been understood that there were norms, or standards, or customary practices in the conduct of war.[37] Napoleon's thirst for power and conquest caused the European powers not merely to declare war upon him, but to outlaw him in 1815. His exile to St. Helena was a form of punishment, though accomplished without a formal trial. There were war crimes trials after the First and Second World Wars, which introduced plotting aggression as a crime, as well as crimes against humanity, and somewhat later genocide was agreed to be an international crime deserving of trial and punishment. The United States was a notable participant in, indeed the driving force behind, the war crimes trials after 1945, and some American legal authorities—as well as jurists from other nations—began to argue for a permanent international criminal tribunal. The end of the Cold War offered both opportunities and inhibitions to the Americans. With American power spread round the world and embodied in everything from naval bases to expeditionary armies, it became a matter of concern to protect the far-flung American military from legal harassment for crimes real or imagined while abroad.

The American approach thus became somewhat ambiguous and self-contradictory. On the one hand the United States (and its allies) claimed to embody the rule of law, but the United States in particular wanted its military while out of the country to be subject only to American law, administered at home. There was, as well, an element of American exceptionalism, and it was deeply rooted in American politics. And so two forms of legalism clashed inside the American government and political system. The Rome Statute of 1998, which gave birth to the International Criminal Court (ICC) in 2002, provided that the court would only take over a case when national authorities failed to prosecute or otherwise deal with it, but that gave insufficient reassurance to American nationalists. And so the United States, under Clinton, helped negotiate the Rome Statute, and under George W. Bush, his Republican successor, withdrew its signature in 2002. The statute does not apply to non-signatories, and so the United States has remained outside the ICC's purview. (It has been plausibly argued that Clinton's signature meant little or nothing, because the US Senate, even under Clinton, would never have ratified the Rome Statute.) Bush went one step further, pressing governments around the world, including signatories, to agree to exempt American troops on their soil from prosecution.[38]

Canada was strongly in favor of the ICC, Canadian representatives were very active in negotiating the details for the future body, and a Canadian jurist, Philippe Kirsch, was prominent in negotiating the statute and in establishing the court after 2002, serving as one of its first justices. Opponents of the ICC in the United States, and sympathizers outside, argued that acceptance of the ICC, or promotion of its objects, was fundamentally an anti-American act, interfering with the United States' ability to protect itself and its allies. Here, then, was another difference, real or potential, between Canada and the United States.

On top of the ICC and the land mines, there was the Kyoto Protocol of 1997, the result of a UN conference in the city of that name. The Protocol dealt with the problem of climate change, which the conference accepted as being caused by human actions, particularly the burning of carbon. The Kyoto Protocol was the culmination, or so it was hoped, of a generation of increasingly anxious discussion of changes in the climate, their implications, and how they might be mitigated or prevented. The increase in carbon dioxide in the atmosphere produced a greenhouse effect, raising world temperatures with alarming and reasonably predictable consequences for melting glaciers and the ice caps around the North and South Poles. That in turn would raise sea levels, drowning coastal areas and even some island countries. The scientific data and the conclusions drawn from the data compelled the signatures to the Kyoto agreement or protocol. Countries subscribing to the Protocol agreed to reduce carbon emissions on a prescribed schedule. In 1997 implementation could still be seen as years away (the deadline was 2010), so there was no immediate pain to accompany the political gain of vocally supporting a good cause that was attracting enthusiasts in every country, including Canada. The Chrétien government took up the cause enthusiastically—some of its members more enthusiastically than others.

The problem with implementing Kyoto from a domestic Canadian perspective was that the Liberals were highly vulnerable to criticism in oil-rich Western Canada because of a failed attempt to impose a National Energy Program (NEP) back in the 1980s. Oil, of course, produced carbon, but oil was also the source of riches for the Canadian West, and also for the country as a whole. In the view of many Western Canadians and most right-wing Canadians in every province, the federal government had already attempted (and failed) to steal Westerners' petroleum birthright and must promise not to do it again. Indeed, it should be prevented from doing so, by shrinking government or disabling it, as soon as the Conservatives came to power. This view was enhanced by regular emissions of rhetoric from Canada's oil capital, Calgary, denigrating environmentalists and praising free-market economics. With this kind of disapproval in the background Chrétien approached the problem of regulating carbon emissions, greenhouse gases, petroleum, and the pollution-producing oil sands of Alberta with extreme caution, which is to say, not at all. From that perspective, the Liberal government's policy on Kyoto was politically a ticking time bomb.

There were similarities in the United States. The Clinton administration signed Kyoto but could not ratify it. Even more than in Canada, there was a very serious oil lobby centered in Texas and Oklahoma, and those and other oil-producing states were very influential in the US Congress. Perhaps, had the Democrats won the presidential election of 2000 and carried Congress with them, there might have been a chance for American ratification of Kyoto; but in 2000, although the Democrat, Al Gore, got a plurality of votes, he did not get the necessary majority of the electoral college, thanks to a decision of the US Supreme Court, where enough of the justices had been appointed by Republican administrations, and enough of those appointments hearkened to the sentiments of their past. Accordingly, on January 20, 2001, George W. Bush of Texas became president of the United States. One of his first acts was to cancel the American signature on Kyoto.

## *Saying No to Power*

When George W. Bush came into office, he was thought to be unschooled in the higher arts of government, uninformed and incurious. He was said to be a reader, and interested in history, from which he picked up legends of Winston Churchill standing firm against dictators and warning against the fascist menace that turned out to be all too real. A bust of Churchill, lent by an eager Tony Blair, sat in his office. Political commentators took comfort in the fact that he had a number of old Washington hands available to help him—Dick Cheney, the vice-president, his friend Donald Rumsfeld, the secretary of defense, and General Colin Powell, the secretary of state. All were veterans of the Nixon, Ford, Reagan, and G.H.W. Bush administrations. If experience counted for anything, they were primed to apply it. No doubt the Bush administration was absolutely to the right of its predecessor, and more nationalist and more inwardly directed, even more "exceptional," but initially there was no particular concern that its beliefs would seriously or negatively affect Canadian–American relations.

There should have been, for Cheney and Rumsfeld and many other administration appointees and supporters had signed on to what was called "The Project for a New American Century," which proposed nothing less than a perpetual (and of course benevolent) American hegemony. There was no other superpower to challenge the United States, and this happy situation should continue, must continue, into the indefinite future. What they proposed, in a statement in 1997, was a policy of "military strength" and "moral clarity." The one would of course sustain the other. "Moral clarity" directed the attention of conservatives and "neo-conservatives" to Iraq, and its dictator, Saddam Hussein, and in 1998 a group of right-wing politicians and intellectuals urged Clinton to go in and finish the job begun by the first President Bush. Clinton had many things on his mind in 1998, to be sure: there had been a sex scandal, and he was about to be impeached by the Republican majority in Congress. Though he would survive and remain president, he definitely was in no position to undertake a bold policy of any kind.[39]

The Chrétien government had its own domestic preoccupations, but Canadian–American relations carried on as normal through the spring and summer of 2001. Chrétien and Bush met at a "summit of the Americas" in Quebec City in April 2001, and then at a G-8 summit in Italy, against a background of anarchist rioting.[40] After summiteering, Bush had his summer vacation, during which he briefly considered intelligence reports that suggested that a radical Islamist group, al Qaeda, led by a Saudi named Osama bin Laden, was determined to attack the United States on American soil. Bin Laden's object was to secure the end of what he considered to be Western, Christian, domination of the Muslim world; he was evidently moved to action by the stationing of US troops on what was to him the sacred soil of Saudi Arabia. The threat should have rung a bell with both American and Canadian authorities, because in 1999 there had been a failed attempt, narrowly thwarted, to move explosives from Canada to Los Angeles airport, using a petty criminal from Algeria as the conduit.[41]

Using a group of Islamist fanatics—all residents of the United States, legally admitted to the country—bin Laden hijacked four American airliners and rammed three of them into targets in New York and Washington on September 11, 2001.[42] The result, not surprisingly, was a continent-wide panic. North American air space was closed, and aircraft heading for the United States were either turned back to their point of origin or forced to put down in Canada, where more than thirty thousand passengers descended on some very surprised and sometimes quite remote Canadian communities. In the crisis, the Canadian government offered both practical support and active sympathy. Although some American officials (including Bush, in a private phone call on September 12) offered thanks, Bush publicly omitted Canada from his list of countries to be thanked. David Frum, a Bush speechwriter and a native of Toronto, told the *Globe and Mail* that the omission was no accident.[43] Failing any other explanation, it seems that ideology was at work—a view of Canada as being at odds with the vision of the world and society held by American conservatives and neo-conservatives.

Bush responded to the al Qaeda attacks by invading their host country, Afghanistan, in October 2001, and in co-operation with local insurgents, captured the capital Kabul and installed a new government. The American intervention also involved a collection of American allies, including Canada; the co-operation of neighboring states, most importantly Pakistan, Iran, and Russia; and, crucially, it was authorized by the UN. There was no significant difference between Canada and the United States over Afghanistan, and over the next ten years Canada generally followed the American lead when it came to Afghan affairs. With a military strictly limited in size, Canada did not have the luxury of choosing multiple targets or spreading its troops even thinner in a variety of theaters. And at first, in 2001–3, it seemed as if the Afghan war was basically won and required only a limited number of American and allied troops to support the new government. It was a mission that Canada and other militarily limited countries could contemplate without concluding that it would be a bottomless pit.[44]

This picture suited the American government very well. The reasoning, not at first shared with the allies, was that Iraq was a much more appropriate and important target for American arms. By the summer of 2002 the Bush administration was preparing public opinion for an invasion of

Iraq and the overthrow of Saddam Hussein. Washington began to leak "intelligence" that showed that Saddam, a secular dictator detested by the Islamist al Qaeda, was nevertheless their sponsor and protector. Saddam, it appeared, had "weapons of mass destruction" (WMD), a clunky phrase that was fearfully repeated again and again through 2002. Time was of the essence: television audiences were repeatedly told that they dare not let a "smoking gun become a mushroom cloud"—in other words, Saddam had or soon would have atomic weapons and it was necessary to strike first.[45]

It is not necessary to rehearse here the history of the approach to war in Iraq. The administration made strenuous efforts to recruit allies for the war and in that task had the wholehearted co-operation of the British prime minister, Tony Blair. The important point for Blair and his ministers and senior officials was that the Americans had decided to go to war and that Britain could not afford not to participate. By joining in, it could hope to moderate American policy while buying influence through its military contribution. Blair later claimed that he believed the evidence of Saddam's evil intent, and that is possible, but it should be noted that by the end of 2002 gaping holes had appeared in Bush's and Blair's case for the existence of WMD, and the implausibility did not decrease as the deadline for war (March 2003) approached.[46]

The Canadian government was distressed by the approach to war. It was scrambling to prevent draconian American measures to stiffen the border in the name of security, by implementing Canadian security measures and streamlining cross-border procedures; and with security in flux after the al Qaeda attacks, it was extremely important to reach a harmonious agreement with the Americans. The importance of an amicable relationship was thus more evident than usual. As Bush's determination became evident, questions were asked about Canada's probable response. Chrétien was reported to be skeptical of the case for war, although Bush in a meeting in Detroit on September 9, 2002, seems to have done his best to make the case for removing Saddam.[47] In response, Chrétien told the president that a war authorized by the UN was one thing, but a war not validated by the UN was quite another. Canada would support the first, but not the second, of those options. The two men then proceeded to an easier or more agreeable question, border security and border transit, which they handled dispassionately and evidently constructively.

In March, with American and allied troops assembled on Iraq's borders and war obviously imminent, there was a last-minute scramble at the UN in the vain hope that the Security Council would authorize Bush's war.

Canada, through its UN delegate, tried to gain time, to postpone events, to discover through a last-minute inspection whether Saddam really had the WMDs—the heart of Bush's case for war. But though that was the excuse for invasion, the object of the proposed invasion was regime change, not disarmament, a point the prime minister deplored.[48] The American delegation at the UN evidently did not appreciate the Canadian efforts, and the Canadian ambassador learned, in a conversation with the prime minister, that the Americans were trying to secure his removal. That would not happen, the prime minister reassured the ambassador. By this point, intelligence officials knew very well from their colleagues in Washington that there were no WMDs—something that could have been deduced from Powell's inadequate speech the month before.[49] Bush's high officials, led by Vice-president Dick Cheney, had arranged the evidence to suit themselves, to get the invasion they wanted.

As is well known, Chrétien decided not to go to war. He had to assess the political balance in Canada and gage how public opinion would react. There had been anti-war demonstrations across the country, but the one in Montreal was huge, impressive, and politically significant. Quebec was about to have a provincial election, and there was a chance that the federalist provincial Liberals would win. But the PQ government would have been most gratified if Chrétien opted for war, for that would be proof positive that English and French Canadians were on different tracks, politically, culturally, and emotionally. The prime minister's decision was therefore fraught, and not simply because the American case for war was bogus.

Naturally American embassy reports to Washington simply assumed the merits of the US government's case for invading Iraq. As for Canada's and Chretien's behavior, they stressed both Chretien's limitations and his concern for politics in Quebec: "He is first and foremost a domestic politician from Quebec, the home of Canada's tenacious and pacifist francophone linguistic minority. His political roots are dug deeply into old-line Liberal Party soil and he is unsympathetic to, and out of touch with, U.S. foreign policy concerns."[50]

Quite a few people were "unsympathetic" to "US foreign policy concerns" as expounded and implemented by the Bush administration. Many American diplomats, unless they were neo-conservatives or otherwise committed to using war as an instrument to reconstitute the Middle East via Iraq, deplored what Bush was doing. One diplomat, then serving in Brazil (he came later to deal with Canada) put it this way: "I have yet to meet a[n] [American] Foreign Service Officer who felt that we made the right choices and implemented the right course of action in the invasion and occupation of Iraq. There must be some out there. None of the Foreign Service Officers with whom I discussed Iraq, even those who favored taking down Saddam's regime, had 'drank [sic] the kool-aid'."[51]

Chrétien consulted his cabinet, but the final decision was his. (Only one junior minister seems to have dissented.) His decision came as a surprise to the American ambassador in Ottawa, and to the Canadian ambassador in Washington. The cases are slightly different: the American ambassador genuinely believed that Chrétien would say "yes" to Bush and Blair, while the Canadian ambassador simply did not know which way the decision would go. The decision was announced in the House of Commons; the American network CNN seems to have been tipped off and ran the scene live, and so American viewers were treated to a panorama of rapturous applause from the Liberal majority in the House for the prime minister's statement.

It might be thought from this episode that Canadians did not participate in the Iraq war that followed. That would be a misconception, for there were a fair number of Canadians attached to American units for training, and when the war started, so did they, accompanying US troops in the invasion. But that was not what Bush was seeking. The Americans were building a "coalition of the willing" designed to show the world but more particularly the American electorate that the United States did not stand alone. Canada was to be part of a list of names—perhaps a name more recognizable than most, since it was after all the immediate neighbor to the United States, and a country for which most Americans had friendly if undifferentiated feelings. The actual military aid that Canada could give was derisory, apart from the qualities of the individuals assigned to American units during the war.

The question lingers, Was the Canadian decision not to go to war at the side of the United States in 2003 well founded? Did it perhaps derive from a misconceived sense of idealism or, worse, a sense of anti-Americanism and a belief that Canadian values were superior to those of the United States? Did Canada violate its own self-interest by refusing to prove itself a reliable ally, and thus store up trouble for the future?[52]

It was not a new question, and in the course of Canadian history those in charge in Ottawa have answered it in different ways. In 1885, Sir John Macdonald answered "no" to the importunities of the British government over the Sudan. But Sir Wilfrid Laurier answered "yes" to the South African War, as did his successor, Sir Robert Borden, to participation in the Great

War of 1914. But Mackenzie King, assured by the British government that civilization and the rule of law were at stake in going to war with Turkey in 1922, was not moved and managed to say "no" without actually uttering the word.[53] Later, in 1939 and in 1950 over Korea, the answer was once again "yes," though we should remember that the Korean War was duly authorized by the UN Security Council and thus passed the new test of international legality imposed by the UN Charter. In 1965 the Americans did not explicitly ask for Canadian help in Vietnam, and certainly Canada did not give it; but it was a war which most Americans, within two or three years, had decided was a bad war, and Canada harvested no blame for refusing to go.[54]

There is therefore no clear Canadian tradition, or rather, there are two alternative traditions, both stretching back into colonial times. Chretien, inadvertently or not, came to stand for one; the leader of the opposition in Parliament in 2003, Stephen Harper, expounded the other. It was Canada's tradition, and Canada's duty, to stand by its allies in their time of need, he argued. Their cause was just, or so he assumed; such a thing as doubt hardly needed to be mentioned. Harper's speech had a whiff of the Anglosphere, the conception that English-speaking countries had similar values and ought to club together to advance and protect them. In an extreme form, it is the view that only English-speaking countries can be relied on. Harper certainly connected with the Anglosphere in his speech, for it was cropped from a speech made by the Australian prime minister two days earlier.[55]

In such an analysis, the actual issue, war or peace, invasion or not, was dwarfed by the context of Canada's strategic situation, as well as a larger issue of morality—assuming that the English-speaking powers had chosen to be on the right side of the right issue. Allan Gotlieb, Canadian ambassador to the United States from 1981 to 1989, in a 2005 article[56] drew attention to the practice in Canadian diplomacy of fixing on the situation at hand—realism, to the exclusion of "romantic" considerations. As he pointed out, it was a productive approach, which one might argue was characteristically Canadian. But who was the realist in 2003 and who the romantic? Surely the romantic was Harper, with his appeals to sentiment, and the realist was Chrétien, who rejected a policy that was, to put it bluntly, both stupid and false. Bush's choice of war was foolish, and his prosecution of the war, stupid. The war certainly got rid of Saddam Hussein, but hanging Hussein did nothing to stop a conflict that consumed eight long years, thousands of American lives, hundreds of thousands of

Iraqis, and a trillion borrowed dollars—the borrowing being necessitated by Bush's simultaneous lowering of tax rates on the rich.

Chrétien's policy was Canada's policy. That policy was, however, not uniquely and solely Canadian. Canada had allies and sympathizers at the UN, and it also had allies in the Anglosphere. The anglospheric sympathizers with Canada included several members of Tony Blair's cabinet, who resigned over his support of the invasion; in Blair's justifications of the war, the first casualty was truth, and not only members of his cabinet but senior officials of the Foreign Office found it too much to stomach. Anti-war opinion included various US foreign service officers, who resigned their posts rather than support the war. The resolution authorizing war passed Congress only on division, and neither the Senate nor the House of Representatives was unanimous.[57] As usual, currents of politics and political ideas cross boundaries even if they also find a national home. Pearson in 1949 and 1956 similarly spoke for opinions in the United States or the United Kingdom that were for the time being suppressed or defeated. Part of Pearson's gift, and Chrétien's too, was that they spoke for more than Canada.

## *13*

# *Back to the Future?*

BETWEEN 2004 AND 2011 Canada held four general elections and enjoyed seven years of minority government. Frequent elections had happened before in Canadian history, in fact, quite often: three in 1921–1926, two in 1957–1958, four in 1962–1968, two in 1972–1974 and again in 1979–1980. Sometimes minorities presaged an emerging majority, but sometimes not. In retrospect, the period after 2004 was a gradual transition from Liberal rule to Conservative, but, in a country with an alternating party system, that was not unusual either. And for almost 150 years it had been the same parties, Conservative or Liberal, Liberal or Conservative, with only one coalition government, 1917–1921, to vary the formula. Informally but importantly, it only rarely seemed to make much difference, since Liberals and Conservatives grew their policies out of whatever the political nation had reached a consensus upon. That was particularly true in the years after the Second World War, where great thundering change and electoral alternation seemed to have no relationship whatsoever, once the excitement of the election period had passed.

Structurally, at least, this was a pattern that should have been familiar in the United States, where it had been the case for just a bit longer—since 1861, to be precise, as between Republicans and Democrats. It should be no great surprise that transborder similarities in the party system, in politics, policy, and partisanship, continued to replicate themselves after 1990 or 2000. It is also no surprise that ideas and policies from Great Britain continued to inform North American events.

Similarity is not identity. Sovereignty, responsible government, and Canada's bilingual body politic all continued to operate. There was history, too, variously interpreted, and to those constant guardians of differentiation should be added Canada's galloping cultural diversity, the fruit of heavy immigration, first from Southern Europe and then Asia—Korea, India, the Philippines, and eventually China. Proportionately to its millions of new citizens, Canada looked and sounded different from the United States.

That did not mean the United States was homogeneous, merely that it was diverse in a different direction. Most notably there was the flood of "Hispanic" immigration to the United States over the border from Mexico or across the Caribbean to what had been the American Old South.[1] If Canada looked different from the United States, the United States sounded different from Canada. The immigrants were desirable because they provided cheap and plentiful labor, but soon they were desirable because they earned money and were consumers of American commerce. In the blink of an eye, signs in banks and on stores in New York City or Washington, DC, acquired Spanish translations, with very little of the linguistic warfare that accompanied French or English differences in Canada. True, there was some dissent, most notably from a political scientist at Harvard University, Samuel Huntington.

Huntington was noted for drawing lines—between groups of Europeans, for example, Muslims and Orthodox forming an odd pair on one side, Latin Christians (including Protestants) on the other. It was a "clash of civilizations," and they were still clashing in the 1990s, in Huntington's opinion. The United States, Huntington correctly pointed out, was mainly the creation of Anglo-Protestants in the eighteenth century, who had given the United States its particular orientation and, in his view, its unique success. Huntington's sense of American uniqueness, with a nod to the country's British ancestry, prevented him from fully appreciating that his analysis could also apply to English Canada; there his vision was obscured by the presence of Quebec, which was included in a category of countries that the United States was not and should not be like.[2]

Huntington was precisely the kind of American that generations of Canadians had links with—the sense of common culture, common political values, and common destiny that had helped propel the United States into the world wars. That is not to mention the implied disdain for others not so descended—a point on which Canadians and Americans of earlier generations would probably have concurred. These were the Americans that Sir Robert Borden orated to in 1916 and that Mackenzie King visited at Williamsburg in 1940 (the Rockefellers) and Hyde Park (Franklin Delano Roosevelt). Unlike the Rockefellers and Roosevelt, Huntington himself was not a particularly conscious promoter of the continental version of Anglo-Saxon harmony, though he might have been if he had ever given it some thought.[3]

Nevertheless, in the 2000s, the sense of common culture and common experience between Canada and the United States was not altogether absent. Accused of ignoring Canada and Canadians, President George W. Bush excused himself by saying that Canadians were after all "just family." He had a point, particularly for his age cohort (he was born in 1947). For the baby boom generation, the United States was an alternative homeland culturally, including family structure and material rewards. "I think it's fair to say," the sociologist and pollster Michael Adams wrote in 2010, "that in the 1950s the Canadian dream was virtually indistinguishable from the American dream of material progress and soft hedonism: a house in the suburbs, a smart set of wheels, a martini before dinner after a hard day's work."[4] The operative word is *dream* since for most Canadians in the 1950s flashy cars and martinis were merely images they saw on American TV shows carried on the CBC. The house in the suburbs was more achievable.

Adams was writing about his own childhood and adolescence, a world shaped by American products, explained by American academics, and led by American presidents. The world was fenced in mentally by the terrors of the Cold War, materially by a steady and predictable prosperity, and by traditional institutions—Huntington's Protestant churches, but also the Catholic Church, not to mention the social clubs of the period, like the Kiwanis and Shriners, which spanned the border. So did "international" trade unions, protected by a labor shortage, which made their members valuable and very employable, and provided the social and economic platform on which Canadian and American—North American—society was built. They were protected, as well, by Protectionism with a capital P, for tariffs were high, especially Canadian tariffs, and foreign products virtually unknown or, if known, exotic, like Rolls-Royce or Peugeot. It was, to a remarkable degree, materially a closed society that existed in two compartments, Canadian (poorer but essentially the same) and American (richer and more abundant). The key in both countries, however, was that the difference in income between top and bottom was at a historically low point; that the public sector in both was powerful and prestigious; and that the Cold War validated a strong communal political purpose.

Government programs like social security contributed to the standard of living, especially if the "security" component is factored in. Here Franklin Roosevelt's "freedom from fear" and "freedom from want" combined—freedom from fear of impoverishment surely contributed to peace of mind and thus to an absence of stress—stress being a recognized contributor to ill health. As one historian put it, "Security of expectations is important to people and to society as a whole."[5]

Apart from nuclear weapons and the Cold War, the "postwar," extending into the 1970s, seemed very secure. To Americans and Canadians in the 1950s the world of giant corporations, imposing behind their skyscraper walls, apparently impervious to change, and masters of their own social structure, to some extent supplemented government, or provided a somewhat smaller and better-paid version of the civil service. "So far as the management of my own company is concerned," proclaimed an oil company president in the late 1940s, "we have formed the habit of thinking in terms of…lifetime employment."[6] It was not unusual to work for the same company one's entire working life, paralleling and usually exceeding the conditions of work and reward offered by governments to their civil servants.[7] This was as true of Canada as of the United States, though since Canada was smaller and poorer, Canadian benefits lagged behind those that very rich American corporations could offer. But while the Canadian government's social safety net was expanded in the 1960s to take on medicare for all Canadians, the American version stalled short of universal, single-payer health care. The result was a divergence in Canadian and American patterns of life. Such divergences had occurred before, but previously they had usually signified an advantage to the United States.

This was different, partly because it coincided with a reversal of the post-1939 tendency toward greater equality of incomes. The growth of lower-class and middle-class incomes slowed in the 1970s while those of the top income brackets did not. Comparing the United States and Canada between the 1970s and 1990s, the income share of American lower and middle earners declined as a percentage of GDP; in Canada the share of the lowest 20 percent actually rose, largely thanks to income transfers by government.[8] Other factors moved the two countries apart as well. Life expectancy, approximately the same in both countries in 1950, with a slight advantage for females in the United States, also diverged. Where the two countries had spent about the same amount on health as a percentage of GDP in the early 1970s, the American percentage rose significantly more than the Canadian over the next twenty years. Throughout this period American per capita GDP remained higher than Canadian— the traditional and never-insignificant measure of the income gap between citizens of the two countries.

Spending and consumption patterns did not always differ. The economist Joseph Stiglitz suggests that lower-income earners mimic the behavior of the top one per cent, running harder to make the money to imitate the desired life style. Wives joined the workforce long ago, at first hoping to make extra money—adding to lifestyle. As incomes stagnated, extra work became necessary to buy basic things.[9] The troubles of the 1960s did push Canada and the United States apart. The social and intellectual revolution in Quebec in the 1960s added a different variable—and Quebec had an influence on the whole of Canada and also directly on its English-speaking inhabitants. If the two countries shared materialism, they also shared material culture, and in such areas as music the two were indistinguishable— partly thanks to British imports like the Beatles and the Rolling Stones. Cultural sharing was not restricted to English-speaking countries: English became the lingua franca of popular music whether one was in Russia or Australia, and the impact should not be underestimated.

American political culture took another turn in the 1980s, which was soon followed, for somewhat different reasons, by British political culture. Both, exercised a strong influence over politics and policy in Canada, and despite local variations the center of political gravity in all three countries was considerably farther to the right than it had been in the 1960s or 1970s.

Government, Ronald Reagan told Americans when he was inaugurated as president in 1981, was not the solution, but the problem. Government was therefore going to be less prominent and less favored—though not less expensive, because of the huge sums of money Reagan poured into the American armed forces. Canada did not follow where Reagan pointed, at least not on the federal level, and did not follow even when a Progressive Conservative government took office in 1984, under Brian Mulroney.

The other income gap, between the rich and the poor, was what likely mattered most. The poor got poorer, faster, in the United States, and the effect was visible from the Canadian border, because the northern tier of states declined first and fastest.[10] The contrast became an issue in the 1988 election in Canada, fought over the free-trade agreement with the United States. "I do not want the cities of Canada to look like Detroit, New York or Chicago," an opposition member of Parliament asserted.[11] It all depended what part of New York or Chicago or Detroit one chose, for some parts were far above what Canadian cities usually achieved. To excited hearers in 1988 it meant slums and universal ruin. There may have been a connection here to atavistic patterns of memory that would have pleased the long-dead British colonial administrators who conceived of "Canada" as a better alternative to republican anarchy in 1791.[12]

Paradoxically, while many Americans became poorer, the United States considered as a statistical aggregate remained richer than Canada, and

Americans, consequently, remained richer than Canadians. Having more money, did Americans live better, or longer, as a consequence? Did they spend it in such a way as to reverse the decline of communities on the American side of the border, or in such a way as to ease their lot? The answer varies with locality and social class, but the answer is not positive for the most part.

Americans spent more, for example, on health care. One might have expected better health outcomes in the United States from the extra income and extra spending, but that was not the case. The conclusion of Arumand Siddiqi and Clyde Hertzman, Canadian social scientists interpreting the data, was that "[r]edistribution and public provisions trump economic well-being and direct health spending." In public spending, they found Canada more closely resembled Western European countries and Japan, while the United States was "an outlier."[13] From another point of view, several health economists cited the lack of efficiency in American health spending, while pointing out that only by that standard was Canada superior.[14] Large numbers of Americans suffered from insecurity in basic health care. Canadians might grumble, quite legitimately, about line-ups and lists and wait-times; but for all Canadians there was a list to be on. The same was definitely not true in the United States.[15]

These considerations match the conclusions of American sociologist Robert Putnam. Putnam observed, "The last third of the twentieth century was a time of growing inequality and eroding social capital.... [S]omewhere around 1965–70 America reversed course and started becoming both less just economically and less well connected socially and politically."[16]

The trend moved faster in the United States than elsewhere, and it created dissonances across the Canadian–American border. Canadian medicare was so well entrenched by the 1980s that it was inconceivable that any sane political leader would wish to tamper with its universal coverage or its single-payer (government) finance. Nor could right-wing politicians quarrel with the statistics that showed Canadian longevity to be greater than American—and a by-product of the more efficient manner in which Canada spent health dollars. But in the United States by the 1980s these Canadian examples were dismissed by the right wing as not merely inapplicable but dangerous—signifying "strong local cultural resistance," in the rather reserved view of a student of health-care programs. Another health expert added that in his view, "It is difficult to imagine a lesson that is more foreign to the American experience.... [The] Canadian lessons... are not just different—they challenge the central features of American political culture, at least as they have manifested themselves in health care policy."[17]

Memories were short. In the 1950s and 1960s Canadian and American health-care plans and projects had closely resembled one another, a point that opponents of universal health care in the United States did not want Americans to remember. In the 1960s Americans could console themselves that health insurance was provided as an employment benefit, in a world where jobs lasted for decades, if not forever. As corporate prosperity eroded and the great American corporations began to shed employees, health costs in the United States were increasingly borne by individuals.[18] It is not surprising that in the 1980s and 1990s the American right wing responded to the Canadian welfare state, and especially its health plan, with a vigorous denial that a Canadian precedent was compatible with American history, and thus applicable to the United States. It was exceptionalism, but in reality, as the economist Paul Krugman wrote, that exceptionalism meant that "[t]he United States is unique in being a place where the cost of illness and medical expenses can bankrupt you, where the inability to pay for basic medical care can lead to a downward spiral in your health, and eventually death."[19]

It was a prospect that discouraged many Americans, and small wonder that it discouraged many and probably most Canadians, and made them aware that life in the United States was a cash-and-carry affair. No cash, then no carry, at any rate not at a level above dire poverty. By the 1980s the positive impression traditionally made by American society, by its wealth and abundance, and its ability and willingness to share its goods widely among its population, was diminishing. As always, American self-study set the pace, and Canadian observers struggled to keep up. *Bowling Alone* was the title of the 1990s equivalent of *The Organization Man*, and where the earlier work had stressed co-operation even to the extent of losing oneself in a job or an organization, *Bowling Alone* suggested that things had gone into reverse, atomizing parts of society previously closely linked and stretching and breaking the bonds of community that had kept the country together. Certainly the example of American health care raised the question of the similarity and compatibility of the two countries, and it proved to be a persistent issue, as the United States struggled with the question of what, if any, government-sponsored system should be put in place.

The United States in the 1990s and even more in the 2000s was not at all the positive model for Canadians that it had once been. This conclusion was fiercely resisted in conservative quarters. As a result there was a dichotomy in Canadian perceptions of the southern neighbor, with the Canadian right wing and conservative think tanks media trumpeting the virtues of the market in enhancing American productivity (a clear measure of goodness and thrift) and the vice of Canadian backwardness.[20] Yet at the same time market forces were reducing the standard of living of many Americans, and the economic security—the freedom from want—of large parts of the population was eroding.[21]

Ross Perot, the third-party candidate for president in 1992, had predicted a loud sucking noise, as North American industries packed up their factories and machinery, fired their work forces, and departed for Mexico. It wasn't that speedy or that simple, and there were good reasons to wish that the Mexican economy would grow by producing and exporting goods that had formerly been made in Canada and the United States. Some Canadian factories found a halfway house in the American South or Southwest, or more generally in states where labor laws were weak and wages low.

On the other hand, the Canadian dollar plunged on foreign exchange markets in 1997–8 and remained low relative to the American dollar until 2007.[22] Low exchange rates benefited Canadian exports and encouraged manufacturers to keep their Canadian operations going—even to expand them. But all the while the auto industry slowly moved production south. The Canadian dollar's low exchange rate kept jobs and production relatively steady until the rise in the exchange rate and the Great Recession of 2008 dealt the industry a succession of blows from which it has never fully recovered. Mexican auto production, in 1994 roughly 7 percent of the North American total, rose to 20 percent by 2014 while Canada's fell from 17 percent in 1994 to 14 percent in 2013.[23]

What this could mean for Canadian industry, and Canadian localities, was illustrated in 2010–12 when Caterpillar, an American multinational firm specializing in engine production, bought the Electro-Motive company located in London, Ontario. Electro-Motive was a unionized firm, and wages were high—the traditional pattern in manufacturing in Southern Ontario. Caterpillar did not like the pattern. After preparing the way by opening plants in San Luis Potosí, Mexico, and a non-unionized site in Muncie, Indiana, Caterpillar offered its London workers a 50 percent pay cut, take it or leave it. Leave the company did, in February 2012.[24] Muncie workers were happy to take the lower wages Caterpillar offered, and there was certainly no problem in Mexico. Caterpillar's owners and management were no doubt pleased. The Ontario government was distressed and grumbled accordingly, while the Conservative government in Ottawa lay low and said little. Canadian costs were high, and Mexican costs were low. It was the market at work.

Harper did not want to stress that what disadvantaged Ontario—a surge of demand for the Canadian dollar, driving up its value—meant that oil exports were booming. The high exchange rate for the Canadian dollar versus the US currency reflected booming oil sales for most of the Harper government's tenure, and selling oil ranked right at the top of Harper's priorities. Its governing economic philosophy also accepted that wages and working conditions must be competitive, and, by extension, that they must be reduced until they matched or outmatched what other jurisdictions could offer. When that happy day occurred, industry might return to Southern Ontario.

## *Choosing the Wrong Moment*

The Harper government's minority status in Parliament from 2006 to 2011 limited some of its options when it came to recasting Canadian policies or institutions. It would have liked to match the George W. Bush administration, which was more than ideologically compatible: what the United States wanted to buy—energy security—corresponded with Canada's desire to sell. By overwhelmingly sourcing its petroleum from the Middle East—an unstable region populated with unreliable allies—the United States was handing over trillions of dollars to incompatible and sometimes covertly hostile countries.

Canada was much preferable on all counts. Not only was Canada preferable, its government was enthusiastic. Canada could be another Saudi Arabia, thanks to its oil sands, but it would be a *good* Saudi Arabia. Stephen Harper saw the country's future as a petro-state—indeed, as *the* petro-state, "an energy superpower." It was a time of opportunity, but for various reasons the opportunity was missed.

Canada was already the largest exporter of petroleum to the United States, and much of the flow was from the sticky "oil sands" near Lake Athabasca—renamed from the less positive-sounding "tar sands" that generations of Canadians had read about in their geography texts.[25] Methods had been developed to convert the viscous tar into usable oil, and this was being done on a huge and impressive scale, through open-pit mining, which was on one level—engineering—most impressive, but on another indubitably unaesthetic.

The Harper government believed it had a mandate and a national duty to develop the oil sands: the benefits to Canada's balance of payments were undeniable, and the petroleum could also be a lever to pry consideration from a neighbor that was only too prone to ignore Canada. It helped that Harper's own base was Calgary, the center of the oil industry. He lived for years in atmosphere in which the "oil patch" could do no wrong, and much good, as Alberta's recent prosperity showed—compared with the bad old days of disinvestment and poverty in the 1980s for which the Liberals and Pierre Trudeau were blamed. Those who favored this line of thought were disinclined to take the sharp recession of 1980–1 into account; Trudeau, the East, and the Liberals (really socialists in this optic) sufficed. For several generations Canadians had urged the fact that Canada was both closely allied to, and a very secure source of petroleum for, the United States. To this was added the notion that Canada produced "ethical oil"—that is, that Canada was a liberal democracy unlike Venezuela run by Marxist thugs or the Gulf or Saudi Arabia, whose sheikhs were known to use their oil money at times to promote the spread of their own very conservative if not fanatical version of Islam.

Canadians are little accustomed to being unpopular in the United States, except in some political ponds on the far right. As we observed at the beginning, the Canadian image was the clean-cut Mountie Dudley Do-Right capering with moose and beavers while fending off mustachioed villains. (It was an image that Canadians also appreciated, and so told themselves appropriately blissful stories on television, replicating Dudley's happy innocence.[26]) It seemed that the Harper government's desire to link Canadian oil supply to American energy demand fitted the image of reliable Canada. If security and predictability of supply was desired, Canada could offer it, as long as the pipelines to bring the oil to the United States were built. Dudley was prepared to share the family jewels with his American cousins, for Alberta's oil sands were one of the biggest petroleum reserves on earth. Of course, it was not just prosperity and security for the United States: Alberta would thenceforth have access to a secure market, and for the indefinite future.

When *National Geographic* magazine hit the stands in March 2009 it appeared that moose and beaver had better think of emigrating to healthier climes. Canada's pristine wilderness was pristine no longer, the land scarred by vast open-pit mines, dug out by earth-moving machines, with monstrous trucks carting tons of tar for conversion on the spot to heavy oil. Fetid tailings ponds, also large and impressive and toxic, completed the picture. The photo essay that accompanied the article could have been designed by Hieronymus Bosch: Northern Alberta had become the antechamber of Hell.[27] Canadians and their government had become Hell's gatekeepers and promoters.

The timing of the *National Geographic* article was unfortunate for the Alberta oil patch, but more misfortune was on the way, for in 2008 Trans-Canada Pipelines had applied for American permission to build a cross-border pipeline, called Keystone XL, designed to carry oil-sands petroleum from Alberta to the American Gulf Coast. Pipelines had once been the shiny symbol of modernity, carrying energy reliably and in the most technologically advanced way from producer to market. The ability of pipelines to carry oil safely came under serious scrutiny when another Canadian-owned pipeline sprang a leak near Kalamazoo, Michigan, in 2010. More than 800,000 gallons (more than 3,000 cubic meters) of heavy oil spilled into the Kalamazoo River. Four years and many hundreds of millions of dollars later, the spill was still not completely cleaned. American regulatory bodies, including the Environmental Protection Agency (EPA), were not impressed. Canada's image took another hit, as the EPA referred to the Keystone Cops (silent movie era clown-cops) as the actual management of the Kalamazoo spill. The unfortunately named Keystone pipeline became an issue in the American elections in 2012 and 2014, while the pipeline and Alberta sparked considerable interest among journalists. The *Washington Post* listed some of the questions this new pipeline posed:

> It is also a sort of Rorschach test of how Americans view energy issues: "Are we energy rich or energy poor? How do energy policies affect job creation, tax revenue and U.S. manufacturing competitiveness? How pressing are climate change concerns? Can we drill our way to energy security or should we conserve our way there?"[28]

The Canadian government's response to these questions was apparently firm but actually evasive. Harper pressed for an affirmative American decision to permit the Canadian pipeline to cross the border and carry on to the Gulf Coast. He wanted it as soon as possible, not merely to get things going—investment and then oil flowing—but because of the possibility of alternative oil. If Canadian oil was ethical and secure, how much more secure and ethical would American-sourced oil be? To ask that question was to answer it, and the answer was not to the Canadian government's liking. American oil production was rising, imports were falling, and the policies of half a century, based on scarce domestic supply, were being reversed. And there were other problems.

It took a spill of a different kind to underline the problems Canada faced as an "energy superpower." In July 2013 a collection of oil tank cars (called a "ghost train" because there was no driver) slipped their moorings and rumbled down a track into Lac Mégantic, Quebec, incinerating the small town's business district and killing forty-seven people. The oil cars carried not Canadian heavy oil but American crude, from a field called the Bakken on the border of North Dakota and Saskatchewan. (The geological formation, called the Williston Basin, also includes parts of Manitoba and Montana.) The field had been known for more than fifty years before its oil began to be extracted, using hydraulic fracturing technology—"fracking," for short.

The technology was not new, but for the first time it could be economically applied on a massive scale to extract gas and oil. The process uses large amounts of water, combined with chemicals; where it has been employed there have been complaints of serious water pollution and instances of harm to humans and animals in the vicinity of fracking wells. Naturally the oil and gas products contribute to further global warming, but the fact that fracking can be applied in many places in many countries is irresistible to revenue-hungry governments and to politicians chasing the will o' the wisp of energy independence. Politicians' horizons are notoriously short term, usually stretching as far as but not beyond the next election. Presidents, prime ministers, premiers, and governors have heard the call for immediate action, and jobs, however temporary.[29]

Using fracking, the United States could theoretically meet all its petroleum needs, oil and gas, for years to come, though at a cost, for the Quebec train wreck was followed five months later by an American one in North Dakota. Not just the West and Southwest, but the Great Lakes states (and also Ontario and Quebec) had possible fields, ironically replicating, and reopening, oil fields first exploited in the 1850s. Viewed simply in transnational terms, the United States would no longer need to import dodgy Middle Eastern and Venezuelan petroleum, produced by populist dictators and sheikhs, nor even the "ethical" Canadian product.[30] This realization compressed the time frame in which the "energy superpower" could flex its petroleum muscles. Some might argue that it undermines Harper's energy strategy, with baneful consequences for the country as a whole, and for Alberta in particular; if we take a purely Canadian perspective, it is possible that the eastern provinces could eventually use a safe or at any rate safer version of fracking and thus obviate western imports. Already pipelines in the Great Lakes region are carrying oil and gas in different directions than those intended when they were first laid down in the 1950s.[31]

It is a truism that governments act only when they are forced to do so, or see an objective so obvious and so irresistible that they lust after it and lunge to possess it. The late twentieth and early twenty-first centuries have been a time of shrinking government and slow-motion action. The prophecies and portents of climate change, though they might be intellectually grasped, have yet to enter the Canadian political agenda or that of other countries. That was probably the main defect of the Kyoto Protocol of 1997: the understanding and hence the will to enforce it had not percolated down to the level where it might compel political action. The ravages of pollution in China and frequent extreme weather may alter this perspective, although how soon this may be remains a moot point. And it is probably true that those countries with the most to lose from the current carbon-intensive energy regime will do their utmost to keep things as they are. Like southern slaveholders in the 1850s, such countries, definitely including Canada, can measure the loss in petroleum-bound capital. They do not want their bubbles coming out of the ground to become bubbles bursting in the air.

Getting on the wrong side of an ethical tsunami can, in the longer run, be disastrous. Resistance is futile. American slaveholders postponed the crisis of their peculiar system for thirty years, using the American political system to their short-term political advantage. Their resistance did not save them and their enslaved assets and the value of their human property descended to nothing. If pollution becomes sufficiently grave, carbon assets could become valued at zero, or less than zero if clean-up costs from the mining, refining, and consumption of carbon are taken into consideration.

## Canada Changes Direction

The implications of oil policy, ethical or not, were not immediately apparent when Harper took office at the beginning of 2006. Instead, attention focused on political foreign policy, and there was plenty to focus on. The American ambassador, David Wilkins, told Washington in January 2006 that "[relations] with the U.S. will be tricky for Harper, who along with many members of his caucus has an ideological and cultural affinity for America."[32] Wilkins meant that many Canadians were suspicious of the United States in general, and the Bush administration in particular. Harper knew this, and he did not try to swallow Bush and his wars all at once. The new prime minister's politics were carefully incremental, aiming to change Canada one step at a time, away from liberalism and liberal traditions, to a conservative alternative. In foreign policy, Harper's most notable step was to align Canada with Israel on any and every issue that affected the Jewish state, which meant that the United States suddenly had a voting partner at the UN in sustaining Israel. Support for Israel fitted easily with disdain for the majority of United Nations members who opposed Israel with varying degrees of fervor. Arguably, as Colin Robertson, an ex-diplomat and prominent foreign affairs commentator, has suggested, Harper wished to do away with Canada's tradition of multilateralism, dating back to the 1940s.[33] It fitted also with an appeal to the Canadian Jewish community, with predictable electoral impact.

The Liberals of the 1940s had seen multilateralism as an alternative to dependence on the United States as well as a useful means of influencing the Americans themselves in the direction of consensus diplomacy. They used the wartime experience to put to sleep, though not to death, the demons of isolationism and ethnic conflict that had bedeviled the definition and conduct of Canadian external relations before 1939. And in terms of the domestically prestigious area of political foreign policy, Canadian governments had considerable success in using foreign policy to cement national unity.

In terms of Canadian–American relations, in all their complexity and variety, not a lot changed: the Americans continued to be obdurate over the signature issue of softwood lumber, free trade or no free trade, and Harper, like his Liberal predecessors, had little option but to swallow hard and accept American terms for yet another modus vivendi on the eternal softwood question. Meanwhile, in NAFTA and related trilateral "North American" forums, Canadian diplomacy secured little; simultaneously, Canada's economic standing declined, relative to Mexico, making Canada economically as well as politically the third partner in the North American free-trade area.

It must have seemed of little consequence that Harper and his followers had little regard for environmentalists—a part of his general disrespect for the class of *bien-pensants* who had for so long misguided the country under the Liberals. Their day was done. The Kyoto accord was done too, though Harper waited until he had a majority to follow George W. Bush in repudiating the treaty. Canada's lack of enthusiasm and commitment on climate change was by then plain, and government scientists who might think differently were ordered to keep their lips buttoned and to refer any inquiries to government flacks, whose task it was to say as little as possible on any subject that could conceivably embarrass what was for a time grandly and absurdly styled "Canada's New Government."[34]

None of this caused any problems with the environmentally skeptical Bush administration. Bush, after all, had created a model for Harper in silencing government scientists who took a view of the environment and climate change that contradicted his own.[35] His repudiation of Kyoto gave Harper a valuable precedent when he eventually rescinded Canada's approval of the treaty. There was, however, some dissonance that followed the arrival of Barack Obama in the White House. There was not much doubt that the Harper government would have been happy to see a continuation of Bush, or rather the victory of the Republican candidate, Senator John McCain. McCain even staged a campaign event in friendly Ottawa, though the government prudently refrained from any public endorsement of the Republicans, their candidate, or their platform. The media did somehow get their hands on a Canadian diplomatic document summarizing a conversation with an Obama campaign aide. The aide pooh-poohed any notion that Obama might be inclined to protectionism, at a time when NAFTA and its opening of the American market was a sensitive subject among voters in the Midwest.[36] In fact, Obama's position on protection and globalization differed little from that of his predecessors, Republican or Democratic.

Given the balance of power in the US Congress, and the necessity of keeping together as broad a coalition as possible, Obama moved cautiously on climate change. He had all the more reason to do so after the failure of a UN-sponsored conference in Copenhagen, which Harper reluctantly attended because Obama was also going, and because he still did not have a parliamentary majority to back him up. Initially, Harper signaled caution as he sized up Obama and his politics, accepting that if the United States moved decisively on climate change, Canada would follow suit.

Obama did pay a quick winter visit to Ottawa in February 2009, his first abroad, following an occasional tradition that had begun in Franklin Roosevelt's day when American presidents' travel options were limited by custom, time, and technology. "Your enormous popularity among Canadians (an 81 percent approval rating) is to Conservative Prime Minister Stephen Harper both a blessing...and a curse, because no Canadian politician of any stripe is nearly as popular, respected or inspiring as you are to Canadian voters," the US embassy in Ottawa told the president prior to the visit.[37] They might have added, but did not, that Obama's relatively liberal and interventionist views on the economy were also a curse as far as Harper was concerned.

Some years later, a well-informed account of their relations commented, "Mr. Obama, according to one of Mr. Harper's university contemporaries, represented many of the characteristics he most disliked: An oratorically gifted Harvard Law grad embraced by the Hollywood culturati and preaching the politics of hope."[38]

Some of the vibrations that accompanied the visit, at least on the Canadian side, were not entirely reassuring, yet there was no real cause for concern. But anyone looking at Obama's ministerial appointments in Washington would have detected that Obama valued expertise and experience, and that he had been at pains to give science a place of distinction, even honor, in his administration.[39] Some of that was mere gloss, and Obama's environmental record would prove inconsistent, fluttering in the electoral winds, but there was nevertheless evidence that Obama wanted to do something positive for the environment even if, in the presence of American energy interests and their political operatives, he could not quite figure out how.

# Conclusion

CANADA OSCILLATES ON the American horizon somewhere between an anomaly and a conundrum. It is definitely foreign yet somehow familiar— not quite American, but not quite un-American. What the difference is, apart from Quebec and as a source for the weather, is not immediately apparent to the casual visitor.

There is a border, established in 1783 after the American Revolution and refined and extended since then. Most of the time since the eighteenth century the border has been porous, with a free flow of migrants north and south. A shared geography creates mutual problems of navigation and pollution, part of the management or preservation or destruction of a common environment. Canada and the United States inherited a political culture from their common parent, Great Britain, and Britain and British culture have remained a constant and important factor in both countries.

There has been another initially common element in the history of northern America. There were earlier wars than the American Revolution that drove another empire, France, off the continent, leaving behind a French-speaking settler remnant that was scattered from the Gulf of St. Lawrence down the Mississippi to New Orleans. The British and British-Americans viewed these francophones rather dubiously, along centuries-old lines of religious and political hostility. Ironically after 1783 the French-speakers of the St. Lawrence valley were for a time the largest single group of British subjects remaining on the continent, and they remain to this day a significant and defining part of twenty-first century Canada. What remains south of the border is mostly place names—"Seul Choix," "Coeur d'Alène," "Bâton Rouge," all anglicized and pronounced in a way that their founders or discoverers could never have imagined. There are, fortunately, other areas where imagination would not have predicted the outcome. Most English-speakers before and after the Revolution would have considered their French neighbors unassimilable and indigestible. Yet in Canada the French and Catholic majority in Quebec easily adapted to the British political (parliamentary) system, which gave them status and significance. With status came respect, sometimes grudging, sometimes not, and with respect participation and power. Seventy years before the United States, Canada had a Catholic head of government, and a few years later someone who was both Catholic *and* French.[1] The difference, however, is more one of phase than principle. The arguments for and against Catholic politicians were the same in both countries; and they can be replicated along other fault lines of ethnicity and religion.

These subjects and more bear on the question of the exceptional nature of American society. All countries are exceptional, it goes without saying. Are the Americans more exceptional than others? The Canadian case is illuminating on that score.

Those who study the northern neighbor more closely seldom agree on what they have seen. There are professional biases and ideological preferences. The American right dreads the possibility that Canada's experiences on subjects like government-funded health care might be applicable at home. The American left takes the same problem and reverses the spin. In between are those whom Canada professionally concerns. The best documented, thanks to interviews and Wikileaks, are members of the foreign service. American diplomats' views of Canadian identity-angst in the years after 2003 were free of right-wing Canada-bashing, and were usually emollient, as conveyed in dispatches home, and presumably meant to reassure readers in Washington.[2] But in soothing potentially hurt feelings back home, they hit on the contradictory nature of Canadian feelings about the United States. Yes, Canada had an anti-American tradition, but it was ambiguous—inferiority and resentment often mixed with contradictory feelings of appreciation and admiration.[3] Nationalism was sometimes written off as "Canada's perennial desire to differentiate itself from its larger neighbor," a fairly standard interpretation, often coupled with the argument that Canada had a weak sense of national identity and thus was prone to aggressively assert such differences as there were.[4] The evidence for anti-Americanism—culled from the media—was also subject to sudden change, suggesting that the roots of anti-Americanism—if it was anti-Americanism—were shallow. Bush and Republicans were very unpopular in Canada, prompting cries of anti-Americanism from right-wing Canadians. The 2008 presidential election laid much of that anti-Americanism to rest and had a remarkably beneficial effect on Canadian perceptions of the United States.[5] Were Canadians' perceptions of the United States before and after 2008 all that different from those of Americans?

What the diplomats did not address was the question, noted above, of whether Canada in some other way was becoming more separate, more different, from the United States, partly as a consequence of a divergence of social and fiscal policies that made Canada seem more European, or at any rate less American. Nor was it usually their business to analyze similarities in ideas, non-governmental institutions, technologies, professions and the like—what travels under the name of "transnational history."[6] Rather, commentators whether official or not concentrated on the end product—what showed up in public opinion polls or in the media. That evidence is necessarily impressionistic, though frequently gleaned from poll data measuring "feelings" or "sentiments" as gauges of identity. The question is complicated in Canada and the United States by regionalism, making New England different from the Rocky Mountain states, and the Maritimes from Alberta and Saskatchewan. But is New England all that different from adjacent parts of Canada, or Alberta from Montana?[7] Andrew Kohut, director of the Pew polling organization, saw the glass of resemblance as half full where his Canadian counterpart Michael Adams saw it half empty. "We found the gap between Americans and Canadians is not a national gap, it's a regional one," he told the Canadian Society of New York.[8] In other words, in some parts of North America there is no a gap at all.

The principal complication in Canada's version of transnationalism has always been the existence of a solid French-speaking minority in Canada, which at the beginning of the twenty-first century hovered around 25 percent of the population. Its principal, majority, concentration was the province of Quebec, which in poll data on social and political attitudes was indeed quite distinct, first as a conservative Catholic bastion down to the 1960s, and as a socially and ideologically liberal stronghold thereafter. Much of Quebec's distinctiveness vis-à-vis the rest of the country has to do with the revolution in attitudes and customs inside the Roman Catholic Church worldwide after 1960; seen from this perspective, much of what happened in Quebec mirrored what occurred in Spain or Ireland, or other previously conservative Catholic countries.

The spread of free thought and secularism in Catholic Quebec (and, to a considerable degree, also in the religious and irreligious parts of the rest-of-Canada) has been set against the religiosity of the United States, and the contrast is undeniable. It is also rather overdrawn. Canada like the United States boasts a large population of evangelical Christians who have played a significant role in politics and government, especially in and around the Harper government after 2006.

Can it be said that the United States' growing numbers of "Hispanics"[9] somehow forms a parallel to Quebec and its distinctive language?[10] The polls raise the possibility that "Latinos" in the United States will acquire or have acquired views akin to their European or Canadian "Latin" cousins, at the socially or even politically liberal end of the spectrum. To the Canadian pollster and sociologist Michael Adams, Quebec had become "the most postmodern region on this continent," but, according to Adams's research data, it differed less from Alberta than from the American region closest in socio-cultural attitudes, New England.

On the other hand, there is the possibility—really the certainty—that Canada and the United States share transborder intellectual, professional, social, and economic links, listed in a descending order of abstraction. The mix varies from generation to generation, and from region to region, but the connection is always there. There are also strategic, historical, and geographic considerations, not to mention the vexed question of energy.

Canadians habitually take comfort in the fact that for a hundred years their country had been more economically significant to the United States, in terms of investment and trade, than had any other. This apparently immutable truth allowed most Canadians to omit from their consciousness the fact that numbers of countries had grown larger economies than theirs over the last decades of the twentieth century, and that Mexico too might soon be a larger economy than Canada, and could equal or surpass Canada in trade with the United States. (It had not escaped some Canadian diplomats, and helps account for Canada's promotion of the G20 in addition to the G8 group of Western industrial nations.) It was true that Mexico enjoyed what could be termed cultural deficits with the United States, and with Canada too. The extremes of poverty and wealth that afflicted Western countries in the years after 2000 were present in spades in Mexico. (Mexico may have boasted among its citizens the richest man in the world during this period.) Basic issues of law and order, coupled to the rampant drug trade and the gangs that exploited it, acted as a retardant on closer relations between Mexico and the two anglospheric countries to the north. But these were not eternal considerations: other countries had passed from anarchy to order in a relatively short time and acquired the reputation of strongholds of stability and civility—most obviously like England in the later seventeenth century.

In the course of this narrative it has been obvious that Great Britain retained and retains still a unique foothold in the English-speaking imagination that is at variance with that country's obvious decline in military and economic power and political prestige. Nevertheless, as a British negotiator told a Frenchman at the time of the Treaty of Paris in 1783, the Americans might have become independent, but they all spoke English. The observation was both perceptive and prophetic. Thanks to the spread of English, Great Britain enjoys soft power in abundance, ironically enough for a country that since the Second World War has spent lavishly to maintain its military standing and hence, it is believed, its influence with other countries. The significance of Britain's cultural industries, from universities to publishing to television, is that they project the British experience beyond the seas, but most particularly into countries where it is historically connected, if not grounded. In the 1940s, there was of course Churchill, and since the 1940s there has been "Churchillianism," the worship of Churchill or his surrogate, the British Lion, which has become a kind of definition of Anglo-Saxon pride. Yet the image has fed into a tradition of forcefulness in foreign policy, as each successive external enemy has been fitted with a Hitler uniform and toothbrush mustache—from Mohammad Mossadegh in Iran in 1953 to Gamal Abdel Nasser in Egypt in 1956 to countless other Third World despots, or purported despots, who can only be confronted with firmness and resolution. It is not so much Churchill's actual historical record that is in question, though he made his share of mistakes in his long career, but the red-faced historical parody of that record.[11]

Similarly the Britain of the later 1940s had an irresistible attraction for the reform minded and for experimenters in various kinds of social policy. This was the Britain of the Beveridge Report, although arguably that document could draw on the experiment and experience of the American New Deal for much of its force and attractiveness. The application of Labour-government-inspired policies was much more apparent in Canada than in the United States, although it was almost accidental that Canada became the North American laboratory in which universal health insurance was worked out in the 1960s. It might just as easily have been Lyndon Johnson's America, but for the accident of a jungle war that Churchillian delusions of power, force, and morality had helped to bring on.

This book has concentrated on points of similarity between Canada and the United States, influenced by Great Britain, yet the fact of different political sovereignties cannot be ignored. The border postpones some events and subtly modifies others so that when they arrive in the adjacent countries the connection with their origin is obscured, and sometimes ignored altogether. Canadian events are often out of phase with American ones, and this has sometimes meant that events in the republic have taken a different course than they would have under a different constitution north of the border. There is the immutable fact that a country with ten times the population will definitely have more of some things—wealth, variety—than its smaller neighbor, though Canada, with its French aspect, has something that the United States does not. American constitutionalism has had its impact on Canada, through the shared practice of federalism, while Canada's constitutional practice has not entirely escaped notice south of the border. No doubt the United States has been from time to time more individualistic than Canada, and more inclined to place "liberty" at the top of its political values, but there have always been Canadians who would agree wholeheartedly with that perspective, willing to adopt the American example in gun ownership or in resistance to most kinds of government authority.[12] The proportions of people holding these and other views differs, and sometimes differs greatly; but there is no idea, good or bad, that pops up in the United States that will not find disciples in Canada.

The similarities have from time to time caused observers to call for the abolition of the border and the combination of Canada and the United States into a single country. In 2013 a well-known business journalist, Diane Francis, proposed that Canada and the United States set aside their differences and take the logical step of making "the merger of the century." The two countries should join together, reflecting their common interests, she wrote, drawing on her observations as a journalist, but also as an American immigrant to Canada. "Americans," she wrote, "are not foreigners; they are kin. Americans and Canadians are no longer distant cousins but siblings."[13]

Francis has a point, though the distance between Canada and the United States over time has been less than she thinks. Connections lingered after 1783. Some of these were political—the two parts of North America were bound together by proximity and shared all the problems of a long and not always watery border. Moreover, both British North America and the United States of America defined themselves by their relations to Great Britain, at least for the first forty years of their existence. Laws, political traditions, even the resemblance of Congress to Parliament and the President to the King made their worlds familiar, if not friendly. The two "siblings," to use Francis's term, were also united by the fact that the Royal Navy guarded the shores of both through a century in which the United States only occasionally had a navy and sent its small army to do battle with the natives of the American plains and Pacific coast.

This unconscious dependence ironically resembles Canada's post-1945 reliance on the fact of American power to keep hostile countries at bay. Not a few Americans complain of the lotus-eating Canadians; but they themselves cultivated the lotus for a century and a half before Britain's decline gave the United States a world role.

But let's return to the nineteenth century. The border was porous, allowing immigrants and smugglers freedom of action, and remained so until the late nineteenth century. And culture simply ignored the frontier, although, as we have seen, cultural exchange was trilateral, always involving Great Britain. In a cultural sense, as Francis observes, Americans and Canadians were not and are not "foreigners," at least not on the English-Canadian side. In most American studies of transnationalism Canada does not usually rate a mention. Transnational historians studying voluntary or non-governmental organizations in the United States end up with lists that could equally apply to Canada, from missionaries to service clubs to trade unions to temperance societies to libraries.

Canada and the United States were also defined and linked by prosperity and opportunity and thus were lodestars for Europeans seeking security, whether economic or political. Americans, with considerable justice, and Canadians, with a bit less, expected prosperity as a matter of right, even though in both countries there were always groups that had not found security or prosperity and lived on charity.

It is not surprising that these positive and negative resemblances—these traditions—outlasted even the emergence of the United States as a superpower after 1945. Canada's political influence in Washington diminished as the United States acquired much greater partners like the British, the Japanese, and ultimately the Chinese, but clever and politically skillful Canadian prime ministers like Mackenzie King and Brian Mulroney found ways to make Canadian opinions heard and to secure objectives they judged valuable for the national interest.

King's and Mulroney's talents would have been wasted had they not rested on a substratum of tradition and resemblance and good feeling. The link between tradition feeding resemblance and resemblance feeding good feeling is obvious. Poll data can be used to confirm this phenomenon. On the question of "trust"—how much confidence Canadians have in Americans, and Americans in Canadians—the figures were 63 percent and 64 percent in 2005.[14]

Mackenzie King knew there were limits as to how far Canadian public opinion would allow him to go in dealing with Americans. In his day the limits were defined by the anti-Americanism—aroused in the 1911 election, an experience that King never forgot, because it almost put an end to his political career. King also understood that anti-Americanism was the obverse side of British Empire patriotism, which defined a majority of Canadians down to the Second World War, and perhaps beyond. It was for that reason that King stopped exploratory talks looking to economic union with the United States in 1948.

By Brian Mulroney's time, forty years later, British-Canadian patriotism was a fading memory. What worried Canadians was economic security and social security, especially as reflected in universal health care, or medicare. But as we have noted medicare was both recent and not uniquely Canadian. There was an American version of medicare—with the same name—that emerged about the same time as its Canadian counterpart. But unlike the Canadian program, it was truncated, beginning only at age sixty-five, and the political will to complete it to cover everyone did not exist in sufficient quantity in the American political class.

There are other differences, such as guns and gun control, some economic regulations, and perhaps the role of religion. Yet commentators from the 1980s forward have noted that many Americans share "Canadian" attitudes on all these subjects and many more, and whole American regions seem to have more attitudinal similarity to Canada than to other parts of their own country.

In terms of the ideologies that underlie policy, it is also hard to see much of a difference. Canada and the United States shared the theories (and some of the instruments) of protectionism, and merrily thumped each other with the tariff club for more than a century, until economic thought changed, and lower tariffs and globalization became all the rage. Keynesian economics had their day in both countries, and Canadians played a prominent role in injecting Keynes's thought into the American economic mainstream. And after Keynes, Reaganomics—the worship of defunct Austrian economists—spread effortlessly through the policy ether.

Diane Francis makes a classic transnational argument, reasoning from similarities to the logical conclusion of political union. The difficulty is that transnationalism depends on borders as much as it transcends them. It is even possible that borders provide the necessary security or psychological reassurance in which similarities can take root and flourish. To reverse Diane Francis's proposition, why merge when so much is already the same, and the result, for whatever combination of reasons varying with the generation, is the creation of trust and mutual reliance? The trust is more than a matter of a moment, a decade, or even a century. It reverts to the pre-revolutionary roots of Canada and the United States and, for that matter, Great Britain. Those common traditions received powerful reinforcement from the accident of geography, isolating North America on three sides from every possible power save one, Great Britain. The Revolution obviously made an important difference, but socially and economically and even politically it was less than is commonly supposed. It did not sever cultural and economic ties with Britain, while Britain recovered handily from its defeat in 1783. Napoleon Bonaparte did the rest, by coercing his Spanish ally and attempting to re-found France's American empire, then selling off the continental part to the United States in the Louisiana Purchase. It was an action that affected British North America as well as the United States by establishing the enduring fact that the United States was then and would be for the indefinite future lager and richer than the British possessions.

Napoleon was not finished. Revolutionary and Imperial France's war with the British Empire and Napoleon's unique qualities as a tyrant and aggressor (and a brilliant general) gave one last shared of hope to Thomas Jefferson and his political friends. The War of 1812 was a testament to the fact that the many of the Revolutionary generation saw their work as incomplete until Canada took its natural place as a star on the American flag. As in the Revolution it would do so with French help, through Napoleon's inevitable and much longed-for defeat of the British and their allies in Europe. Jefferson and his successor as president, James Madison, miscalculated. Stalemated on land and defeated at sea, the United States could not hope for rescue from Bonaparte, whose empire fell apart in the spring of 1814, eight months before the United States and Great Britain concluded what was the next-to-last phase of the Napoleonic Wars. The War of 1812 was the last serious attempt to resolve the separation of Canada by violence, and by invoking France in the cause. The hankering for Canada abated, but it did not die, and when it reappeared it was in another form.

Expansion to the West and slavery in the South sucked the air out of the United States' political atmosphere for the fifty years after the War of 1812. The slavery question was a great transnational event, involving Canadians as well as Americans. Canada as such sat on the sidelines, a British colony protected in part by the British but really and mostly by the all-consuming nature of the American Civil War and its aftermath. The generation of politicians who fought the Civil War had little time to spare for Canada, but if they did, like Secretary of State William Henry Seward, they expected Canada to fall peacefully into the lap of the Union. The same was true of the next generation of American politicians, like Theodore Roosevelt or W.H. Taft. Neither would contemplate seizing Canada by coercion. Nevertheless through some unpredictable future circumstance, Canadians would eventually see the light and join the American Union. When that occurred, they would be welcome. They would find little difference, and indeed lives lived in Canada by 1900 varied little from lives lived in the United States, except for a 25 percent differential in the standard of living.

It was difficult for Theodore Roosevelt and his contemporaries to grasp the contemporary emergence in Canada of a local nationalism—or rather two local nationalisms, English and French. What seems to have impressed Roosevelt most was Canada's participation in the First World War. By his reasoning its level of sacrifice in the conflict validated Canada's place among nations. His eventual successor as president, his cousin Franklin D. Roosevelt, does no seem to have questioned either Canada's standing as an autonomous nation or its simultaneous membership in the British Empire. When the decline of the Empire after 1945 obscured Canada's British identity, Canadian nationalism was sufficient to sustain the northern side of the 49th parallel. War—the Second World War followed by the Cold War—did the rest.

There is no template for bilateral relations between states. There are other countries where a border bisects a common language, and other countries that were once united in some distant past. There are countries where political ideology flows from one side of the frontier to the other, and many countries where the lifestyles and culture are close enough to create a community of interest and sometimes a community of politics. These factors call into question such terms as "exceptionalism" as applied to the United States, especially when on so many points it shares characteristics with its political and cultural twin. George W. Bush called the relationship "family." He was probably not recalling Leo Tolstoy's comment, "Happy families are all alike; every unhappy family is unhappy in its own way." In this case, Canada and the United States are alike—transnational —while each reserves the right to be unhappy in its own way—sovereign.

# Notes

INTRODUCTION

1. The term "Great Neighbor" comes from an almost forgotten book edited by Henry Angus, *Canada and Her Great Neighbor* (New Haven: Yale University Press, 1938).

2. "I will say this: He has absolutely destroyed every stereotype people have about Canadians," Bill Clinton said on the *Jimmy Kimmel Show*, *National Post*, April 9, 2014. The stereotype was probably the usual one, that Canadians were worthy and respectable, nice people, if a bit dull.

3. Konrad Yakabuski, "The Return of 'Blame Canada'," *Globe and Mail*, October 30, 2014, dealing with the reaction of some American politicians demanding a more restrictive northern frontier in the wake of two terrorist attacks *in* Canada in October 2014.

4. See Jeffrey Simpson, *Star-Spangled Canadians: Canadians Living the American Dream* (Toronto: Harper Collins, 2000) for a variety of Canadians living in the United States.

5. Edward McClelland, "America's Middle-class Defeat: How Canada Shamed the Wealthiest Nation on Earth," *Salon*, May 31, 2014, http://www.salon.com.

6. A.R.M. Lower, *My First Seventy-Five Years* (Toronto: Macmillan, 1970), 151.

7. Quoted in Marcus Cunliffe, "They Will All Speak English": Some Cultural Consequences of Independence" in *In Search of America: Trans-Atlantic Essays, 1951–1990* (New York: Greenwood Press, 1991), 55. The Scot was Caleb Whitefoord.

8. The "race" question did not vanish, and lingered in British North America, but because of the small numbers of black residents in Canada, it was possible for politics to ignore their unequal treatment.

9. See the excellent article by Peter Beinart, "The end of American exceptionalism," *National Journal*, February 3, 2014, http://www.nationaljournal.com/magazine/the-end-of-american-exceptionalism-20140203.

CHAPTER I

1. The Five Nations occupied the land now in upstate New York between the Hudson River and Lake Erie, sometimes extending north of the Great Lakes, where they conflicted with their linguistic relatives, the Huron (Wendat). From east to west, the Five Nations were Mohawk, Onondaga, Oneida, Cayuga, and Seneca. In the 1720s they were joined by the Tuscarora migrating north from the Carolinas and became the Six Nations.

2. The phrase comes from the Sermon on the Mount in the Gospel of Matthew and was used by Governor John Winthrop in a sermon in 1630, as he was about to found the colony of "Massachusetts Bay." It has unfortunately been used ever since as a kind of signature of the doctrine of American exceptionalism.

3. Charles I is commemorated in the name of the river Charles that flows past Cambridge and Boston in Massachusetts.

4. The best rendering of *stadtholder* is "chief magistrate." The Netherlands was technically a republic and remained so until the beginning of the nineteenth century. However, the stadtholder's office was hereditary in the House of Orange.

5. Tim Harris, *Revolution: The Great Crisis of the British Monarchy, 1685–1720* (London: Allen Lane, 2006), 313.

6. Quoted in Harris, *Revolution*, 324.

7. Quoted in Harris, *Revolution*, 325.

8. See Alan Taylor, *American Colonies* (New York: Penguin, 2001), 276–82.

9. "Declaration of Boston," 1689, quoted in Daniel K. Richter, *Before the Revolution: America's Ancient Pasts* (Cambridge, Mass.: Belknap Press of Harvard University Press, 2011), 300.

10. It is, properly, "Rule Britannia!" with an exclamation mark. Appropriately enough, the libretto was by a Scot and the music by an Englishman.

11. It should be added that despite Louis's persecution, the Huguenots never completely disappeared from France. Huguenots had already participated in the early colonization of New France, and from time to time slipped into the colony, but their presence was officially discouraged, and they could not hope to practice their religion openly.

12. Richard White, *The Middle Ground: Indians, Empires, and Republics in the Great Lakes Region, 1650–1815* (Cambridge and New York: Cambridge University Press, 1991).

13. Andrew Preston, *Sword of the Spirit, Shield of Faith: Religion in American War and Diplomacy* (New York and Toronto: Knopf, 2012), 50–1.

14. Taylor, *American Colonies*, 389–90.

15. Taylor, *American Colonies*, 381–2.

16. Angus Maddison, *The World Economy: Historical Statistics* (Paris: OECD, 2003), Table 2c.

17. The American advantage may have been eroding. While per capita Americans in 2014 were better off than Canadians, the American advantage disappeared at

the median income level and was reversed the farther down the income scale one went: David Leonhardt and Kevin Quealy, "The American Middle Class is No Longer the World's Richest," *New York Times*, April 22, 2014.

18. And in the north too, to some extent; but the use of slaves in great houses was not universal in the north as it was in the southern colonies.

19. Slavery was not absent from New France, though the number of slaves was not especially great. Most slaves were actually native captives from wars in the interior, such as the Fox Wars.

20. Taylor, *American Colonies*, 371, quotes a French officer on the "habitants" (farmers) of New France: they would, he wrote, "be scandalized to be called peasants," and indeed were "of a better stuff, have more wit, more education, than those of France." Allan Greer, in *Peasants, Lords and Merchants: Rural Society in Three Quebec Parishes* (Toronto: University of Toronto Press, 1985), 138–9, concludes that the rents, dues, and tithes paid by "habitants" to seigneurs and the clergy did not constitute a significant burden on rural families. On the other side, the rents and dues definitely allowed the seigneurs to maintain their social and political standing.

21. See David Hackett Fischer, *Albion's Seed: Four British Folkways in America* (New York: Oxford University Press, 1989).

22. The war did not really begin in 1744 but rather in 1739, as between Great Britain and Spain; or if you prefer, it began in 1743, between British and French armies on the continent of Europe. A formal declaration of war was, however, only issued in 1744.

23. Quoted in Richter, *Before the Revolution*, 380–1.

24. Such was the view of the governor general, Count de la Galissonière, cited in Theodore Draper, *A Struggle for Power: The American Revolution* (New York: Vintage, 1997), 82–3.

25. Every able-bodied man in New France was a member of the militia. Militiamen were in effect conscripted into service, although the frequency and duration of their service were limited.

26. Quoted in the Jean-Louis LeLoutre biography, *Dictionary of Canadian Biography (DCB)*, online. See also the informative biography of the French commissioner in Cape Breton, Charles des Herbiers de la Ralière in the *DCB*, in which the Duke of Newcastle is quoted.

27. In the view of British legal authorities, the capitulation had the force of international law, unless specifically revoked.

28. "We are the first ring of bells cast for the British Empire in North America," was inscribed on the bells of North Church in Boston, in 1744: David Hackett Fischer, *Paul Revere's Ride* (New York: Oxford University Press, 1994), 12.

29. Quoted in Richter, *Before the Revolution*, 398.

30. Beyond the regular colonies, there were anomalies. There was Newfoundland, which, as one historian has put it, was "not quite a colony" and was governed by naval

officers (Sean T. Cadigan, *Newfoundland & Labrador: A History* [Toronto: University of Toronto Press, 2009], chapters 3 and 4). There was also St. John's Island, now Prince Edward Island, which was separated from Nova Scotia in 1769 and got its own governor and, remarkably, an assembly. It was truly minute, with perhaps 2,000 people in the 1770s. See Harry Baglole, "Walter Patterson," *DCB* online.

31. Quoted in Alan Taylor, *The Divided Ground: Indians, Settlers and the Northern Borderland of the American Revolution* (New York: Knopf, 2006), 6.

### CHAPTER 2

1. There were of course other theories that applied to females, designed to illustrate the incapacity of women to take part in politics or government.

2. The phrase belongs to Edward Channing, a later historian, and is quoted in Hiller Zobel, *The Boston Massacre* (New York: Norton, 1970), 6.

3. In hindsight, the term *Loyal* seems heavily ironic, but that was probably not the original intent. Adams and company would have said they were loyal to the true principles of the Constitution.

4. On Samuel Adams's mode of reasoning, I am impressed by the analysis of Hiller Zobel, *Boston Massacre*, 18–9, and I agree with Zobel's other conclusions on the character of events in Boston. On Adams's connection with Ebenezer Mackintosh and his mob, and his analysis of the role of mobs in politics, see ibid. 27–8.

5. Peter Oliver, *Origin and Progress of the American Rebellion* (Stanford, Calif.: Stanford University Press, 1961), 39.

6. Quoted in Zobel, *Boston Massacre*, 34.

7. The Sons of Liberty reappear in a counter-factual novel by the actor Richard Dreyfuss and the quasi-historical novelist Harry Turtledove, *The Two Georges* (Tor Books, 1996) in which the American Revolution did not succeed, and an undivided America survived as a British dominion under a governor general, Sir Martin Luther King. The Sons of Liberty are presented as a subversive and racist collection of terrorists who are eventually outwitted and arrested by Governor General King and the Royal American Mounted Police.

8. Vernon P. Creviston, "'No king unless it be a constitutional king': Rethinking the place of the Quebec Act in the coming of the American Revolution," *The Historian*, 73:3 (Fall 2011), 463.

9. Bernard and other governors began to clamor for troops as early as 1765: Theodore Draper, *A Struggle for Power: The American Revolution* (New York: Vintage Books, 1997), 258–9.

10. Quoted in John Shy, *Toward Lexington: The Role of the British Army in the Coming of the American Revolution* (Princeton: Princeton University Press, 1969), 295–6.

11. Mein's writing is a fertile oasis in the desert of revolutionary prose. He is quoted in Zobel, *Boston Massacre*, 156.

12. Shy, *Toward Lexington*, 316.

13. J.L. Bell, in his blog *Boston 1775*, February 21 and March 11, 2007, http://boston1775 .blogspot.ca/2007/03/mather-byles-sr-and-three-thousand.html, makes a plausible case that Lillie's comment, published in January 1770, was appropriated by a Congregational minister, Mather Byles, in March 1770, as he witnessed the very large funeral procession for those killed in the "Boston Massacre." In the minister's version, he asked a young friend, "which is better—to be ruled by one tyrant three thousand miles away, or by three thousand tyrants not a mile away?"

14. As the law of the time allowed, the two who were convicted pleaded "benefit of clergy"—a medieval remnant—and were branded on the hand, and released.

15. David Hackett Fischer, *Paul Revere's Ride* (New York: Oxford University Press, 1994), 39.

16. A very clear summary is Gilbert Doré, "Why the Loyalists Lost: Imperial Unity and Parliamentary Sovereignty: The Loyalist Alternative to the American Revolution: The political and ideological perceptions of William Smith, Jr., Joseph Galloway and Thomas Hutchinson," *Early America Review*, Winter 2000, http://www.earlyamerica.com/review/winter2000/loyalists.html.

17. Robert A. Gross, *The Minutemen and their World*, 2nd ed. (New York: Hill and Wang, 2001), 63.

18. Sarah C. Chambers and Lisa Norling, "Choosing To Be a Subject: Loyalist Women in the Revolutionary Atlantic World," *Journal of Women's History* 20:1 (2008), 39–62. The authors seem to me to unfairly depreciate the opinions of sixteen-year-old Kezia Coffin, who wrote these words in her diary, December 1, 1775, as "obviously much influenced by her mother," also called Kezia Coffin, who was herself a fierce Loyalist.

19. Quoted in Hackett Fischer, *Paul Revere's Ride*, 51.

20. Gross, *Minutemen*, 137, 167–9, describes what happened in Concord, where there were indeed several "Tories." One of them, the brother-in-law of the radically inclined Congregational minister, fled to Boston with two British officers he had been entertaining, a few days before the battles of Concord and Lexington.

21. A recent example of the quiet treatment of the Loyalists is John Ferling, "Myths of the American Revolution," *Smithsonian Magazine*, 40:10 (January 2010), 48–55, in which Ferling only once mentions the Loyalists, and, in discussing the role of African Americans in the war, fails to mention that more African Americans opted to fight for the British, and personal freedom, than soldier at the side of their ex-owners—including George Washington—in the rebel army.

22. This is the striking theme of Maya Jasonoff's book, *Liberty's Exiles: American Loyalists in the Revolutionary World* (New York: Knopf, 2011).

23. John Coffin of Boston was fortunate enough to have his own ship, onto which he loaded his family and sailed to Quebec City in August 1775, in time to participate in the defense of the city against American invaders in December of the same year: Marie-Paule LaBrèque, "John Coffin" (1729–1808), *DCB* online.

24. The occasion was the official signature of the parchment copy of the Declaration, August 2, 1776: the phrase is quoted in Walter Isaacson, *Benjamin Franklin* (New York: Simon and Schuster, 2004), 313.

25. Seymour Martin Lipset, a distinguished sociologist, was the strongest proponent of the idea that the American Revolution marked the triumph of equality, individualism, and democracy, as opposed to the Loyalists' acceptance of hierarchy, authority, and government intervention. These values made Americans distinct from all other nationalities. In Lipset's history, the Loyalists can be seen as proto-Canadians. See Lipset, *Continental Divide: The Values and Institutions of Canadians and Americans* (New York: Routledge, 1990).

26. Cecil Roth, "Some Jewish Loyalists in the War for American Independence," American Jewish Historical Society, *Publications*, 38 (Sept. 1948–June 1949), 81–107.

27. Quoted in Chambers and Norling, "Choosing to be a Subject," above, note 18.

28. The speedy creation of a sizeable army from the depleted British military establishment was a major administrative achievement, as Piers Mackesy shows in his excellent *The War for America 1775–1783* (Cambridge, Mass: Harvard University Press, 1964), 61–4.

29. General James Robertson, quoted in Mackesy, *War for America*, 88.

30. Michael S. Adelberg, "An Evenly Balanced County: The Scope and Severity of Civil Warfare in Revolutionary Monmouth County, New Jersey," *Journal of Military History*, 73:1, January 2009, 28. Out of six thousand adult males in the county, 605 served at one time or another in Loyalist units, while others performed at least occasional service. Adelberg estimates about 30 per cent of the county favored the Crown, a slightly larger number supported the rebels, and the rest could be qualified as neutral.

31. A loyalist officer probably caught the moment best when he wrote, "The friend and the foe from the hand of rapine shared alike"; quoted in David McCullough, *1776* (New York: Simon and Schuster, 2005), 261. There is a more extensive quote in George F. Scheer and Hugh Rankin, *Rebels and Redcoats* (New York: New American Library, 1957), 237.

32. McCullough, *1776*, 258; Elkanah Watson, *Men and Times of the Revolution, or, Memoirs of Elkanah Watson: including Journals of Travels in Europe and America from 1777 to 1842* (New York: Dana and Company, 1856), 24.

33. Elizabeth Mancke, *The Fault Lines of Empire: Political Differentiation in Massachusetts and Nova Scotia, ca. 1760–1830* (New York and London: Routledge, 2005), 83–7.

34. Quoted in Maura Jane Farre, *Popish Patriots: The Making of an American Catholic Identity* (New York: Oxford University Press, 2012), 239.

35. Carleton to Dartmouth, November 11, 1774, *Documents Relating to the Constitutional History of Canada: 1759—1791* (Ottawa: King's Printer, 1907), 414.

36. See Gustave Lanctot, *Canada and the American Revolution, 1774–1783* (Cambridge, Mass.: Harvard University Press, 1967), 78. Those who did not volunteer were

noted for future reference. As a contemporary wrote, "That was where the traitors could be recognized most clearly."

37. Quoted in Lanctot, *Canada and the American Revolution*, 84.

38. Coffin biography, *DCB* online.

39. Quoted in Lanctot, *Canada and the American Revolution*, 154.

40. Carleton to General John Burgoyne, May 29, 1777: C.P. Browne, "Guy Carleton,
1st Baron Dorchester," *DCB* online.

41. Lanctot, *Canada and the American Revolution*, 155–61.

42. Haldimand was baptized François-Louis-Frédéric. He was born near Neuchatel
in 1718, and at an early age chose soldiering for his career, serving in various
armies until he joined the British army in 1756, in company with various other
Swiss, several of whom were to have distinguished careers in the British service:
Stuart Sutherland, Pierre Tousignant, and Madeleine Dionne-Tousignant. "Sir
Frederick Haldimand," *Dictionary of Canadian Biography*, online.

43. Barbara Graymont, "KOÑWATSI'TSIAIÉÑNI," *DCB* online. This is the
Mohawk name for Mary or Molly Brant.

44. Alan Taylor, *The Divided Ground: Indians, Settlers and the Divided Borderland of
the American Revolution* (New York: Knopf, 2006), 47–8.

45. Quoted in Julian Gwyn, "Sir William Johnson," *DCB* online.

46. Browne, "Guy Carleton," *DCB* online.

47. Jasanoff, *Liberty's Exiles*, 41–2, places the figure of regular Loyalist troops at
nineteen thousand, compared with a Continental army force total of twenty-five
thousand at its maximum. The real difference in size between Loyalist and rebel
forces lay in the militia, which was much larger on the rebel side.

48. Jasanoff, *Liberty's Exiles*, 49.

49. There were separate treaties for the United States, France, Spain, and (eventually) the Dutch Republic. They are collectively known as the "Peace of Paris," but
most references are to the one with the United States, called "The Treaty of Paris."

50. Cadigan, *Newfoundland and Labrador*, 76.

51. Haldimand was writing to his fellow general, Baron von Riedesel, in April 1783;
quoted in Taylor, *Divided Ground*, 112.

52. Quoted in Graymont, "KOÑWATSI'TSIAIÉÑNI."

53. There is a striking debate among historians in a Book Review Colloquium on
Alan Taylor's book *The Civil War of 1812*, in the *Huntington Library Quarterly*,
74:1 (March 2011), 99–124. The participants were John Brewer, Elizabeth
Mancke, Daniel K. Richter, and Sean Wilentz, with a response by Alan Taylor.
Much of the discussion focused on whether the war could possibly be a "civil
war" and on the distinction between subjects and citizens. Taylor's critics were
focused, as Taylor was not, on the American side of events; his useful notion of
civil war between groups of Americans in Canada is lost, one more time, in the
press of greater events in the United States itself.

54. Jasanoff, *Liberty's Exiles*, 89.

55. Quoted in David McCullough, *John Adams* (New York: Touchstone, 2002), 348–50, 71.

## CHAPTER 3

1. Quoted in Stephanie Kermes, "'I wish for nothing more ardently upon earth, than to see my friends and country again': The Return of Massachusetts Loyalists, " *Historical Journal of Massachusetts*, 30:1 (winter 2002), 46.

2. Louis Gentilcore, "The Coming of the Loyalists," Plate VII, *Historical Atlas of Canada*, vol. 2 (Toronto: University of Toronto Press, 1993). Using muster rolls, ration lists, and numbers of "settled refugees," Gentilcore finds thirty-five thousand for the Maritimes in 1785, two thousand for Great Britain, and fifteen thousand for Quebec; but for 1790 he finds two thousand in Africa, and in 1791 twenty-five thousand for Upper and Lower Canada, the year Quebec was divided into the two provinces.

3. http://www.ukpublicspending.co.uk/total_spending_1783UKmn. Gross domestic product at the time was around £160 million. On the British government's financial problem and its policy, see John Ehrman, *The Younger Pitt*, vol. 1, *The Years of Acclaim* (London: Constable, 1969), 239–40. Interest on the national debt, much of it accumulated to pay for the war, was the largest single item in peacetime expenditure. In 1786 expenses fell as low as £17 million, largely thanks to swingeing cuts in military costs.

4. Jasanoff, *Liberty's Exiles*, 138. The estimate dates from a compilation made in 1915: Ehrman, *Younger Pitt*, 1, 362n.

5. Christopher Moore, *The Loyalists* (Toronto: McClelland and Stewart, 1984), 179.

6. Marston's quotation and Jasonoff's comment are from Jasanoff, *Liberty's Exiles*, 170.

7. Col. Edward Winslow: A Harvard man, Winslow had accompanied the British troops as they struggled to retrieve themselves from the debacle at Concord and Lexington in 1775, and served with the British throughout the war. Winslow is quoted in Moore, *Loyalists*, 187.

8. Quoted in W.G. Godfrey, "Thomas Carleton," *DCB* online.

9. Quoted in W.G. Godfrey, "James Glenie," *DCB* online.

10. See William Westfall, *Two Worlds: The Protestant Culture of Nineteenth-Century Ontario* (Montreal: McGill–Queen's University Press, 1990), 94–95.

11. The Anglicans were to get money from the sale of the clergy reserve but did not at any point become active landlords or landholders.

12. Alan Taylor, *The Civil War of 1812: American Citizens, British Subjects, Irish Rebels & Indian Allies* (New York: Knopf, 2010), 37.

13. Taylor, *Civil War*, 37–8.

14. Gad Horowitz, *Canadian Labour in Politics* (Toronto: University of Toronto Press, 1968), 3.

15. Lipset was much more than a student of Canada; a socialist-turned-neoconservative, he was one of the United States' leading social scientists: on this point, and

the place of Canada in his work, see the detailed obituary assessment of his work relating to Canada by Randall White, "Rethinking the Continental Divide," *Counterweights*, Feb. 8, 2007, http://www.counterweights.ca/2007/02/american_exceptionalism/.

16. Bill Schneider of CNN, and later of George Mason University, quoted in White, "Rethinking."

17. Schneider of CNN, as quoted in White, "Rethinking." Lipset, in his *American Exceptionalism: A Double-edged Sword* (New York: Norton, 1996), 92 and elsewhere, lays out Canada's statism and its deferential political culture, inherited from eighteenth-century Loyalists. He points to Canadians' acceptance of the metric system at the hands of the Trudeau government in 1976 as clear evidence of their deferential nature.

18. The Canadian philosopher George Grant might be placed in this category, though he also concluded that by the 1960s, when he was writing on the subject, old differences were eroding.

19. I am indebted for the quote to the very useful essay on the Constitutional Act by W.R. Wilson in his *Historical Narratives of Early Canada*, http://www.uppercanadahistory.ca/pp/pp1.html.

20. Jasanoff, *Liberty's Exiles*, 202, calls the Constitutional Act not so much counter-revolutionary as post-revolutionary.

21. Lipset, *American Exceptionalism*, 35.

22. Lipset, *American Exceptionalism*, 94–5.

23. It was estimated that twenty-one out of seventy-seven seigneuries in the Montreal area were in "English" hands by 1791.

24. Kermes, "'I wish for nothing," 45–6; Jasanoff, *Liberty's Exiles*, 317–9.

25. Rush and Adams are quoted in Gordon Wood, *Empire of Liberty: A History of the Early Republic, 1789–1815* (New York: Oxford University Press, 2009), 544.

26. Kermes, "I wish for nothing," 47 and 48n.

27. Quoted in William L. Welch, "Lorenzo Sabine and his critics," *New England Quarterly*, 78:3 (September 2005), 48–52. Undeterred, Sabine produced an even larger, two-volume edition of his book, *The American Loyalists*, in 1864. The second edition received a much more favorable response from critics, perhaps because the United States was by then embroiled in its second bloody civil war.

28. Ian R. Christie, *Wars and Revolutions: Britain, 1760–1815* (Cambridge, Mass.: Harvard University Press, 1982), 162.

29. Quoted in Jasanoff, *Liberty's Exiles*, 205.

30. Molly Worthen points out that the earliest Quakers were not pacifists during the English Civil War, so Thomas was actually reverting to an earlier Quaker practice.

31. See Harry M. Ward, *Between the Lines: Banditti of the American Revolution* (Westport, Conn: Praeger, 2002), 83, for a round-up in May 1781 of Loyalist guerrillas by rebel troops.

32. The local history is ambiguous on the date, stating only that Thomas Bowerman (1760–1810) was a private in the KRR in 1783, and that in 1789 he was reported as

having received a land grant on East Lake near the Bay of Quinte. Frank J. Doherty, *The Settlers of the Beekman Patent*, vol. II (Poughkeepsie, NY: 1993), 662–3.

33. Ichabod died that year, 1790, which allowed his much younger widow to leave with most of his children for Upper Canada.

34. Thomas Bowerman, in assessment of the township of Hallowell for the year 1808, http://my.tbaytel.net/bmartin/assessmt.htm.

35. Taylor, *Civil War of 1812*, 37.

36. This is the population of European descent. Seven thousand to ten thousand natives should be added to each of these figures.

37. Statistics are sometimes known as "state arithmetic." Their use here should be taken as indicative in a very broad sense, a guide but not an atlas. See Lawrence H. Officer, "What Was the UK GDP Then? A Date Study," 33–4, attached as a PDF to http://measuringworth.com/ukgdp/#. I am grateful to my colleagues Margaret MacMillan and Lori Loeb for leading me to this source.

38. This was, of course, the Industrial Revolution. See David Landes, *The Unbound Prometheus: Technological Change and Industrial Development in Western Europe from 1750 to the Present* (Cambridge: Cambridge University Press, 1969), chapter 2. Ian R. Christie, *Wars and Revolutions: Britain, 1760–1815* (Cambridge, Mass.: Harvard University Press, 1982), 19, argues that the average standard of living increased markedly during the eighteenth century; but neither author produces even a speculative estimate of gross domestic product.

39. There were two other signatories to the treaty, the "Batavian Republic" (the Netherlands), and Spain, both allies of France.

40. This conclusion is very strongly advanced by Paul Schroeder, *The Transformation of European Politics, 1763–1848* (Oxford: Oxford University Press, 1994). It is most succinctly put in his essay, "Napoleon's Foreign Policy: A Criminal Enterprise," *Journal of Military History*, 54:2 (April 1990), 147–62.

41. Schroeder, "Napoleon's Foreign Policy," 148.

42. As quoted in Jane Errington, *The Lion, the Eagle, and Upper Canada: A Developing Colonial Ideology* (Montreal and Kingston: McGill-Queen's University Press, 1987), 24–5.

43. Gilles Chaussé, "Jean-François Hubert," *DCB* online.

44. James H. Lambert, "Joseph-Octave Plessis," *DCB* online. At the same time the Anglican bishop of Quebec was engaged in an ill-judged quarrel with his Catholic counterparts, which may have mitigated the Catholics' joy at their place in the Protestant empire of Great Britain.

45. Graeme Wynn, "Timber Trade History," *Canadian Encyclopedia* online.

46. Douglas McCalla, *Planting the Province: The Economic History of Upper Canada* (Toronto: University of Toronto Press, 1993), 19.

47. Mountain is quoted in Errington, *The Lion, The Eagle*, 25.

48. The first quote is from *The Upper Canada Gazette* in 1798 and the second from a sermon to the Upper Canadian Assembly in 1804: Errington, *The Lion, the Eagle*, 25.

49. The quote is by a Pennsylvania Republican, a member of the party opposing the Federalists: Wood, *Empire of Liberty*, 183.

50. Taylor, *Civil War*, 82.

51. Wood, *Empire of Liberty*, 181.

52. This was Jefferson in 1795, as quoted in Wood, *Empire of Liberty*, 181, with Wood's summation of the context. His dining companion would have been General Jean-Charles Pichegru, who was the flavor of the month among republican generals. Wood also quotes some gruesome images from Jefferson, expressing his hope that the European monarchs, certainly including George III, would all mount a scaffold dripping with blood. Jefferson included nobles and priests in his wish list. Pichegru, ironically, ended up in the pay of the British, and was either murdered or committed suicide in a Napoleonic prison in 1804.

53. Schroeder, *Transformation*, 403.

54. Andrew Lambert, *The Challenge: Britain against America in the Naval War of 1812* (London: Faber and Faber, 2012), 21.

55. Lambert, *The Challenge*, 27.

56. Taylor, *Civil War*, 104–5. The American merchant marine had expanded very fast, thanks to restrictive American laws limiting the coastal carrying trade to American ships, and thanks to demand in the first decade of the war, 1793–1802.

57. http://www.ukpublicspending.co.uk/total_spending_1783UKmn, for the years 1793, 1798, and 1809.

58. Jeremy Black, "A British View of the Naval War of 1812," *Naval History Magazine*, 22:4, August 2008.

59. Taylor, *Civil War*, 116–8.

60. Taylor, *Civil War*, 118.

61. Jefferson to William Duane, August 4, 1812, *The Writings of Thomas Jefferson*, vol. 9 (New York: G.P. Putnam, 1898), 365–6.

62. Lawrence A. Peskin, "Conspiratorial Anglophobia and the War of 1812," *Journal of American History* (December 2011), 647–69.

63. Schroeder, *Transformation of European Politics*, 440. To be fair, while Jefferson did indeed viscerally hate the British, he was not completely blind to Napoleon's imperfections. In a letter composed just before Napoleon's final collapse at the battle of Waterloo, Jefferson expressed himself as follows to a friend: "We concur in considering the government of England as totally without morality, insolent beyond bearing, inflated with vanity and ambition, aiming at the exclusive dominion of the sea, lost in corruption, of deep-rooted hatred towards us, hostile to liberty wherever it endeavors to show its head, and the eternal disturber of the peace of the world. In our estimate of Bonaparte, I suspect we differer....Our form of government is odious to him, as a standing contrast between republican and despotic rule; and as much from that hatred, as from ignorance in political economy, he had excluded intercourse between us and his people, by prohibiting the only articles they wanted from us, that is, cotton and tobacco. Whether the

war we have had with England, and the achievements of that war, and the hope that we may become his instruments and partisans against that enemy, may induce him, in future, to tolerate our commercial intercourse with his people, is still to be seen." *The Writings of Thomas Jefferson*, vol. 11 (New York: G.P. Putnam, 1904), 477–8. Note that despite Napoleon's defects, Jefferson still expected that the United States could make a deal with him, based on their common enmity to Great Britain.

64. Lambert, *Challenge*, 56.

65. Michael Smith, "Upper Canada During the War of 1812," in Gerald Craig, *Early Travellers in the Canadas* (Toronto: Macmillan, 1955), 45.

66. Lambert, *Challenge*, 108–110, 141.

67. On the intersection of American escaping slaves and the ships of the Royal Navy, see Alan Taylor, *The Internal Enemy: Slavery and War in Virginia, 1772–1832* (New York: Norton, 2013), chapter 6.

## CHAPTER 4

1. Strachan is quoted in Troy Bickham, *The Weight of Vengeance: The United States, the British Empire, and the War of 1812* (New York: Oxford University Press, 2012), 147.

2. Robert Kagan, *Dangerous Nation: America's Place in the World from Its Earliest Days to the Dawn of the Twentieth Century* (New York: Knopf, 2006), 167.

3. Adams is quoted in Kagan, *Dangerous Nation*, 167. As Kagan points out (170–1) the British and the Americans agreed not only on the Latin American Revolutions but the Greek Revolution, which occurred at the same time.

4. One of the themes of Alexandre Dumas's nearly contemporary novel, *The Count of Monte Cristo*, published in 1844, is precisely about a romantic foreign cause and the powerful sentiments it evoked in the France of the 1830s.

5. As Robert Kagan points out, *Dangerous Nation*, 169, the Greek agitation is an early example of what would much later be called "the CNN effect." In both cases, a fascination with bloodshed and other atrocities seems indicated.

6. See Stéphane Roussel, *The North American Democratic Peace: Absence of War and Security Institution-Building in Canada-US Relations, 1867–1958* (Montréal and Kingston: McGill-Queen's University Press, 2004).

7. The cost was £800,000 in the currency of the day. To this could be added another £200,000 for other Canadian canals.

8. Anna Jameson, *Winter Studies and Summer Rambles in Canada* (1839), excerpted in Gerald Craig, ed., *Early Travellers in the Canadas* (Toronto: Macmillan, 1955), 123–4.

9. General Winfield Scott of the US Army is a good example of restrained enthusiasm. Scott had fought in the War of 1812, and had been a prisoner of the British after the battle of Queenston Heights. When he first heard of the rebellion,

in December 1837, he wrote to a friend that his heart was with "the oppressed of both Canadas." But within a month he had been assigned by President Van Buren to keep the peace along the border, an assignment he fulfilled with considerable enthusiasm: Scott Kaufman and John A. Soares, "'Sagacious beyond Praise?' Winfield Scott and Anglo-American-Canadian Border Diplomacy, 1837–1860," *Diplomatic History*, 30:1 (January 2006), 57–82.

10. There are historians who characterize the American reaction to the 1837–8 rebellions as far more sympathetic and energetic, arguing that some Americans, at least along the border, really did understand the rebellions as the final, long overdue chapter of the American Revolution. (John Duffy and Nicholas Muller, "The Great Wolf Hunt;" *Journal of American Studies*, 8:2 (August 1974), 153–69; Marc Harris, "The Meaning of Patriot: The Canadian Rebellion and American Republicanism, 1837–1839," *Michigan Historical Review*, 23:1 (Spring, 1997), 33–69.)

"The Great Wolf Hunt" explicitly makes the point that the immediate public response in New York and Vermont and in the frontier was to view the Patriotes as a reincarnation and completion of the Founding Fathers' objectives (see p. 156). Harris emphasizes how the Van Buren administration cast them as dangers (p. 55), but notes that some supported the Patriotes as a means of rebelling against the Van Buren government (p. 56).

11. See Taylor, *Civil War*, 455–6. Van Buren had the support of several former enthusiasts for war in 1812 ("war hawks"), who in 1837 had become prominent and much more peaceable senators.

12. Journals of Queen Victoria, January 10, 1838: these are to be found on a website of the Royal Archives: http://www.queenvictoriasjournals.org/.

13. Kaufman and Soares, "'Sagacious beyond Praise?'," 64–5.

14. The *Caroline* case, consisting of an exchange of letters between Daniel Webster, American Secretary of State, and Lord Ashburton, British minister in Washington, with notes by David Hunter Miller, a prominent American international lawyer in the early twentieth century, has been included in the Yale Law School's Avalon Project, and may be found at http://avalon.law.yale.edu/19th_century/br-1842d.asp.

15. The services of Winfield Scott were once again called for: Kaufman and Soares, "'Sagacious beyond Praise?'," 66–71. In this case, he had the advantage of friendly personal relations with Sir John Harvey, the New Brunswick lieutenant-governor, against whom he had fought in the War of 1812.

16. On the military excitement on the British side from 1836 to 1842, see Kenneth Bourne, *Britain and the Balance of Power in North America, 1815–1908* (Berkeley and Los Angeles: University of California Press, 1967), chapter 4.

17. The term *Whig* recalls the Revolutionary War and had deep roots in American political nomenclature. The term *Democrat* dates both positively and negatively back to the 1790s. The Democratic party as a consistent political organization really is a creation of the 1820s. Both Whigs and Democrats had their southern

wings and as a condition of their existence as national parties both supported or condoned slavery.

18. On the split between "Hamiltonians" (in this period, Whigs) and Jacksonians (Democrats), see Walter Russell Mead, *Special Providence*, 90–91.

19. The journalist was John L. O'Sullivan. In fairness to O'Sullivan, he seems to have thought by the 1840s that the British provinces would peacefully fall into the Americans' lap and not have to be forcibly annexed.

20. Journals of Queen Victoria, December 22, 1837, January 4 and 7, 1838.

21. In the relatively small political class of Great Britain, Durham cut a large figure. It helped that his family was very wealthy, from coal in the north of England. Money led to prominence and a noble title. As a member of the cabinet in 1832 he helped draft the Reform Act; he was also part of the government that passed the abolition of slavery through Parliament. His wife was lady-in-waiting to the queen, and Durham himself appears very frequently either in person or in references by others in Queen Victoria's journals.

22. Edward Grabb, James Curtis, and Douglas Baer, "Defining Moments and Recurring Myths: Comparing Canadians and Americans after the American Revolution," *Canadian Review of Sociology and Anthropology*, 37:4 (November 2000), 373–419. The article is part of a continuing debate over Seymour Martin Lipset's theory of American exceptionalism.

23. In 1834 William IV dismissed his Whig ministry and replaced it with a Tory one. After a general election, the Tories were defeated in the House of Commons, and William was obliged with much grumbling to accept the Whigs back into government. This was the last occasion on which the monarch exercised his/her power to dismiss a government. See H.J. Hanham, *The Nineteenth Century Constitution* (Cambridge: Cambridge University Press, 1969), document 26.

24. Slavery was restricted but not abolished by an act of the Upper Canadian legislature in 1793, and restricted, but not abolished, by judicial decisions in the other provinces. Technically slavery was legal until the 1833 abolition by the British Parliament took effect in 1834.

25. J.M.S. Careless, *Brown of the Globe*, vol. 1, *The Voice of Upper Canada* (Toronto: Macmillan, 1959), 103; Fred Landon, "The Anti-Slavery Society of Canada," *Journal of Negro History*, 4, 1919, 33–40. The whole Brown family was involved: George, his father, and his brother.

26. Lord Elgin to Lord Grey, May 23, 1848, in Sir Arthur Doughty, ed., *The Elgin–Grey Papers*, vol. 1 (Ottawa: King's Printer, 1937), 178.

27. See Michael Hart, *A Trading Nation: Canadian Trade Policy from Colonialism to Globalization* (Vancouver: University of British Columbia Press, 2002), 49–53.

28. Lawrence H. Officer and Lawrence B. Smith, "The Reciprocity Treaty of 1855 to 1856," *Journal of Economic History*, 28:4 (December 1968), 598–623.

29. Figures are derived from Angus Maddison, *The World Economy: Historical Statistics* (Paris: OECD, 2003), Tables 1a and 2a.

30. Maddison, *World Economy*, Tables 1c and 2c.

31. Northumberland Agricultural Society, June 1828, quoted in Errington, *Lion, Eagle*, 188.

32. A forgotten aspect of Irish immigration was the number of adherents to the "Church of Ireland"—the Irish Anglicans—who had a strong influence over the very early politics and development of Upper Canada.

33. After Ireland became independent and eventually got rid of the British monarch, Irish diplomats sent to Canada sometimes referred to it as a transatlantic "Ulster"—the Protestant section of Ireland ("Northern Ireland") that had refused to join the Irish Republic and remained British.

34. Or almost complete: the old Coutume de Paris in force as the civil law in 1760 continued to hold sway in Lower Canada for another decade, when it was replaced by a version of the Napoleonic Code.

35. Quoted in Errington, *Lion, Eagle*, 47.

36. Quoted in Grabb, Curtis, and Baer, "Defining Moments," Stuart, 1988, 213.

37. Quoted in Kagan, *Dangerous Nation*, 250.

38. Alexis de Tocqueville, *Democracy in America*, vol. 1. Third American Edition. (New York: George Adlard, 1839), 429, 347.

39. Henry David Thoreau, *A Yankee in Canada*, chapter 1.

40. Peter S. Onuf, "American Exceptionalism and National Identity," *American Political Thought*, 1:1 (Spring 2012), 86.

41. See Fred Cogswell, "Thomas Chandler Haliburton," *DCB* online. Haliburton's family had originally come from Massachusetts in the 1760s, and Haliburton was sufficiently familiar with the Yankees of New England to be able to portray them in a recognizable fashion.

42. Quoted in Duncan Andrew Campbell, *Unlikely Allies: Britain, America and the Victorian Origins of the Special Relationship* (London: Hambledon Continuum, 2007), 110.

43. In the aftermath of the Civil War, Dickens noted the Americans' "swagger and bombast," which may have been connected to their extensive demands for compensation after the Civil War and their threats toward Canada: Dickens to William de Cerjat, November 30, 1865, in Jenny Hartley, ed., *The Selected Letters of Charles Dickens* (Oxford: Oxford University Press, 2012), 397.

CHAPTER 5

1. Sir Charles Wentworth Dilke, *Greater Britain: A Record of Travel in English-Speaking Countries* (London: Macmillan, 1907), 54. This is a reprint of the second, 1885, edition.

2. Ibid. Roy Jenkins in his *Dilke: A Victorian Tragedy*, 2nd ed. (London: Collins, 1958), 35, gently calls Dilke's view of Canada "an extreme position," to be explained by his strong pro-American sentiments.

3. William H. and Jane H. Pease, "Josiah Henson," *DCB* online. Henson later gave lecture tours advertising himself as "the real Uncle Tom."

4. Robin W. Winks, *Canada and the United States: The Civil War Years*, 2nd ed. (Montreal: Harvest House, 1971), 8. Winks, relying on much older scholarship, estimated the black population of British North America at 60,000 in 1860. Some of that number can be traced back to the slaves freed during the American Revolution or the War of 1812 as an act of war against their hostile proprietors.

5. Quoted in Winks, *Canada and the United States*, 9.

6. Winks, *Canada and the United States*, 33–6.

7. *New York Times*, July 10, 1861.

8. Quoted in Amanda Foreman, *A World on Fire: Britain's Crucial Role in the American Civil War* (New York: Random House, 2010), 177.

9. J.M.S. Careless, *Brown of the Globe: Statesman of Confederation, 1860–1880* (Toronto: Macmillan, 1963), 53–4.

10. The phenomenon is known as "cognitive dissonance"—the habit of rejecting information that does not conform to one's preconceived convictions.

11. Robin Winks' careful history, *Canada and the United States: The Civil War Years*, does not attempt an estimate, but satisfactorily refutes some of the wilder speculations of historical enthusiasts.

12. J.C. Dent, *The Last Forty Years: The Union of 1841 to Confederation* (Toronto: McClelland and Stewart, Carleton Library, 1972), 280.

13. See the perceptive and amusing description of Colonel George T. Denison in Carl Berger, *The Sense of Power: Studies in the Ideas of Canadian Imperialism, 1867–1914* (Toronto: University of Toronto Press, 1970), 15–7.

14. Careless, *Brown*, vol. 2, 52–3, outlines the reasoning of pro-Confederate Canadians.

15. Winks, *Canada and the United States*, 330.

16. The historian Amanda Foreman in her book *A World on Fire: Britain's Crucial Role in the American Civil War* is oblivious of the role of the Canadian government in responding to the various border problems of the Civil War, conveying the erroneous impression that Governor General Lord Monck, when it came to relations with the United States, ruled by fiat. A better sense of the operation of government in Canada is conveyed in Careless, *Brown*, and Winks, *Canada and the United States*.

17. Peter Vronsky, *Ridgeway: The American Fenian Invasion and the 1866 Battle That Made Canada* (Toronto: Penguin, 2011). Walter Stahr, *Seward: Lincoln's Indispensable Man* (New York: Simon & Schuster, 2012), wrongly describes the battle as a Canadian victory. The Canadian dead numbered thirty-one in a number of local skirmishes.

18. The subject appears to have been on Seward's mind in 1866 and 1867: Stahr, *Seward*, 498.

19. Barbara J. Messamore, "Diplomacy or Duplicity? Lord Lisgar, John A. Macdonald, and the Treaty of Washington, 1871," *Journal of Imperial & Commonwealth History*, 32:2 (May 2004), 33.

20. Quoted in Allan Nevins, *Hamilton Fish: The Inner History of the Grant Administration* (New York: Frederick Ungar, 1957), 397.

21. Lord Kimberley, colonial secretary, to Sir John Young, governor general, July 28 and August 10, 1870, quoted in Messamore, "Diplomacy or Duplicity?," 34. Young would later be ennobled as Baron Lisgar.

22. Messamore, "Diplomacy or Duplicity?," is a fair and nuanced appreciation of the role of British officials and politicians in 1869–72, which highlights their difficulties in getting the Canadians, represented by Macdonald, to see the advantage of conciliating the Americans. Messamore's work supersedes that of Donald Creighton embodied in his 1950s biography of John A. Macdonald. Creighton's theme is basically repeated in Richard Gwyn, *Nation Maker: Sir John A. Macdonald: His Life, Our Times* (Toronto: Vintage Canada, 2011).

23. To be fair, the Americans had hesitated when confronted with evidence that British Columbians or inhabitants of Rupert's Land might not actually want to join the United States: see Stahr, *Seward*, 498–9.

24. *Record of the Proceedings of the Halifax Fisheries Commission, 1877*, vol. 1, 53–4 (Washington: Government Printing Office, 1878). The commission consisted of one Canadian, one American, and a Belgian chairman. The American foreshadowed Congress's displeasure by dissenting from the award.

25. Kagan, *Dangerous Nation*, 277–9.

26. Gary B. Magee and Andrew S. Thompson, *Empire and Globalisation: Networks of People, Goods and Capital in the British World, c. 1850–1914* (Cambridge: Cambridge University Press, 2010), 45.

27. Every historian puts it differently. See Michael Fellman, "Sleeping with the Elephant: Reflections of an American-Canadian on Americanization and Anti-Americanism in Canada," in Ken Coates, ed., *Parallel Destinies: Canadian-American Relations West of the Rockies* (Montreal and Kingston: McGill-Queen's University Press, 2002), 275.

28. Christopher Pennington, *The Destiny of Canada: Macdonald, Laurier and the Election of 1891* (Toronto: Penguin, 2011), 53.

29. Angus Maddison, *The World Economy: Historical Statistics* (Paris: OECD, 2003), Tables 1c and 2c, showing per capita GDP.

30. See Carl Berger, *The Sense of Power: Studies in the Ideas of Canadian Imperialism, 1867–1914* (Toronto: University of Toronto Press, 1970), 155.

31. Carl Berger gives several convincing (and amazing) examples of the imperialist-conservative conception of French Canadians, who were held to be placid, traditional, and anti-materialistic: Berger, *Sense of Power*, 142–3.

32. This too was a point traditional Canadian Protestants held in common with their American counterparts, and of course it can be traced back to a common history in the seventeenth century.

33. Pennington, *Destiny of Canada*, 68–9.

34. Quoted in Pennington, *Destiny of Canada*, 116–7, 180. Given the size of several American presidents of the day and their likely beer-guzzling habits, this was a dangerous argument to make.

35. Pennington, *Destiny of Canada*, 285.

36. Quoted in Robert Bothwell, "Foreign Affairs a Hundred Years On," *Canada Among Nations 2008: 100 Years of Canadian Foreign Policy*, ed. Robert Bothwell and Jean Daudelin (Montreal and Kingston: McGill-Queen's University Press, 2009), 27.

37. Kagan, *Dangerous Nation*, 280. See the extremely positive view of the American nationalist intellectual Walter Russell Mead, on the origins of the "Anglosphere," in which he sites nineteenth-century Canada: Mead, *God and Gold: Britain, America, and the Making of the Modern World* (New York: Knopf, 2007), 115–9.

## CHAPTER 6

1. Figures are derived from the tables in the immensely useful Angus Maddison, *The World Economy: Historical Statistics* (Paris: OECD, 2003).

2. Smith argued as early as 1863 that Canada should be handed over to the Americans: Ernest R. May, *American Imperialism* (New York: Atheneum, 1968), 97. His flirtation with Canadian nationalism in the 1870s should probably be taken as an aberration.

3. Ramsay Cook, "Goldwin Smith," *DCB* online: Formerly a professor at Oxford University in England and Cornell University in the United States, Smith had moved to Canada and lived grandly on an estate in central Toronto. After a brief spell as a Canadian nationalist, he began to urge annexation to the United States in 1877 and remained true to that proposition for the rest of his life.

4. Moffett, who died in 1908, was also Mark Twain's nephew.

5. Buffalo had 423,000 people in 1910, compared with Toronto's 376,000 in 1911. Buffalo, moreover, had its parks and parkways laid out by the Olmsted firm of town planners. Visitors in 1910 would not have been in doubt as to which was the more progressive and impressive city.

6. US Census Bureau, "Region and Country or Area of Birth of the Foreign-Born Population, With Geographic Detail Shown in Decennial Census Publications of 1930 or Earlier: 1850 to 1930 and 1960 to 1990," http://www.census.gov/population/www/documentation/twps0029/tab04.html.

7. Canada's GDP by 1914 was a third larger than Australia's: Maddison, *World Economy*.

8. Canadians sometimes found American ceremonies, for example the opening of a congressional session, commonplace.

9. David Cannadine, *Ornamentalism: How the British Saw Their Empire* (London: Allen Lane, 2001).

10. Victoria's great-great-granddaughter, Elizabeth II, may yet surpass her in length of reign.

11. Sargent did, however, decline a knighthood and maintained his American citizenship. Henry James received the Order of Merit (or OM, an invention of

Edward VII) on taking out British citizenship in 1914; Bryce got one, in addition to a peerage; and the OM was later given also to Mackenzie King in lieu of a title. Tom Stoppard, Lucian Freud, Florence Nightingale, Lester B. Pearson, and Jean Chrétien are among the other Meritorious over time.

12. There are two other railway lords: Mount Stephen and Shaughnessy, and a newspaper baron, Atholstan. All dwelt in Montreal, in its famous "Square Mile" on the lower slopes of Mount Royal. The American-born Sir William Van Horne had to be content with a knighthood.

13. I am grateful to my colleague Julie Gilmour for these enlightening details of Mackenzie King's peregrinations around the world and the Empire. The full story is in Julie F. Gilmour, *Trouble on Main Street: Mackenzie King, Reason, Race and the 1907 Vancouver Riots* (Toronto: Allen Lane, 2014).

14. C.P. Stacey, *A Very Double Life: The Private World of Mackenzie King* (Toronto: Macmillan, 1976).

15. The reward for such services was sometimes an appointment to the Order of St. Michael and St. George, and its various ranks, often satirically interpreted: the knighthood, KCMG, was translated as "Kindly Call Me God," while the higher ranking GCMG was "God Calls Me God."

16. Besides the remittance men, there were often British immigrants from good families drawn to the romance of ranching: Peter Pagnamenta, *Prairie Fever: British Aristocrats in the American West, 1830–1890* (New York: Norton, 2012). By the 1880s young Britons were increasingly drawn to the Canadian West, which after 1885 was accessible by railway.

17. A fictional but believable remittance man, Bertie Buzzard-Cholmondeley, featured in the columns of the satirical *Calgary Eye-Opener*, which flourished at the turn of the twentieth century. Many Canadians, however loyal to the Empire in theory, harbored a prejudice against Englishmen and English accents.

18. Karen Dubinsky, *The Second Greatest Disappointment: Honeymooning and Tourism at Niagara Falls* (Toronto: Between the Lines, 1999).

19. Bill Waiser, *Saskatchewan: A New History* (Calgary: Fifth House, 2005), 69.

20. Ibid.

21. Despite his dismissive comment, Kissinger took an intelligent interest in Canadian–American relations, essentially from a cultural standpoint. He was, however, impatient with the minutiae of a relationship that seemed mainly to consist of fish and wood pulp.

22. The term derives from Engels, not Marx.

23. The term is obsolete slang for "beneath one's dignity," "not done."

24. John W. Leedy was Populist governor of Kansas, 1897–9. When he died in Edmonton in 1935, the Kansas legislature voted $1,000 to pay his funeral expenses, since he was indigent.

25. Theodore Roosevelt to John Hay, July 10, 1902. Theodore Roosevelt Papers, Manuscripts division. The Library of Congress. http://www.theodorerooseveltcenter

.org/Research/Digital-Library/Record.aspx?libID=0182738. Theodore Roosevelt Digital Library. Dickinson State University.

26. Douglas Brinkley, *The Wilderness Warrior: Theodore Roosevelt and the Crusade for America* (New York: Harper Perennial, 2010), 194.

27. Quoted in Edmund Morris, *Theodore Rex* (New York: Random House, 2001), 463.

28. Brinkley, *Wilderness Warrior*, 226.

29. Quoted in Edmund Morris, *The Rise of Theodore Roosevelt* (New York: The Modern Library, 2001). Hanna responded, "You're crazy, Roosevelt! What's wrong with Canada?" Roosevelt did live to sixty, but by then (1918) he had changed his view of Canada.

30. Roosevelt seems to have entertained a prejudice against French-Canadians and perhaps more broadly against the French: Brinkley, *Wilderness Warrior*, 243.

31. Brinkley does, however, speculate that Roosevelt was prepared to use force to preserve the scenic grandeur of Niagara Falls (*Wilderness Warrior*, 638–9). This seems improbable, for although there was plenty to complain of on the Canadian side, the American side was no prize either: Dubinsky, *Second Greatest Disappointment*, 94.

32. A point made in the Canadian House of Commons by Laurier's Quebec nemesis, Henri Bourassa: in response, all Laurier could mumble was that the "grasping" United States would take by force what it could not get by arbitration, or so the *New York Times* reported to its readers, *NYT*, October 23, 1903.

33. See the authoritative article by Alvin C. Gluek, "The Invisible Revision of the Rush–Bagot Agreement, 1898–1914," *Canadian Historical Review*, 60:4 (1979), 466–84. The Rush–Bagot agreement allowed four armed vessels on each side; the Americans at the time had nine. But shortly thereafter, for various reasons, the Americans lost interest; the "fleet" shrank, and the Great Lakes returned to their previous state of passive indifference, militarily speaking.

34. The Newfoundland government had in 1902 negotiated a limited commercial treaty, trading fishing privileges for American fishers off Newfoundland for partial access for Newfoundland fish, free of duty, to the American market. Gloucester, Massachusetts, was instrumental in blocking ratification of the treaty: Sean Cadigan, *Newfoundland & Labrador: A History* (Toronto: University of Toronto Press, 2009), 173–4.

35. Edmund Morris, *Theodore Rex*, 463–4. Roosevelt would have preferred his close friend (and best man at his second wedding), the diplomat Cecil Spring Rice, or Arthur Lee, another friend, but unfortunately from the wrong party; he was a Conservative MP and, through his American wife, a very wealthy one.

36. For those who are unfamiliar with the old usage of *slate*, this means wiping off the blackboard—or, in today's terms, deleting.

37. Root seems to have been one of the first American secretaries of state to attempt some serious voyaging abroad, both to get local impressions and to negotiate. He also visited Newfoundland in 1905 and Mexico in 1907.

38. "Pelagic sealing" is catching/killing seals at sea, as opposed to their breeding grounds on land.

39. Maurice Pope, ed., *Public Servant: The Memoirs of Sir Joseph Pope* (Toronto: Oxford University Press, 1960), 182. Laurier assigned Pope, a senior civil servant, to handle these issues, and relations with the Americans generally.

40. See Alvin C. Gluek, "Canada's Splendid Bargain: The North Pacific Fur Seal Convention of 1911," *Canadian Historical Review*, LXIII:2, 1982, 185.

41. "Root's Object Peace: Visit to Canada's Governor May Have Results: Many Questions at Issue," *New York Times*, January 13, 1907.

42. A.C. Gluek, "Programmed Diplomacy: The Settlement of the North Atlantic Fisheries Question, 1907–12," *Acadiensis* 6:1 (Autumn 1976), 44–70.

43. Gluek, "Canada's Splendid Bargain," 189.

44. Gluek, "Canada's Splendid Bargain," 179–201.

45. Root quote and other data from Robert E. Hannigan, "Reciprocity 1911: Continentalism and American Weltpolitik," *Diplomatic History*, 4:1 (January 1980), 1–18.

46. Canadians at the time, like Americans, were strongly fixed in their partisan identities. Only a small minority could usually be counted on as "independent," or "unreliable," as partisans thought of them. In 1910 the reliably Liberal voters of the West appeared to be on the verge of changing their party allegiance, which in the culture of the time was equivalent to a political tsunami.

47. On the Canadian party system, see John English, *The Decline of Politics:* (Toronto: University of Toronto Press, 1977).

48. Taft and Theodore Roosevelt both emphatically and very publicly denied any annexationist intentions: Doris Kearns Goodwin, *The Bully Pulpit: Theodore Roosevelt, William Howard Taft, and the Golden Age of Journalism* (New York: Simon & Schuster, 2013), 660.

49. See J.L. Granatstein, *Yankee Go Home? Canadians and Anti-Americanism* (Toronto: Harper Collins, 1996), 57–64.

50. "Kipling's Warning against Reciprocity," *New York Times*, September 8, 1911.

51. "Laurier blames the United States," *New York Times*, September 10, 1911.

52. Goodwin, *Bully Pulpit*, 665–6.

53. Taft to Roosevelt, January 10, 1911, quoted in Hannigan, "Reciprocity 1911," 17.

54. Helen Taft Manning made French Canada her particular subject and wrote a distinguished history on the subject of Lower Canada in the early nineteenth century. She became professor of history at Bryn Mawr, as well as dean of the college.

## CHAPTER 7

1. As a result, most Japanese immigrants were women, coming to join their families.

2. On the effect in India, see Seema Sohi, *Echoes of Mutiny: Race, Surveillance & Indian Anticolonialism in North America* (New York: Oxford University Press, 2014).

3. Sir Joseph Pope to Sir Robert Borden, November 4, 1915, LAC-BAC, Ottawa, Sir Joseph Pope Papers, folder 11.a.

4. Sir Cecil Spring Rice to Sir Edward Grey, Foreign Secretary, July 31, 1913, copy in LAC-BAC, Sir Robert Borden Papers, file OC [O'Connor] 162.

5. The "linchpin" idea appears first, as far as I have been able to discover, in H.B. Gates, *The Dominion of Canada: Its Interests, Prospects and Policy* (Montreal: n.p., 1872).

6. There is an interesting argument to the contrary in Robert E. Hannigan's well-researched and closely reasoned *The New World Power: American Foreign Policy, 1898–1917* (Philadelphia: Pennsylvania University Press, 2002), 143–57.

7. Gary B. Magee and Andrew S. Thompson, *Empire and Globalisation: Networks of People, Goods and Capital in the British World, c. 1850–1914* (Cambridge: Cambridge University Press, 2010), 70.

8. The most obvious of the British imports was the Orange Order (see chapter 3), which played a large and sometimes dominant part in the life and lifestyle of Ontario: Magee and Thompson, *Empire and Globalisation*, 87. It should be added that the British government throughout the nineteenth and twentieth centuries viewed the Orange Order and its doctrines with aversion.

9. Magee and Thompson, *Empire and Globalisation*, 30.

10. The most obvious example is Richard Hannay (a British-colonial but not a Canadian), who appears in John Buchan's very successful novel, *The Thirty-Nine Steps*, first published in 1915. Hannay appears in two later novels, *Greenmantle* and *Mr. Standfast*. There are less heroic and more specifically Canadian-colonial types, like the successful but unpleasant Canadian financier Rex Mottram in Evelyn Waugh's *Brideshead Revisited* or the Nova Scotian Cedric Hampton in Nancy Mitford's *Love in a Cold Climate*. Eventually there would be the character based on the Canadian diplomat Charles Ritchie in Elizabeth Bowen's *The Heat of the Day*.

11. A point Carl Berger makes in his *Sense of Power*, 49.

12. Magee and Thompson, *Empire and Globalisation*, 167.

13. James Belich, *Replenishing the Earth: The Settler Revolution and the Rise of the Anglo-World, 1783–1919* (Oxford: Oxford University Press, 2009), 49ff.

14. Magee and Thompson, *Empire and Globalisation*, 182.

15. Hannigan notes that Borden's finance minister hastened down to Wall Street to reassure investors; but it is probable that Wall Street's significance is somewhat exaggerated. Canadian governments did not, by and large, borrow in New York, and Canada lagged behind Mexico and Cuba, and Latin America generally, as well as the Far East and Europe as a venue for US investment: William O. Scroggs, "The American Investment in Canada," *Foreign Affairs*, XI:4 (July 1933), 716–9.

16. Robert Craig Brown, "Sir Robert Borden," online *DCB*.

17. "Thinks Anglophobes Few: J.A. Stewart Writes about Adverse Action on Peace Centenary," *New York Times*, July 2, 1914.

18. Michael Bliss, *Northern Enterprise* (Toronto: McClelland and Stewart, 1987), 303–4.

19. Maddison, *World Economy: Historical Statistics*, GDP Levels, 27, Canada.

20. J.L. Granatstein, *Canada's Army: Waging War and Keeping the Peace* (Toronto: University of Toronto Press, 2002), 72. After the United States joined the war, American pilots, including the future novelist William Faulkner, trained jointly with Canadians at schools in and around Toronto.

21. The cousin later retailed the story to Wilson's biographer and, in one form or another, it appears in most of his biographies. It was an admiration he shared with Laurier, who in 1897 had actually met the "Grand Old Man"—popularly abbreviated to "the G.O.M.," which according to Gladstone's rival Benjamin Disraeli actually meant "God's Only Mistake."

22. Alan Kramer, *Dynamic of Destruction: Culture and Mass Killing in the First World War* (Oxford: Oxford University Press, 2007), chapter 1.

23. One estimate places Canadian participation at over 13 per cent of the male population of Canada.

24. Roosevelt's biographer notes that Roosevelt was conversant with German culture, and greatly liked Germany, but that on the other hand he felt "a solidarity with the English and their empire." Edmund Morris, *Colonel Roosevelt* (New York: Random House, 2010), 374–5.

25. Wilson's reaction to the sinking by a German submarine of the *Lusitania*, in which 1,198 lives were lost, including many Americans, was to isolate himself and engage in deep reflection: he walked anonymously and without escort through the streets of Washington; and to assure the public that he was giving this serious matter prolonged and responsible thought, in his next major speech he told his audience that there was such a thing as being "too proud to fight." John Milton Cooper, Jr., *Woodrow Wilson* (New York: Vintage, 2011), 285–7.

26. Maddison, *World Economy: Historical Statistics*.

27. "Discuss Peace Centenary," *New York Times*, August 11, 1912. The main proponents of a commemoration of peace were British and American, with Canadians apparently as an afterthought. Sir Robert Borden had, however, been consulted and would cooperate. The main event was to be a replication of the peace signing at Ghent, to be held on December 25, 1914.

28. The Pilgrims Society had been founded in 1902 by a former American ambassador to Great Britain. It continues to exist, and its patron is currently Queen Elizabeth II.

29. It did not help that the British ambassador, Sir Cecil Spring Rice, was known to be a close friend of Wilson's bitter critic, ex-president Theodore Roosevelt. The ambassador's circle of acquaintances and informants was thought to be closer to the Republican opposition than to the Democratic administration. Spring Rice's reporting from Washington to London was consequently not as helpful as it might have been. He was finally expelled from Washington when he made one

untimely joke too many about Wilson and his family. See Morris, *Colonel Roosevelt*, 516, 518.

30. Peter Clarke, *Mr. Churchill's Profession: The Statesman as Author and the Book That Defined the "Special Relationship"* (New York: Bloomsbury Press, 2012), 93.

31. "Roosevelt Extols Canadians in War: Greeted by Cheering Crowds at Toronto, Where He Speaks for Victory Loan," *New York Times*, November 27, 1917.

32. The author has no idea what Roosevelt meant by this.

33. The *New York Times* gave its readers a verbatim transcript of Roosevelt's speech, which suggests it was not delivered on the spur of the moment.

34. Toronto reserved a very different reception for the Democratic politician, three-time presidential candidate and former secretary of state William Jennings Bryan. Bryan had opposed American entry into the war, and in February 1918 a Toronto mob booed him off the stage at a temperance convention.

35. Reading (formerly Sir Rufus Isaacs), like Taft and Charles Evans Hughes on the American side, passed from politics to the judiciary and back; he had held cabinet rank before, as attorney general, and would return to a later cabinet after serving as Viceroy of India.

36. See Borden to Leo Amery, August 22, 1918, Borden Papers, Peace Conference Series, file 18.

37. Sir James Dunn to Borden, November 3, 1918, and Borden speaking at the Imperial War Cabinet, minutes for November 20, 1918, quoted in Robert Bothwell, *Loring Christie: The Failure of Bureaucratic Imperialism* (New York: Garland, 1988), 166.

38. Quoted in Lawrence Martin, *Presidents and Prime Ministers: Washington and Ottawa Face to Face: The Myth of Bilateral Bliss, 1867–1982* (Toronto: Doubleday, 1982), 83.

39. Borden to Leo Amery, August 22, 1918, Borden Papers, Peace Conference Series, file 18.

CHAPTER 8

1. Technically, only Pearson had been professionally appointed, after sitting a competitive qualifying examination; Wrong, a lecturer in history at the University of Toronto, had merely been appointed, because of pressure of time, at the suggestion of his family friend, Vincent Massey. John Hilliker, *Canada's Department of External Affairs*, vol. 1, *The Early Years, 1909–1968* (Montreal and Kingston: McGill-Queen's University Press, 1990), 115–9.

2. William H. McNeill, *The Pursuit of Truth: A Historian's Memoir* (Lexington, Kentucky: University of Kentucky Press, 2005), 124.

3. There is a perceptive contemporary summary of Mackenzie King's style of politics in John MacCormac, *Canada: America's Problem* (New York: Viking, 1940), 87–93. MacCormac, a Canadian and a Great War veteran, had been the *New York Times* correspondent in Canada from 1933 to 1939.

4. Churchill quoted in Kathleen Burk, *Old World, New World: The Story of Britain and America* (London: Little, Brown, 2007), 468–9. Sir Robert Vansittart of the Foreign Office went Churchill one better, when he commented that "The Anglo-Saxon element" in the United Sates had sunk below 25% of the population and "at the present rate will be 10% or 5% within a biological twinkling." To Vansittart, this thinning English blood seems to have increased the chances for an Anglo-American war: FO 800–261–0-2 Part 3, untitled memorandum, September 15, 1927. Vansittart, like Mackenzie King, defined himself as "pro-American."

5. Quoted in Burk, *Old World, New World*, 469.

6. Charles Stacey, *Mackenzie King and the Atlantic Triangle* (Toronto: Macmillan, 1976), 2.

7. Austen Chamberlain to Esme Howard, August 10, 1927, FO 800–261–0-2 Part 3.

8. Esme Howard to Austen Chamberlain, June 23, 1927, FO 800–0-2 Part 1. Howard argued the sentiment in a letter to Chamberlain on September 1, 1927, ibid., part 4. Howard's comment shows that some British policy-makers, some of the time, had heeded Arthur Meighen's warning at the Imperial Conference of 1921. Chamberlain strongly discouraged any public exposure of Canadian (and Empire) vulnerabilities as likely to worsen, not improve, relations with the United States. He repeated this contention in a further letter to Chamberlain on September 1, 1927.

9. Mackenzie King Diary, LAC, October 25, 1929. King defined himself in this period as "pro-American," in the King diary, August 4, 1927—in conversation with the Prince of Wales, yet another self-described "pro-American."

10. *Historical Statistics of Canada*, 2nd ed., Table 389.

11. The British prime minister, Stanley Baldwin, was watching. Mackenzie King was in attendance too.

12. John Kenneth Galbraith, quoted in John Herd Thompson and Allen Seager, *Canada 1922–1939: Decades of Discord* (Toronto: McClelland & Stewart, 1985), 146.

13. See Bruno Ramirez's very interesting if rather dry and technical study of Canadian emigration patterns, *Crossing the 49th Parallel: Migration from Canada to the United States, 1900–1930* (Ithaca, N.Y.: Cornell University Press, 2001).

14. Arthur Irwin, "Can we stem the exodus?" *Maclean's*, 11:3 (May 15, 1927), 34.

15. The popular British television series *Downton Abbey* got it right when it showed its noble hero's "safe" Canadian investments vanishing in the early 1920s. Even as late as the 1960s disconsolate British investors were writing letters to Canadian newspapers asking Canada to make good on their vanished money.

16. John Darwin, "Imperialism in Decline? Tendencies in British Imperial Policy between the Wars," *Historical Journal*, 23:3 (September 1980), 662.

17. Willingdon took advantage of a visit to Canada by the British prime minister, Stanley Baldwin, to urge a "big" British presence in Canada, and Baldwin took his views home with him for consideration: P.A. Keppel, Foreign Office, memorandum, September 30, 1927, FO 800–261–0-2.

18. Hickerson described his Canadian interests to John Kirton and me in an interview at the offices of the Atlantic Council of the United States in Washington, DC, December 1978.

19. Jack Benny and Red Skelton were examples.

20. "Richard Rodriguez Considers the North American Free Trade Agreement," essay, PBS, July 22, 2005: http://www.pbs.org/newshour/bb/entertainment/july-dec05/rodriguez_7-22.html

21. There is an intriguing reference by Franklin Roosevelt in conversation with Mackenzie King in April 1940 to the possibility of settling "Anglo-Saxon" Americans in the Canadian West: King, memorandum, dictated May 7, 1940, but referring to a conversation at Warm Springs, Georgia, two weeks earlier: enclosed with King Diary, April 23–24, 1940. King, incidentally, demurred, citing high unemployment in Canada as a factor in avoiding any immigration scheme.

22. In keeping with constitutional evolution, it became the tallest hotel in the renamed British Commonwealth.

23. On Skelton, see Norman Hillmer, "O.D. Skelton and the North American Mind," *International Journal*, 60:1 (Winter 2004/2005), 93–110.

24. Dandurand is quoted in C.P. Stacey, *Canada and the Age of Conflict*, vol. 2: *1921–1948, The Mackenzie King Era* (Toronto: University of Toronto Press, 1981), 61.

25. Stacey, *Age of Conflict*, 2, 112–3.

26. Stacey, *Age of Conflict*, 2, 127.

27. Wilson B. Brown and Jan S. Hogendorn, *International Economics in the Age of Globalization* (Toronto: University of Toronto Press, 2000), 245–6.

28. The "forgotten man" theme is prominent in the 1936 movie *My Man Godfrey*, featuring William Powell and Carole Lombard.

29. Wallace Stegner, *Wolf Willow: A History, a Story and a Memoir of the Last Plains Frontier* (New York: Viking, 1966), 9.

30. Robert C. McMath, "Populism in Two Countries: Agrarian Protest in the Great Plains and Prairie Provinces," *Agricultural History* 69:4 (Autumn 1995), 543, notes the very high levels of federal government assistance in the plains states as early as 1934. In South Dakota, 39 percent of the population was getting some form of federally funded help.

31. Neatby, *Mackenzie King*, vol. 3, 96, 308.

32. McMath, "Populism," 543–4.

33. A spectacular bank failure in the 1920s had caused the government of the day to establish much stricter oversight of banks and their practices.

34. There is a convenient summary of the RTAA in Brown and Hogendorn, *International Economics in the Age of Globalization*, 247–8.

35. Mackenzie King diary, October 24, 1935; "the American" reference is from Norman Armour to State Department, October 24, 1935, *Foreign Relations of the United States* [FRUS], *1935, The British Commonwealth, Europe*, 29.

36. Bruce Hutchison, *The Incredible Canadian* (Toronto: Longmans, Green, 1953), 277. As Hutchison notes, ibid., 278, "King kept Roosevelt's confidences," a crucial aspect of their friendship.

37. Mackenzie King to Thomas King, Sept. 1, 1927, quoted in Brian McKercher, "The Cold War North Atlantic Triangle, Great Britain, the United States and Canada, 1945–1990," in Antoine Capet and Aïssatou Sy-Wonyu, eds., *The "Special Relationship" : la "relation speciale" entre le Royaume-Uni et les Etats-Unis* (Rouen: C.É.L.C.L. Rouen, 2003), 138.

38. King Diary, November 8, 1935: At the end of King's first visit to Washington, Roosevelt mentioned the notion of Canada as a linchpin in almost classic form: Roosevelt "thought that Canada and the United States understood each other better than the United States and Great Britain; that he believed I could help him in his relations with England...."

39. Hutchison, *Incredible Canadian*, 278.

40. Roosevelt to King, May 18, 1942, in Jean-François Lisée, *Dans l'oeil de l'aigle* (Montreal: Boréal, 1990), 454–5.

41. Sir John Simon to Stanley Baldwin, July 20, 1932, quoted in John Darwin, "Imperialism in Decline?," 660. Both Simon and Baldwin were cabinet ministers at the time; Simon was thought to have a notably unromantic and unsentimental personality, which makes this effusion the more remarkable.

42. This episode is considered in J.L. Granatstein and Robert Bothwell, "'A Self-Evident National Duty': Canadian Foreign Policy, 1935–39," *Journal of Imperial and Commonwealth History*, 3:2 (1975), 221. The title is from a remark by Mackenzie King, referring to Canada's responsibility to come to Britain's aid in case of real danger threatening the motherland.

43. Sir Maurice Hankey, quoted in Ann Trotter, "The Dominions and Imperial Defence: Hankey's Tour in 1934," *Journal of Imperial and Commonwealth History*, 2:3 (1974), 328.

44. This persistent fantasy (where Canada is concerned) is continued in Brendan Simms, *Europe: The Struggle for Supremacy, 1453 to the Present* (London: Allen Lane, 2013), 356, where "the dominions" are reported as strongly against going to war. It was first discredited in C.P. Stacey, *Arms, Men and Governments: The War Policies of Canada, 1939–1945* (Ottawa: Department of National Defence, 1970), 7. The Mackenzie King diary for August 31, 1938, available on the Internet, backs up Stacey's point, which is also made at greater length in H. Blair Neatby, *William Lyon Mackenzie King*, vol. 3, *1932–1939: The Prism of Unity* (Toronto: University of Toronto Press, 1976), 287–93.

45. Franklin D. Roosevelt address at Queen's University, Kingston, Canada, August 18, 1938, http://www.presidency.ucsb.edu/ws/index.php?pid=15525.

46. On Canadian opinion, see R.A. MacKay and E.B. Rogers, *Canada Looks Abroad* (Toronto: Oxford University Press, 1938). The book assesses Canadian opinion in an age just before public opinion polls, and divides it by policy preference

as revealed in public statements and newspapers. "The great majority" of Canadians, the authors argue (p. 253), supported membership in the British Commonwealth, English Canadians because of "their traditional loyalty to the Crown," and French Canadians because they saw "the British connection as a guarantee of their minority rights." What is important today is that MacKay and Rogers saw this summary of opinion as entirely unexceptionable, and for that reason their interpretation at the very least reflected what were assumed to be the political realities of the time.

47. On Chamberlain, see the excellent book by R.A.C. Parker, *Chamberlain and Appeasement: British Policy and the Coming of the Second World War* (Basingstoke: Palgrave, 1993).

48. There is a fair assessment of King's interview with Hitler in Stacey, *Age of Conflict*, vol. 2, 210–13.

49. Parker, Chamberlain, 11.

50. Neatby, *King*, vol. 3, 310.

51. Visitors to the national park at Hyde Park, New York, Roosevelt's estate, receive a brief and somewhat confused mention from the park service guide as to King's presence during the royal visit. In a movie about the royal visit, *Hyde Park on the Hudson* (2012), King is entirely omitted, along with any Canadian reference, in order to make room for some fanciful twists in an implausible plot. He would have been pleased that one reviewer dubbed the film "inert and inconsequential."

## CHAPTER 9

1. A University of Toronto historian, Frank Underhill, had predicted that a second world war would be the ruin of the British Empire, for which comment he almost lost his job at the hands of enraged provincial politicians in 1939. Underhill was, of course, right. See Michiel Horn, "The Wood Beyond': reflections on academic freedom, past and present," *Canadian Journal of Higher Education* 30:3 (2000), 157

2. A point also made by Frank Underhill, a Great War veteran, as early as 1923.

3. The Germans, it is true, did establish a weather station secretly on the coast of Labrador, and the Japanese by submarine and balloon did hurl some projectiles over the West Coast. There was also a very lively anti-submarine war in and around the Gulf of St. Lawrence, and along the Atlantic coast of North America, and in the Caribbean.

4. Roosevelt had met Churchill at a banquet in London in 1918 and had been unfavorably impressed.

5. The occasion is described in the King Diary, August 13–15, 1929.

6. Bruce Hutchison describes the incident in his book, *The Incredible Canadian: A Candid Portrait of Mackenzie King, His Works, His Times, and His Nation* (Toronto: Longmans, Green, 1953), 278. King himself is the likely source of the story. The conversation probably occurred in 1908.

7. The King Diary, August 28, 1939, refers to Churchill's "war-like" ways, at a time when King was desperately hoping for peace. In his diary entry of September 15, 1939, King seems almost to hold Churchill (and Lloyd George) responsible for the long drift to war after 1919.

8. King's remarks during Churchill's visit to Ottawa in December 1941 were notably fulsome. See, for example, King Diary, December 29, 1941.

9. C.P. Stacey, *Mackenzie King and the Atlantic Triangle* (Toronto: Macmillan, 1976), 55. Stacey reinforces his case by quoting to the same effect L.B. Pearson, who closely watched the prime minister from his vantage point as under-secretary for external affairs in Ottawa, 1946 to 1948.

10. All these topics and more can be found in the diary entries for King's visit to Roosevelt at Warm Springs, Georgia in the spring of 1940: King diary, April 23–24, 1940.

11. Churchill made a notable exception for the South African statesman Jan Smuts; otherwise, prime ministerial visitors from the dominions were respectfully entertained, humored, and sent on their way home as soon as could be managed.

12. The mood of the times is well represented in the King diary from mid-May to the end of June 1940.

13. The idea was that the Germans would soon be capable of landing in North America, which, in the panic after France for a time seemed Inscribed by Roosevelt on the agreement: Hutchison, *Incredible Canadian*, 289. conceivable.

14. King diary, February 3, 1941. His informant was Arthur Purvis, who directed British supply purchases in North America. This is an unusually long diary entry, indicative of the importance King gave the subject.

15. Inscribed by Roosevelt on the agreement: Hutchison, *Incredible Canadian*, 289. "Lend-Lease" was a marvellously misleading term for a program that neither lent nor leased. Neither money nor equipment was ever returned to the United States, which wrote off the sums as a contribution to the common defense.

16. H.G. Nicholas, ed., *Washington Despatches* (London: Weidenfeld and Nicholson, 1981), September 18, 1943, 247, 194.

17. As Howe liked to say to his cabinet colleagues (he was a minister for twenty-two years), he was the only one in the room who had actually chosen to be a Canadian.

18. Groves was a man of contradictions. Anti-Semitic, like many American army officers of his generation, he made an exception for Robert Oppenheimer, who supervised the design and manufacture of the first bombs. He made another exception for Bertrand Goldschmidt, a refugee from Nazi-occupied France, and offered to keep him at the end of the war if only he would exchange his French citizenship for something reliable—Canadian or American.

19. Patriotism is notoriously the last resort of a scoundrel, and the adage applies in this case. This was the advice of the international uranium speculator and embezzler

Boris Pregel, who immediately became an object of interest to American and Canadian security and intelligence. Pregel did, however, have a connection to the American vice-president, Henry Wallace, and in the secrecy-obsessed atmosphere of the war a link to the vice-president could not be dismissed out of hand. Fortunately for Canada, Groves's xenophobia and anti-Semitic prejudices were operating at full throttle when it came to Pregel, who was not only a foreigner but Jewish. For Groves, Canadians were not really foreigners, and as for Jews, see note 18, above.

20. J.H. Perry, *Taxes, Tariffs and Subsidies: A History of Canadian Fiscal Development,* vol. 2 (Toronto: University of Toronto Press, 1955), 328, shows that 56.6 per cent of federal government expenditure from 1939 to 1946 was paid by revenue.

21. Perry, *Taxes, Tariffs,* vol. 2, 368. The rates include compulsory savings, another device to produce revenue and reduce the taxpayer's propensity to consume. The compulsory savings were returned to the taxpayers after the war.

22. Richard S. Sayers, *Financial Policy, 1939–1945* (London: Her Majesty's Stationery Office, 1956), 322.

23. Angus Maddison, *The World Economy: Historical Statistics* (Paris: OECD, 2003), table 2c.

24. M. Todd Bennett, *One World, Big Screen: Hollywood, the Allies, and World War II* (Chapel Hill: University of North Carolina Press), 2012.

25. One story was recounted to the author by a former USO (United Service Organization) travelling road-show manager many years later. He brought his troupe to Ottawa, where they performed at a movie theatre, the closest thing that Ottawa then had to a real theatre, and King attended. Afterward Ingrid Bergman, who was part of the show, complained that the prime minister had been more than usually attentive.

26. One estimate has some 50,000 (southern) Irish men and women joining the British forces in World War Two. This compares with 150,000 between 1914 and 1918, when Ireland was still part of the United Kingdom.

27. Five hundred thousand is a cumulative figure, covering units stationed in Britain over the whole period 1939–45.

28. See Spike Milligan, *Adolf Hitler: My Part in His Downfall* (London: Michael Joseph, 1971), for a vivid description of Canadian interaction (brawls) with the locals, in uniform and out. See also Jonathan Vance, *Maple Leaf Empire: Canada, Britain and Two World Wars* (Don Mills: Oxford University Press, 2012), 177.

29. There is a sensible discussion of the often contradictory reactions of Canadian troops to life among the British, and the morale problems that caused their commanders to seek a role in what became the Dieppe fiasco, in David Reynolds' excellent book, *Rich Relations: The American Occupation of Britain, 1942* (New York: Random House, 1995), chapter 9.

30. David Reynolds, *In Command of History: Churchill Fighting and Writing the Second World War* (London: Penguin, 2005), 345. See also C.P. Stacey, *A Date with History* (Toronto: Deneau, 1982), 100.

31. The exception was the First Special Service Force, a commando unit consisting of both Canadian and American troops, formed in 1942 and disbanded in 1944. The distance between the Canadian and American armies is reflected in Rick Atkinson's *Liberation Trilogy* (published 2002–13) on the allied campaigns in Western Europe in which the Canadians appear only sporadically, when they appear at all. On this and on other points, see Reynolds, *Rich Relations*, 338–41.

32. Reynolds, *Rich Relations*, 341–2.

33. The outstanding exception was Lord Elgin in the 1850s, though Elgin was not the head of a sovereign government. Prime Minister Stanley Baldwin visited Canada, not the United States, in 1927. His successor, Prime Minister Ramsay MacDonald, met with President Herbert Hoover in the White House in October 1929; nothing permanently useful emerged from their conference, which, as the date indicates, was soon overtaken by events.

34. The American instrument was the Lend-Lease Agreement, which propped up the British and allowed them to remain solvent for the duration of the war. In return the British promised the Americans that they would do something about imperial preference.

35. Nicholas, ed., *Washington Despatches,* December 3, 1944, 472.

36. Canada had representation in Paris and Tokyo before the war, as well as London and Washington. But the legations in Paris and Tokyo were relatively insignificant, and no serious (or rather major) policy matters were ever conducted through them. The other focus for Canadian diplomacy was the League of Nations in Geneva, which itself could be said to embody the functional principle, and which in many of its organs worked just as Mitrany hoped and prescribed.

37. A splendid example is this point of view is Steven Pinker, *The Better Angels of Our Nature: Why Violence Has Declined* (New York and London: Penguin, 2011).

38. King diary, December 5, 1942.

39. Roosevelt's attitude to the British Empire has been the subject of much dispute. While he was quite ready to accept Canada's membership in the Empire, though he may have regarded it as an amiable eccentricity that would be corrected in the course of time by union with the United States, he was quite unwilling to deploy American resources to prop up the non-self-governing part of the Empire, in Africa or Asia. This is a principal theme in Nigel Hamilton's *The Mantle of Command: FDR at War, 1941–1942* (Boston: Houghton Mifflin, 2014).

40. The individual concerned, Harry Ferns, had also been a communist before the war, and it is true that communists as a matter of faith and tactics supported colonial independence as a means of undermining the imperialist powers. But other Canadian civil servants, such as R.B. Bryce, later deputy minister of finance and Clerk of the Privy Council, had been communists or near-communists in the 1930s and suffered no ill consequences from the fact. See Harry Ferns, *Reading from Left to Right* (Toronto: University of Toronto Press, 1983), 165–70.

41. See the wonderful memoir by Douglas LePan, *Bright Glass of Memory* (Toronto: McGraw-Hill Ryerson, 1979), which contains an essay on a seminar John Maynard Keynes ran for Canadian officials at Cambridge in the spring of 1945.

42. Ken Coates and William Morrison, *The Alaska Highway in World War II: The US Army of Occupation in Canada's Northwest* (Toronto: University of Toronto Press, 1992). The US historian Rick Atkinson, in his *The Guns at Last Light* (New York: Henry Holt, 2013), has a very revealing section describing the US army's supply and logistics units in Europe in 1944. If the US army in Northwest Canada was anything like that, it would have been surprising if they did not stir up some resentment.

43. King diary, March 13, April 15, 1945. "Poor little Falla," King wrote in his diary on April 15, after the funeral, "my thoughts were of him." referring to Roosevelt's Scottie dog.

44. In Canada, four departments were outstandingly led after 1945: the three on the domestic side were Reconstruction and Supply, under C.D. Howe; Finance under J.L. Ilsley and Douglas Abbott; and Health and Welfare, under Brooke Claxton. The fourth was External Affairs under Louis St. Laurent. On reconstruction programs, including tax incentives for industrial reconversion, see Robert Bothwell and William Kilbourn, *C.D. Howe: A Biography* (Toronto: McClelland and Stewart, 1979).

45. One source places "Baby Boom" as a coinage of 1941; "Baby Boomer" or "Boomer "apparently dates from the early 1970s.

46. David K. Foot, *Boom, Bust & Echo: How to Profit from the Coming Demographic Shift* (Toronto: Macfarlane, Walter & Ross, 1996), and Doug Owram, *Born at the Right Time: A History of the Baby-Boom Generation* (Toronto: University of Toronto Press, 1996), are the best-known studies of the Baby Boom and the Baby Boomers.

47. Perry, *Taxes, Tariffs and Subsidies*, Table XXXI, vol. 2, 399.

48. Quoted in Robert Bothwell, *Alliance and Illusion: Canada and the World, 1945–1984* (Vancouver: University of British Columbia Press, 2007), 33.

49. "Customs Union with Canada: Canada Needs Us and We Need Canada in a Violently Contracting World," *Life*, March 15, 1948, 40.

CHAPTER 10

1. The song is from the George Gershwin 1935 musical, *Porgy and Bess*. The exact wording of these lines varies with the production. See John English, *The Life of Lester B. Pearson*, vol. 2, *The Worldly Years 1949–1972* (Toronto: Knopf, 1992), 24.

2. Ironically, most of those who worried about American domination were far to the left of King politically. There were also some traditionalists who had not come to terms with the realities of Britain's economic decline.

3. Foreign Affairs Oral History Collection (FAOH), Library of Congress, interview with Theodore Achilles, for the Harry Truman Library, November 13, 1972.

Achilles, a senior American diplomat, and his friend Jack Hickerson both favored Article 2 of the treaty but their views were lost without Canadian help. Eventually, at Canadian insistence and with the active support of Hickerson and Achilles, Article 2, covering economic and cultural cooperation, was inserted in the North Atlantic Treaty. See Bothwell, *Alliance and Illusion*, 65–71.

4. With the exception of Portugal, a dictatorship that just happened to occupy strategically vital territory for trans-Atlantic communication, and France's Algerian departments, a French colony masquerading as part of metropolitan France.

5. LAC, King diary, September 30, 1945, (dictated) October 1, 1945.

6. See Michel Crozier, *The Trouble with America* (Berkeley: University of California Press, 1984), Part One: "America's Happy Days," reflecting the author's enthusiasm for his experience in the United States in the 1950s.

7. Avner Offner, *The Challenge of Affluence: Self-Control and Well-Being in the United States and Britain since 1950* (Oxford: Oxford University Press, 2006), 361.

8. David Potter, *People of Plenty: Economic Abundance and the American Character* (Chicago: University of Chicago Press, 1954), 95.

9. The last survivor of the mandarins was Mitchell Sharp, civil servant and cabinet minister, who functioned as a dollar-a-year adviser to Prime Minister Jean Chrétien into the twenty-first century.

10. The sums were calculated using a constant measure incorporating purchasing power.

11. Table 2b, "GDP Levels in Western Offshoots," in the immensely useful work by Angus Maddison, *The World Economy: Historical Statistics* (Paris: OECD, 2003), 85ff.

12. The Americans had social security, and Canadians, in the 1940s and 1950s, had only a meager old-age pension.

13. Paul Krugman, *The Conscience of a Liberal* (New York: Norton, 2007), chapter 3.

14. FAOH, interview with Willis C. (Bill) Armstrong, November 29, 1988, http://memory.loc.gov/cgi-bin/query/r?ammem/mfdip:@field%28DOCID+mfdip2004armo3%29.

15. Horace Miner, *St. Denis, A French Canadian Parish* (Chicago: University of Chicago Press, 1939), Everett C. Hughes, *French Canada in Transition* (Chicago: University of Chicago Press, 1943).

16. From the 1930s to the 1960s, Canada's democratic socialists called themselves the Cooperative Commonwealth Federation, or CCF.

17. A. Siddiqi and Clyde Hertzman, "Towards an Epidemiological Understanding of the Effects of Long-Term Institutional Changes on Population Health: A Case Study of Canada versus the USA," *Social Science and Medicine*, 64 (2007), 594.

18. Jan Morris, "City of Wonder, Then and Still," *New York Times*, July 28, 2013.

19. McNeil became a standby on the PBS network's main news program. See Bruce McCall, *Thin Ice: Coming of Age in Canada* (Toronto: Random House, 1997) for a description of a cramped life in small-town Ontario and Tory Toronto in the 1940s and 1950s. McCall too escaped to the United States. Peter Jennings,

slightly later, also decamped for the United States, also to work in broadcast news (ABC), and achieved a prominence and a salary he would not have had in Canada. Lorne Greene, a newsreader at home, became a television drama star; William Shatner exchanged Shakespeare in Canada for *Star Trek* in the United States. The list goes on and is renewed every generation.

20. The socialist book, written with Gary Marks, is *It Didn't Happen Here: Why Socialism Failed in the United States* (New York: Norton, 2000).

21. Seymour Martin Lipset, *Continental Divide: The Values and Institutions of the United States and Canada* (New York and London: Routledge, 1990), 212.

22. "The Quarter's Polls," *Public Opinion Quarterly*, 10:1 (Spring 1946), 107–8.

23. Ibid., 114: 8 percent of Americans polled opted for Britain alone, and 8 percent for Britain and Russia in combination (!). The Canadians did not link the British and the Russians in their answers.

24. FAOH, interview with Philip Trezise.

25. *Forrestal Diaries*, ed. Walter Millis (New York: Viking Press, 1951), 474–5.

26. But not unanimously.

27. FAOH, interview with George Vest, July 6, 1990, http://www.loc.gov/item/ mfdipbib001223/.

28. LAC, Cabinet minutes, December 21, 1950. http://www.collectionscanada.gc.ca/ databases/conclusions/001039-119.01-e.php?&sisn_id_nbr=10424&page_se-quence_nbr=1&interval=20&&page_id_nbr=15840&&&PHPSESSID=hddhtptg pi4go5ucm821tfocs1.

29. LAC, Cabinet minutes, December 28–29, 1950.

30. A minute in the French foreign office reminded its readers that Canada should be viewed, not in terms of its actual, immediate armed strength, but in terms of what it had mobilized during the previous war. From that point of view, Canada was an important ally indeed. The French might also have been mindful that Canada had lent France some hundreds of millions of dollars in foreign aid at the end of the war.

31. FAOH, interview with David Jones, October 5, 2001. Unable to find FAOH for this date with Jones, only found for March 16, 1999.

32. See Reg Whitaker and Gary Marcuse, *Cold War Canada: The Making of a National Insecurity State* (Toronto: University of Toronto Press, 1994), 188ff.

33. See Neville Thompson, *Canada and the End of the Imperial Dream: Beverley Baxter's Reports from London through War and Peace, 1936–1960* (Don Mills: Oxford University Press, 2013).

34. FAOH, interview with Thomas G. Weston, March 4, 2005, http://www.loc.gov/ item/mfdipbib001665/.

35. FAOH, interview with Louise Armstrong, January 13, 2000, http://www.loc .gov/item/mfdipbib001312/. Louise was the wife of Bill, above, note 14.

36. Several US diplomats posted to Ottawa, like Willis Armstrong, had themselves been the targets of McCarthyite inquisitions in Washington.

37. Louise Armstrong interview, http://www.loc.gov/item/mfdipbib001312/.

38. Louise Armstrong interview, http://www.loc.gov/item/mfdipbib001312/. She added, "But their own domestic material is so high class, I'd much rather listen to some of those Canadian stations than our own." This comment may have applied more accurately in 2000, when the interview was done, than it did ten or fifteen years later.

39. The documentary record of the 1959 visit is summarized in an article by Phillip Buckner, "The Last Great Royal Tour: Queen Elizabeth's 1959 Tour to Canada," in *Canada and the End of Empire*, ed. Phillip Buckner (Vancouver: University of British Columbia Press, 2005), 66–93.

40. But only on the Egyptian side. While the Israelis welcomed the UN force, called UNEF (United Nations Emergency Force) they would not let it be stationed on their side of the border.

41. Functionalism, the reader will recall, is a slightly pretentious term for the ability to make oneself useful.

42. On Western opposition to nuclear weapons, see Lawrence Wittner, *Resisting the Bomb, 1954–1970* (Stanford, Calif.: Stanford University Press, 1997); on the more specifically Canadian anti-nuclear movement, see Patricia McMahon, *Essence of Indecision: Diefenbaker's Nuclear Policy, 1957–1963* (Montreal: McGill-Queen's University Press, 2009), 63ff.

43. FAOH, interview with Donald A. Kruse, March 17, 1997.

44. Lawrence S. Wittner, *Resisting the Bomb: A History of the World Nuclear Disarmament Movement*, volume 2 (Stanford, Calif.: Stanford University Press, 1997), 196–203, and Patricia McMahon, *Essence of Indecision: Diefenbaker's Nuclear Policy, 1957–1963* (Montreal and Kingston: McGill-Queen's University Press, 2009).

45. See the moving discussion of the contrast between the 1950s and 2000s in Port Clinton, an Ohio community not far from the Canadian border, by Robert Putnam, the Harvard sociologist: "Crumbling American Dreams," in the *New York Times* blog, "The Great Divide," August 3, 2013, http://opinionator.blogs.nytimes.com/2013/08/03/crumbling-american-dreams/?ref=global-home&_r=0

46. Three books by American intellectuals both explained and helped shape the 1950s and 1960s: John Kenneth Galbraith, an ex-Canadian, *The Affluent Society* (Boston: Houghton Mifflin, 1958); William Whyte, *The Organization Man* (New York: Simon & Schuster, 1956); and David Riesman, Nathan Glazer, and Reuel Denny, *The Lonely Crowd: A Study of the Changing American Character* (New Haven: Yale University Press, 1950). See the perceptive column by Robert Fulford, *National Post*, July 3, 2006. Fulford noted that although Riesman wrote about the world of the 1950s, "much in *The Lonely Crowd* seems to describe the life North America lives today."

47. FAOH, interview with Emerson Brown, February 2, 1990.

48. Willis Armstrong commented: "Not the best choice because he was so overbearing in style. The Canadians didn't like him." FAOH, interview with Willis Armstrong

November 29, 1988. Emerson Brown spoke of the impression the ambassador made on his own staff in Ottawa: "I do know that Butterworth had a plane that he flew around in and he literally had a red carpet rolled out for him." In justice to Butterworth, he had had a distinguished career prior to his Canadian episode; and he had, by some accounts, also been a victim of the McCarthy attacks on American diplomats—a point he shared with Pearson who was a perennial target of the American witch-hunters.

49. Joe Scott, who headed the Canadian desk in the State Department in the late 1960s, told me that when one of Butterworth's staff in Ottawa was removed because he and the ambassador could not get along, the ambassador was told that the next personnel displacement would be his own recall to Washington.

50. Actually the LBJ Ranch.

51. FAOH, Philip Trezise interview with Willis Armstrong.

52. Reisman was for thirty years the Canadian government's principal adviser on trade—especially trade with the United States. The job followed him from department to department—from finance to industry, back to finance, and finally to a quasi-independent office when he was hired to manage the free-trade negotiations with the United States, 1985–88.

53. FAOH, interview with Julius Katz, May 12, 1995, http://www.loc.gov/item/mfdipbib000592/.

54. FAOH, interview with Julius Katz, May 12, 1995, http://www.loc.gov/item/mfdipbib000592/.

55. LAC, RG 2, cabinet conclusions, January 13, 1965. The brother-in-law was Charles M. (Bud) Drury; Reisman was his deputy, and so logically Drury reported for his work to the cabinet. The cabinet conclusions are not a verbatim transcript, and Gordon may have spoken, but if he did, it was not a major intervention, and there is no hint of dissension on the principle of free trade.

56. Greg Donaghy, *Tolerant Allies: Canada and the United States, 1963–1968* (Montreal: McGill-Queen's University Press, 2002), 130–131. On the other hand, Canadians seeking to prove their country differed on Vietnam cited the speech approvingly—often without having read it.

57. FAOH, interview with Dwight Mason, August 3, 1993, http://www.adst.org/OH%20TOCs/Mason,%20Dwight%20N.toc.pdf: "However, a basic rule of U.S.-Canadian diplomacy is that in the end, we all have to live together in North America, and therefore we must never allow one issue to affect other issues. This is the "no linkage" policy. So just because we're having a trade dispute doesn't mean we're going to have trouble in some unrelated area. The fact is there's a very serious effort to avoid linkages, because we both recognize that if we ever linked things, there's no limit to the gridlock that could result."

58. Robert M. Ball, "Perspectives On Medicare: What Medicare's Architects Had In Mind," *Health Affairs*, 14:4 (1995), 62–72.

## CHAPTER 11

1. Canada was a member of three International Commissions for Supervision and Control or ICSC, one for each of the three Indochinese states, Vietnam, Laos, and Cambodia, along with neutral India and communist Poland from 1954 to 1973. See Bothwell, *Alliance and Illusion* (Vancouver: University of British Columbia Press, 2007), 195–211. The commissions were almost always abbreviated in general usage to "International Control Commission," or ICC.

2. This time there was only one commission, and its title was International Commission for Control and Supervision (ICCS). It had four members rather than three, two Western-oriented, two communist. Like its predecessor, it ceased to function in a very short period of time. Canada withdrew long before the official death of the ICCS.

3. In a conversation with me, one of Nixon's close advisers suggested that Nixon's resentment of the stylish Trudeau was based on a form of sexual jealousy—Trudeau, after all, had dated Barbra Streisand and a bevy of other women. Nixon had not.

4. There is a suggestion in an interview of Vladimir Toumanoff, June 18, 1999, FAOH, http://www.loc.gov/item/mfdipbib001188/, that Kissinger scribbled "Trudeau S.O.B." on a memo during one of his meetings with Nixon.

5. Rick Pearlstein, *Nixonland: The Rise of a President and the Fracturing of America,* (New York: Scribner, 2008).

6. David Greenberg, *Nixon's Shadow: The History of an Image* (New York: Norton, 2003), 306.

7. The phrase comes from Greenberg, *Nixon's Shadow,* 308.

8. Pearson was, to say the least, skeptical of Trudeau's promise to do things better; as for Diefenbaker, since fulmination was his natural mode of expression, it is hard to tell what he really thought.

9. Robert Bothwell, Ian Drummond, and John English, *Canada since 1945: Power, Politics and Provincialism* (Toronto: University of Toronto Press, 1981), 458.

10. The full quote is "Canada is divisible because Canada is not a real country," and was uttered on January 27, 1996, according to Wikipedia.

11. Memorandum from Secretary of State Rogers to President Nixon, November 24, 1970, *Foreign Relations of the United States, 1969–1976,* vol. XLI, *Western Europe, NATO, 1969–1972,* 408.

12. Jean-François Lisée, *Dans l'oeil de l'aigle: Washington face au Québec* (Montréal: Boréal, 1990), 201–3.

13. Secretary's Analytic Staff Meeting, March 8, 1974, Digital National Security Archive, Kissinger Transcripts, item 01062.

14. Enders was a professional diplomat, and one of the brightest, as well as the tallest, in the US foreign service. As American ambassador in Cambodia, he had materially helped in Kissinger's conduct of the war, and after the war this got

him into hot water with the Democrats in Congress. To take Enders off the firing line, Kissinger sent him to Ottawa, which in a more normal course of events would not have been his natural posting.

15. Enders to State Department (Secretary of State), November 18, 1976, "Trudeau on tactics vis-à-vis the separatists," secret, no distribution, http://www.wikileaks .org/plusd/cables/1976OTTAWA04579_b.html. Trudeau raised not only his worry about US attitudes, but whether Canadians would start thinking and talking about joining the United States.

16. A variant of this analysis can be found in Colin Woodard, *American Nations: A History of the Eleven Regional Cultures of North America* (New York: Viking, 2011), which in turn is similar to Joel Garreau, *The Nine Nations of North America* (Avon Books, 1982). Both authors argue the similarities between Canadians and Americans, but in essence see English-speaking Canadians as add-ons to the inhabitants of adjacent American regions. The French-Canadians, especially in Woodard, are romanticized by leaving out large chunks of their intractable history.

17. State Department, "The Quebec Situation: Outlook and Implications," August 1977, reproduced in Lisée, *L'œil*, 461–80.

18. There is a later parallel in the active use of American good offices in resolving the Northern Ireland imbroglio under Bill Clinton, with the very active support of both the British and Irish governments. That occurred after thirty years of bombs and riots—something that did not happen in Canada.

19. The main NATO policy was called the "two-track" decision of 1979. Whereby the NATO countries on the one hand negotiated with the Soviet Union for détente and the removal of Soviet missiles, and on the other hand, the deployment of NATO missiles to counter the Soviet build-up. One of the Western weapons at issue was the cruise missile, an American device, which Trudeau had allowed to be tested in Canada, since the terrain so closely resembles Siberia's. On these points, see Bothwell, *Alliance and Illusion*, 362.

20. The Foreign Investment Review Act (FIRA), an outgrowth of the nationalism of the 1960s and 1970s.

21. FAOH, Paul Robinson interview by Willis Armstrong, 1989, http://www.loc.gov/ item/mfdipbib000984/ and interview of Paul Robinson by Robert Bothwell and John Kirton, Chicago, 1987. In an eccentric way, and from a conservative point of view, Robinson, a Chicago businessman of Canadian descent, was extremely pro-Canadian. To Willis Armstrong, he said, "There are no two people in this world closer to each other than the United States and Canada, not only by blood and by language, but by basic outlooks on life. That doesn't mean there aren't differences; there are. We, as Americans, want to make sure that we are aware of these." On Quebec separatism, Robinson had firm views: "I detest separatism as much as the Canadians, or good Canadians, do. I was invited by the Lévesque government on November 11th, I remember, 1981, Remembrance Day, our Veteran's Day. I laid the wreath in Quebec City. Lévesque was, I thought, a despicable man. He refused to wear the king's uniform during the war. He came in the U.S. Army as a cameraman."

22. FAOH, interview with Dwight Mason, August 3, 1993, http://www.loc.gov/item/mfdipbib000758/.

23. Andrew Marr, *A History of Modern Britain* (London: Pan, 2008), 400.

24. Trudeau stated that Canada was "100 percent behind the British." Mark MacGuigan, *An Inside Look at External Affairs during the Trudeau Years*, ed. P. Whitney Lackenbauer (Calgary: University of Calgary Press, 2002), 43–4.

25. John Graham to author, August 22, 2013.

26. Quoted in Marr, *A History of Modern Britain*, 382.

27. As sometimes happened with lucky conservative governments, their low-tax, low-spending (on some things) policies were bolstered with an infusion of oil revenue: Marr, *Modern Britain*, 438.

28. After seventy years of usually mythical reports of Soviet gold buying radical support, the Soviet Union really did support the British miners.

29. Douglas Brinkley, ed., *The Reagan Diaries*, vol. 1 (New York: Harper Collins e-books, 2009), Diary 20, 1 July 1981: "Margaret Thatcher is a tower of strength and a solid friend of the U.S."

30. *Reagan Diaries*, vol. 1, Diary 25, September 1984.

31. *Reagan Diaries*, vol. 1, Diary 18, February 1986.

32. FAOH, interview with Thomas Niles, June 5, 1998.

33. Confidential interview, 1989.

34. Derek Burney, "What America Stands to Lose if NAFTA Is Reopened," *Globe and Mail*, February 29, 2008; John Ibbitson, "U.S. Candidates in Canadian Eyes," *Globe and Mail*, 21 June 2008.

35. Some of the then-gruesome wines of New York state could be compared in every respect in the 1960s to the wines of Southern Ontario, from the few good or at least passable ones, to the many bad ones. The improvement on both sides of the border is notable, though it seems to this prejudiced consumer that the Ontario wines are now, on the whole, better than the product from across the lakes.

36. Paul Krugman, "The Undecade," *The New York Times*, February 7, 2013.

37. It was perfectly obvious that the Soviet ruling class was a gerontocracy, with its average age well over 70, and with its leaders either senile or dependent on life support—as in the cases, respectively, of Leonid Brezhnev and Yuri Andropov, who split his time as Soviet leader with a dialysis machine.

38. The "end of history" recalls the "end of ideology" school of the 1950s, both presentist doctrines that inflate short-term developments into political laws of great significance. The "end of history" school is associated with Francis Fukuyama, an American political scientist and sometime diplomat.

CHAPTER 12

1. Tim Adams, "Robert Skidelsky: 'Why Don't More People Aspire to Living a Good Life?' The Economic Historian Talks about His Utopian Philosophy, Our Damaging Pursuit of Money and the Problem with Happiness." *Guardian*,

August 25, 2013. See also Steven Pearlstein, "Can We Save American Capitalism?" *Washington Post*, August 31, 2012.

2. Christian Caryl, *Strange Rebels: 1979 and the Birth of the 21st Century* (New York: Basic Books, 2013), 160–1.

3. The parallel with Great Britain is particularly striking, a mix of public (crown) corporations with private enterprise—the "mixed economy" of mid-century. True, there were fewer government companies in Canada, but the principle was the same, and it emerged strongly when in the 1960s first Saskatchewan and then Canada adopted universal government medical insurance. There was no particular practical difference between Labour/Tory Great Britain and Tory Ontario as to the mix of government and private institutions favored by the Liberals in Ottawa in the same time period as a means of securing the public interest in economic affairs. As far as the United States was concerned, the public power movements in Canada and the United States in the early twentieth century are strikingly similar in assumptions and objectives.

4. Clement quoted in Steven Chase and Campbell Clark, "For Canadian Conservatives, Thatcher was a 'Saviour'," *Globe and Mail*, April 9, 2013, at the time of the death of Thatcher.

5. The most prominent was Milton Friedman of the University of Chicago, whose "unapologetic support for laissez-faire" made him one of the earliest and best-known figures among right-wing economists. See Angus Burgin, *The Great Persuasion: Reinventing Free Markets since the Depression* (Cambridge, Mass.: Harvard University Press, 2012), 222–3.

6. Michael Harris [a journalist, not the former premier of Ontario], *Majority of One: Stephen Harper and Canada's Radical Makeover* (Toronto: Penguin, 2014), kindle loc 601.

7. Adrian Morrow, "Hudak Revamped Policy after Visiting Stalwarts of US Right," *Globe and Mail*, June 1, 2014.

8. Tony Judt, *Postwar: A History of Europe since 1945* (New York: Penguin, 2006), 536–7.

9. The best account of these highly significant events is Edward Greenspon and Anthony Wilson-Smith, *Double Vision: The Inside Story of the Liberals in Power* (Toronto: Doubleday, 1996).

10. This was a point made for Chrétien in his briefing notes for Clinton's state visit in February 1995: DFAIT Records, file 2950–01/USA, "Visit to Ottawa of the President of the United States, Bill. J. Clinton, February 23–24 1995."

11. This was actually a rather old issue. Scotland had had its own Parliament until 1707 when it joined the "Union" with England, creating Great Britain as a country and British as a nationality. Britain's abounding prosperity and its evident success as a country down to the 1940s—the Scots helped run the Empire and profited from it—kept nationalists north of the border a tiny, disgruntled, and uninfluential minority. For how could you argue with success? By the 1990s it was debatable

whether Britain was any longer a successful country, Scotland's great industries were in radical decline, and in any case Margaret Thatcher struck many Scots as a "conspicuously English figure," and her policies irritated the majority of Scottish voters. There was a consequent rise in Scottish nationalist sentiment. See Andrew Marr, *A History of Modern Britain* (London: Pan, 2008), "The Tartan Pizza," 523–7.

12. Needless to say, the separatists liked to talk of the "betrayal" of Quebec by Trudeau in securing the Constitution of 1982. On this point, see Ron Graham, *The Last Act: Pierre Trudeau, The Gang of Eight and the Fight for Canada* (Toronto: Penguin, 2011).

13. One of Johnson's daughters did, however, come to live in Toronto for a considerable period, and her mother with accompanying secret service agents visited her from time to time.

14. Because Joe Clark was prime minister only from June 1979 to March 1980, he is generally omitted from general histories except for, as in this case, a footnote. But it should be emphasized that Clark did Carter an immense favor by authorizing the rescue and escape from revolutionary Iran of six US diplomats after the Iranians seized the American embassy. The sequence of events was not exactly as depicted in the dreadful Hollywood film *Argo* (2012). The Clark government also gave Canadian consent to NATO's two-track policy in 1979.

15. Quoted in Lawrence Martin, *Iron Man: The Defiant Reign of Jean Chrétien* (Toronto: Viking, 2003), 171. Clinton had actually met Mulroney in Vancouver in April 1993, in the context of an encounter with the Russian president, Boris Yeltsin. The 1995 visit to snowbound Ottawa was therefore his second to Canada.

16. FAOH, interview with David T. Jones, October 5, 2001 (second of three).

17. FAOH, interview with Victor D. Comras, April 16, 2002. Comras headed the Office for Canadian Affairs in the State Department in 1998. He added: "It's true that if you look at the political spectrum in Canada and compare it to the political spectrum in the United States, some differences can be discerned. Our conservative groups are somewhat more pronounced. Their middle of the road is somewhat to the left of ours."

18. Canadian quotes are from Chretien's 1995 briefing book referenced in footnote 9. The minister-counselor at the US embassy made essentially the same point: FAOH, interview with David T. Jones, (third of three), March 19, 2002.

19. FAOH, interview with David T. Jones, October 5, 2001 (second of three).

20. FAOH, interview with Lynne Lambert, January 24, 2002.

21. David T. Jones, "An Independent Quebec: Looking into the Abyss," *Washington Quarterly*, 20:2 (Spring 1997), 21–36.

22. Speech by Bill Clinton on federalism, October 8, 1999, http://ideefederale.ca/wp/wp-content/uploads/2009/09/Speech_by_President_Bill_Clinton_on_federalism.pdf

23. On taking the "long view" with its intimations of inevitability, see Walter Russell Mead, *God and Gold: Britain, America and the Making of the Modern World* (New York: Knopf, 2007).

388 *Notes to Pages 305–311*

24. Intervals of war were mixed with intervals of peace, and when peaceful the region had many people who preferred and profited from peaceful ways. A book, *Balkan Ghosts* (1993) by the American author Robert Kaplan, had a considerable and baneful influence in persuading readers, including the US president Bill Clinton, that barbarism in the Balkans was intractable and endemic.

25. A movie, *Welcome to Sarajevo*, uses a Canadian character to illustrate well meaning but futile humanitarianism. *Hotel Rwanda* uses a version of Dallaire played by the Hollywood star Nick Nolte to make the same point.

26. Stéphane Roussel, *The North American Democratic Peace: Absence of War and Security Institutions Building in Canadian-U.S. Relations (1867–1958)* (Montreal: McGill-Queen's University Press, 2004).

27. The Canadian government did have misgivings about the inclusion of Portugal, a dictatorship, and the Algerian departments of France in the alliance. But pressures to include Portugal because of its strategic Atlantic islands and French insistence that Algeria was a sine qua non for French membership overcame Canadian hesitations.

28. Lloyd Axworthy and Alan Rock, "Looking Back at Kosovo Can Move the Syria Conflict Forward," *Globe and Mail*, August 26, 2013.

29. FAOH, interview with Thomas M. T, Niles, June 5, 1998, http://www.loc.gov/item/mfdipbib000869/.

30. FAOH, interview with David T. Jones, March 16, 1999, http://www.loc.gov/item/mfdipbib001375/.

31. FAOH, interview with Thomas Weston, March 4, 2005 ff, http://www.loc.gov/item/mfdipbib001665/.

32. Inderfurth had a varied career, serving on the National Security Council and the US senate staff, and as a correspondent. From 1997 to 2001 he was assistant secretary of state for the South Asian region.

33. FAOH, interview with Karl Inderfurth, April 27, 2001. The questions by the interviewer, Charles Stuart Kennedy, are a striking contrast in tone and ideology with Inderfurth's position, and are an excellent illustration of the top-down alliance attitude when it came to Canada: "Did you find a problem with the Canadians being quite aggressive and in a way sanctimonious about this? They didn't have any troops in the DMZ in Korea. There is a dangerous situation and you have to use every means you can."

34. John English, "The Ottawa Convention on Anti-Personnel Landmines," in Andrew F. Cooper, Jorge Heine and Ramesh Thakur, eds., *The Oxford Handbook of Modern Diplomacy* (Oxford: Oxford University Press, 2013), 805.

35. FAOH, interview with Karl Inderfurth, April 27, 2001.

36. Ironically Axworthy had been a vitriolic critic in the 1960s of Pearson being too accommodating to the Americans. He claimed in 1963 that Pearson had "renege[d] on past principles" in supporting the acquisition of nuclear weapons for Canadian forces. Axworthy is quoted in John English, *The Worldly Years: The Life of Lester*

*Pearson, 1949–1972* (Toronto: Knopf, 1992), 251. On Axworthy, see Bothwell, "Lloyd Axworthy," *National Post*, September 19, 2000; Norman Hillmer and Adam Chapnick, "The Axworthy Revolution" in *Canada Among Nations 2001: The Axworthy Legacy*, edited by Fen Osler Hampson, Norman Hillmer, and Maureen Molot (Toronto: Oxford University Press, 2011), 65–88; and John English, "In the Liberal Tradition: Lloyd Axworthy and Canadian Foreign Policy," in ibid.

37. There is a reference by Captain Fluellen in Shakespeare's Henry V: "'tis expressly against the law of arms," referring to a French atrocity in which non-combatants were massacred during the battle of Agincourt: See *Henry V*, Act IV, scene 7.

38. This was embodied in the American Serviceman's Protection Act (ASPA) of 2002, which required the US government to negotiate exemptions for American personnel with individual governments. NATO countries, however, were in turn exempt from the Act, and so Canada was not confronted with an American demand for exceptional treatment.

39. This was the Monica Lewinsky affair. When in 1998 Clinton did authorize both air strikes on Iraq to rein in Saddam Hussein and al Qaeda bases in Sudan and Afghanistan, to retaliate for attacks on US embassies in Africa, he was accused of trying to divert attention away from his troubles. A satirical movie, *Wag the Dog*, released in the fall of 1997, catches the cynical spirit of the age.

40. In 2002 Canada hosted a G8 summit at Kananaskis, Alberta, which Bush attended and where, according to his custom of giving nicknames, he dubbed Chrétien "Dino" (for Dinosaur, a character in the television series *The Flintstones*).

41. The criminal, since convicted of much more serious crimes, was named Ahmed Ressam, who lived semi-clandestinely in Montreal, first as a refugee claimant and then as an illegal immigrant evading deportation. The inefficient and understaffed Canadian immigration service failed to locate Ressam before he moved on with his explosives to the United States, where he was arrested before he could detonate them.

42. Many Americans, including then-Senator Hillary Clinton and, years later, Barack Obama's cabinet secretary Janet Napolitano of the Homeland Security Department, asserted that the terrorists had arrived through Canada, as Ressam had. Efforts to get a public retraction from Clinton were unavailing, and Napolitano's regrets were very grudgingly offered.

43. "Canada was purposely cut from speech, Frum says," *Globe and Mail*, January 8, 2003, A7. Frum's further comments in the article do not add much to our knowledge of exactly why this happened. See also the memoir by the US ambassador, Paul Celucci, *Unquiet Diplomacy* (Toronto: Key Porter, 2005), 85, which claims there was "no deliberate snub." But Frum was on the spot, and Celucci was in Ottawa, which suggests that Frum is probably the better source.

44. On the Afghan war, see Carlotta Gall, *The Wrong Enemy: America in Afghanistan, 2001–2014* (Boston: Houghton Mifflin, 2014). Canada's eventual mission in Kandahar fell victim to the limited number of Canadian troops available to be deployed.

45. On pre-war propaganda and its impact in Canada, see Paul Rutherford's excellent book, *Weapons of Mass Persuasion: Marketing the War against Iraq* (Toronto: University of Toronto Press, 2004).

46. Especially painful was a speech by the secretary of state, Colin Powell, to the UN Security Council on February 5, 2003. A travesty of facts and logic, it finished Powell's then considerable reputation as a serious actor in international affairs. Powell later, and appropriately, expressed his profound regret that he had ever given it. Two of his senior staff, Dick Armitage and Col. Lawrence Wilkerson, have said much the same thing.

47. "Bush, Chrétien, Tout Border Security," CNN, http://edition.cnn.com/2002/ ALLPOLITICS/09/09/bush.chretien/

48. While visiting Mexico City in February 2003 Chrétien was asked about regime change in Iraq, and replied, according to an American diplomatic cable, "that this was a dangerous concept, and that 'if you start changing regimes, where do you stop?'" US embassy, Ottawa, to State Department, March 3, 2003, https:// www.wikileaks.org/plusd/cables/03OTTAWA589_a.html

49. Timothy A. Sayle, "'But He Has on Nothing at All!' Canada and the Iraq War, 2003," *Canadian Military History*, 19:4 (Autumn 2010), 12.

50. US embassy, Ottawa to State Dept., March 28, 2003, signed by ambassador Celucci, https://www.wikileaks.org/plusd/cables/03OTTAWA917_a.html

51. FAOH, interview with Lawrence Cohen, July 12, 2007, http://www.loc.gov/ item/mfdipbib001531/.

52. This is the theme of a powerful article by Allan Gotlieb, a former under-secretary for external affairs and former ambassador in Washington: "Romanticism and Realism in Canada's Foreign Policy," *Policy Options*, February 2005.

53. This is the so-called Chanak crisis named after the epicenter of the Anglo–Turkish confrontation in 1922.

54. Australia, by contrast, did send a substantial number of troops to Vietnam, and in return received no influence over the aims or the prosecution of the war, but suffered riots and other forms of civil strife over the unpopular conflict. In the same vein, Australia became part of the Coalition of the Willing in 2003.

55. Readers can compare the two and their near-identical phrasing and structure: John Howard's was in the Australian Parliament on March 18 and Harper's in the Canadian on March 20. Evidently Harper had some very lively and up-to-date speechwriters.

56. See above, note 47.

57. Senator Robert Byrd's (Democrat, West Virginia) speech against the war was as notably good as Colin Powell's UN oration was bad.

CHAPTER 13

1. *Hispanic* is one of the oddest categories in American immigration, spanning as it does several continents and a kaleidoscope of geographical origins, from

Tierra del Fuego in South America to Catalonia on the Mediterranean. But Hispanics do (or once did) speak the same language, often in dialects incomprehensible to the various nationalities and regions that the term covers.

2. "It would not be the United States," he wrote in 2004: "it would be Quebec, Mexico, or Brazil." See Samuel P. Huntington, "The Hispanic Challenge," *Foreign Policy*, March 2004. Huntington approvingly quoted Theodore Roosevelt to the effect that the United States must have one flag, and one language, English.

3. The author recalls accidentally tuning into a CBC interview with Huntington who was in Canada promoting his last book, *Who Are We? The Challenges to America's National Identity* (2004). Huntington's impact on his Canadian listeners might have been greater if he had pointed out some of the common features of Canadian and American history, but he did not.

4. Michael Adams and Amy Langstaff, *Stayin' Alive: How the Baby Boomers Will Work, Play, and Find Meaning in the Second Half of Their Adult Lives* (Toronto: Viking Canada, 2010), 10–11.

5. James Wooten, quoted in Peter Gosselin, *High Wire: The Precarious Financial Lives of American Families* (New York: Basic Books, 2008), 38–9.

6. Eugene Holman, quoted in Gosselin, *High Wire*, 52. The company in question was Standard Oil of New Jersey.

7. Gosselin, *High Wire*, 41.

8. Arjumand Siddiqi and Clyde Hertzman, "Towards an Epidemiological Understanding of the Effects of Long-Term Institutional Changes on Population Health: A Case Study of Canada versus the USA," *Social Science and Medicine* 64 (2007), 589–603, Table 1, section "Income share by quintile."

9. Joseph Stiglitz, *The Price of Inequality: How Today's Divided Society Endangers Our Future* (New York: Norton, 2014), 130–2."

10. It is quite probable that as early as the 1980s the poor were better off in Canada than in the United States, though the United States was much the richer country, in terms of per capita GDP.

11. Quoted in J.L. Granatstein, *Yankee Go Home: Canadians and Anti-Americanism* (Toronto: Harper, 1996), 260. Anyone looking at the obsolete and sometimes crumbling public facilities of Toronto or Montreal in the 2010s might wish for government as enlightened as in those two cities. Detroit, granted, is another case entirely.

12. The discussion of the free-trade election in Granatstein, *Yankee*, gives a fair account of events and catches the spirit of the time.

13. Siddiqi and Hertzman, "Epidemiological Understanding."

14. Douglas Barthold, Arjit Nandi, Jose M.M. Rodriguez, and Jody Heymann, "Analyzing Whether Countries Are Equally Efficient at Improving Longevity for Men and Women," *American Journal of Public Health*, published online December 12, 2013.

15. Robert G. Evans, "Extravagant Americans, Healthier Canadians: The Bottom Line in North American Health Care," in David M. Thomas and Barbara Boyle

Torrey, eds., *Canada and the United States: Differences That Count* (Toronto: Broadview Press, 2008), 135–64.

16. Quoted in Richard Wilkinson, *The Impact of Inequality: How to Make Sick Societies Healthier* (New York: Norton, 2005), 46.

17. Theodore R. Marmor, Richard Freeman, and Kieke G.H. Okma, "Comparative Policy Analysis and Health Care: An Introduction," in Marmor, Freeman, and Okma, *Comparative Studies of the Politics of Modern Medical Care* (New Haven: Yale University Press, 2009), 5.

18. Diana Petramala and Sonya Gulati, "Comparing and Contrasting Canadian and American Consumers: Some Stylized Facts," TD Economics Observations, December 18, 2013, 4: "prime working aged Americans spend six times more on health care (insurance)" than Canadians in the same category. On the other hand, American families' disposable income was much higher than Canadians'.

19. Paul Krugman and Robin Wells, quoted in Evans, "Extravagant Americans," 137.

20. This approach was particularly associated with the *National Post* newspaper, founded or re-founded (on the ruins of the old *Financial Post*) by Conrad Black, which was remarkably strident in trumpeting the virtues of the American model around the year 2000. The *National Post* was far from alone, though it was probably the most coherent expression of its point of view.

21. Gosselin, *High Wire*, 255–82 on the transformation of American pensions between 1980 and 2000.

22. It took 1.61 Canadian dollars to buy an American dollar in January 2002, an all-time low for the Canadian currency, but only .92 Canadian to buy one American dollar in November 2007, an all-time high. http://www.tradingeconomics.com/canada/currency

23. Canadian Press (CP) "Canadian auto sector stalled due to shift in production locations: RBC Survey," CTV News, May 28, 2014: http://www.ctvnews.ca/business/canadian-auto-sector-stalled-due-to-shift-in-production-locations-rbc-survey-1.1841899.

24. Norm de Bono, "Caterpillar's Closing London plant cost $38 M," *Toronto Sun*, April 25, 2012. The article noted, among things, "Cat recorded record earnings and profits across the board in its new financial report. It posted more than $60 billion in earnings in 2011 and this year projects that to top $72 billion."

25. Extracting oil from the tar sands was a gleam in the eye of successive Canadian governments. The oil-from-tar technology owed a great deal to federal subsidies, especially in the 1970s, a point that would later be forgotten.

26. Consider the US embassy's criticism of the CBC for its television series *The Border*—the American side of the border, in which American civil servants, and police and the CIA too, were painted in very dark colors, or so it argued. The complaints unconsciously echoed similar American complaints from the 1950s. See above, note 18.

27. Robert Kunzig, "The Canadian Oil Sands: Scraping Bottom," *National Geographic*, March 2009, with photo essay by Peter Essick, which may be viewed at http://ngm.nationalgeographic.com/2009/03/canadian-oil-sands/essick-photography.

28. The *Washington Post* ran a series on the pipeline route, from its origins in Alberta, down to the Gulf: http://www.washingtonpost.com/blogs/keystone-down-the-line/2012/06/17/keystone-highway-down-the-line. The quote is from a prologue to the series, by Steven Mufson.

29. See Madelaine Drohan, "Harper Ties Keystone to 'Facts', but Which Ones?" *Globe and Mail*, September 30, 2013. As Drohan notes, a push by Harper for the support of American business interests for the Keystone pipeline was overshadowed by the simultaneous release of a UN climate panel report (IPCC) on global warming, its human origins, and its drastic consequences.

30. Mike Berners-Lee and Duncan Clark, *The Burning Question: We Can't Burn Half the World's Oil* (Greystone/David Suzuki Foundation, 2013), 91: according to the authors, the United States ranks first in carbon reserves, at 17.8 percent of world resources, while Canada ranks ninth, at 3.2 percent.

31. The tone of East–West relations in Canada is caught in Mary Janigan, *Let the Eastern Bastards Freeze in the Dark: The West versus the Rest since Confederation* (Toronto: Knopf, 2012). Compared with Western Canadian resentment of Eastern Canada, Canadian anti-Americanism may be a picnic.

32. David Wilkins, US ambassador, to Secretary of State, January 23, 2006, http://www.wikileaks.org/plusd/cables/06OTTAWA194_a.html. Wilkins was a South Carolina Republican who found the Conservative government in Ottawa refreshing, and definitely something to be encouraged, as Mulroney's had been by Reagan in the 1980s. There is an implicit suggestion that the Conservatives were more pro-American than the recently departed Liberals had been, and of course the Conservatives were still a minority. Wilkins recommended strengthening Harper's position by showing cooperation on some outstanding Canadian–American dispute such as softwood lumber or the Devils Lake diversion, a link between the Mississippi watershed and that of Hudson Bay. What kind of affinity Wilkins was speaking of may be seen in Tim Hudak's Washington trip of 2012, references above (chapter 12, note 5). His sponsor and guide, David Frum, was a well-known member of the right-wing intelligentsia in the United States. Frum's sister, Linda, who shared his right-wing politics, was appointed by Harper to be a Conservative senator in Ottawa.

33. Colin Robertson, "Stephen Harper's World View," *iPolitics*, December 15, 2013, and also published, with some other essays, in a circular, *CDFAI*, December 17, 2013. CDFAI is the Canadian Defence and Foreign Affairs Institute.

34. By itself, at least. Irony was in short supply in Harper's Ottawa.

35. See Verlyn Klinkenborg, "Silencing Scientists," *New York Times* editorial page, September 22, 2013. The editorial adds that while George W. Bush set the precedent

for ignoring and muzzling government scientists, "nothing [in the United States] came close to what is being done in Canada." See Chris Turner, *The War on Science: Muzzled Scientists and Wilful Blindness in Stephen Harper's Canada* (Vancouver: Greystone Books, 2013).

36. Michael Luo, "Memo Gives Canada's Account of Obama Campaign's Meeting on NAFTA," *New York Times*, March 4, 2008.

37. Quoted in Vincent McDermott, "The Five Most Intriguing Canadian Wikileaks Revelations," *National Post*, January 12, 2010. The original is from the Ottawa Embassy to the National Security Council and the Secretary of State, January 22, 2009: http://www.wikileaks.org/plusd/cables/09OTTAWA64_a.html.

38. Edward Greenspon, Andrew Mayeda, Rebecca Penty, and Theophilos Argitis, "How Keystone XL Soured the 'Special Relationship' between Stephen Harper and Barack Obama," *National Post*, April 24, 2014.

39. Steven Chu, Obama's first energy secretary, was a Nobel Prize–winner in physics, and was skeptical of fossil fuels because of their impact on climate change. Chu served for all of Obama's first term, 2009 to 2013. He could hardly have been impressed by Harper's policy of muzzling government scientists. Harper's various ministerial appointments (four different people as the minister covering energy between 2006 and 2013, and five in the environment portfolio) were not exactly comparable.

## CONCLUSION

1. The first Catholic prime minister in Canada was Sir John Thompson in 1892; the first French Catholic was Sir Wilfrid Laurier in 1896. The first Catholic president of the United States was John F. Kennedy in 1961.

2. The authors could hardly have known that their analyses of Canada and Canadians would be read much sooner than expected, thanks to the Wikileaks affair.

3. See chapter 13, note 19, quoting a US despatch noting Canada's "habitual inferiority" complex.

4. This is a point made by an American student of Canada, Charles Doran, in 1984, and later critiqued by Louis Bélanger, "The Institutional Conundrum of North American Integration: A Power-Based Analysis," in Greg Anderson and Christopher Sands, eds., *Forgotten Partnership Redux: Canada-US Relations in the 21st Century* (Amherst, NY: Cambria Press, 2011), 201.

5. US embassy, Ottawa, to State Department, April 16, 2009, recounting the adventures of an American embassy officer attending a "human rights law" class at the University of Ottawa: http://wikileaks.org/cable/2009/04/09OTTAWA298 .html. John Kirton, "Soft-Power Partnership in a Multipolar World," in *Forgotten Partnership Redux: Canada-U.S. Relations in the 21st Century*, edited by Greg Anderson and Christopher Sands (Amherst, NY: Cambria Press, 2011), 98.

6. David Thelen, "The Nation and Beyond: Transnational Perspectives on American History," *Journal of American History*, 86:3 (December 1999), 967–8. Thelen dates the term "trans-national" back to a 1916 essay by Randolph Bourne, "Trans-National America."

7. Michael Adams, *Fire and Ice*, (Toronto: Penguin, 2000), 79ff.

8. Adams, *Fire and Ice*, 88; Shawn McCarthy, "Social Gap between Canada, U.S. Regional, Pollster Says," *Globe and Mail*, December 11, 2003, http://www.theglobeandmail.com/news/national/social-gap-between-canada-us-regional-pollster-says/article1048752/.

9. *Hispanic* can mean anyone of Portuguese or Spanish descent or culture, meaning that the category links Catalans with Ecuadoreans and Bolivians. It does not, however, include Filipinos, so that Ferdinand Marcos or Corazon Aquino, despite their indisputably Spanish names, are not Hispanic.

10. See especially Laurie Goodstein, "Latinos Grow Cool to G.O.P., Poll Finds," *New York Times*, September 27, 2013; "Latino Religion Survey Reveals Rise in Unaffiliated and Evangelical Hispanics," *Huffington Post*, September 30, 2013, US edition, http://www.huffingtonpost.com/2013/09/27/latino-religion_n_4005525.html.

11. Contemporary Churchillians irresistibly recall the red-faced, paunchy character of Colonel Blimp from David Low's classic cartoons of the 1930s and 1940s, complacent and oblivious of the imminent danger from Germany, relying instead on Britain's glorious past. The original Colonel Blimp was ironically portrayed by Low as the embodiment of everything Churchill appeared to be against. One must ask whether Churchill would be a Churchillian.

12. These stereotypes appeared, forcibly, in the more than 650 comments on a *New York Times* column, "Life in Canada, Home of the World's Most Affluent Middle Class," by Ian Austen and David Leonhardt, on April 30, 2014. But they also tended to confirm that many Americans and many Canadians would like to switch identities—in other words, that differences and resemblances transcend national boundaries.

13. Diane Francis, *Merger of the Century: Why Canada and America Should Become One Country* (Toronto: Harper Collins, 2013), 342.

14. World Values Survey, quoted in Francis, *Merger*, 266.

# Index

Simon, Sir John, 200, 373n41
Simpson's department store, 272
Six Nations, 51–52
Skelton, O.D., 179, 189–90
skepticism, 199
Skidelsky, Robert, 294–95
slate, 143, 366n36
slavery, 4, 87, 116, 345, 366n4
  Anti-Slavery Society, 103, 360n24
  British North America and, 103
  in Canada, 103, 360nn24–25
  1815–1854, 99, 360n19
  Jefferson, Thomas, and, 54
  in New France, 349n19
  oil in Canada compared to, 333
  in southern colonies, 349n18
  Underground Railroad, 103
  in United States, 99, 103, 360n19
  War of 1812, 87
  Washington, George, and, 54, 56, 351n21
Smith, Goldwin, 129–31, 159, 364nn2–3
Smith, Michael, 85
Smuts, Jan, 375n11
"snowbirds," 274
socialism, 240
  labor-socialism, 294–95
  in Saskatchewan, 230, 238, 262, 379n16
societies, 56–58
  Anti-Slavery, 103, 360n24
  Pilgrims, 167–68, 369n28
soft power, 6
softwood lumber, 288–89, 334, 393n32
Somalia, 304
Sons of Liberty, 36–37, 350n7
South African War, 131, 138, 318–19
southern colonies, 349n18
southern states, 104
Soviet Union (USSR), 205, 282
  atomic bomb of, 243
  Canada and, 292–93
  collapse of, 293, 385n38
  Gorbachev, Mikhail, of, 292–93
  Khrushchev, Nikita, of, 252
  Lenin of, 136, 365n22
  LPP and, 246–47
  missiles of, 282–83, 291

Stalin, Joseph, of, 207–8, 242–44
  as superpower, 266
  Trudeau, Pierre, and, 292, 385n37
Spain, 82, 92
  religions in, 10–11
Spanish-American War, 120, 131
sports, 1–2
Spring Rice, Sir Cecil, 156, 369n29
Srebrenica, 305
St. Albans raid, 115–16
stability, 44
Stacey, Charles P., 181, 209, 375n9
Sudan, 251, 318
Stalin, Josef, 207–8, 242–44
Stamp Act, 35, 37–38
standard of living, 229, 236, 272
  in British colonies, 23
  difference in, 122, 184, 218, 235, 346
Stegner, Wallace, 193
Stelco, 272
stereotype, 347n2
Stiglitz, Joseph, 324
St. John's Island. *See* Prince Edward Island
St. Laurent, Louis, 247–48
St. Pierre and Miquelon, 92
Stowe, Harriet Beecher, 109
Strachan, John, 91, 96–97
strategy
  dominion, 210–11
  of NATO, 291
Strathcona, Lord, 132
Streisand, Barbra, 276, 383n3
Suez crisis, 251, 310–11, 381n40
Sumner, Charles, 113, 117
superpower
  energy, 329, 332
  Soviet Union as, 266
  United States as, 8, 263–64, 266, 293, 314

Taft, William Howard, 145–48, 150–53, 161, 221
tariffs, 148–51, 173–74
  in Canada, 182–83, 190–92, 254
  for colonial Canada, 121, 124–25
  Fordney–McCumber, 177, 182